About the Underground Guide Series

Welcome to the underground!

Are you tired of all the fluff—books that tell you what you already know, ones that assume you're an idiot and treat you accordingly, or dwell on the trivial while completely ignoring the tough parts?

Good. You're in the right place.

Series Editor Woody Leonhard and Addison-Wesley bring you the Underground Guides—serious books that tackle the tough questions head-on but still manage to keep a sense of humor (not to mention a sense of perspective!). Every page is chock full of ideas you can put to use right away. We'll tell you what works and what doesn't—no bull, no pulled punches. We don't kowtow to the gods of the industry, we won't waste your time or your money, and we *will* treat you like the intelligent computer user we know you are.

Each Underground Guide is written by somebody who's been there—a working stiff who's suffered through the problems you're up against right now—and lived to tell about it. You're going to strike a rich vein of hard truth in these pages, and come away with a wealth of information you can put to use all day, every day.

So come along as we go spelunking where no book has gone before. Mind your head, and don't step in anything squishy. There will be lots of unexpected twists and turns . . . and maybe a laugh or two along the way.

The Underground Guide Series

Woody Leonhard, Series Editor

The Underground Guide to Word for Windows™:
Slightly Askew Advice from a WinWord Wizard

Woody Leonhard

The Underground Guide to Excel 5.0 for Windows™:
Slightly Askew Advice from Two Excel Wizards

Lee Hudspeth and Timothy-James Lee

The Underground Guide to UNIX®:
Slightly Askew Advice from a UNIX Guru

John Montgomery

The Underground Guide to Microsoft® Office, OLE, and VBA:
Slightly Askew Advice from Two Integration Wizards

Lee Hudspeth and Timothy-James Lee

The Underground Guide to Telecommuting:
Slightly Askew Advice on Leaving the Rat Race Behind

Woody Leonhard

The Underground Guide to Computer Security:
Slightly Askew Advice on Protecting Your PC and What's On It

Michael Alexander

The Underground Guide to Microsoft® Internet Assistant:
Slightly Askew Advice on Mastering the Web with WinWord

John Ross

The Underground Guide to Color Printers:
Slightly Askew Advice on Getting the Best from Any Color Printer

M. David Stone

The Underground Guide to Windows® 95:
Slightly Askew Advice from a Windows Wizard

Scot Finnie

The Underground Guide to
Color Printers

Slightly
   Askew
      Advice
         on
           Getting
              the
                 Best
                    from
                       Any
                          Color
                             Printer

M. David Stone

Series Editor Woody Leonhard

ADDISON-WESLEY DEVELOPERS PRESS

Reading, Massachusetts • Menlo Park, California • New York • Don Mills, Ontario
Wokingham, England • Amsterdam • Bonn • Sydney • Singapore • Tokyo
Madrid • San Juan • Paris • Seoul • Milan • Mexico City • Taipei

Many of the designations used by manufacturers and sellers to distinguish their products are claimed as trademarks. Where those designations appear in this book, and Addison-Wesley was aware of a trademark claim, the designations have been printed in initial capital letters or all capital letters.

Adobe, Adobe Photoshop, and PostScript are trademarks of Adobe Systems, Incorporated.
Bubble Jet and BJC are trademarks of Canon Inc.
Canon and BJ are registered trademarks of Canon Inc.
Corel is a registered trademark of Corel Corporation.
CorelDRAW and Corel PHOTO-PAINT are trademarks of Corel Corporation.
FARGO is a registered trademark of FARGO Electronics, Incorporated.
Phaser is a trademark of Tektronix, Inc.
PrimeraPro is a trademark of FARGO Electronics, Incorporated.
SJ-144 is a trademark of Star Micronics Co., Ltd.
SuperScript is a registered trademark of NEC Corporation.
Tektronix is a registered trademark of Tektronix, Inc.
Other brand and product names may be trademarks or registered trademarks of their respective owners.

Screen shots of CorelDRAW and Corel PHOTO-PAINT courtesy of Corel Corporation.
Screen shots of Hewlett-Packard printer drivers courtesy of Hewlett-Packard Company.
Screen shots of Adobe Photoshop courtesy of Adobe Systems Incorporated.
Except where indicated otherwise, the photos in this book are taken from the Corel Professional Photo Series
Screen shots of the NEC SuperScript 3000 printer diver courtesy of NEC Technologies, Inc.
Screen shots of Tektronix printer divers courtesy of Tektronix, Inc.
Screen shots of Windows Paintbrush courtesy of Microsoft Corporation.

The author and publisher have taken care in preparation of this book, but make no expressed or implied warranty of any kind and assume no responsibility for errors or omissions. No liability is assumed for incidental or consequential damages in connection with or arising out of the use of the information or programs contained herein.

Library of Congress Cataloging-in-Publication Data

Stone, M. David.
  The underground guide to color printers: slightly askew advice on
getting the best from any color printer / M. David Stone.
    p.   cm. — (Underground guide series)
  Includes index.
  ISBN 0-201-48378-5
  1. Color printers (Data processing systems)   I. Title.
II. Series.
TK7887.7.S76   1996
004.7'7—dc20   95-43285
                                                              CIP

Copyright © 1996 by M. David Stone

All rights reserved. No part of this publication may be reproduced, stored in a retrieval system, or transmitted, in any form or by any means, electronic, mechanical, photocopying, recording, or otherwise, without the prior written permission of the publisher. Printed in the United States of America. Published simultaneously in Canada.

Series Hack: Woody Leonhard
Sponsoring Editor: Kathleen Tibbetts
Project Manager: John Fuller
Production Coordinator: Ellen Savett
Technical Editor: Michael J. Zulick
Cover design: Jean Seal
Text Design: Kenneth L. Wilson, Wilson Graphics & Design
Set in 10-point Palatino by Rob Mauhar, CIP of Coronado

1 2 3 4 5 6 7 8 9 -MA- 0099989796
First printing, February 1996

Addison-Wesley books are available for bulk purchases by corporations, institutions, and other organizations. For more information please contact the Corporate, Government, and Special Sales Department at (800)238-9682.

Find us on the World-Wide Web at:
http://www.aw.com/devpress/

To Marie and Baba, both

Contents

Acknowledgments xi
Foreword xiii
Do You Need This Book? xv

Chapter 1 **A Colorful Can of Worms** 1
Speaking in Colors 1
The Taxonomy of Color Printers 9
More Ways to Slice and Dice 22
What You See Is Sometimes Surprising 32
WYSAWYG: What You See Ain't What You Get 44
The Psychology of Color 47

Chapter 2 **Getting Pretty Good Color with Hardly Any Effort** 51
A Bigger Image 52
Paper Matters 53
Ribbons Matter Too 55
Changing Ribbons 59
Watch Out for Streaks 62
First Get It Right in Black and White 66
Less Is More 67
Be Consistent 69
Don't Choose Colors, Choose a Color Scheme 70
Warm and Cool Colors 71
Monochromatic Color Schemes 71
Use the Colors of the Rainbow 72
More Color Schemes: You Like It? It's Yours. 75
Backgrounds 77
Making Edges Stand Out 78
Ten Rules for Text and Color 80
Get It Right in Black and White II: The Handout 81
Different Printers Print Different Grays Also 91

Chapter 3 **Printers Aren't Monitors** 95
- The Primary Issue 96
- Why Colors Don't—Can't—Match 105
- More Reasons Why Colors Don't Match 117
- Color (Mis)Matching 120

Chapter 4 **More Ways Printers and Monitors Don't Match** 135
- There's Graphics, and Then There's Graphics 135
- Some Monitor Basics 152

Chapter 5 **Pick Your Poison** 173
- Color Printers: The Expert's Tour 174
- Ink Jet Printers 180
- Wax Jet Printers 195
- Color Laser Printers 197
- Thermal Wax and Thermal Dye 204
- What Language Does It Speak? 208
- Printer Size—Paper Size 213
- Two Buying Tips 215

Chapter 6 **A Bit of Color** 219
- Color Models Revisited 220
- Color Matching Revisited 224

Chapter 7 **Making Color Work** 237
- Color (Harmony) Theory 238
- Color Schemes 242
- Psychology of Color 248
- Spot Color and Color Matching Systems 250

Chapter 8 **Color Photos** 253
- Getting a Photo into Your Computer 253
- A Look at Resolution 260
- Gamma: The Third Letter in the Greek Alphabet 285
- Color Matching with Scanners 288

Chapter 9 **Get to Know Your Printer Driver** 289
- Full Manual Control 290
- Automatic Pilot 295

PostScript   298
Windows 95   305
And Finally . . .   306

Glossary   307

Index   331

Acknowledgments

Some books are tightly focused enough so one person can write them based on his or her own experience and knowledge, without help from anyone. This isn't one of those books. This one is wide ranging enough—covering everything from printer technology to color theory—that I doubt there's anybody who's an expert in everything in here. Fortunately, I had the phone numbers (and some home addresses) of various experts to fill in the gaps.

I'd like to thank Rod Belshee of Tektronix, who was foolish enough to offer to read the manuscript and good-natured enough to spend the time reading it and to offer any number of valuable suggestions; Kevin Draz, Lori Grunin, and Luisa Simone, who all let me call as needed and who cheerfully provided answers in their various fields of expertise; Alfred Poor, who also let me call and ask questions (but that's nothing new); and Mike Zulich, who not only did the technical edit on this book, but also let me pick his brains on various subjects.

I'd also like to thank the printer manufacturers—Tektronix, NEC Technologies, Hewlett-Packard, FARGO, and Canon—who were kind enough to provide printers for the examples needed to write this book. Special thanks to Julie Galla and Carrie-Lynn Bendzsa at Corel Corporation, and to Torey Bruno, driver program manager at Adobe, for providing help far beyond the minimum required.

Finally, I'd like to thank Woody Leonhard, whose enthusiastic comments about my writing are always a great ego boost (I only hope I'm half as good as Woody's compliments make me sound), and Kathleen Tibbetts, whose patience and good humor make her a pleasure to work with.

Foreword

Color. It's *everywhere*!

Thanks to dramatic decreases in the price of color output—both the printers themselves and the consumables they gobble—the entire world of PCs is starting to shift to color printing.

That's the good news. Here's the bad news: if you want to do anything fancier than print a color calendar for the kids, or reproduce a bit of canned clip art, this stuff gets complicated, quick. You don't stand a snowball's chance in fiery burnt umber of producing a professional-looking color piece unless you know what you're doing. The difference between a quality, high-impact printed page and a garish, amateurish blob can be just a few notches on a Contrast slider somewhere.

The trick, as always, is to know where to look, and what to twiddle.

In this Underground Guide, PC guru M. David Stone takes you through the depths of the color conundrum—from CMYK color models to printer technologies—and shows you in his inimitably clear and funny way what to get, how to use it . . . and where the bodies are buried.

The book is packed with down-to-earth advice that you won't find anywhere else, from a guy who's obviously fought it out in the trenches. If you're looking for straight answers to your tough color questions, well, you found the right place.

So take this book, go out there and sling a little mud! Light ochre, if you would, please, and don't forget to deepen the shadows. Thanks.

Woody Leonhard
Series Hack

Do You Need This Book?

Color printers aren't just for artists anymore. You can now get brilliant color from printers that cost about the same as a desktop laser printer, or, for about the same price, get both both black and white output and acceptable color in a single printer.

But if you're reading this, you probably know that already. Odds are that you've gotten your hands on a color printer (or are about to) or that someone has hung one on your office network. You may not know much about using color beyond the obvious fact that it can add impact to everything from business presentations to party invitations. But you may have already discovered color printing's dirty little secret for yourself: Printing in color is not just a matter of creating a colorful image on screen and printing it.

You may have noticed, for example, that the colors you see on screen rarely match the colors you get on the printed page. Or that some colors go well together on screen but don't work together on paper. Or that some pairs of colors that provide ample contrast between, say, text and background on screen turn into virtually the same color on paper.

With color, it's WYSIANWYG: What You See Is Almost Never What You Get.

You may even have noticed that the colors you see on your screen vary with the time of day. (Really. This is not a takeoff on the old joke about programs that work or don't depending on the phase of the moon. On-screen colors change as your monitor warms up, and they change—very slightly—with changes in room lighting. That means they change with time of day—and with the phase of the moon, for that matter, if you work by moonlight.)

Depending on your printer, you may have found that some colors print as solid blocks of a single color, while others print as a mottled mix of colors. And if you've tried scanning and printing photos, you may have been disappointed by the lack of resolution in the output, compared to the quality you should be getting—if you ever learn how to adjust your settings.

If any of this sounds familiar, and you wish you had a better grasp of how to take advantage of your color printer, this book is for you. If you're just starting to work with a color printer or are on the verge of buying one and want to avoid finding the pitfalls of color printing the hard way, this book is for you too.

WHAT YOU'LL FIND HERE

My primary aim is to give you a bagful of handy tricks for taking best advantage of your color printer—from suggestions for color schemes that work well for graphics to hints about setting line screens for improving the look of photos. (And if you don't know what line screens are, you *really* need this book.)

Along the way, we'll dip into such theoretical issues as color models and color perception. (Did you know, for example, that there are several different ways to describe and create colors? Or that the paper you use can affect your perception of the colors you print—not the colors themselves, just your *perception*?) But even when discussing the theoretical, I'll stay focused on practical applications—the things that matter for helping you get the results that you want out of your printer.

We'll also take a tour of the various color printing technologies, with an emphasis on explaining the limitations and capabilities of each. If you're shopping for a color printer, you'll find lots of useful information here to help you make your choice. But the real point is to let you know what you can expect from each technology, so you don't wind up spinning your wheels trying to get something out of your printer that it's not capable of producing.

Because there are so many aspects to color printing, and because they are as thoroughly tangled as strands of angel hair in a pasta dish, we'll start with a broad-brush overview of everything you ought to know, followed immediately by some practical tips for getting decent results right from the start.

For the bulk of the book, starting with Chapter 3, we'll cover each of the strands—from printer technology to color models to color schemes, to scanning and printing color photos—in far more detail. I'll then give you a short course in how to teach yourself everything there is to know about your printer by taking a careful look at your printer driver.

Be sure to read Chapter 1.

Not so incidentally, I've designed this book so you don't have to read it from beginning to end to make sense of it. For the most part, you should be able to go to just those chapters—or even those sections of chapters—that interest you, without having to read everything that comes before. However, I recommend that you read Chapter 1 all the way through before sampling other parts of the book. It covers everything once over lightly, and it gives you a wide-ranging background for putting the detailed information from any given chapter in context. You'll also find occasional warnings in a few sections suggesting that you read specific earlier chapters first.

Do you use a PC? A Mac? A printer I don't cover here? Doesn't matter.

One other thing before we get started. If you page through this book, you'll see examples created with specific printers and specific programs. You may or may not see any examples created with the printer you have or the programs you use. Don't let that bother you, but be aware of what it means.

Sure, if this were a how-to book about using a specific printer with a specific program, I could lead you through a detailed, keystroke-by-keystroke explanation of how to get the most from your printer. But then you wouldn't necessarily learn how to apply the same underlying techniques to other programs and other printers.

The point here is to teach you how to explore any printer and any program so you can get the most out of it. One of the reasons I'm using a variety of printers for the examples in the book is precisely to show you a range of possibilities and give you a larger set of strategies to call on as well as features to look for.

You should treat the examples here as just that—examples. Draw on them as a basis for understanding your own printer and programs. Use them as a guide for learning what to look for. But don't let yourself be limited to the examples I use. And if your printer, or software, happens to be represented here, don't fall into the trap of following the examples for that printer only and ignoring the rest.

For the record, the printers I'll use for the examples in this book are the Hewlett-Packard DeskJet 560C, DeskJet 660C, DeskJet 1200C/PS, DeskJet 1600CM, the Canon BJC-600e, the FARGO Primera Pro, the NEC SuperScript Color 3000, and the Tektronix Phaser 340. (And this is one of the few times I'll use the full, official name for any of these.) The programs I'll primarily use are CorelDRAW, PHOTO-PAINT, and Photoshop, (okay, since it's for the record: CorelDRAW version 5.0 and 6.0, Corel PHOTO-PAINT version 5.0, and Adobe Photoshop 3.0).

I'll be using a PC for generating the examples in this book. If you're a Mac user, however, you shouldn't let that throw you. All of the examples and certainly all of the principles I'll cover apply to printing color from a Mac as well as from a PC. The printer doesn't care what kind of computer it's getting its marching orders from, so it doesn't matter whether you're a PC power user or a Mac maven. Follow me through, and by the time we're done, you'll not only know why your printed output doesn't match what you see on the screen, you'll know what to do about it.

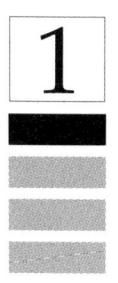

1 A Colorful Can of Worms

> There are more things in heaven and earth, Horatio,
> Than are dreamt of in our philosophy.
>
> William Shakespeare
> *Hamlet* Act 1 Scene V

Before you delve too far into any one area dealing with color, it helps to know a little about a lot of areas—and there are more than you may realize. So I'm going to use this chapter to lay an inch-thick, mile-wide foundation for understanding color and color printers.

Among the topics we'll look at are the technologies for color printing, the differences between color in printers and color in monitors, some different ways to describe color, issues that affect the perception of color, and even the psychology of color. To get all this, and more, into one chapter, we're not going into anything in much depth. But virtually everything I'll touch on here we'll come back to in greater detail later. Think of this chapter as an executive summary, if you like, or as the *Reader's Digest* version of the rest of the book—except that in this chapter, I'll concentrate on giving you the background you need and on making you aware of problems, rather than solutions.

SPEAKING IN COLORS

> In Paris they simply stared when I spoke to them in French; I never did succeed in making those idiots understand their own language.
>
> Mark Twain

Let's start with some essential color vocabulary (other than the blue streak of expletives that color printers sometimes encourage). The three key alphabet soup terms are: RGB, CMY, and CMYK.

First some background, which you may remember from high school physics. (I see Tim has his hand raised in the back of the class. What's that, Tim? You don't remember any high school physics because you made a point of skipping the course? Well, don't let that scare you; this is stuff that artists learn too. So, if you didn't learn it in a physics class, you may remember it from art class.)

When Isaac Newton was fooling around with prisms more than 300 years ago, he showed that white light consisted of a collection of other colors. Shine white light though a prism, and the prism will break it down into the rainbow-like spectrum (as shown in black and white in Figure 1.1). It works the other way too: Add the colors of the spectrum back together, and you wind up with white.

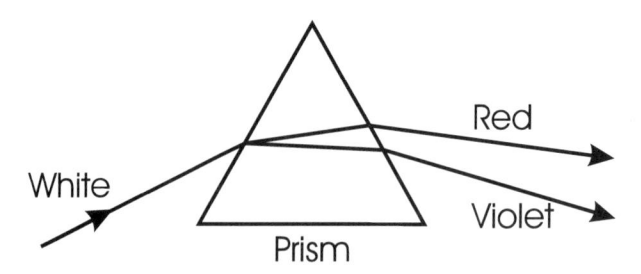

Figure 1.1 The color spectrum (in black and white). If you shine white light through a prism to break up the colors, you get the full spectrum, from red to violet.

Mixing colored light

Whether you remember any physics or not, you certainly know that you can mix colors to get other colors—if only from a vague memory of using fingerpaints. If you haven't tried mixing colored light recently, though, you may not know (or may have forgotten) that mixing colors works differently with light than with paint.

Add two relatively dark colors of light together, and you wind up with a lighter color. In some ways this is surprising, since it's the opposite of what you would expect from working with pigment-based color all your life. Mix two dark colors of paint, after all, and you'll wind up with an even darker color. But it makes good sense if you stop to think about it. If adding all the colors of the spectrum together gives you a bright white, then the more colors you add together, the closer you should get to white—which means each added color should make the mix lighter and brighter, instead of darker and duller. Still, this difference between mixing colors in paint and in light is one of the reasons why adjusting color on a monitor or in software by setting red, green, and blue levels can be frustrating. It's somewhat like trying to perform an intricate task with your hands by looking in a mirror, with everything working backwards from what you'd expect. You can learn to do it, but it takes practice.

If you overlap circles of red, green, and blue light, as shown in Figure 1.2, you'll find that a relatively dark green and dark red add together to give you a bright yellow; a dark green and dark blue (dark enough so that you'd more likely think of it as violet) add to give you cyan (which is a light blue); and a dark blue and dark red add to give you magenta (which is a purplish red). The three colors together—red, green, and blue—all add up to white. More important for the moment, if you vary the intensity of the three primary colors—red, green, and blue—you can produce just about any color you want, which is one of the reasons these are called primary colors. (And I mean *just about* any color. There are some colors you won't get, but we'll come back to that in Chapter 3.)

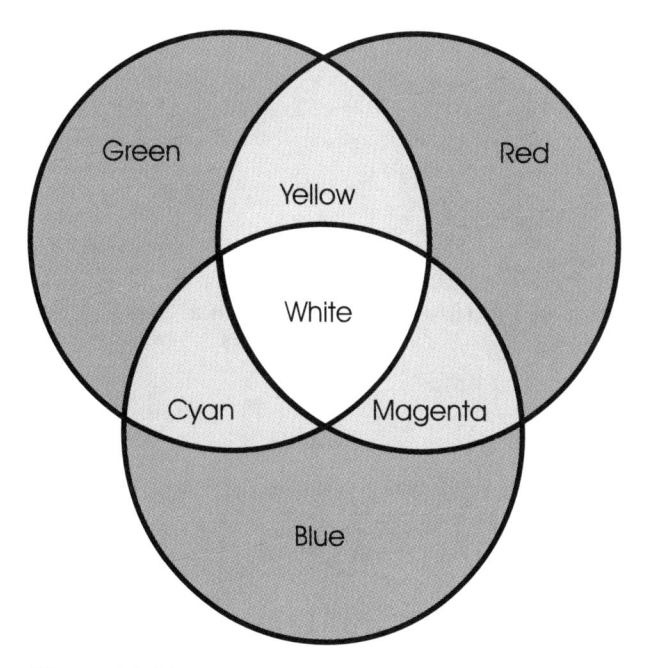

Figure 1.2 You don't even need all the colors of the spectrum to get white light. Overlap red, green, and blue lights, and you'll wind up with white.

Color printers, of course, have nothing whatever to do with creating colors using light of any color. They're much closer in spirit to using fingerpaints—at least to the extent of starting with light, bright pigments, and mixing them together to create darker colors. However, almost every color output device . . . (Sorry for the technojargon, but I'm talking here about both color printers and color monitors, and *output device* is the only phrase I know that covers both. Uh . . . let's start again.)

It takes just three colors to make a rainbow.

Virtually every color output device, including every printer, creates all the colors it's capable of producing by mixing just a few basic colors. More precisely, if we ignore black for the moment, every output device creates every color it's capable of with just three colors. For color monitors—as well as for color video and film recorders—those colors are red, green, and blue. For printers, those colors are cyan, magenta, and yellow. But there's a minor problem here; namely, video monitors and most kinds of printers can't actually mix colors together.

How to Mix Colors Without Actually Mixing Colors

> I'm not confused, I'm just well mixed.
>
> Robert Frost

When you go to your local paint store to get just the right peach color for your breakfast nook, the friendly neighborhood store owner will try to match the swatch of cloth you brought by literally mixing paints together. You then slap the mixed paint on your walls and hope it dries to the right color. Likewise, if you mix colored light beams as shown in Figure 1.2 so they overlap each other, you're literally mixing the colored light.

Video monitors and most printers can't do that. Monitors create images by aiming electrons at the screen. The electrons hit dots of phosphor, which glow in red, green, or blue, depending on the phosphor. Since the phosphor dots are in fixed positions, as shown in Figure 1.3, you can't actually mix the colors.

Figure 1.3 Monitors produce colors with red, green, and blue phosphor dots.

Beam me a little more red, Scotty.

What monitors do instead is use three dots—one red, one green, and one blue—for each picture element, or pixel, in the image. These little triangles, or triads, of dots are physically close enough to each other so the human eye (or brain) treats each triad as a single dot, mixing the colors that the monitor can't mix. By adjusting the electron beam to change the intensity of each dot within each pixel, the monitor effectively mixes the three primary colors to create all the other colors you can see on the screen.

> **Don't just take my word for this. If you have good enough eyesight, or, better yet, a good magnifying glass, you can see it for yourself on most monitors. The easiest approach is to load Windows or any other program that will let you put a white background on the screen, and then look closely at the screen with a loupe or magnifying glass. From up close and personal, you should be able to see distinct red, green, and blue colored dots, even though the background looks white from only a few inches away.**
>
> **If you don't see the dots, it doesn't mean they aren't there. One way monitors differ is in the size dot that they use. Obviously, the smaller the dots on your monitor, the harder it will be to see them, particularly if your magnifying glass isn't strong enough. You should have no problem seeing the dots on a color TV because a color TV works the same way but has much bigger dots. (Actually, most TVs today have somewhat elongated dots, with red, green, and blue dots—or short vertical stripes, if you prefer—in trios next to each other. But the basic idea is the same, only the placement and size of the dots are different.)**

Most printers do something similar to this, placing colored dots on the paper in groups and letting the eye and brain meld the groups of dots into colors that the printer can't mix. (I see that Arnold, in the second row, has an objection. Yes, Arnold, I know there are exceptions; that's why I said *most* printers. We'll get to the exceptions when we look at printer technologies in depth.)

Dithering

Unlike monitors, which can vary the intensity of each primary color, printers are stuck with the colors they've got, in just two intensities: on and off. (At least, most printers are, and those are the only ones we're concerned with right now.) So instead of mixing colors by varying the intensity of each color within a pixel, printers vary the number of dots of each color within a pixel and the position for each color dot. The technique is called dithering.

Printers are also free to lay the dots down in any pattern they like, not just the simple three-dot triangle that monitors use. The number of dots for each picture element, and the arrangement of those dots, is up for grabs, though the simplest arrangement is a square of so many dots by so many—five by five, say, or six by six.

Most important, because the arrangement is usually repetitive, like a tiled floor, you can often see dithering patterns in printed output. These patterns are most obvious in large solid blocks of dithered color, and in dithered versions of continuous tone images, where the colors change gradually and continuously, as in a photograph. There's lots more to say about dithering, but this bare-bones description is all you need in order to understand the comments in this chapter. Right now, let's get back to explaining RGB, CMY, and CMYK.

Color Models

> A good model can advance fashion by ten years.
>
> Yves Saint-Laurent

Devices that depend on red, green, and blue to produce colors are RGB devices. Devices that depend on cyan, magenta, and yellow are CMY devices. But the initials RGB and CMY mean much more than that. Each of these approaches to creating colors also provides a way to describe colors—as a specific percentage of red, green, and blue or of cyan, magenta, and yellow. So each one also provides a color model. (Yes, Arnold, I know this isn't strictly true because hardly anyone talks about a CMY model, but I'll get to that in a minute. Just pretend I'm right for now.)

The RGB and CMY color models

The RGB model describes each color in terms of its red, green, and blue components. The CMY model describes each color in terms of cyan, magenta, and yellow. Figure 1.4, for example, shows a section of CorelDRAW's Uniform Fill dialog box, with a specific color defined in terms of red, green, and blue.

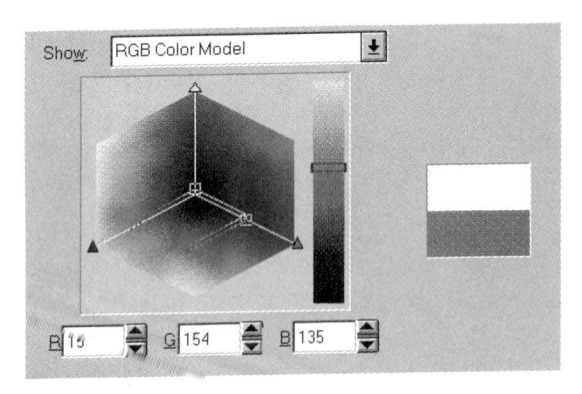

Figure 1.4 15 red; 154 green; 135 blue; hike!

Color models and color spaces

Notice that the Show text box at the top of Figure 1.4 reads RGB Color Model. Just below that is a representation of the RGB color space.

Okay, so I've slipped in another new term. You prefer a formal introduction? How's this: A color space is simply the spatial representation of a color model. (Yes, Arnold, that's not precisely right, but it's close enough for this discussion.)

I see Mary shaking her head in the front row. What's that, Mary? Oh. I've just defined color space in terms of space and color. Maybe you'll prefer this definition (for Mary only, the rest of the class can ignore it): A color space is the mathematical representation of the visual sensation of color. By mapping the colors along x, y, and z (in this case, red, green, and blue) axes, you can build a spatial representation of all the colors available from mixing specific amounts of each primary color. Okay? Now where was I before Mary's question?

Just below the representation of the RGB color space in Figure 1.4 are three text boxes, labeled R for red, G for green, and B for blue. The numbers in those boxes define a specific color by the amount of red, green, and blue in that color: red 15, green 154, and blue 135 (out of a maximum value of 255 in each case).

Figure 1.5 shows the same section of the same CorelDRAW dialog box, with the same color as in Figure 1.4. But in this figure, the color is defined in terms of cyan, magenta, and yellow (and black, but we're still ignoring black for the next paragraph or three).

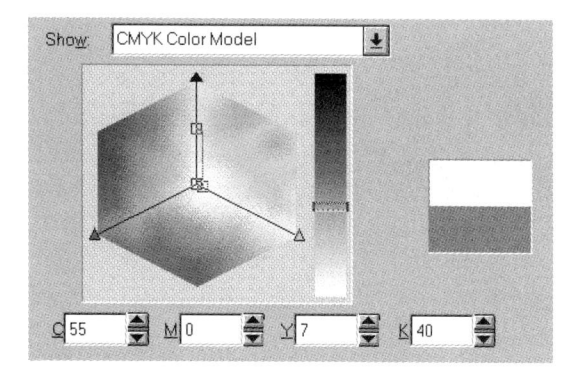

Figure 1.5 Proof, in black and white, that the R15, G154, B153 of Figure 1.4 equals C55, M0, Y7, K40—whatever that means.

As you can see, Figure 1.5 is similar to Figure 1.4. In this case, though, the Show text box at the top of the figure reads CMYK Color Model. Just below that is a representation of the CMYK color space. And below that are four text boxes, labeled C for cyan, M for magenta, Y for yellow, and K for black. (Yes, it should logically be B for black, but then you might confuse it with B for blue. Of course, I've never heard of anyone thinking the M stands for maroon, or the C for chartreuse, but don't let that bother you. Foolish consistency and all that.)

Here again, the numbers in the boxes define a specific color, in this case, by the amount of cyan, magenta, yellow, and black: cyan 55, magenta 0, yellow 7, and black 70 (out of a maximum value of 100 for each in this particular representation).

Four-Color Printing

> Personally, I can't see why it would be any less romantic to find a husband in a nice four-color catalogue than in the average downtown bar at happy hour.
>
> Barbara Ehrenreich

CMY plus black equals CMYK

The CMY model has one shortcoming. In theory, cyan, magenta, and yellow mixed together should yield black. In reality, it usually yields a not-quite black with a muddy brown or bluish tinge. Conventional wisdom insists that the only way to reach true black with any kind of CMY device (whether it's on your desktop or in a professional print shop) is to add some K and make it a CMYK device.

The need for adding black is why full-color pages (like the ones you'll find elsewhere in this book) are often called four-color pages. Four-color pages, of course, are produced with a four-color printing process, which is called four-color process printing.

The need for adding black also explains why CorelDRAW offers a CMYK color model, but not a CMY color model (or I would have used it in my example). And CorelDRAW isn't alone on this by any means. You'd have to look far and wide to find a program that lets you define colors with a CMY model.

Having said that, however . . . please put your hand down, Arnold . . . I have to point out that you may wind up printing with just CMY anyway. Despite the conventional wisdom that CMY doesn't cut it without some K thrown in, most color printers that use ribbons to put color on paper—by transferring wax or dye from ribbon to paper—will let you leave the K out.

Using CMY without the K

Typically, for these printers, you can buy both three-color (CMY) ribbons and four-color (CMYK) ribbons, and you can use either kind. (Yes, Arnold, black is a color.) And typically, you can see the difference, with CMY ribbons yielding a visibly brownish or bluish black.

A few printer manufacturers, however, sell three-color ribbons only for at least some of their printers. I've also seen black output from three-color ribbons—from some Tektronix printers in particular—that's suitably black. (So much for the conventional wisdom.)

So don't assume that a color printer that leaves out the K won't give you the dark blacks that you want. (But don't assume that it will print them for you, either. There's a reason for the conventional wisdom.) Note in passing that when you use a printer with a three-color ribbon, the printer itself is printing based on a CMY color model, translating the black component to some combination of cyan, magenta, and yellow.

The advantage of using a three-color ribbon is simple: It costs less. Any time you use any color on the ribbon, you also have to use or bypass equal amounts of all the other colors. So with a three-color ribbon, you use up only three-fourths as much ribbon as with a four-color ribbon.

Put it another way: For every three images you can print with a four-color ribbon, you can print four images with the same length of three-color ribbon. That's twelve color panels either way, divided as three of each color on a four-color ribbon, or four of each on a three-color ribbon. Even if the ribbon costs only a dime a panel (and for some printers, ten cents a dance is a lot less than it costs as I write this), that will save you $10 for every 100 images you print—or $100 for every 1000 images. This logic doesn't apply to printers that don't use ribbons. Ink jet printers, for example, spray-paint the paper and can use just as much ink as they need for each color, without wasting any. So with an ink jet printer, adding a black ink saves money: You can print black with the black ink only, instead of having to combine cyan, yellow, and magenta inks.

All of which brings us to the color printers themselves.

THE TAXONOMY OF COLOR PRINTERS

> In a museum in Havana there are two skulls of Christopher Columbus, "one when he was a boy and one when he was a man."
>
> Mark Twain

To have any hope of understanding color printers, you first have to realize that there are more ways to slice and dice the category than there are ohs and ahs of amazement on a typical infomercial. You can divide them by price, by technology, by resolution, by the kind of paper they use, by the printer command languages they follow, and more. Here's a quick look at the most important ways you can categorize these suckers. (We'll take a similar tour, in more detail, in Chapter 5.) I'll start with the technology.

Bangers, Spitters, Heaters, and Zappers

> Inanimate objects are classified scientifically into three major categories-those that don't work, those that break down and those that get lost.
>
> Russell Baker
> *New York Times,* June 18, 1968

Broadly speaking, there are four kinds of color printers: bangers, spitters, heaters, and zappers. There are a couple of different technologies included in each group, but the point is that there are only a limited number of ways you can get ink onto paper. (Yes, Arnold, it's true that some printers use wax, or dye, or toner, or whatever, but I'm using *ink* in a generic sense, meaning anything with pigment in it that leaves marks on the paper.)

Dot Matrix Printers

> There is no terror in a bang, only in the anticipation of it.
>
> Alfred Hitchcock

One way to put ink on paper is to put a ribbon next to a piece of paper and slam something solid into the ribbon to transfer the ink. That's how dot matrix printers work—as well as obsolete daisywheel printers and even typewriters.

Daisywheel printers, for those who have never seen one, use a typing element that you can also find in some typewriters. The element is shaped like a wheel, with a hub and spokes, but no outer rim, so it looks vaguely like a daisy. (Well, if you squint at it in the right light and have a good imagination and ignore the fact that it's all black, it looks vaguely like a daisy.) The characters are on the far end of the spokes. When printing, the wheel spins to bring the right character to the ribbon at the right time for the printer to hit the spoke and slam it into the ribbon.

The one thing these bangers all have in common—aside from being noisy—is that they're best restricted to black and white printing. (And given the price of ink jet and laser printers today, I'd argue that they're best restricted to black and white printing only when you need to print through multipart forms, but that's a little off the subject of color printers.)

Color dot matrix printers are fine for black and white.

You can find any number of dot matrix printers that claim color capabilities. They've been around for years. I've never heard of color daisywheel printers—and don't think I want to be enlightened if there are any.

If your only need for color is to highlight an occasional word or sentence in your text or print the negative balance in your checkbook in red, these printers are eminently . . . uh . . . adequate. At least, they are adequate within the limitations of dot matrix printers for printing text, which is pretty limited.

If you want to print color graphics or, heaven forfend, color photos, you don't even want to consider printing on a dot matrix printer—unless, of course, you actually want muddy colors and poor resolution. Bottom line: Color bangers don't count.

Ink Jet Printers

> Gimme the Plaza, the jet and $150 million, too . . .
>
> Headline reporting Ivana Trump's divorce settlement demands of husband Donald.
> *New York Post,* February 13, 1990,

A second choice for getting pigment on paper is to spray paint the page. Ink jet printers spit ink out of their nozzles and aim the individual dots at the paper. The spray is fine enough for claimed resolutions of 300 dpi (that's 300 dots per inch) and up, depending on the printer.

A 300-dpi resolution is high enough so ads can lay claim to laser printer quality for these beasts. But keep in mind that the ink from ink jet printers goes on wet. That means it tends to spread a bit when it hits the page because it's absorbed by the paper—a tendency known as bleeding (or blooming or wicking, depending on who you're talking to). How much it spreads depends a lot on the paper you're using, but the point is that 300 dpi from an ink jet printer doesn't yield the same crisp edges for text and lines as 300 dpi from a laser printer.

> **Now here's the interesting part: The spreading, or bleeding, of ink from an ink jet printer isn't entirely a Bad Thing, at least not for a *color* ink jet printer. I mentioned earlier that when you're printing colors that are mixtures of other colors, you often get visible dithering patterns. But with ink jet printers, when the dithered dots of ink bleed into each other, you're actually physically mixing the inks. In addition to blurring edges slightly, that also blurs the dithering patterns, neatly turning a flaw into a slight benefit.**
>
> **Not so incidentally, some people use *bleeding, blooming,* and *wicking* more or less interchangeably. Others draw a distinction between the three terms. By some definitions, bleeding applies only when two different color inks spread into each other. Blooming refers to the tendency of an individual dot to grow larger by spreading. Wicking refers to the tendency for ink to spread along individual fibers in the paper as it spreads. But by these definitions, when two side-by-side dots of different colors bloom, they generally bleed into each other as well. More often than not, they wick as they bloom. For our purposes, bleeding covers any tendency to spread—bleeding, blooming, or wicking.**

Color quality from ink jet printers varies from dull and disappointing to vibrant and exciting, although the results for any given printer also vary with the paper you're using. The best ink jet printers can go toe to toe with more exotic technologies on output quality. (They'll usually lose in the comparison, but at least they're in the same league.) The worst are right up there with dot matrix color printers.

Wax Jet Printers

> I recently learned something quite interesting about video games. Many young people have developed incredible hand, eye, and brain coordination in playing these games. The air force believes these kids will be our outstanding pilots should they fly our jets.
>
> Ronald Reagan
> Quoted in *Reagan's Reign of Error*, "Temptation of Pride" (ed. by Mark Green and Gail MacColl, 1987)

Ink jet printers aren't the only printers that spray paint the page. Another kind of printer works almost identically, except instead of spraying drops of ink, it sprays drops of wax.

Some people call these solid wax printers since they start with sticks of solid wax. (Picture big crayons, though not necessarily in a crayon shape. And be sure to peel off the paper wrapper in your picture before you put the crayon in the printer). But that doesn't really describe this class of printers, because they have to melt the wax before they use it, so they're really printing with liquid wax. (No one calls them liquid wax printers, though.)

Tektronix—the leading manufacturer of this class of printers—used to call them phase change printers, since they melt the wax so they can spit the drops out on the page, and then the liquid quickly dries to a solid as it cools. You have to be a physicist to appreciate this name, though. It's based on the physical definition that each state of matter—solid, liquid, gas, and plasma—is a phase. So, changing from a solid to a liquid, or from a liquid to a solid is a change in phase. (I see Mary nodding her head in agreement.)

Most people aren't physicists, however, so the phase change name never caught on. Even Tektronix has given up on it, now preferring solid ink printer instead—using *ink* instead of *wax* to include printers that work the same way but melt other materials, like polymers, instead of wax. (File this under breaking developments for up and coming technologies. As I write this, there ain't no such printers for the desktop, so if you can't find any, don't think you missed something.)

Of course, *solid ink* has the same shortcoming as *solid wax* in not really describing what these printers do. And some might quibble with calling wax an *ink* since it's ink only in the most generic sense.

The name I prefer is wax jet printer (but you knew that from the section title). After all, these printers work the same way as ink jet printers, except they spit wax instead of ink.

As far as I know, I'm a lone voice in the wilderness on this one. I invented the name, and I haven't heard many people use it. So don't be surprised if people try correcting you when you talk about wax jet printers. But the reason I like the name is that it's descriptive enough so they'll usually know what you're talking about, even if they haven't heard it before. And *wax jet* is what I'll use for the rest of this book. Besides, I have hopes for the term. A few people I've used it in front of have said that they liked it, including some who work for a major manufacturer of wax jet printers.

> **What's that, Arnold? Yes, I know that at least one wax jet printer—from Tektronix—doesn't work exactly the same way as an ink jet printer. Instead of spraying wax directly on paper, it sprays the wax on a drum that then rolls the ink onto the paper. But it is still spraying the wax, and by my lights that still makes it a wax jet.**

Wax jet printers, by the way, don't have the problem with bleeding that ink jet printers have. The wax dries too quickly for that. Edges on text and lines are crisp and clean, and any given resolution in dots per inch looks essentially the same on a wax jet as on a laser printer. The bad news is that dithering patterns also stand out crisp and clear.

Color quality for wax jets is among the best you'll find. The worst looking output I've ever seen from a wax jet printer still offered brilliant, vibrant color—much more so than most ink jet printers. The best looking output easily blows away anything you can get from an ink jet printer. (At least, that's true so far. Ink jet printers have been improving remarkably over the last few years and may get better yet.)

Thermal Wax Printers

> "The time has come," the Walrus said,
> "To talk of many things:
> Of shoes—and ships—and sealing wax—"
>
> Lewis Carroll
> *Through the Looking-Glass*

In case you're wondering, wax jet printers aren't one of the heaters, even though they heat the wax to melt it before they can print. They're one of the spitters, along with ink jet printers. The heaters are the printers that apply heat directly to a ribbon to transfer color from ribbon to paper.

The best example in this category is the thermal wax transfer printer, which I'll usually shorten to thermal wax printer. Keep the full name in mind, though, because it does a good job of describing what the printer does.

Thermal wax printers use a ribbon coated with wax. The printhead heats the wax enough to melt it to a tacky consistency, so when the printer presses the ribbon firmly against the paper, the wax will stick to the paper.

The ribbons in color thermal wax printers are generally as wide as the page they're meant to print on, with panels of color that are as wide as the ribbon and as long as the page they're meant for. The printers print in three or four passes—meaning that the paper literally passes through the printer three or four times—depending on whether you're using a three- or four-color ribbon. (Typically the page comes almost completely out of the printer with each pass and then gets sucked back in.) Each pass uses one color panel—cyan, magenta, yellow, or black—to print one color for the entire page.

Before Arnold raises his hand, let me rush to qualify this description from two different directions and try not to trip over myself in the process:

First, the length and width of the panels don't exactly match the paper size, but the concept is right, and the description is close enough for right now. (I'll refine it when I talk about the different printer types in depth in Chapter 5.)

Second, the color panels don't *have* to print a page at a time. You could design one (well, okay, *you* couldn't design one, and neither could I, for that matter, but *someone* could) that would print, say, a half-inch wide strip at a time, printing the first strip in each color, then moving down half an inch to print the next strip, and so on. If you were printing, say, only a half a page, you could save a lot of ribbon.

In fact, someone has designed a thermal wax printer—the Star SJ-144—that works exactly this way. The Star printer uses a ribbon that you would probably call a half-inch wide, but keep in mind that the half-inch width is matched to the length of the page you're printing on, so it might be more appropriate to call it a half-inch long. The color panels on the ribbon are each long (or wide) enough to reach across the 8.5-inch width of a letter-size page.

This hasn't been an overwhelmingly popular design, because the printer tends to leave hairline thin lines of white between strips of brilliant color. But it does make for a far less expensive printer mechanism than in traditional thermal wax printers, which need to control a much larger ribbon and control the paper so the colors from each pass all line up precisely right.

Output for thermal wax printers varies. Almost any thermal wax printer will give you vibrant colors along with crisp clean edges. But with some printers, solid areas of color may not fill in as solid, wall-to-wall color because some bits of wax don't transfer to the paper. And as with wax jets, the bad news is that thermal wax printer's sharply delineated edges on lines go hand in hand with dithering patterns that stand out sharp and clear. Resolution for this technology is typically 300 dpi and up.

Thermal Dye Printers

> Wit lies in recognising the resemblance among things which differ and the difference between things which are alike.
>
> Madame de Staël

First cousin to thermal wax printers in every way, and completely different as well, are thermal dye transfer printers. (Hold on to that thought. I'll explain it a little later.) If you've never heard of a thermal dye transfer printer, it may be because most manufacturers call them dye sublimation printers, or dye subs for short. Some people call them dye diffusion printers.

I usually call them dye subs when I'm speaking about them. It's short, it's snappy, and it rolls off the tongue. The only problem, as a friend of mine pointed out to me several years ago, is that it's wholly inaccurate.

No, Arnold, it's not inaccurate because of its psychological meaning. (And, by the way, I wish you would sublimate the instinct to interrupt.) There's another meaning straight out of physics. To sublimate is to change from a solid to gas, or gas to solid, without ever becoming a liquid. For example, dry ice, or frozen carbon dioxide, is called dry ice because it doesn't melt and get wet. It sublimates (or sublimes) directly from solid to gas.

(Well, okay, it says here—in my handy copy of Microsoft Bookshelf—that it's actually known as dry ice because *dry ice* used to be a trademark. But it's a sure bet that one of the reasons the trademark owners picked that name, and one of the reasons it stuck so well that it lost trademark status, is because frozen carbon dioxide doesn't melt into a liquid.) It also says here, for those who are interested, that dry ice sublimates at minus 78.5 degrees Celsius (or Centigrade, which is the way I learned it).

Why Dye Sublimation Printers Aren't

> This is either a forgery or a damn clever original!
>
> Frank Sullivan

The friend who pointed out that dye sublimation printers don't sublimate (whose name, by the way, is Mike Zulich, and who was kind enough to be technical editor on this book) realized that if the dye were really sublimating in these printers, no reasonable person would want to be anywhere near them when they were operating—at least, not the sort of person who worries about breathing potentially harmful vapors of gaseous dye floating around the printer. (And never mind that the dyes are supposed to be harmless. Sometimes it pays to be paranoid.)

He also pointed this out to a leading manufacturer of dye transfer printers, who admitted that, yes, the dyes don't really sublimate. In fact they can't since there's no air space between the ribbon and the paper to give the dyes room to turn into a gas. (Mike could get answers like this from leading manufacturers because he was the project leader on *PC Magazine's* hardware team when he asked. The manufacturer will remain nameless, to protect the guilty.)

No sublimation here

What the dyes actually do is diffuse into the paper, or, more precisely, into the polyester coating on the paper or transparency, with the diffusion helped along by heat from the printhead. In other words, the physics of the process is diffusion, not sublimation. And that explains why some people call them dye diffusion printers.

In fairness to the manufacturer not named above, as well as other manufacturers who insist on calling these printers dye sublimation printers, I have to take a short tangent here to point out that there's a reason why these printers are widely misnamed. According to my contact at the same unnamed company, these printers are direct descendants of a printer-like technology used in the garment industry to dye synthetic cloths, such as polyesters, with patterns. It seems that in the original beasts, developed in the 1950s, the dyes really did sublime because there was some air space between the cloth and the carrier with the dye in it. (Which means, by the way, that polyester leisure suits have a sublime history.)

My nameless contact at this unnamed company (well, okay, it's Tektronix, which makes terrific thermal dye printers) says that when the company's engineers were busy developing their first thermal dye printers, they insisted on calling them dye diffusion printers. At the time, however, the technology was even more exotic than it is now, and those few people who knew about this class of printers at all knew them as dye sublimation printers. Since nobody knew what a dye diffusion printer was, Tektronix decided to stay with the dye sublimation misnomer, along with most of the rest of the industry. In other words, the name is a historical accident that we're stuck with, just like we're stuck with *dialing* a phone number, and probably will be, even after everyone who has ever used a rotary dial phone is long since gone.

Where the thermal dye printer name comes from

Yes, Mary? You're wondering why, if these printers are really dye diffusion printers, I keep calling them thermal dye transfer printers. Well, I'll grant that the dye diffusion name tells you the physics of how the dye gets transferred to the paper (should anyone care). But it's just as accurate to call them thermal dye transfer printers because they use heat to encourage the dye to transfer to the paper.

Besides, as I said before, they're first cousin to thermal wax transfer printers, so it makes sense to give them a parallel name. And to keep the parallel, I'll usually call them thermal dye printers for short.

Thermal Dye and Thermal Wax: The Same, but Different

> The odd thing about being a vegetarian is, not that the things that happen to other people don't happen to me—they all do—but that they happen differently.
>
> George Bernard Shaw

Let me backtrack a bit: What I actually said before was that thermal dye printers are first cousins to thermal wax printers in every way, and completely different as well. By now you know at least one difference: One kind of printer uses wax that sticks to a piece of paper; the other uses dye that diffuses into a polyester coating. You also know at least one of the similarities: They both use heat. But the similarities go far beyond this. And so do the differences.

The biggest difference between thermal wax and thermal dye printers is output quality. At least, that's the biggest difference unless you're paying for the prints yourself. Then the biggest difference is cost.

As a class, thermal dye printers have, beyond argument, the highest quality color output of any color printer technology. Colors in graphics are vibrant and fully saturated and solid areas are solidly filled in. Even better, you won't see a dithering pattern with these printers because they don't use dithering to create colors.

The dyes in thermal dye printers are translucent, or transparent, depending on who you're talking to. Some people prefer to call them transparent because the primary dictionary meaning for translucent applies to things that diffuse light enough to keep you from seeing clear images—like looking through wax paper. But the primary dictionary meaning for transparent applies to things that you can see through as if there were nothing there. That's not much of an improvement since you can certainly see the colors in the dyes. One of the secondary definitions for translucent, however, is *clear*. And one of the secondary definitions for transparent is *can be seen through*. So either word applies.

Whether you call the dyes translucent or transparent, thermal dye printers can overlay the dyes on top of each other and actually mix the colors on the page. For graphics, the dither-free color gives thermal dye output a slight advantage over wax jets and thermal wax printers. For photos, it blows everything else out of the water.

One price you pay for this gorgeous output is that you have to use the special, polyester-coated paper, which has much the same look and feel as a glossy photograph. The other price you pay is money.

Thermal dye prints are expensive. Prices may change by the time you read this, but on the day I'm writing it, the cost for thermal dye prints ranges from about $2 to $7 *per page*—and the price has been pretty much the same for years. The only good news about these prices is that the prints you're likely to be most interested in are at the low side of the range. Transparencies cost more than paper, and oversize pages cost more than standard letter-size pages. If all you want is letter-size paper output, it shouldn't cost you much more than $2 per print. But that's still enough to give you pause before running off twenty party invitations for your eight-year old's birthday. The same set of party invitations on a thermal wax printer will be closer to fifty cents a page. (Prices for other kinds of printers can be as low as ten cents a dance or well over a dollar, but figuring price per page is a tricky issue that we'll look at in Chapter 5.).

Now that I've sold you on how different these technologies are, how dumb would it sound if I told you they are more alike than they are different? Don't answer just yet.

What I haven't told you is that the mechanics of printing with a thermal dye printer are virtually identical to the mechanics of printing with a thermal wax printer. Both kinds of printers use a ribbon, a printhead that heats the ribbon while holding it firmly against a piece of paper, and a colorant (there's one of those jargon words again; it just means some material that holds color, like wax or dye) that moves between ribbon and paper.

If you ignore the material the ribbons are made from, the ribbons in thermal dye printers are essentially identical to ribbons in thermal wax printers—generally as wide as the page they're meant to print on, with panels of color that are as wide as the ribbon and as long as the page they're meant for.

The printing process itself for thermal dye printers is also identical to the process for thermal wax printers, with the paper passing through the printer once for each color panel, and the printer laying down one color on each pass—cyan, magenta, yellow, or black—for the entire page.

So just how similar are these technologies? Would it sway your opinion if I told you that some printers offer both thermal dye and thermal wax output in the same box?

Two For the Price of One

> If man could be crossed with a cat it would improve man, but it would deteriorate the cat.
>
> Mark Twain

Look down there at the desk! It's a thermal wax printer! It's a thermal dye printer! It's both!

The typical dual mode printer lets you change from thermal wax to thermal dye and back again simply by changing the ribbon and paper. In some cases, you have to tell the printer driver to change mode as well. In other cases, the printer can figure it out for itself. (This doesn't require sensor readings from the bridge of the *Enterprise*. A marking system on the ribbons that's similar to bar codes in concept but much simpler, or a small physical difference between, say, the ribbon cartridges or paper trays for each mode is enough to clue the printer in.) The key difference between modes is in how fast the printer moves the paper (much slower for thermal dye), and how much heat the printhead puts out.

Yes, Tim? You wonder why anyone bothers building—or buying—a printer that's thermal wax only or thermal dye only when they can have both at once? Well, not everyone is convinced that dual mode printers are a Good Thing.

The good, the bad, and the gorgeous

It happens that you can't design a printer to give the best possible output for both modes, so you have to make compromises in one mode or the other, if not both. Another issue is that changing ribbons and paper is a chore—not much of a chore, compared to, say, working on a chain gang, but still a chore. And if you switch between the two modes very often, changing ribbon and paper gets old real fast.

I don't know how you feel about it, but I find that my laser printer, with a 250-sheet paper tray, runs out of paper annoyingly often. Maybe I just get annoyed easily, but, after all, the only time the paper runs out is in the middle of a print job—usually one that needs to be finished ten minutes ago. The thought of having to switch ribbon and paper several times a day with a dual mode printer isn't overly inviting.

On the other hand, if I used one of the modes most of the time and reserved the other for birthdays and other special occasions, a dual mode printer would look a lot more attractive. It would look even more attractive if I could use it to save money—relying on thermal wax mode for, say, proofs and everyday printing, even though I absolutely had to have the thermal dye capability for occasionally dressing up my output in its Sunday best. (I'm sure I'm only being paranoid by thinking that whenever I needed to print something, the printer would have the wrong ribbon and paper loaded anyway.)

Laser Printers

> One cool judgment is worth a thousand hasty counsels. The thing to do is to supply light and not heat.
>
> Woodrow Wilson

Next (and last) on the list are laser printers. Yes, Arnold, I mean laser and laser-like printers as a single category. More precisely, to use a term that almost no one ever uses, I mean electrophotographic printers.

Electrophotographic printers include laser, LED, and LCD printers. (They also include a *really* exotic breed called ion-deposition printers. Odds are you've never heard of these even if you knew what an electrophotographic printer was.) All of these printers work essentially the same way, and all have essentially the same capabilities. (Well, the first three, at least, work the same way and have the same capabilities. The ion-deposition printers work slightly differently and have different capabilities, but let's ignore them for the moment.)

Laser, LCD, and LED printers all work by zapping a photosensitive drum (or photosensitive belt) with light to draw the image for a page—text and all—as an electrostatic charge. Toner, which is basically plastic dust (with some other stuff mixed in), then sticks to the drum or belt the same way, and for the same reason, that dust sticks to your monitor screen—because of the electrostatic charge.

To be precisely correct (and to get Arnold to put his hand down), I should explain that the drum or belt starts out with an electrostatic charge, and the light removes the charge from the areas it hits. In fact, there are two approaches to laser printers. In one kind, the light draws the negative of the image, removing the charge from the places you don't want it. The charged areas on the belt then pick up the toner and hold it in place.

In the other kind, the light draws the actual image, removing the charge from the areas where you want toner. This kind of printer also charges the toner, so it's repelled by the charged areas of the drum or belt and sticks to the uncharged areas. No matter how the image gets drawn, however, the point is that the toner sticks to the drum or belt through an electrostatic charge.

Next, the drum or belt transfers the toner to a piece of paper, also by way of an electrostatic charge. The last step on the way to the output bin is the fuser, which heats the toner (read: melts the plastic) to fuse it to the paper.

If you want a graphic demonstration of the importance of fusing the toner, try opening the cover to a laser printer after it's fed a piece of paper. If you time it right, just before the page hits the fuser, you'll get a piece of paper with the toner all nicely in place, but only until you touch it or breath on it. Don't do this too often, however. In fact, don't do it on purpose at all; breathing toner is not healthy. But if you get a paper jam at the output tray and you happen to notice that the toner comes off on your hands when you free up the paper, now you know why. If you're wondering where the fuser is, just look inside the printer, close to the output tray, for something labeled *Warning. High Temperature.*

The only real difference between laser, LCD, and LED printers is in how they produce and control the light that zaps the drum and gives it an electrostatic charge. (There are no prizes for guessing which kind uses a laser, which kind uses a liquid crystal display, and which kind uses light-emitting diodes.)

If you want to impress your friends with how much you know about printers, point out that LCD printers are really liquid crystal shutter printers because the LCDs in these printers are really liquid crystal shutters. Lasers and LEDs are light sources; LCDs are not. The LCD, or technically the liquid crystal shutter, in an LCD printer sits between a light source—typically a halogen lamp—and the drum. Each liquid crystal acts as a shutter to let light shine through or not.

Aside from the possibilities for impressing your friends, the distinction between liquid crystal display and liquid crystal shutter is too subtle to matter much. In fact, the distinction between laser, LCD, and LED is more subtle than is usually worth bothering with.

LCDs and LEDs aren't lasers, but . . .   Given how similar these printers are, it's not surprising that most people use *laser* to mean *laser or laser-like printer*. I vote with most people on this, and that's how I'm going to use the word too. It's a lot easier than saying *laser or laser-like printer* each time, or worse, *electrophotographic printer*.

As it happens, all of the color laser printers that are available as I write this are true laser printers, but that won't be true for all time (or even for the lifetime of this book). And what's true for the current crop of laser printers should apply to all the variations on the laser theme.

> **File this one under completely tangential information, but since I mentioned ion-deposition printers, it wouldn't be fair to go too far without explaining what they are. These printers are *really* zappers. Instead of using a photosensitive drum, they paint the electrostatic charge on the drum directly with a stream of ions. (Ions, for Tim and others who skipped high school physics, are electrically charged atoms or molecules.) Ion-deposition printers are fast—up to about 90 pages per minute—but they don't offer the kind of crisp, clean edges that laser printers are known for, which is why their natural home is in a high-volume data processing department, where speed is more important than quality.**

Color quality from laser printers varies all over the map—or a good part of it. The worst looking laser output is on a par with the best ink jet printers, or a little worse. The best lies somewhere between the best wax jet and the least of the thermal dye printers. (I say *least* rather than *worst* because I've never seen any thermal dye printer produce anything less than superb output. Some printers offer more superb output than others, but *worst* has such a negative connotation.)

The worst color laser printers (and for laser printers I don't mind the word) print color that's a little dull, like a coat of paint that should have an undercoat but doesn't. The best of the breed offer a near match for the fully saturated, vibrant colors you'll find in a wax jet printer. But the color quality from laser printers, unlike the color from wax jets, varies depending on the smoothness of the paper you're printing on.

Edges on text and graphics for these printers are . . . well . . . laser quality, which means that dithering patterns stand out sharp and clear. However, some laser printers offer a high enough resolution—at 600 by 600 or 1200 by 300 dpi—to make the dithering far less obvious. Other laser printers mix the toner on the page for each dot, to provide something approaching continuous tone output.

I'm hedging like crazy here because I'm oversimplifying a bit. The printers I'm thinking of—the Tektronix 540 Plus and the Apple Color LaserWriter 12/600 PS—actually combine continuous tone mixing of colors with dithering. And that's the closest you'll find to continuous tone lasers for under $10,000. (You can also find true continuous tone lasers if you're willing to include printers that cost some multiple of $10,000 plus change. These are not exactly aimed at the home office, and I'll ignore them for our purposes.) Let's leave the discussion at that for now. There's no need to go into details on this once-over-lightly pass. We'll take a closer look at combining continuous tone with dithering in Chapter 5.

MORE WAYS TO SLICE AND DICE

> I see no reason for calling my work poetry except that there is no other category in which to put it.
>
> Marianne Moore
> In accepting the National Book Award for poetry, May 1959.

I said it before, and I'll say it again: There are lots of ways to slice and dice color printers besides printer technology. It's useful to keep at least some of the more important possibilities in mind.

The choices I mentioned before are price, resolution, printer language, and the kind of paper the printer uses. Still other ways are how well a printer prints on different kinds of paper (like copy paper versus laser paper), how well it handles different kinds of printing (like paper versus transparencies), whether a given printer is designed as a dedicated color printer, or whether you can use it as your workhorse for monochrome as well.

Here's a quick look at each of these cubbyholes. (Again, this is a once over lightly. We'll look at some of these in more detail in Chapter 5 also.)

High-end, Low end, and Mid-end Printers

> "Too caustic?" To hell with the cost. If it's a good picture, we'll make it.
>
> Samuel Goldwyn

High end, low end, and middle range are relative terms, and their definitions (since I get to define them) depend more on features and output quality than on price. There's some logic to this: You can take a low end printer and try to sell it for $10,000, but it will still be a low-end printer. (You won't sell many at that price, but I'll bet you sell some.) As a rule, though, high-end color printers are over $3000, with most over $5000, and low-end printers are under $500. The mid-range covers everything in between.

High end   High-end color printers produce vibrant color output using the more exotic technologies we've looked at: thermal wax, thermal dye, wax jet, and color laser. They are also designed for networks and are loaded with expensive hardware—from network connectors, to lots of memory, to fast internal processors so they can quickly process an image for printing.

At $3000 and up (mostly up), these printers are hard to justify unless you're a graphics professional or like to buy expensive toys. But they can also wind up in offices where the powers that be appreciate the value of letting everyone add a little color to their lives—not to mention adding it to their reports, presentations, and correspondence.

Do the math: Hanging one $5000 printer on a network with, say, twenty people is cheaper than putting a $300 color ink jet printer on each desk. And everyone's output will look a lot better. The single $5000 printer will also generally print color pages faster, which makes it a lot easier to print 20 overhead transparencies at the last minute before a meeting or 200 copies of a brochure.

Another advantage is that a $5000 printer generally needs less care and feeding than a $300 printer. If you have to print those 200 copies of a brochure, you won't have to stand over the printer to add more paper or make sure it doesn't run out of ink. You can simply make sure it's loaded with paper when you start and come back later to pick up the finished job.

Mid-range printers produce color output that runs from acceptable to terrific. This category includes the printer that you're most likely using (or considering buying) if you're reading this book—unless you're lucky enough to be plugged in to a network with one of those $5000 toys. **Mid range**

Most printers in this range are under $2000, and most of those are under $1000. They may be based on ink jet, thermal wax, or thermal dye technology—or they may offer both thermal wax and thermal dye printing in one package. But unlike the high-end thermal wax and thermal dye printers, these printers keep cost down by leaving out all the network features and the expensive hardware that goes with them. That means it's not unusual to get high-quality color output at a mid-range price.

Low-end printers, at $500 or less, are far more affordable and are based on the more common technologies of ink jet and even (ugh!) dot matrix printing. But the color quality varies from disappointing to a bad joke. With a little luck, prices on color printers will eventually fall enough to turn some of today's mid-range printers into the next generation's low end and make the current low end go away. **Low end**

Lots of Dots

> It was said of old Sarah, Duchess of Marlborough, that she never puts dots over her i's, to save ink.
>
> Horace Walpole

You can also classify printers by resolution. Dots per inch is a good place to start. All other things being equal (which, of course, they rarely are), more dots per inch means better resolution, which means more detail, sharper edges, and less obvious dithering patterns.

For most kinds of color printers—including ink jets, wax jets, thermal wax, thermal dye, and laser printers—300 dots per inch has become a minimum standard. (Yes, Arnold, I know if you look hard enough you can find an occasional printer with lower resolution. But I can think of only two offhand.)

When 600 dpi doesn't mean 600 dpi

With monochrome laser printers migrating to 600 dpi as the new monochrome laser standard, more and more color printers are offering higher resolutions as well. Watch out when you run across references to 600 dpi or higher, however, especially if the references are in ads and you're looking for a new printer.

In this book, when I talk about 300 dpi or 600 dpi I mean *300 by 300* dpi or *600 by 600* dpi. And when I talk about printers with different horizontal and vertical resolutions, like 600 by 300 dpi (which we'll come to later), I'll always give both numbers. But I've seen manufacturers casually refer to, say, 600 dpi resolution when they really mean 600 by 300 dpi. For most printers that offer it, 600 by 300 dpi makes a noticeable difference compared to the same printer at 300 by 300 dpi. But it still isn't 600 by 600 dpi. Caveat emptor, indeed.

Now here's the shocker: Resolution depends on more than just dots per inch. For any given technology, more dots per inch usually improves the output, but 360 dpi on, say, an ink jet printer, still won't be a match for 300 dpi on a laser printer. Since the laser printer dots don't bleed and the ink jet dots do, the laser printer will still have crisper, cleaner edges, with smaller, more precise dots than the "higher resolution" ink jet printer. And this isn't the only factor that can affect resolution. So don't assume that dots per inch tells the whole story.

Printer Language

> I speak Spanish to God, Italian to women, French to men and German to my horse.
>
> Attributed to Charles V King of Spain, Holy Roman Emperor

In the bad old days when every program had to come with its own printer drivers, printer language—the set of commands that a printer takes its marching orders from—was critical. If you had a printer with an obscure language, it might not work with some of your programs.

Today, if you use Windows or Windows 95 or OS/2 or the Mac, you need only a single driver for your operating system. Install the one driver, and any program that runs under that operating system can use it. (Yes, Arnold, Windows isn't really an operating system, but Microsoft likes to call it one, so let's not quibble.)

Even better, most color printers come with their own drivers for Windows, Windows 95, OS/2, and the Mac. (Well, not always for OS/2, but usually for Windows, Windows 95, and the Mac, at least.) In some cases, you get all three drivers when you buy the printer. In others, you have to specify which version of the printer you want. (But I'll assume you're smart enough to get the right driver for your preferred operating system. After all, you showed a high level of intelligence in picking out this book to read.)

All this makes printer language less of an issue than it once was, but it's still important. Lots of people are still married to WordPerfect for DOS, for example. If you're one of them, and you want to print in color from WordPerfect, you'd better be sure that WordPerfect comes with a driver for your printer, or, better yet, that your printer offers a WordPerfect driver. In fact, you'll need a driver if you simply want to print monochrome text and graphics. But even if you never go near a DOS program, printer language makes a difference.

If you have to print the same file on two different printers—at home and at the office, say, or in your office and at a client's office—and the printers use different languages, you'll find that changing languages can change layout and color. If you have a printer that understands more than one language, changing language can even change layout and color on the same printer.

One of the printers I used for testing for this book is the Hewlett-Packard DeskJet 1200C/PS, which understands both PCL-5C and Adobe PostScript Level 2. (More on these in a moment.) One of the files I used prints with dark orange and bright yellow in PCL mode, but with dark orange and yellowish orange in PostScript mode. And when I printed the same file on a Hewlett-Packard DeskJet 560C, which uses a different version of PCL, the colors came out as light orange and yellow. This is an experiment you might want to try yourself. Create a file with blocks of various colors in it, print it using two different printer languages, and compare the results. If you can't get at two printers (or one bilingual printer), take a look at the sample color output elsewhere in this book to see what I'm talking about.

PCL, which is short for Printer Control Language, and PostScript are the two most popular printer languages. Both come in more than one version, but there are fewer variations on PostScript than on PCL. We'll dissect the variations in Chapter 5. For now, there are only a few things you have to know.

Hewlett-Packard created PCL, but lots of other manufacturers use it in their printers. The hard part is keeping up with the variations, since HP keeps changing PCL to fit the features in new printers, while other manufacturers add their own changes as well. I'll ignore the variations for the moment.

PCL

PostScript comes originally from Adobe, but there are lots of cloned versions of PostScript. I'll ignore these variations for now also, except to point out that PostScript Level 2 is concerned with (among other things) maintaining color consistency from one printer to another.

Not so incidentally, printing a page in PCL is usually faster than printing the same page on the same printer in PostScript. But if you need to print the same file on different printers, you'll get greater consistency with two PostScript printers than with two PCL printers.

Operating system specific languages

There are two other language categories for printers: Operating System Specific and the ever popular Other. An operating system specific language is just what it sounds like—a language that's specific to a given operating system. These languages differ from traditional printer languages in that the printer driver doesn't have to translate images from the way a program describes them to the way the printer describes them. It simply uses the same description.

If that didn't make sense, don't reread it just yet. This is one of those ideas that doesn't quite click without a specific example.

Windows, for instance, has its own set of commands for putting images on the screen. The set of commands is the graphical device interface, or GDI. A Windows GDI printer uses the same GDI commands. And because Windows and the printer are both using the same commands, (all together, now) the printer driver doesn't have to translate images from the way the program describes them to the way the printer describes them. (See, it does make sense.)

Printers that use Windows GDI or other operating system specific printer languages are usually available for more than one operating system, so you can get the printer for Windows or for the Mac, for example. However, you can't generally use these printers with DOS programs.

Other languages

PostScript and PCL aren't the only traditional printer languages (as opposed to operating system specific printer languages) that include commands for color. You can find color printers that use standard dot matrix command sets—including, say, IBM commands and Epson commands—or oddball command sets of their own.

You'd probably guess that most color dot matrix printers would use standard dot matrix command sets, and you'd be right. But just because a printer isn't a dot matrix printer doesn't mean it doesn't use a command set that originated on dot matrix printers. The Star SJ-144, which is a thermal wax printer, uses Epson and IBM dot matrix printer command sets. So does the Canon BJC-600e, which is an ink jet printer.

Printers in this category can have all sorts of variations, depending on the language. Their most obvious shortcoming is that if you print the same file on several printers, you'll find little consistency in color from one to the next, even for printers that use the same language.

Does It Work with Copy Paper?

> My own experience has been that the tools I need for my trade are paper, tobacco, food, and a little whisky.
>
> William Faulkner

You can also divide color printers by the kind of paper they use. This is an easy one: Ink jets, wax jets, lasers, and some thermal wax printers can use any paper you have handy, including plain old copy paper. Thermal dye printers and some thermal wax printers can't. (Any printer can print on transparencies—using different transparency stock for different printers—but that's another issue entirely.)

This matters because special paper tends to be expensive, and that can add anywhere from a few pennies to almost a dollar to the price per page. It also matters because special paper tends to stand out as different. If you're printing photos on a thermal dye printer, you may think that the special-purpose, heavy-weight paper that makes the output look and feel like a glossy photo is a Good Thing. But if you want to slip one or two color pages into an otherwise black and white report, or you want to add a color graphic in the middle of a page of text, you probably don't want the paper itself to stand out as different.

In case you're wondering, the reason some thermal wax printers can print on standard copy paper while others can't is that it takes an extra step to print on copy paper. Some printers offer the extra step. Others don't.

How thermal wax printers turn copy paper into coated paper

Thermal wax printers normally use special paper, notable for its smooth surface, so they can lay down an even coat of wax. (Don't confuse this special thermal wax paper with that evil-looking thermal paper that comes out of cheap fax machines. Thermal wax paper is much more like plain paper in look and feel.) If you try printing on copy paper with a printer that's set up to use thermal wax paper, you'll leave lots of white specks where the wax didn't transfer to the paper, as in Figure 1.6.

Figure 1.6 This is what you can normally expect if you try printing with a thermal wax transfer printer on copy paper—at least, for a printer that isn't set up to use copy paper.

The trick for printing on standard paper is to add an extra panel to the thermal wax ribbon. The extra panel lets the printer lay down a coating on the first pass, presto chango turning plain old copy paper into thermal wax paper, and turning the spotted black and white horse in Figure 1.6 into the black horse in Figure 1.7.

Figure 1.7 This is the same horse as in Figure 1.6, but this is what it should really look like—and what it will look like from a thermal wax printer if you use thermal wax paper, or if the printer has a special ribbon for printing on standard copy paper.

Does It Print Well on Copy Paper?

> A verbal contract isn't worth the paper it's written on.
>
> Samuel Goldwyn

Printing on copy paper is one thing. Printing well on copy paper is something else altogether. From a printer's point of view, copy paper is a little like the paper you learned how to write on in first grade—the kind with lines about an inch apart and marbled with slices of porous wood. Put a drop of ink on the paper, and you can watch the drop spread out as the paper absorbs it. Draw with a crayon, and you can see small gaps because the paper's so rough that the crayon hits the peaks and misses the valleys. And whatever color ink or crayon you use is dulled down by the dingy yellow background.

Well, okay, I'm exaggerating—but just a little. The ink from ink jet printers does in fact bleed into the copy paper, making edges less sharp and colors duller than they can be. Even laser printers and thermal wax printers lose some sharpness and color vibrancy because of the relatively rough surface and off white color. All three kinds of printers can benefit from high-quality laser paper. (So can monochrome laser and ink jet printers, for that matter.)

> **If you're not familiar with laser paper, you should correct that oversight immediately. Put down the book, go to the closest office supply store, and buy some laser paper. Go ahead; I'll wait. Dum . . . de . . . dum . . . de . . . dum . . . de . . . dum.**
>
> **Ah, you're back. Now take one sheet of the laser paper and compare it to a sheet of the copy paper you've been using. Notice that it's a little heavier weight and a little brighter white (in most cases, at least). But most important, it's smoother to eye and touch. (If you have calluses on your fingertips from typing on a hot keyboard all day, you may not be able to feel the difference in smoothness, but I promise you that it's there. If you can't see it with your naked eye or you're not sure that you see it, try a magnifying glass or loupe. Or try rubbing both sides of the paper against your lip to feel the difference. But watch out for paper cuts.)**
>
> **Now print some text in black and white, using any handy laser or ink jet printer. Print the same text on both the laser paper and the copy paper. (Be careful to print on the right side of the paper. It's not so easy to see the difference, but there is a preferred side for printing. There should be an arrow or other indication on the package to tell you which side that is.) Finally, compare the two printed pages. The text on the laser paper should look sharper and darker. If you repeat this test with a color graphic, the colors on the laser paper should look more vibrant.**

Now here's the weird part. And I see Tim's already discovered it by the puzzled look on his face and the loupe in his hand. If you look at the text output on both kinds of paper with a loupe or good magnifying glass, you'll be hard put to see any improvement in the sharpness of the edges on the laser paper. In fact, the image on the laser paper will be *worse* in some ways.

If you're using a laser printer, you'll likely see some scattered specks of stray toner on the laser paper that you won't see on the copy paper. If you're using an ink jet printer, the text on the copy paper may actually have better formed edges than the text on the laser paper. So how come the text looks sharper and darker to the naked eye? It's a simple illusion: The brighter white background provides greater contrast, so your brain says that the text is darker.

Laser paper costs roughly twice as much as copy paper, or about a penny a page. (But you know that from having just bought some, right?) You'll have to decide whether the extra quality is worth the extra cost. But you'll certainly want to consider it when it's time to spruce up for special occasions. (And that applies to black and white printing too.) Not so incidentally, wax jet printers can also benefit from the sharper contrast between the printed output and a whiter, brighter white.

Having gotten your hopes up, I also have to point out that even laser paper won't show off ink jet and thermal wax printers at their best. For that you need special paper—with different paper available for different printers. You already know the bad news: Special paper tends to be expensive. The good news is that for thermal wax printers, at least, what you lose by paying extra for the paper, you make up for in savings on the ribbons.

What About Transparencies?

> In my own time there have been inventions of this sort, transparent windows . . . tubes for diffusing warmth equally through all parts of a building . . . short-hand . . . But the inventing of such things is drudgery for the lowest slaves . . .
>
> Seneca (c. 4 BC–AD c. 65)
> *Epistulae ad Lucilium,* Epistle 90, sct. 25

If you spend a lot of time slaving away at creating transparencies for presentations, you may care more about what printer output looks like on transparencies than on paper. And, as you may have found out the hard way already, great-looking output on paper doesn't necessarily translate to great-looking output on transparencies.

Ink jet printers are known for doing poorly on transparencies, printing washed-out colors, rather than the fully saturated colors you need to stand up to the bright city lights in a projector. There's at least one exception to this rule, however. The Hewlett-Packard DeskJet 1200 spray paints transparencies that can go toe to toe with other technologies. (There are probably some other exceptions as well, but none that I can vouch for from personal experience.)

Wax jet printers have traditionally been known for doing poorly on transparencies. Those little dots of wax that look so great on paper because they cool to a solid without bleeding into the page turn into thousands of tiny lenses on a transparency because they dry to a semi-spherical shape. Here again, there's at least one exception to the rule. The Tektronix Phaser 340 flattens the dots to avoid the lensing effect, while still keeping all the benefits that go with the technology—especially the fully saturated colors and sharp edges.

Thermal wax transfer printers are known for printing great transparencies, with fully saturated colors that stand up to bright lights. Thermal dye printers can be as good or better—particularly if you use photos in your transparencies—but they can also suffer from washed-out colors. Very few people use thermal dye printers for transparencies because the difference in price per page—which is measured in dollars—is much greater than the difference in quality.

Laser printers, finally, are a mixed bag. Laser printers that print washed out colors on paper will print washed-out colors on transparencies too. Printers that print fully saturated colors on paper may or may not print fully saturated colors on transparencies. Some do. Some don't.

The only way to test a transparency is to throw it on a projector. If you hold a transparency up against a white background, like a white piece of paper, you can see the transparency well enough, but you can't really judge how it will hold up to light. Thermal dye output, for example, should look too dark against a piece of white paper, or it's pretty well guaranteed to look too light on the screen.

How good a transparency looks also depends on the projector. A yellowish bulb, for example, will make white and yellow areas on the transparency look the same. A transparency that looks just fine on one projector, with a bright (Read: high wattage) bulb may look too dark on another projector with a dimmer bulb, while a transparency that looks washed out on the first projector may look fine on the second.

Dedicated Color or Monochrome Plus Color?

> When choosing between two evils, I always like to pick the one I never tried before.
>
> Mae West
> As Frisco Doll, in the film *Klondike Annie* (1936).

The ideal color printer would not only offer the best possible color output on plain copy paper but would offer high quality black and white output as well. That would let you use one printer for all your printing, mix text and color graphics in the same document or even on the same page, and never have to collate color pages from one printer with text pages from another.

Unfortunately you can't find a printer that does all this at the same time—even if you don't care about price. So the best you can do is choose between two evils: a dedicated color printer if you insist on the best possible output, or less-than-ideal color if you insist on a printer that will let you print monochrome or color, or mix the two on a single page.

What's that, Arnold? Yes, you're right. Technically there ain't no such thing as a dedicated color printer, at least, not in the sense of a printer that can print only color.

If you like, you can take a thermal dye printer and print text—at two or three dollars a page and a speed measured in minutes per page—but you'd have to have a lot of money and a lot of time on your hands. You'd also have to be willing to live with the heavy-weight, polyester coated paper and the glossy look of the page. By my lights, that turns thermal dye printers into dedicated color printers for all practical purposes. Thermal wax printers fall into the same category.

What's a dedicated color printer?

Some ink jet printers also fall in the dedicated color category, but they're mostly obsolete. Any color ink jet printer you can buy today should also print monochrome text and graphics quickly enough, and well enough, to serve for monochrome printing also. (At least, any ink jet printer you should be willing to buy today should meet that description. Can't tell what's hiding in bargain basements, cable TV shopping channels, or the next tag sale you come across.)

Most color ink jet printers and all color laser printers fall in the all-around workhorse category, suitable for color or monochrome printing (except for those that simply do a lousy job). Use these for your day-to-day black-and-white output, and you won't pay much of a premium in speed or price. In fact, you won't pay any premium for printing in black and white on a color ink jet and only a small premium on most color lasers, which cost about a penny more per black-and-white page than a typical monochrome laser printer.

Wax jets have a foot in both worlds. Most wax jet printers to date are best understood as dedicated color printers. Speed for monochrome pages is on the slow side, and the wax is a bit shiny, so text pages don't look quite right. But there's at least one exception. (Well, okay, there is only one exception as I write this, but if it gets popular, you can expect imitators.) The Tektronix Phaser 340 offers a four-pages-per-minute speed and text that doesn't have any more shine than text from a color laser printer.

And that, finally, finishes the whirlwind tour of color printers and how to categorize them. Let's switch gears and talk a little bit about color.

WHAT YOU SEE IS SOMETIMES SURPRISING

> When we got into office, the thing that surprised me most was to find that things were just as bad as we'd been saying they were.
>
> John F. Kennedy
> Speech at dinner honoring Kennedy's 44th birthday, May 27, 1961

A cautionary tale: Everyone here is probably too young to remember this, but there was a time when monospaced, Courier font was the standard for letter-quality text. Even after the laser printer came along, the standard persisted for a while. Then people started buying extra fonts for their laser printers and started playing with them. Desktop publishing was born. And with it, came ransom-note typography.

Ransom note typography

Ransom note typography gets its name from the classic ransom note. As any mystery buff will tell you, ransom notes are painfully pasted together from words and letters cut from a random selection of magazines. Each magazine typically uses its own font and font size, and the cuttings are slapped together with no regard to how well the fonts go with each other. This isn't surprising for ransom notes since the people who write them are generally not too concerned with the niceties of typography. But too many people who try their hands at desktop publishing—or even sprucing up a letter—manage to produce something similar, like the sample in Figure 1.8.

Picking The Wrong Font

The essence of ransom note typography is to pick one or more unusual fonts, and use them in a way that's somehow inappropriate, which usually means the font takes something away from the text, rather than adding to it.

Difficult To Read Typefaces

If I had to choose a font that was difficult to read, it would be hard to top a script font. IF I WANTED TO MAKE IT REALLY HARD TO READ, HOWEVER, I'D PUT IT IN ALL CAPS.

How To Make a Page Really Ugly

If I wanted to work at making a page really ugly, I'd add several unusual, difficult to read typefaces on the same page. (But I'll just use two in this example. It's enough to make the point.)

It also helps (ha!) to add some dingbats or other symbols, in this case from the Botanical font.

I'm using one of the botanical symbols, the ❁, to indicate the end of each section. If I were using a readable font, this would be a potentially useful technique–to signal the end of an article in a newsletter, for example. But with this script font, which is already difficult to read, adding the botanical symbol is gilding an already gilded lily.

Figure 1.8 You too can use fancy fonts to create really ugly pages.

Something about having too many fonts to play with draws some people into picking unusual fonts just for the sake of having something unusual. Other people pick fonts that are readable enough in themselves, but don't go together very well, as in Figure 1.9.

Picking the Wrong Font, Part 2
You don't have to choose completely unreadable fonts to qualify for ransom note typography. In this case I've chosen Avant Garde for the headings and Swiss for the body text. The result is perfectly readable, but just doesn't look right.

Readable, but Not Pretty
The problem here is that the font I'm using for the heading and the font I'm using for body text are similar, but different. They are both sans serif fonts, meaning that they don't have the extra little strokes that you'll find at the ends of letters in a serif font, like Times New Roman. (I'd show an example here but that wouldn't be fair, since the additional font would make the page look even worse. Well, okay, I'll add the example to the bottom.)
Despite their essential similarity as two sans serif fonts (or rather, because of that similarity) their differences nag at the edge of your awareness as being a little off. Take a close look, and you'll see that the lower case t, for example, is different in the heading than in the body text.

An example of a Serif Font
This is an example of a serif font, using Times New Roman for the body text, and the slightly different Book Antiqua for the heading. Note the extra little finishing strokes at the end of each letter so that a T, for example, is more than just one vertical stroke and one horizontal stroke.

Figure 1.9 It's not hard to create ugly pages without fancy fonts too.

Now that laser printers have been around for a while, most people who are drawn to the sort of typography shown in Figure 1.8 have learned to restrain themselves a bit (if only because someone in their office with better taste or a better feel for typography has imposed office-wide standards). And most people who make the sort of mistake shown in Figure 1.9 have learned to do better as well, but you'll still see occasional examples from one category or the other from people who haven't learned better.

Yes, Mary? You're wondering what this has to do with color printers? Well, I'm making a point by analogy, which is always a slippery way to argue, but in this case is exactly right.

The problem with having a color printer is that to use it effectively, you have to know at least a little about color. Unless you're either an artist or color blind, you probably don't think that's a big deal. After all, you deal with color every day, and you've dealt with it all your life.

You've probably decorated your house or apartment, and chosen colors for rugs, furniture, and wall paint. You may have played with the color settings in Windows or other programs to customize your screen. And unless you're in the military or other job with a prescribed uniform, or you're one of the lucky folks who works in blue jeans and a T-shirt, you probably consider color combinations every time you dress in the morning. So working with color is second nature. Straightforward. Intuitive. Easy. Right?

Buzzzzzzz.

Wrong.

If working with color is so easy, how come most people have to bring a couch cushion or the equivalent along with them when they're trying to pick the right color paint for their living room? And how come they have to spend so much time trying to decide which color goes best with the couch? And after spending all that time deciding, how come it still sometimes turns out that the paint doesn't go with the couch after all?

Working with color ain't easy.

And if working with color is so easy, how come graphic artists have to go to school to learn how to use color? (Put your hand down, Arnold, that's a rhetorical question.)

The answer is that working with color isn't easy.

Six Reasons Why Colors Can Surprise You

> Be astonished, O ye heavens, at this, and be horribly afraid.
>
> Jeremiah 2:12

In Chapter 7 we'll take a reasonably close look at color and I'll discuss such issues as color schemes that generally work well together. Right now, I just want to make sure you're aware of some of the reasons why colors don't always work the way you expect them to.

One: Sometimes Colors That Match, Don't Match

> You look rather rash my dear your colors don't quite match your face.
>
> Daisy Ashford
> *The Young Visiters,* "Starting Gaily"

Have you ever tried to put together a suit at a department store by picking out a jacket and pants or jacket and skirt that are sold separately, and trying to match the colors? Or have you ever tried to match a swatch of cloth from a piece of furniture to get, say, the same color drapes? If so, you've probably run into the

The famous jacket and pants problem (or jacket and skirt problem)

situation where two colors that matched perfectly in the store magically turned into two different colors the first time you wore the suit in daylight or saw the furniture and drapes together at home.

No, you weren't suffering from delusions at the store, and no one snookered you by switching the material when you weren't looking. You just stumbled over a minor rock on the road to color.

Two colors that look the same under one kind of light source—fluorescent light, say, at the clothing or drapery store—don't necessarily look the same under another kind of light source such as incandescent light at home or daylight when you step out the door. (Don't worry yet about why this happens. We'll come back to that in Chapter 6. Just be aware that it does happen.)

Two: The Color of Light

> "YES," I answered you last night,
> "No," this morning, Sir, I say.
> Colours seen by candle-light,
> Will not look the same by day.
>
> Elizabeth Barrett Browning
> "The Lady's 'Yes,'" st. 1

Quite apart from the issue of colors matching or not depending on lighting is that any given color looks different under different color lights. No, I'm not talking about *colored* lights, like red, green, and blue lights, although those kind of lights will certainly affect colors also. I'm talking about lights with different amounts of various colors.

Incandescent vs. fluorescent

Incandescent light, for example, has a distinctly yellowish tinge and tends to bring out reds, yellows, oranges, and yellowish-greens. Classic fluorescent lights (as opposed to the yellowish fluorescent lights you can use to replace incandescent bulbs) look white because they have more blue and violet, and they tend to bring out blues, violets, and cyan.

> Next time you're at the supermarket, check out the lighting around the vegies and the meats. No matter what kind of lighting is in the rest of the store, odds are that you'll find incandescent lights, or something even yellower, around the produce to bring out the reds, yellows, and orange colors, and around the meats to bring out the red. Stores that use white fluorescent lights around the vegetable and meat department don't sell as much because very few fruits and vegetables—and certainly no red meats—look fresh and healthy when you emphasize blue, violet, and cyan. (And, by the way, since I mentioned the new yellowish fluorescent lights: If you haven't tried using them to replace incandescent bulbs yet, you should. They're a bit pricey, but they really last a lot

longer than incandescent bulbs. I have three bulbs in a ceiling fixture in my office and used to have to replace bulbs often enough to be annoying. I switched to the fluorescents about a year ago and haven't had to replace a single bulb yet. Yes, Arnold? True enough; this doesn't have anything to do with color or printers. But it is a tip.)

Three: Turn Down the Light and Change the Color

> There is a certain relief in change, even though it be from bad to worse; as I have found in traveling in a stage-coach, that it is often a comfort to shift one's position and be bruised in a new place.
>
> Washington Irving
> *Tales of a Traveler,* 1824

Early on in this chapter, I talked about color models as ways to describe color, and I talked specifically about RGB (red-green-blue), CMY (cyan-magenta-yellow), and CMYK (cyan-magenta-yellow-black) color models. Among the color models I haven't mentioned yet is the HSB model, for hue, saturation, and brightness.

Unlike the RGB, CMY, and CMYK models, which describe colors strictly in terms of other colors—red, green, and blue, or cyan, magenta, yellow, (and black)—the HSB model describes color in terms of perception. The hue of any color comes closest to describing the raw color—as red, orange, green, blue, yellow, or whatever. Saturation measures how much of the color there is. The same hue, for example, serves for both pink and red. There's just more of it in red. Think of pastels and you'll have a good sense of colors that aren't heavily saturated. Zero saturation means there's no color, which leaves you with white, black, or some shade of gray.

The HSB (hue, saturation, brightness) color model

Brightness is a measure of how much white or black is in the color. For any given hue, at any given saturation, you can make the color lighter or darker by adjusting brightness. Brick red, for example, is a darker version of red—or red with some black in it, if you prefer.

Zero saturation with maximum brightness is an alternate pronunciation for white, no matter what hue, because zero saturation means zero hue. Zero brightness is always black, no matter what the hue or saturation.

Don't worry if you didn't follow this thumbnail description, or the logic behind it, completely. The only way to get a good feel for how hue, saturation, and brightness interact is to work with the HSB color model to pick colors. If you have a program that uses the HSB model, you'll learn it quickly enough.

The important point for right now is that you understand the basics. Hue is the choice in raw color. Saturation is the amount of color, which can range from none (which gives you white, black, or gray) to a little (which gives you off-white, off-black, or tinted gray) to full (which gives you a robust color in any hue).

Brightness determines whether you get white, black, or gray at zero saturation. It also determines whether a given color looks light (like yellow or red) or dark (like a mustard color or brick red).

> **Don't confuse the idea of saturation in the hue, saturation, brightness model with the issue of whether a printer can print fully saturated colors. The two kinds of saturation are not quite the same thing. In the HSB color model, saturation tells you how much color is in a color. (Or, if that doesn't go down well, try it this way: Saturation is a measure of how much hue is in a given color.) When you're talking about printers, rather than color models, saturation is a measure of how well the printer covers the page with whatever color it's using. Better yet, think of it this way: In the one case, the issue is how well the hue saturates the color. In the other, the issue is how well the color saturates the page.**
>
> **This means a printer can print in fully saturated colors even with colors that aren't saturated from the HSB color model's point of view. It can even print fully saturated grays, which have a saturation, in the HSB model, of zero. The same color from the same printer can even be fully saturated on paper, but not on transparencies—which is a fairly common problem for ink jet printers. The saving grace for this dual purpose word is that it's usually clear which kind of saturation someone's talking about—just listen for the words *printer* or *color model* nearby.**

An experiment in the dark

With me so far? Okay, try this experiment (preferably at night since you need a dark room for it to work well). Take something orange and something red—an apple and an orange will do nicely. Then go into a room, turn off the lights, and close the door, with your back to the door, but standing where you can open it easily. Wait a minute or two to give your eyes a chance to adjust to the dark. At this point, both the apple and orange (if you can make them out at all) should be the same color: Black. Perceived brightness for both is zero.

Now, with your back still to the door, open the door just enough so you can barely see some color for the orange. Take a second and try to honestly name the color you see.

Don't cheat. Knowing it's orange will influence your perception, but just because you know it's orange, doesn't make it orange. In reality, the color will likely be a pale orange or pale yellow—pale meaning little saturation. At the same time, the apple should be impossible to honestly describe as red. Sure, you *know* it's red, but can you really tell that from what you see? I'll bet it could just as easily be a dark blue, and you wouldn't know the difference. *Tell* yourself that it's dark blue (try hard to believe it) and see if you agree.

With your back still to the door, so your body is shielding the apple and orange a bit from the light, slowly open the door in stages. You should gradually see the apple become unarguably red and the orange become more definitively orange and more saturated. Finally, turn around to face the door and walk into the light. As you move into better lighting, the colors will brighten. Now you can go ahead and eat the evidence, secure in the knowledge that it's a healthy snack.

There are two points to this exercise. The first is to give you a better sense of what hue, saturation, and brightness are. The second is to drive home the fact that all three can change with changes in the amount of light. For the orange to look pale yellow, you have to affect both hue and saturation. And even after you can clearly see the orange and red colors, there's a fairly obvious change in brightness and saturation as you continue moving from dark to light.

Four: Colors Affect Colors

> It is a fact so obvious as to be misunderstood that one cannot ordinarily look into a window from outside. Even an open window is merely a rectangle darker than the exterior wall . . .
>
> Tom Clancy
> *Clear and Present Danger*

The color you see depends partly on the colors around it. Remember the last time someone sat in the power seat, putting himself or herself between you and the bright daylight glare of a window? (Nice, huh?) Did you happen to notice that his or her face seemed darker than it was before it was framed by the window?

If it's bright enough outside, you'll see the face against the window as a dark silhouette. But if you draw the curtains, the same face in the same lighting suddenly becomes easy to see. If you've never noticed this effect, take a moment to see it for yourself.

If you don't have a window, another person, and a bright, sunny day handy, here's a simple way to get the same result. Look directly at a handy light bulb (okay, *squint* directly at a handy light bulb) and hold your arm out with your fingers closed and your thumb up, thumbnail facing you, like an artist doing whatever it is that artists do with their thumbs up. Hold your hand so your thumb is between your eyes and the light. You should see very little beyond the silhouette of your thumb against the light.

Now grab something opaque in your other hand and stick it between the light and your thumb. Presto chango, you should immediately be able to see all sorts of detail in your thumb. (Now wait a while for the spots to disappear from in front of your eyes.)

This change in appearance of one area in your vision because of another area is called simultaneous contrast, and it's not limited to what happens when you stare at a bright light. Figures 1.10 and 1.11 are illusions of sorts that demonstrate

Simultaneous contrast

the same effect. In both figures, the two squares in the center are both the same size and same color (well, the same gray in this case). But the square that's surrounded by the lighter color (meaning the lighter gray in one case and white in the other) looks smaller and darker than the square that's surrounded by the darker color (meaning the darker gray or black).

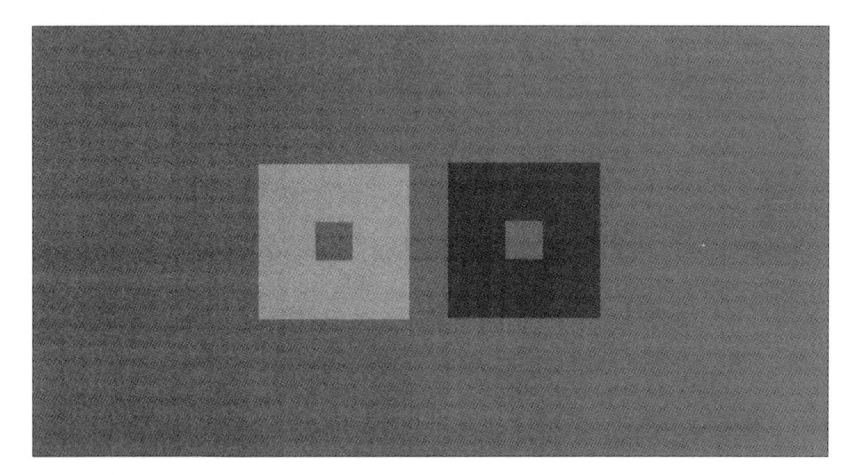

Figure 1.10 The square on the left looks smaller and darker, but isn't.

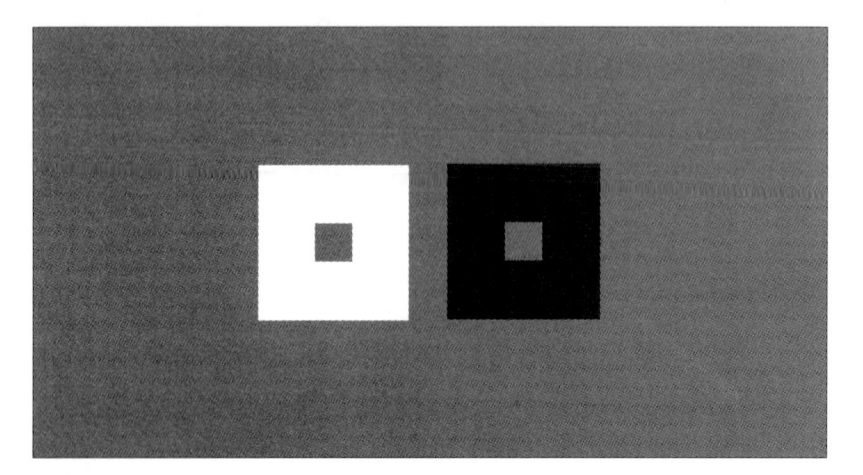

Figure 1.11 Here again, the square on the left looks smaller and darker, but isn't.

This same phenomenon of simultaneous contrast affects your perception of colors. Surround a small patch of green with a bluish background, for example, and you'll swear that the green has a yellowish tinge. Surround the same patch of green with a yellowish background, and you'll swear it has a bluish tinge. And any given color can appear darker or lighter, more green or more yellow, or whatever, depending on the colors around it. (You don't have to take my word for this. I've included some samples that show this effect in the color section of the book.)

Simultaneous contrast has the greatest effect when one color completely surrounds another, but it crops up even when two colors are merely near each other or there's simply a lot of one color close by. This is not just a curious optical illusion; it makes a difference in the real world. Really.

Remember the test print with laser paper and standard copy paper? That's the one where the edges were just as good on the copy paper as on the laser paper when you looked through a loupe—and maybe even better. But the output on laser paper looked darker and crisper to the naked eye. I sped past that observation before and mumbled something about the whiter, brighter background giving a better contrast. But what's really going on is a prime example of simultaneous contrast.

Remember the laser paper

Simultaneous contrast means that a dark area surrounded by a light area will look smaller and darker than it otherwise would. Take that one step further: The lighter the surrounding area, the darker and smaller the dark area will look. Laser paper takes advantage of that phenomenon by providing a glistening white background. That's why the text looks darker. Even if the characters print a little less crisply on the laser paper, they still *look* crisper because the white background also makes the dark area look smaller.

Five: Size Affects Color

> There is no need to worry about mere size . . . Sir Isaac Newton was very much smaller than a hippopotamus, but we do not on that account value him less.
>
> Bertrand Russell
> "The Expanding Mental Universe," in *Saturday Evening Post* (July 1959)

I hate to contradict Bertrand Russell, but sometimes you do need to worry about size. Oh, not if you're comparing Isaac Newton to a hippopotamus, perhaps, but if you're talking about color, then, yeah, you need to worry about size.

Have you ever picked out a paint for a room and then been surprised by how it looked on the wall? The next time that happens, get out the sample you started with and compare it to the finished, dried paint. Yup, it's the same blue, you say. So how come it looks so different on the wall? So much *bluer*?

Congratulations. You've just run into the effect that size has on color. The rule of thumb is that the bigger the patch of color, the more saturated it will look. This is something that I can't show you in gray and white because any shade of gray has zero saturation by definition. But I can show you how to demonstrate this for yourself.

42 *Chapter 1*

Figure 1.12 is a blueprint (or would that be grayprint?) for an image you can create using your favorite graphics program. (This works on screen as well as on the printed page, so you may not want to bother printing it out.) Simply place one large block of color covering about three-quarters of the page (or a good chunk of the screen), as shown in the figure. Then create a small block of the same color, keeping a good size gap between the second block and the first.

Figure 1.12 If this were in color, the large block would look more saturated than the small one, Try it for yourself.

If you look at the large block, then look at the small one, you should see the small block as having a somewhat paler color. You may have trouble seeing this effect because you know better—the same way some people have trouble experiencing stereo, with sound coming from between the two speakers, if they can see the two speakers. If so, it may help to cover each block as you look at the other. The bigger the difference between the two size blocks, the easier time you'll have seeing a difference in saturation. But the effect is real, I promise.

Six: Your Color or Mine

> Bias and impartiality is in the eye of the beholder.
>
> Lord Barnett
> July 12, 1990

Color is subjective. Yes, Mary, you can measure wavelengths of light and get objective measurements of those wavelengths. But the colors you see are subjective.

True story: At some point after I knew I was going to write this book, but before I'd started working on it, I was sitting at my desk, and asked my wife to hand me a book from the shelf she was standing next to.

"The blue one," I said, and she proceeded to hand me the one I would have called cyan.

"No," I said, "the blue one; just to the right."

"Oh, you mean the purple one."

"Uh, huh. That's right, the purple one. Thank you, hon."

You don't believe me? Try this: Go grab a carrot and an orange. Is the carrot orange? Yes, absolutely. Is the orange? Surely. Are they the same color? No way, no how. (Unless you have some very funny looking carrots and oranges.)

Still not convinced? Okay, try this: Take a half dozen or so tomatoes in various stages of ripeness and get, say, three or four people to write down which tomato is the reddest, which is the most orange (orangest?), and how they'd classify each if they had to classify it as red or orange. (Leave the green tomatoes out of this.) Odds are you'll have some disagreements. Who's right and who's wrong? Everyone.

I see Tim nodding in agreement (I guess those art classes paid off, Tim), but Mary doesn't look satisfied. What's that, Mary? You're thinking that all I'm talking about is a matter of naming or misnaming colors—that different people simply use different names for the same color. Surely there is some single standard for orange that's really orange, the same way there's a standard way to measure a foot and compare individual rulers to that standard. And likewise, you're thinking, there should be a standard for blue, and red, and so on, right? Wrong.

Not only is there no such thing as a standard orange in that absolute sense, but there can't be since your perception of a so-called standard wouldn't be (couldn't be) . . . well . . . standard. That's the whole point I've been getting at: Your perception of any color—its hue, saturation, and brightness—will change under changing conditions.

If colors that match at some times don't match at other times . . .

If the color of light affects the color you see . . .

If the intensity of light affects the color you see . . .

If nearby colors affect the color you see . . .

If the size of the patch of color affects the color you see . . .

. . . then there can't be a standard for color because there's simply no objective way to say that *this color* is orange and anything that doesn't match exactly isn't. Got it? Good.

Because that's not even the half of it. You can take two colors that are fairly close as measured by the wavelength of light and find some people who will see them as different colors and others who will see them as the same color. In the extreme case, you wind up with people who are color blind (actually, more often color deficient, but let's not quibble), and can't, for example, tell the difference between red and green. But even for people who aren't color blind, there are differences in the colors they'll perceive because there are physiological differences from one person's eye to the next.

Bottom line: You have your own idea of orange—and red, and green, and blue—and I have mine, and they're almost certainly not the same. And that's okay. It doesn't make you a bad person.

Here's a colorful irony: If you go to almost any graphic design shop, the artist in charge—the one who gets to make the final decisions about colors—is normally the oldest and most experienced artist in the shop. But one of the reasons for physiological differences from one person's eye to another is age. As you get older, you lose some of the ability to differentiate colors, the same way you lose some hearing. So the artist making the final decisions about color is usually the one who has the least acute color vision.

WYSAWYG: WHAT YOU SEE AIN'T WHAT YOU GET

> Not to get what you have set your heart on is almost as bad as getting nothing at all.
>
> Aristotle

This is going to be a short section. All I want to establish here is that you shouldn't expect to see the same colors on the printed page as on your monitor. Once you realize that little fact, you're less likely to pull your hair out in frustration when the page doesn't match the screen.

Printers are not monitors. (This should not be an earth-shattering revelation.) Just the difference in color models—the difference between monitors as RGB devices and printers as CMYK devices—is enough to guarantee some mismatches in color, but I'll save that discussion for a later chapter. There are plenty of other reasons why your printed page won't match your monitor. I'll touch on enough of them here to make the point.

Yes, Arnold, I know there are a whole bunch of features in various products whose sole purpose is to help you match the colors on the screen to the colors on the printed page. But unless you're a graphic artist who absolutely must see the colors on screen as closely as possible to the way they'll come out of the printer, they take more effort than they're worth—and they may take more effort than they're worth even if you are a graphic artist. Let's save that discussion for Chapter 3; however, right now, I just want you to understand the problem that gives those features and products a reason for being.

Warming up

To begin with, your monitor doesn't always match itself. If you turn it off every night, when you first turn it on in the morning, the colors won't be the same as the night before. They also won't be the same as they'll be an hour later when the monitor's fully warmed up. If you have an energy-saving monitor, which counts the minutes since you last messed with the keyboard or mouse and powers down every so often, you may run into this same warm-up issue several times a day.

Brightness and contrast

Changes in monitor color aren't just an issue of warming up the monitor. Any time you change the brightness or contrast control on your monitor, you're also changing the color. You can prove this easily enough. Simply load any program that includes some colors in its display or load a file with some color graphics in it. Then adjust the brightness and contrast and watch what happens to the colors.

On my monitor, I can start with a pale yellowish-orange with brightness and contrast cranked all the way up and change it to a rust color by turning brightness way down and then adjusting contrast. I can also turn a blue into a violet, a bright yellow into a muddy yellow, and a brown into something approaching maroon. I can even make two shades of blue look very different from each other, so one can serve in foreground and stand out clearly from the background, or make them look virtually the same, so the foreground disappears into the background.

Just as important, changing the brightness and contrast changes the whiteness of the Windows (or OS/2 or Mac) background. Keep in mind also that your perception of a color will change depending on the background.

> **After you finish messing with your monitor, you'll want to adjust it properly again. Here's a useful trick for setting it up—at least on a DOS-based system. First, go to DOS or open a full-screen DOS window, so you have a black screen. (The last I looked, you could do this with OS/2 also. Mac users are on their own here.) Then adjust the brightness level so you can see the background as a faint white. (If necessary, adjust the size of the screen image first, so you can easily see to the edge of the image. If the edge is hiding under the monitor bezel, it's hard to see the background because you don't have a fully black screen to compare it to.) Once you can see the background, back off just enough so it disappears. Then adjust the contrast to taste. (And readjust the image size if you messed with it in the first place.)**
>
> **Yes, Tim, I know this makes it sound as if there's a preferred setting for contrast and brightness that you can set once, leave alone, and have the same colors on the monitor all the time (ignoring the warm-up issue). 'Taint so. If**

you try this under different lighting conditions, you'll wind up with different settings because the more light in the room, the more you'll have to crank up the brightness to see the background. You'll also have to readjust the controls as the monitor ages.

Lighting

While I'm on the subject of lighting conditions, that's an issue also. Unless you're in a completely enclosed office, with no light creeping in from around window blinds or from the room across the hall, the lighting in your office varies with time of day. Changes in lighting will not affect colors on screen as much as they will colors on paper because the screen provides its own light. That means you can easily run into a situation where a printed color and screen color will match at one time of the day, but not another. (Remember the famous jacket and pants—or jacket and skirt—problem.)

Paper

Finally, for now, there's the issue of background color. I already mentioned that changing brightness and contrast will change the background on your screen and affect your perception of color on the screen. The same issue crops up at your printer, in the form of your paper color.

Yes, Tim, you're right. We've already gone over this ground when we compared text output on copy paper and laser paper. But there's a little more to say.

I already mentioned that if you try printing the same color graphic on the two kinds of paper, the colors will usually be more vibrant on the laser paper. More precisely, now that everyone here knows about the hue-saturation-brightness model, the color on the laser paper will usually be brighter and more fully saturated.

You can prove this to yourself easily enough by printing a small square of color—say, 2 inches by 2 inches—on each kind of paper and comparing them But keep in mind that other effects may complicate the issue. If you print a small patch of color with a heavy black border, for example, you may not see any difference in the colors because the black surrounding the color in both cases may have more effect on your perception of the color than the white of the page.

I see Mary looking skeptical. Okay, Mary, I admit it, the difference in color between printing on copy paper and on laser paper isn't all that much, but every little change in color perception adds up. For those printers that do their best stuff on special-purpose paper, the difference in color between using copy paper and using the special paper is far more dramatic.

Keep in mind too that if you use colored paper—gray, tan, off-white, or whatever—for your reports and letters, those background colors will have even more effect on the colors you see. The point is that if you print the same file, on the same printer, but use different paper, the colors will change.

Now here's the really nasty part. Take a sheet of whatever paper you normally use and hold it up against your screen. I'll bet you a chocolate ice cream soda that the color of the paper doesn't match the color of the white background on screen, and I'll bet you a vanilla ice cream soda that the difference is far greater than the difference between copy paper and laser paper.

And you wonder how come the colors you get on paper don't match the colors you see on the screen. Ha.

THE PSYCHOLOGY OF COLOR

> He had that curious love of green, which in individuals is always the sign of a subtle artistic temperament, and in nations is said to denote a laxity, if not a decadence of morals.
>
> Oscar Wilde

Artists, interior decorators, and packaging designers know a secret that most of us either never learned, or don't pay much attention to: People react to color in predictable ways. You don't believe me? Take a walk through your local supermarket and look at the packaging. Don't pay any attention to the food that you can actually see—like vegetables and cheeses. Go straight to the cans and boxes.

Pull two different brands of, say, canned asparagus off the shelf—one premium brand and one el cheapo brand (the store brand should do). I'll bet the premium brand looks more inviting—more appealing, more appetizing, more promising of high-quality asparagus inside—than the other. Right? Hey, cuz, wake up: You're reacting to the *label* on the can. You have no idea what's inside either can *because you can't see the food.* That's what the psychology of color is about.

Here's another example: A few years ago my local A&P began experimenting with generic food packaging. This was a little like generic aspirin in concept—drop the brand name and the fancy packaging and just sell the product. After all, corn flakes are corn flakes, right?

Well, apparently not. The generic corn flakes and other purported food (I never tried any) came in purely black and white packages. More precisely, they came in white packages with black lettering—Helvetica, if memory serves, which was fully in keeping with the generic spirit of the products. (I see Tim shaking his head in wonderment already.) The packages looked a little like Figure 1.13.

It was an inspired packaging theme if you didn't want to sell any corn flakes. I swear that the black-and-white boxes were actually less appealing than the olive drab cans of C-rations that the Army hands out. I don't remember how long this particular experiment lasted, but it wasn't very long because the generic packaging simply wasn't selling any food. That's also what the psychology of color is about.

Corn Flakes

Would you buy a box that looked like this, in black and white?

Probably not.

Figure 1.13 Would you buy a box of corn flakes with packaging like this?

Why bother learning the psychology of color?

Yes, Arnold? You're wondering why you should care, and what, if anything, this has to do with color printers? Just this: If you're going print in color and, more important, design documents to print in color—anything from business reports, to brochures, to one-page advertising handouts, to party invitations—you'll be more effective if you know a little about the psychology of color.

Warm and cool colors

For example, you probably know the terms *warm color* and *cool color*. But did you know that warm colors tend to attract attention, so that warm colors are a good choice for things in a graphic that you want to highlight, while cool colors are a better choice for backgrounds?

Yes, Arnold? You know the terms but you're not quite sure what they mean? Well, I don't want to get into too much detail here, but I'll sketch in a couple of specifics just to make this a little more concrete.

You can divide all colors into warm and cool categories, but the division isn't all that neat. Yellow, orange, red, and most browns are warm colors. Blue, blue-green, and violet are cool colors. So when you design a graphic, you'll generally want to use blue, blue-green, or violet as the background, and yellow, orange, red, and brown for the foreground.

No, I didn't forget green and magenta. I skipped over them on purpose. These can fall into either category, depending on what you've got around them. Stick some green in a sea of blue, and it will appear a little yellowish, making it a warm color. Put it near red, and it turns into more of a bluish-green, making it a cool color. (There's that issue of colors affecting colors again.) Pretty much the same happens with magenta, but if you want to experiment with these colors, I'd recommend using yellow with magenta instead of red. Red and magenta look pretty horrible together.

Okay; that's one example of the psychology of color. Here are a few more:

Did you know that young children are most likely to pick out toys with bright, primary colors? Did you ever notice that people who live in tropical regions tend to prefer bright, saturated colors (think of Hawaiian shirts), while people who live in temperate zones tend to prefer more subdued colors? (That's probably not just a coincidence; nature in tropical regions is a riot of color compared to temperate zones.)

So which colors are you going to use on the invitations to your six-year-old daughter's birthday party? And which ones to invite your friends to a party with a tropical theme? (And by the way, if you've recently moved from Hawaii to Boston, you may want to rethink the colors you've planned for almost anything you've put together.)

Whether you've noticed it consciously or not, colors and color combinations send out psychological messages. You want an example? Okay, wait a minute, let me go rummaging through my kitchen. Ah, here's a good one: **You too can send messages.**

I have two bottles of vitamins in front of me from different companies. The label on one uses black text over a background of deep gold with a touch of dark red—a color combination that fairly shouts quality. The label on the other uses brown text on a background that shades gradually from a rich orange at the bottom to a deep dark yellow at the top. The company logo uses red text over orange and bright yellow. The overall effect is similar to a sunrise. And it rings with the psychological overtones of nature, natural, and healthy—all those Good Things you want in your vitamins.

Surely you didn't think these color combinations were an accident, did you? By the way, did you notice that both labels use warm, attention-getting colors?

If you simply become aware of color and your reactions to it, you'll find you can take advantage of the psychological messages yourself and make your own color output that much more effective.

Like so many other topics in this chapter, we'll come back to the psychology of color later—in Chapter 7. Until we get there, you might want to work at being just a bit more aware of color—in everything from advertisements to interior decoration schemes to graphics in magazine articles—to get a first-person viewpoint of one person's reactions to various color schemes.

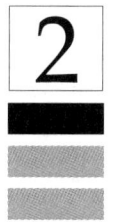

2 Getting Pretty Good Color with Hardly Any Effort

> The secret of the truly successful, I believe, is that they learned very early in life how not to be busy. They saw through that adage, repeated to me so often in childhood, that anything worth doing is worth doing well. The truth is, many things are worth doing only in the most slovenly, halfhearted fashion possible, and many other things are not worth doing at all.
>
> Barbara Ehrenreich
> *The Worst Years of Our Lives,* "The Cult of Busyness" (1991; first published 1985)

Most things in life follow some variation of the 80–20 rule: You can get it 80 percent right for 20 percent of the effort it takes to get it 100 percent right. Color printing is no exception. In this chapter we'll concentrate on getting it 80 percent right.

You need to know a couple of ground rules for this chapter only. Basically the chapter is a bunch of useful tips in no particular order. Since everything is a tip, I'm not going to mark each item with a wand. Instead, I'll save the wand for the occasional tip within a tip.

The concentration here is on practical problem solving. You'll find that most tips cover territory similar to information elsewhere in the book. However, when I cover the information in other chapters, it will be in the context of explaining something—color theory, or design, or the strengths and weaknesses of ink jet printers. In this chapter, I'm only concerned with giving you a pocketful of useful tricks to call on when you need them. I'll often suggest what to do, cookbook fashion, without worrying too much about why—except when you need to understand the reasons before you can make sense of the solutions.

So much for the ground rules. Any questions? Good. Let's get started.

A BIGGER IMAGE

> [Texas] is very considerably smaller than Australia and British Somaliland put together. As things stand at present there is nothing much the Texans can do about this, and . . . they are inclined to shy away from the subject in ordinary conversation, muttering defensively about the size of oranges.
>
> Alex Atkinson
> "The Eyes of Texas Are Upon You," in *Punch* (1959)

Most color printers have larger margins—or nonprintable areas in PrinterSpeak—than you might like. This isn't usually a problem for color ink jet or color wax jet printers because the typical margins on these printers are only a little larger than the typical margins for monochrome laser printers. And, even then, it's usually only the bottom margin that's larger, so the only effect is that you may have to put a footer a quarter inch higher than you really want to.

With thermal dye and thermal wax printers, however, the larger margins can be a lot larger. I've seen some printers that are limited to an 8.1 inch by 8.6 inch image on a standard 8½ inch by 11 inch letter-size page.

Some manufacturers make up for the dead space these printers need by offering oversize paper stock that has perforated, tear-off strips. By printing on the larger paper stock, the printer still gets its large margins, but there's more room for the image, as shown on the right side of Figure 2.1. After you tear off the strip shown on the right side of the figure, you wind up with a letter-size page and a nice size image.

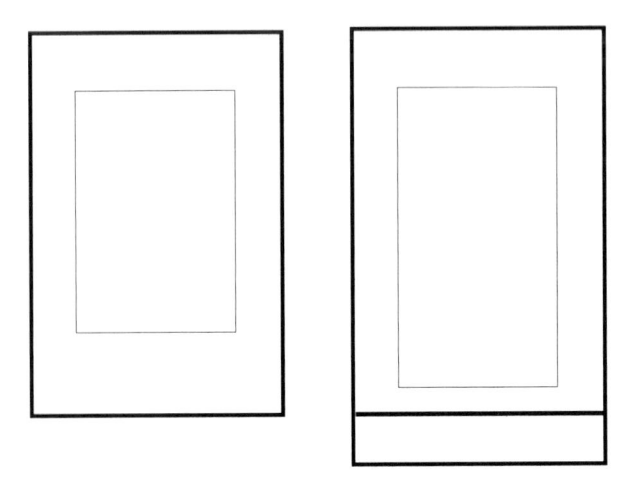

Figure 2.1 For printers that need large margins, adding a tear-off strip, as shown on the right side here, lets you have a large image too. Just tear off the strip, and you get rid of the extra margin.

So what about printers that don't provide perforated, oversize paper? Well, most of them can print on legal size or A4 paper, and they'll print with a larger image on the larger paper.

> **I see lots of puzzled expressions on the mention of A4 paper. That's the standard European letter size. At 210 by 297 millimeters, it's a little narrower but a little longer than U.S. letter size. What's that in inches, you ask? Let me get my calculator out. Let's see . . . 210 millimeters divided by 25.4 millimeters per inch . . . uh huh . . . 297 millimeters divided by 25.4 . . . round off to the nearest tenth of an inch . . . okay. It's 8.3 by 11.7 inches. Compared to 8.5 by 11 inches, that's not a lot of difference, but it's enough to add almost seven-tenths of an inch to the length of the image. By the way, the 8.5 by 11 inch U.S. letter-size paper is also called A size. (And everybody here knows that legal size paper is 8.5 by 14 inches, right?)**

If your printer will print on either of these larger paper sizes, all you have to do to get a large image is use the larger pages and trim the paper yourself. You'll also want to invest in a decent paper cutter. This is one situation where scissors won't . . . uh . . . cut it.

PAPER MATTERS

> Do not on any account attempt to write on both sides of the paper at once.
>
> W. C. Sellar and R. J. Yeatman
> *1066 and All That*

Paper always affects printer output. That means you should pay attention to the paper you use. With thermal dye printers, you don't have a choice. But almost every thermal wax printer (well, virtually every current model of thermal wax printer, at least) will let you print on a range of papers, and so will any ink jet or laser printer.

> **Wax jet printers are the only printers that can print well on any paper, no matter how rough. Because the wax drops are sprayed on the paper, you don't need a smooth surface to guarantee coverage, as with printers that press a drum against the paper. And because the wax dries by cooling and solidifying, it isn't absorbed by the paper as with ink from ink jets. That means wax jets can print on anything that will make it through the paper feed mechanism. And with some wax jet printers (notably the Tektronix Phaser 300i) almost anything that's reasonably flat can make it through—paper towels, tissue paper, wash cloths, whatever. I even know someone who swears that they've seen the Phaser 300i print on taco shells. No kidding. But don't try this at home kids. I've never tried it myself because I have religious objections to running taco shells through a $10,000 printer.**

I mentioned in Chapter 1 that even monochrome laser and ink jet printers do better on special, high-grade laser paper than on standard copy paper. I also mentioned—at length—that for color printers, the effect of paper on the final output is even greater. But don't think for an instant that copy paper and laser paper are your only two choices for printing.

Not only can you find other kinds of paper, like special ink jet paper or thermal wax paper, but you have other choices for copy and laser paper as well. My current preferred copy paper is the Staples house brand, which offers the usual white, 20-pound weight specification, but is noticeably whiter than the brand name paper I used to use. And since it's the house brand, it's also less expensive, which is a nice bonus. (Gee, it's better and cheaper too. Let me think about which one to use.)

Browse through any office supply catalog, and you'll likely see several choices for copy paper and for laser paper. It's probably not worth investing the time in sampling every possibility, but sample as many as you have time for. You may find a better choice than what you're using now.

Also consider other variations. You might want to take a look at slightly heavier weight paper, at say, 28 pounds. Or you might want to consider colored papers. Either of these possibilities can dress up your output for important reports or the like. (But remember that the color of the paper will affect color output. And not all printers can handle 28-pound weight paper, so check your printer's requirements first.)

You can even find laser paper in colors and with unusual textures. (My favorite source for interesting papers is Paper Direct at 800-272-7377.) And don't overlook the special-purpose paper for ink jet printers. You might want to experiment with other brands besides the one the printer manufacturer recommends.

Once you've chosen the papers you like, and you've run them through your printer to make sure they meet some minimum level of usability, create some sample prints on each kind of paper, and file them in a folder or notebook, with each one clearly marked with the name and source of the paper. You may not want to use the highest quality, most expensive paper every time, but you'll have a good reference for picking the minimum quality you're comfortable with for any given print job.

At the very least, you might want to consider using inexpensive paper for test runs and saving the more expensive paper for final output. Well, okay, it's a little more complicated than that since the paper color will affect the colors you're printing. But if you're using, say, white copy paper for your test runs and a brighter white ink jet paper for your final output, the copy paper will still give you what physicists like to call a close approximation.

RIBBONS MATTER TOO

> Between what matters and what seems to matter, how should the world we know judge wisely?
>
> E. C. Bentley

The title for this section is only partly true. Lots of printers don't use ribbons, and for them, ribbons don't matter at all. But for printers that use ribbons—namely, thermal dye and thermal wax printers—the ribbons not only matter, they matter a lot. And that means you want to be sure you choose the right ribbon.

No, I'm not talking about choosing between a thermal dye ribbon and a thermal wax ribbon for dual mode printers—although that's obviously important too. I'm talking about picking the right thermal dye ribbon or the right thermal wax ribbon when you have a choice of more than one.

Some ribbon-based printers don't give you any choice. But thermal dye printers can give you up to three choices: three-color ribbons, four-color ribbons, and monochrome ribbons. Thermal wax printers can give you the same three, plus one more: a plain paper ribbon. In case you're wondering, there's nothing special about dual mode printers in this context. If you're printing in thermal wax mode, you have the same potential choices as for a thermal wax printer. If you're printing in thermal dye mode, you have the same potential choices as for a thermal dye printer.

Choices in ribbons

Logically, a plain paper ribbon can be either a three-color or four-color ribbon, but I've yet to see any four-color versions. (Well, that's not entirely true, but I'll come back to that in a minute.) In general, the difference between a plain paper ribbon and a three-color ribbon is that the plain paper ribbon includes a fourth panel in addition to three color panels. The extra panel lays down a coating on plain paper so you can print without special-purpose thermal wax paper.

> **Yes, Arnold, you got me. What I've just said is that a plain paper ribbon is really a three-color ribbon. If you want to get picky about it, you should call the standard version a three-pass three-color ribbon and call the plain paper version a four-pass three-color ribbon. (And you should call the four-color ribbon, a four-pass four-color ribbon, for that matter.) Except where the meaning is critical, however, and there's room for confusion, I'll stick with three-color ribbon, four-color ribbon, and plain paper ribbon.**
>
> **There's another issue too. I lied when I said I have yet to see any four-color plain paper ribbons. The precise truth is that I've never seen any four-color plain paper ribbons for printers that print a full page at a time. The Star SJ-144, with its half-inch wide ribbons, uses four colors. It also does without a special panel for laying down a coating on the paper thanks to colored wax coatings**

that are specifically designed for plain paper. So logically there are four possibilities for plain paper color ribbons: three-color with a coating panel, three-color without, four-color with, and four-color without. But I've yet to see any printer offer more than one kind of plain paper ribbon. (And this time I'm telling the truth.) So, in most contexts, it makes sense to talk about plain paper ribbons and not worry about the details.

Three-Color Ribbons Versus Four-Color Ribbons

As I mentioned in Chapter 1, for any given printer, printing with a three-pass three-color ribbon is faster because the paper has to go through the printer once for each color. (See, sometimes the number of passes is a critical issue.) Standard three-color ribbons are also less expensive because each image needs only three-fourths as much ribbon as it needs from four-color ribbons or plain paper ribbons.

So why get a four-color ribbon if a three-color ribbon is faster and cheaper? The answer's simple: For those printers that offer a four-color ribbon, the four colors usually give you better-looking color. In particular, a four-color ribbon will usually provide a blacker black—thanks to its black panel—than a three-color ribbon, whose blacks, mixed from a combination of the three colors, will often take on a sepia or blue tinge.

Test your color ribbon in black and white. If there's only one type of color ribbon available for your printer, none of this matters. But if there's more than one type available, you'll want to try them all and compare them. Be sure to print at least two samples in black and white. One should be a graphic with a large, solid black area filled in. The other should include a lot of black text in an assortment of point sizes.

If the black for the three-color ribbon is just as dark as for the four-color ribbon, or at least dark enough for your tastes, there's no point in spending extra money on the four-color ribbon. If the black for the three-color ribbon is noticeably bluish, brownish, or anything other than dark-as-night-in-a-coal-mine black, you'll need to consider whether the extra blackness is worth the extra price—especially if you rarely print anything with much black in it.

What was that, Mary? You were wondering about color? Oh, yeah. Be sure to print and compare some samples with color in them also. The difference in color quality between three-color and four-color ribbons should be somewhere between slim and none, but you'll want to know that for sure, rather than just assume it.

Issues for Plain Paper Ribbons

Did anybody notice how I cleverly sidestepped plain paper ribbons? Testing a plain paper ribbon is a bit more complicated, because first you have to decide which paper to test it on. If you pick a high-quality laser paper, however, you won't be far off the best looking output the ribbon can offer. Here again, print some samples in both black and white and color and compare them to the other choices for the printer.

With a plain paper ribbon, there's a little more to look for. Once again, check out the blacks for an off-black tinge. (Well, if off-white can be a color, why not off-black?) When you're printing on plain paper, though, you may find a noticeable difference in color also, compared to three-color and four-color ribbons.

Watch out for two other quality issues: how well the plain paper ribbon fills in solid areas of color and how well it handles hairline thin lines. First, of course, you'll have to make sure your samples include both large areas of solid colors and hairline thin lines. Don't be cheap with the lines. Include some vertical, some horizontal, some diagonal, and some curved, in the spirit of Figure 2.2. And feel free to use color; Figure 2.2 is all black only because I'm limited to printing it in black and white.

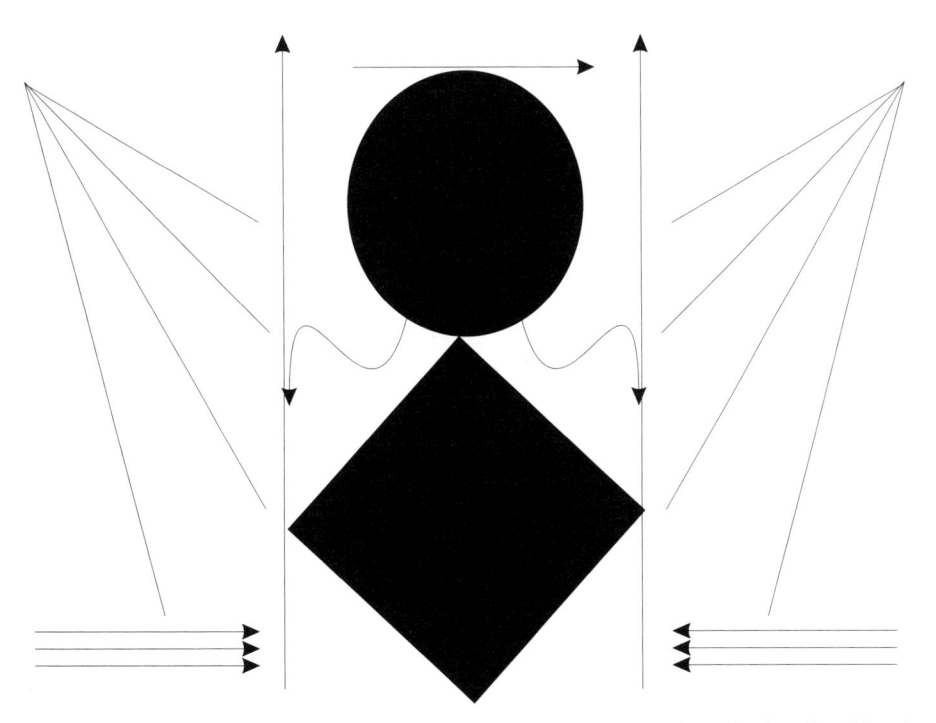

Figure 2.2 You don't need a pretty graphic to test out a ribbon, just blocks of solid color and thin lines.

Check to see if the solid areas are as solid on standard paper as on thermal wax paper. Look at the thin lines closely to see if they're as well formed with the plain paper ribbon as with the standard ribbons. If the three-color and four-color samples look fine, but the solid areas on plain paper are filled with lots of white specks (where the wax didn't meet the paper) or there are small visible gaps in the lines, you probably don't want to use the plain paper ribbon very often.

(Yes, Arnold, it is logically possible that the plain paper ribbon will do a better job than the standard ribbons on special-purpose thermal wax paper. But it ain't likely. As someone once said, the race is not always to the swift, nor the battle to the strong, but that's the way to bet it.)

And look at the paper too.

One last thing to look at is the paper itself. Compare the look and feel of the thermal wax paper to the standard paper you normally use for black and white printing. If you're printing a page that will go in a report, surrounded by pages of text on standard paper, you might be willing to forgive a few flaws in quality in exchange for a page that won't stand out as different just for its paper.

If the printer handles black text well enough, you might even be able to get away with printing body text using the same paper as for the rest of the document. That will let you mix body text and graphics on one page, just as you can with ink jet or laser printers. (I admit that's pushing it, but it's still something to consider.)

On the other hand, some of the special-purpose paper for thermal wax printers isn't all that different from standard paper in weight, look, and feel. If the thermal wax paper is close enough to copy paper and the output quality is noticeably better, you may not want to bother with plain paper printing.

When to Use a Black Ribbon

All of which brings us to monochrome ribbons, which I mentioned way back in the beginning of this section on ribbons and have otherwise ignored.

I know what you're thinking: Why on Earth would anyone want to buy a dedicated color printer and then use a monochrome ribbon to print in black and white? Well, there are a few reasons you might want to, probably including some I've never thought of. But the most common reason is to print an original for someone else to reproduce. If you're sending a brochure to a print shop for photo offset printing, for example, you might want to print the original on a thermal wax or thermal dye printer instead of a laser printer.

For the moment, though, the reason for printing in black and white doesn't matter. The point is that you may want to. When that time comes, you'll almost certainly want to use a one-color black ribbon if one is available for your printer. Printing with a monochrome ribbon is faster (with only one panel to print, the paper will have to run through the printer only once), less expensive (one ribbon panel is cheaper than four), and it guarantees a dark black (this should not be a surprise; the ribbon is black). So what's there to think about? Read on.

CHANGING RIBBONS

> Only man is not content to leave things as they are but must always be changing them, and when he has done so, is seldom satisfied with the result.
>
> Elspeth Huxley
> *The Mottled Lizard*

One of the problems with having a choice of ribbons for thermal wax and thermal dye printers is the temptation to change them. Try to resist it. The issue here is slightly different for dual mode printers and for printers that are either thermal wax only or thermal dye only. Let's take on the single-minded printers first.

Swapping Ribbons for Thermal Wax or Thermal Dye Printers

> When it is not necessary to change, it is necessary not to change.
>
> Lucius Cary, Lord Falkland
> Speech to House of Commons, November 22, 1641

Say your printer takes two kinds of color ribbons: three-color and four-color. And say you've tested both kinds and decided that the three-color ribbon is fine for test prints and for graphics that don't have any black in them. But you've also decided that the blacks are so obviously sepia that you won't be satisfied with them for final output on graphics that include black.

This seems like a perfect situation for keeping both kinds of ribbons handy and switching between them as needed. By using the three-color ribbon most of the time, you can keep costs down, and when the three-color ribbon won't do, you can use the four-color ribbon. But what are you going to do with the ribbon you're not using at any given time?

Most thermal dye and thermal wax printers come with only one ribbon carrier. Unloading the ribbon from the carrier and then reloading it is a minor chore. And when you're done, you have a partly used ribbon left over. The ribbon, with its unused portion on one roll and used portion on another, vaguely resembles a scroll. If you throw it on a shelf or in a drawer, it will likely unroll a bit before you use it again, and you may have to rewind it before you reload it.

What's wrong with that, you ask? Nothing, except that you'll usually lose a set of color panels in the process. Once you've handled part of the ribbon or gotten dust on it, you don't want to use that part. The dust specks can translate into specks of color or streaks of white on the printed image. (More on this a little later.)

To prevent that, you'll want to roll the ribbon past the panel that's been exposed to dust. And if you lose the first color panel in the CMY or CMYK set, the printer will roll past the other panels in the set as well. That means you can count on losing at least one image on a ribbon every time you take it out of the printer.

You can probably buy a second ribbon carrier. That will make it a lot easier to switch ribbons, but it doesn't solve the problem. If you keep the ribbon in the carrier when it's not in the printer, it's less likely to unroll, but it's still likely to get dust on it. That means you're still best advised to roll past the exposed panel before you put the ribbon back in the printer. So, once again, you can count on losing at least one image on the ribbon.

When swapping makes sense; And when it doesn't

This doesn't mean that you should never swap ribbons. If you need to run, say, forty black and white pages, it still makes sense to take out the four-color ribbon and put in a black ribbon. Not only will it save you a lot of time, but it will save money as well since you'll only lose one set of four color panels that way, instead of wasting three color panels for every black panel you use.

On the other hand, if you typically alternate between, say, two test prints and one final print, you're better off just leaving a four-color ribbon in all the time rather than constantly switching between a three-color and four-color ribbon. That way you'll waste only two panels on the test prints, instead of seven panels from swapping ribbons. And you won't have to waste time changing ribbons either.

There's one other issue that you'll want to keep in mind. If you change ribbons a lot without keeping careful track of which ribbon is loaded at any given time, there's a good chance you'll wind up printing with the wrong ribbon fairly often. And if you have to run the print job again because you used the wrong ribbon, that can wind up costing money instead of saving it. It will certainly wind up costing time.

Swapping Ribbons for Dual Mode Printers

> But each day brings its petty dust.
>
> Matthew Arnold

When it comes to swapping ribbons, dual mode printers have one key advantage over thermal wax only and thermal dye only printers: They're designed for it. This particular design difference isn't all that dramatic. It usually includes a second ribbon carrier as a standard part of the package. More important, it includes some sort of dust protection for the ribbon when it's not in the printer. Most often the protection is a dust cover on the carrier that closes over the unused part of the ribbon.

The dust protection with these ribbon carriers is usually good enough that you don't have to waste a set of color panels every time you leave the ribbon out of the printer for more than a minute or two. But it's not perfect.

The dirty secret about dual mode printers is that every time you swap ribbons, you risk getting dust inside the printer. And that means you risk getting random specks of color or random streaks of white on the printed image, as in Figure 2.3.

Figure 2.3 Get dust on a printhead in a thermal wax or thermal dye printer, and you'll wind up with streaks of white on your output.

Did someone ask why dust sometimes leaves colored specks and sometimes leaves white streaks? Think about it: If a dust speck is sitting on the wax or dye side of the ribbon, it will get in the way and keep the wax or dye at that spot on that one color from transferring to the paper. But you'll still get whatever other colors are supposed to print at that spot, and you'll wind up with a colored speck on your output.

If the dust is on the other side of the ribbon, it can rub off on the printhead, or it may settle on the printhead in the first place. Either way, if it's on the printhead, it will get in the way of heating the ribbon enough to transfer the dye or wax. Since the dust stays in one place as the ribbon moves past it, you'll wind up with a streak of white that shows the path of the ribbon across the dust speck.

Three Rules for Changing Ribbons

> Wisdom lies neither in fixity nor in change, but in the dialectic between the two.
>
> Octavio Paz

All this leads to three rules for changing ribbons in thermal dye, thermal wax, and dual mode printers.

Clean the printhead.

Rule One: First, and most important, whenever you change a ribbon, wipe the printhead with a soft, dry cloth. This applies whether you're changing temporarily to a different type of ribbon or replacing a ribbon that's run out. You should also wipe the printhead just before you close the printer.

It's a good idea to wipe the printhead even if all you did was open the cover. You've may have heard of the tradition with samurai swords that if you unsheathe a sword, you have to draw blood with it before you return it to its sheath. I've no idea if that's a real tradition, but you should bring the same spirit to a thermal wax or thermal dye printhead. Once you unsheathe it by opening the printer cover, you must wipe the head. Consider it a Zen experience.

Check the output.

Rule Two: After you change ribbons, check the output for dust specks and lines before you run a lot of ribbon through the printer. The smartest strategy is to never change the ribbon unless you're ready to print immediately afterward. Then print one page, and check it before printing anything else.

If you don't see any white streaks on the first page you print after closing the printer, you would probably think that you're home free. You would be wrong. But we'll cover that issue in the next section.

What's in the printer?

Rule Three: Make sure you know which ribbon is in the printer at any given time. Establish some kind of system—any kind of system—and follow it. A stick-on note on the printer or on your monitor will do. Just make sure you change the note whenever you change the ribbon, and make sure that you check the settings on your printer driver before you print.

What's that, Arnold? Yes, you're right, if the printer driver automatically detects which ribbon is in the printer and sets itself to match, you don't have to make sure the driver is set correctly. In that case, you can skip the stick-on notes. But you should still check the driver to find out which ribbon is loaded. (And be sure you have the right paper loaded too.)

WATCH OUT FOR STREAKS

> As usual I finish the day before the sea, sumptuous this evening beneath the moon, which writes Arab symbols with phosphorescent streaks on the slow swells. There is no end to the sky and the waters.
>
> Albert Camus

Streaks can be a problem for almost every kind of color printer, but for the moment, let's stay with thermal wax and thermal dye printers. (I'll get to ink jets and wax jets at the end of this section.)

I already mentioned, as part of Rule 2 for changing ribbons, that just because you don't see any white streaks when you print a page doesn't mean that you don't have to worry about streaks. If you change ribbons a lot, I'd urge you to check your output the way some politicians like their supporters to vote—early and often. That means early in the day, early in a long print run, and as often as possible—even after every page. At the very least, be sure to check the first few pages immediately after changing ribbons.

You say you're wondering how likely it is for a streak to show up after the printer's been turning out pages without streaks? Good question. The truth is that dust will almost never spontaneously show up in a ribbon-based printer unless someone opens the printer so some dust can get in. But here's the problem: Just because you don't see any streaks on the first page you print after changing a ribbon doesn't mean there isn't any dust on the printhead. Think about it. Suppose you have a page that looks like Figure 2.4.

Figure 2.4 All together now: There are no streaks on this page, right?

64   *Chapter 2*

You print this page, and everything look fine. So you go ahead and print thirty copies of another graphic without bothering to look. Only this time, when you finally get around to getting the paper out of the printer, every page looks like Figure 2.5.

Figure 2.5 If there were no streaks in Figure 2.4, where did these streaks come from?

What happened between Figure 2.4 and Figure 2.5? Nothing. Take a look at Figure 2.6. In Figure 2.6, I've put the graphics from both Figure 2.4 and Figure 2.5 on one page and shown the path of the streaks in black. As you can see, that path happened to miss everything in the first graphic but slashed through a good portion of the second graphic.

The point is that unless the image you're printing runs the whole width of the image area, you can easily have a dust speck sitting on a part of the printhead that didn't try to print anything. And if it didn't try to print anything, you won't see any streaks.

Now ask me how likely that is to happen.

Very likely.

Getting Pretty Good Color with Hardly Any Effort **65**

Figure 2.6 What happens if we put the graphics from Figure 2.4 and Figure 2.5 on the same page?

The moral: If you've recently changed ribbons and one page prints without problems, you can print additional copies of the same image without worrying about it. But if you're going to print a lot of pages with different images, start with a test image that runs the entire width of the page. If you see a vertical streak of white, the cure is the same as the preventative. Open the printer, and wipe the printhead with a soft, dry cloth.

Ink jet and wax jet printers can also leave streaks in their output, but with these printers, the problem has a different cause, a different cure, and a different way of showing up.

Streaking with ink jet and wax jet printers

If you're getting streaks that you don't normally get, at least one nozzle is clogged so it can't spray any ink. The cure is to run the printer's head-cleaning routine. The key difference in the way it shows up is that for most ink jet and wax jet printers, the streaks run horizontally instead of vertically because the printhead moves horizontally across the page.

(Yes, I mean *most* ink jet and wax jet printers. At least one wax jet printer—the Tektronix Phaser 340—uses a printhead that's almost as wide as the page. There's very little movement back and forth, and streaks run vertically instead of horizontally.)

Its easy to miss streaks on ink jet and wax jet printers. The problem can show up as a white gap, but it can also show up as a streak of off colors where one, two, or three colors have made it to the page, but one is missing. That means you can easily wind up printing any number of problem pages before you notice the streaks.

This is a nasty problem and one that's caught me more often that I'd like to admit before I finally wised up. It's no fun having to throw out all those pages you thought were finished, and then have to waste time printing them again. (Not to mention wasting the price of printing the pages, which can be significant if you're covering enough of the page.) The only way to prevent getting caught in this trap is to check the first pages in any given print job carefully, and make sure there's no streaking.

If you think you're seeing some streaking, but aren't convinced, it's worth running the printer's self-test. Most (if not all) ink jet and wax jet printers include a built-in test mode that's designed to help you spot clogged nozzles. It's also a good idea to run the self-test after running the head-cleaning routine, just to make sure the cleaning worked.

Okay, that's enough about hardware for now, let's talk a little about making the output look good.

FIRST GET IT RIGHT IN BLACK AND WHITE

> In it he proves that all things are true and states how the truths of all contradictions may be reconciled physically, such as for example that white is black and black is white.
>
> Cyrano de Bergerac
> *The Other World: States and Empires of the Moon* (1656)

Tim in the back row looks skeptical of this tip already, and he's right to be skeptical. You can design a page that looks great in color but not in black and white or looks great in black and white, but not in color.

But (you knew there was a *but* coming, didn't you?) having said that, it's also true that some basics—notably layout and typography—stay the same whether you're working in black and white or color. Getting it right in black and white means making sure you pay attention to those basics instead of giving all your attention to playing with colors. Colors are important, but first things first.

Getting the black and white part right also means that while you're working on the layout for a page, you can save some money by printing draft copies in black and white instead of color. Any four-color printer that doesn't use a ribbon—including ink jets, lasers, and wax jets—should print black and white pages for much less than color pages. If you have a ribbon-based printer, you can print drafts on your standard monochrome printer instead. (But watch out for differences in layout that can crop up if the printers use different printer languages or different fonts—an issue we'll cover in Chapter 5.)

I'm not about to launch into a discussion of layout and typography here. That's a subject for a book on desktop publishing, and it's a major understatement to say it's not going to fit in a short tip. But that's no reason for you ignore it. Good layout design can help make the page more readable, and that makes it worth the effort.

You may never have thought about it this way, but whenever you put a page together—whether it's a full-page business graphic, a transparency, a newsletter, a report, or even a one-page letter—you're playing the part of a graphic designer. You can simply slap the pages together, or you can invest some time and effort in the design. Either way, you *are* designing them.

If you haven't had any training in graphic design, you may find that thinking about layout and typography takes a little work at first. Instead of forcing text to fit on a page by making the margins smaller, you need to pay attention to whether the page looks too crowded and harder to read with those smaller margins. But don't give up just because you think you don't know what you're doing. Put the effort into making the page attractive and readable to your eye, and it should work for other people, too. You know that old line: *I don't know much about art, but I know what I like.* That's a good place to start.

LESS IS MORE

> It is vain to do with more what can be done with less.
>
> William of Occam

There are no hard and fast rules about using color, which means that a talented artist can make and break rules at will. However, most of us aren't talented artists. The good news is that there are a few rules of thumb that can help all but the colorblind create more visually attractive graphics. (Come to think of it, following the rules may help even more if you're colorblind.)

One of the most important rules is to keep it simple. Your screen and printer may be capable of 16.7 million colors, but unless you're printing continuous tone images (read: photographs), you shouldn't use more than five or six at a time, and less is usually better. If you can keep it down to two or three colors, you should.

(Yes, Arnold, there are exceptions. The most obvious is that you may want to use a gradient fill, which gradually changes from one color to another in a more or less continuous way. Gradient fills often make effective backgrounds. For purposes of this rule, though, consider a gradient fill a single color. Besides, this is only a rule of thumb, not a law of nature.)

The fewer colors you use in a graphic, the easier it is for people to digest what they're looking at. If you want to draw attention to a single bar in a bar chart, for example, you can use one color for all the text and the axes, another for all the bars you're not concerned with, and a third color for the bar that you want to highlight. If you give each bar a radically different color, the one you want to highlight won't stand out. This basic concept works even in black and white. In Figure 2.7, you won't have any way to know which bar I'm trying to highlight because they're all different shades of gray. You might guess that it's either the black bar or the white bar, but you can't be sure.

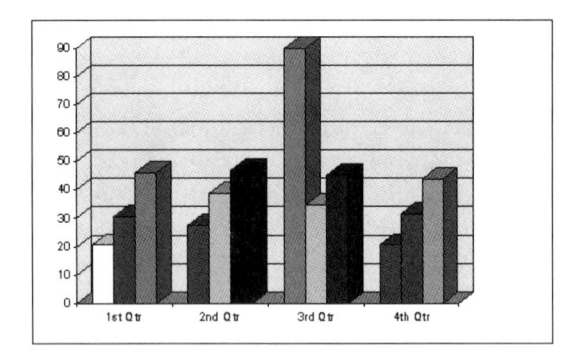

Figure 2.7 One of these bars is meant to be highlighted, but which one?

Give up? Okay, now take a look at Figure 2.8, and tell me which bar I'm trying to draw your attention to.

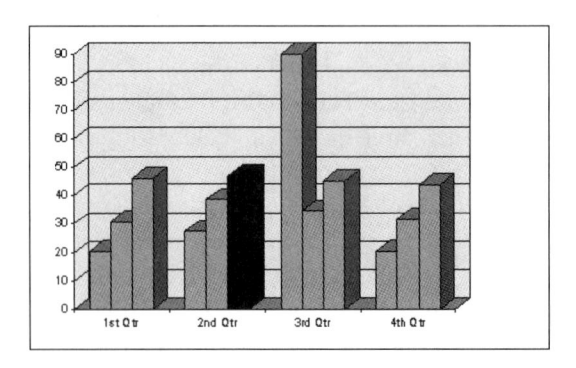

Figure 2.8 Sparing use of color (or, in this case, shades of gray) immediately draws your attention to the one black bar.

Yes, Tim, you're right; I cheated a bit to make it harder on you. If I were really trying to highlight one of the bars in Figure 2.7, I'd probably use white rather than black, but black works too.

BE CONSISTENT

> Consistency is contrary to nature, contrary to life. The only completely consistent people are the dead.
>
> Aldous Huxley
> *Do What You Will*, "Wordsworth in the Tropics" (1929)

> Consistency is the last refuge of the unimaginative.
>
> Oscar Wilde
> "The Relation of Dress to Art," in *Pall Mall Gazette* (Feb. 28, 1885)

Consistency has a bad reputation. All the witty sayings about consistency—and even most of the dull ones—put it down. Consistently. But when it comes to color schemes, particularly for graphics, consistency is a Good Thing, right up there with keeping it simple. Don't let anyone tell you otherwise. In fact, being consistent is a big part of keeping it simple.

Use colors in a consistent way and they'll carry part of the meaning for you. Take another look at Figures 2.7 and 2.8. Figure 2.8 is easier to make sense of partly because it's using the colors (or shades of gray, if you want to get picky) consistently.

In Figure 2.7, the bars are colored (grayed?) haphazardly, in a veritable riot of . . . uh . . . grays. In Figure 2.8, the bars are all the same, except one. It's the different color of the one bar that tells you there's something special about it, but what makes it different is that I've colored the other bars consistently.

Figure 2.9 shows the same graph again, this time with a different but equally consistent color scheme. In this case, the different shades of gray suggest that the

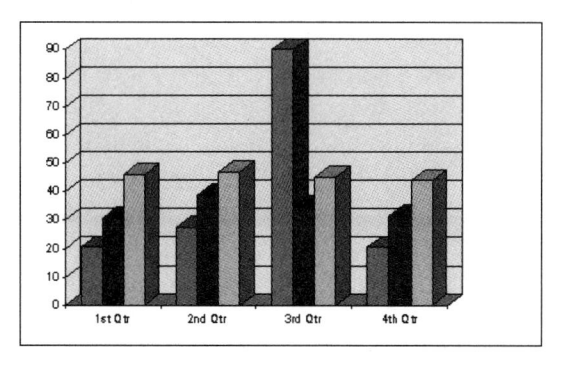

Figure 2.9 Same graph, different color scheme.

first bar in each group of three are all related to each other because they're all colored the same way. The same comment applies for the second bar in each group, and for the third. Consistent coloring ties each of the groups together.

Consistency in a series

Consistent color is even more important when you're creating a series of images—as part of a presentation, for example. Something as simple as keeping the same colors for background, titles, and bulleted text throughout the entire presentation can provide immediate visual clues for placing different parts of each image in context. Similarly, if you want to highlight part of an image, you should use the same color for highlighting throughout the series.

Suppose, for example, that you have a bar graph like the one in Figures 2.7 through 2.9, and you want to make several points about the graph. The trick is to draw attention to different parts of the graph as needed. You might create a separate graph for each point you want to make, using a color scheme like the one in Figure 2.8 to highlight just the part you want to draw attention to in each case.

If you stay with the same scheme throughout the series, using the same colors for highlighted and not-highlighted each time, the part that you want to highlight should be immediately obvious. If you change the highlight or not-highlight color at any point, or add more colors to the mix, you'll likely confuse the issue—as well as confuse anyone who is trying to work his or her way through the graphics.

The other side of this coin is that if you're consistent throughout, and you then change color for some element in one image, you'll provide an immediate visual cue that something is different about that element in this particular case. For example, you might change the text color with each new major topic within a presentation. The change in color will alert the viewer that you're starting a new topic. The point is, if you change colors, make sure there's a reason for it.

DON'T CHOOSE COLORS, CHOOSE A COLOR SCHEME

> There are two things to be considered with regard to any scheme. In the first place, "Is it good in itself?" In the second, "Can it be easily put into practise?"
>
> Jean-Jacques Rousseau
> *Emile*, Preface (1762)

Unless you have an artist's sensibility for color, in which case you can pick any colors that feel right to you and probably do just fine, you're best off sticking with rule-of-thumb decisions and picking your colors from common color schemes. Graphic artists know about and use color schemes, and even good artists consciously use them in their work. So why shouldn't you? We'll cover a few here as a kind of starter kit and a few more in Chapter 7.

WARM AND COOL COLORS

> There is no blue without yellow and without orange.
>
> Vincent Van Gogh

One of the easier color schemes for non-artists to use well is one I mentioned in Chapter 1, which takes advantage of warm colors and cool colors. The warm colors are red, orange, yellow, and yellowish green. The cool colors are bluish green, blue, indigo, and violet. If you forget which are which, remember the mnemonic Roy G. Biv, with G the middle initial and a foot in each camp.

Meet Roy G. Biv.

In general, warm colors tend to stand out, while cool colors tend to recede. So warm colors are best for small areas of foreground information such as text or bars on a bar chart, while cool colors work best for large areas such as the background.

As I mentioned in Chapter 1, green and magenta can be either warm or cool, depending on the colors around them. Surround them with warm colors and they look cool in comparison; surround them with cool colors and they look warm.

If you're having trouble deciding whether green or magenta is working as a warm or cool color, the solution follows a logic similar to that in my favorite manual for training cats. The manual recognizes that cats can't be trained, so you shouldn't waste your time trying to train them. If your cat insists, say, on using your brand new couch as a scratching post, the answer is to put the cat in another room.

If you're not sure whether a particular green or magenta works as a cool color or warm color in a given graphic, that probably means it's not doing the job you want from it. Don't waste time worrying about it. Change the color. If it comes across as a cool color on the screen, but a warm color on the printed page (or vice versa), don't waste time trying to make the printed version match the screen. Change the color.

MONOCHROMATIC COLOR SCHEMES

> Here or henceforward it is all the same to me...
>
> Walt Whitman
> *Leaves of Grass*, "Song of Myself," sct. 23 (1855)

Another color scheme that's relatively easy to use well is a monochromatic color scheme. I'm not talking about using shades of gray—that's an achromatic color scheme. (And besides, you didn't buy a color printer just to print in black and white.) A monochromatic color scheme uses a single hue but varies the saturation and brightness. A combination of dark red, red, light red, and pink would be a good example. So would dark blue, blue, and light blue.

When done right, a monochromatic color scheme can provide a subtle, yet sophisticated distinction among graphic elements. The trick is to pick colors of the same hue that are still different enough that viewers can recognize the differences at a glance.

With monochromatic color schemes you have to be particularly careful to make sure that the colors are significantly different at the printer as well as on the screen. You might want to create a test page for any given hue that you want to use, with blocks of color using different saturation and lightness settings. (Don't forget to include some text identifying the settings for each color so you can reproduce them at will.) This will take a little time to set up for any given hue, but if you keep the test page handy for reference, it can save hours of trial and error when you're creating graphics.

USE THE COLORS OF THE RAINBOW

> I always find that statistics are hard to swallow and impossible to digest. The only one I can ever remember is that if all the people who go to sleep in church were laid end to end they would be a lot more comfortable.
>
> Mrs. Robert A. Taft

One other color scheme belongs in your inventory—namely, the colors of the rainbow. This scheme is a little more limited in scope than the other two I've just mentioned, so let's take a little detour and talk about the sort of situations where you may want to use it.

A special class of graphics

In some cases, particularly if you need to graph statistical or technical data, it's easier to interpret the data if you create a color scale and match the colors to the values. You've certainly seen this approach in topographical maps that use colors for different land elevations and weather maps that use colors for temperatures or pressures.

Using color for a third dimension

You may also be familiar with using the same kinds of contour charts to graph other kinds of information. The only requirement is that the information needs three dimensions to represent it. Here again, you can create a color scale and use color to represent one of the dimensions.

Figure 2.10 should give you a sense of what I'm talking about. The figure, obviously, is limited to a gray scale, but the concept is the same as with color since even the gray scale can let you map the third dimension. (I'm not going to get into explaining the graph itself. If you need this sort of graph, I assume you're familiar with it already. If you don't need it, there's no point in explaining it.)

The other way to show three dimensions, of course, is to use a graph with three axes, as in Figure 2.11.

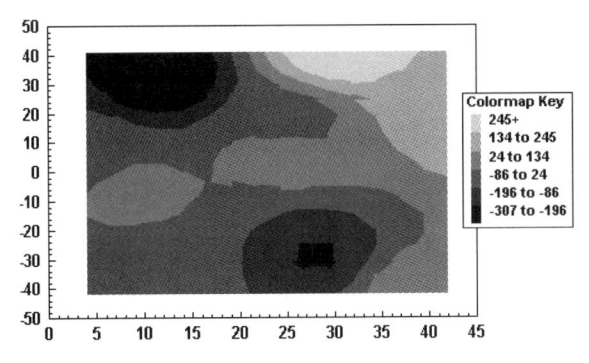

Getting Pretty Good Color with Hardly Any Effort 73

Figure 2.10 If you need three dimensions to map your data, you can create a color key (or in this case a gray-scale key) and use color (or shades of gray) to represent the third dimension.

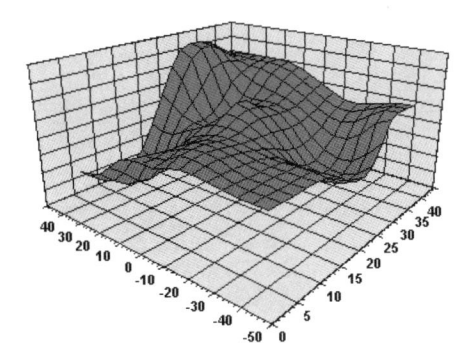

Figure 2.11 Another way to show a third dimension is, well . . . to show a third dimension.

The graph in Figure 2.11 is more eye catching than the one in Figure 2.10, but it's also harder to read since it's not always easy to tell where a given point on the surface is in relation to the z axis. But you don't have to choose one approach or the other. You can get the advantages of both kinds of graphs by combining a three-dimensional surface like the one in Figure 2.11 with a color key like the one in Figure 2.10 (or gray-scale key in this case). Try that, and you'll wind up with something like the graph in Figure 2.12.

The graph in Figure 2.12 is essentially identical in concept to the one in Figure 2.10, but it's a lot more eye catching, thanks to the third dimension. It's also more eye catching than the graph in Figure 2.11 because of the shades of gray. More important, it's easier to read because the shades of gray immediately tell you the approximate value on the z axis for any point on the surface. Change the grays to colors and it will be even more eye catching and easier to read.

Using color with a 3-D graph

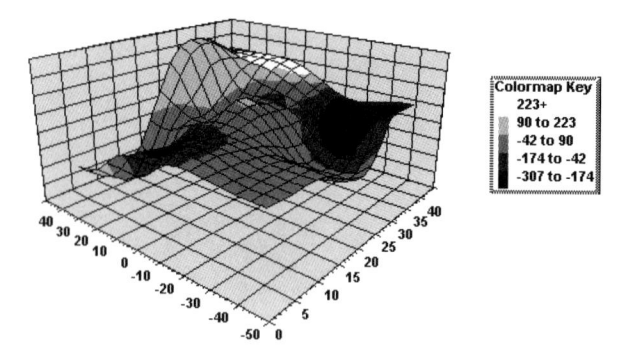

Figure 2.12 You can also show the third dimension in a contour map by both a third dimension and color (or shade of gray) at the same time.

Yes, Tim? This is all very interesting you say, but you don't care because you never deal with any data that needs three dimensions? Well, that's a fair complaint. But even if you've never been anywhere near a contour graph and you have no idea why anyone would use a graph like these, you may still find it useful to create a color key for a simple line graph, like the one in Figure 2.13.

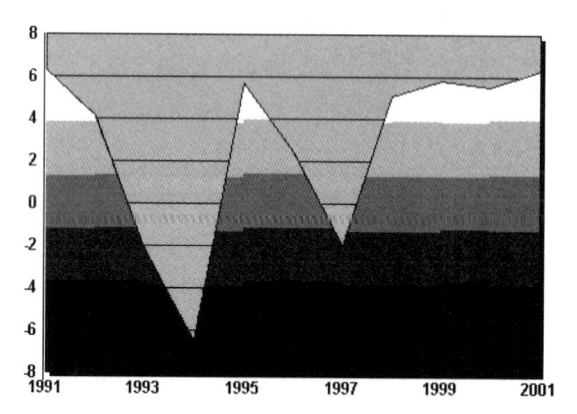

Figure 2.13 Even a simple line graph can benefit from a color scale (or gray scale).

The advantage here over a line graph without the color scale . . . uh, sorry, I mean gray scale . . . is the same as for the three-dimensional surface with a color scale. You can immediately see the value for the y axis at any point on the line without having to look over at the axis. For most graphs, this additional visual information isn't really needed, but it can make the graph easier to read, and it certainly makes it more interesting.

So much for the detour. Now you know the sort of graphics that I'm talking about. The common theme running through these examples is the need for a color scale, with the colors telling you something about the data. In these black and white examples, I've used a scale that runs from black to white. That's a natural progression that works well because everyone has experience with the full range from black to white; it just feels right.

End of digression

If I had the luxury in this book of showing these examples in color, the color scale I'd use would be the rainbow. More precisely, I'd follow the same progression of colors that you'll find in a rainbow: red, orange, yellow, green, blue, indigo, violet—or Roy G. Biv, for short.

Another visit by Roy G. Biv

This scale works for the same reason that the scale from black to white works—because it's a natural progression. Everyone who has ever played with fingerpaints or mixed wall paint knows that red naturally shades into orange, which shades into yellow, which shades into green, and so on.

A small warning goes here: I've oversimplified this discussion just a bit, and Tim's been sitting quietly in the back row, politely biting his tongue, ever since I mentioned indigo. Artists have a long standing joke that no one's seen the color indigo since Isaac Newton. And all jokes aside, it's really tough to see the difference between indigo and violet, which means the rainbow scale really has six colors, not seven.

It also helps to add some intermediate colors—particulary a yellowish-green and a greenish-blue—to remind the eye of the less obvious transitions from one color to the next. Also, don't feel that you have to start at any particular color. Remember, violet shades naturally into magenta, which shades naturally into red, which closes the circle for Mr. Roy G. Biv. You can start a rainbow-based color scale pretty much anywhere on the circle.

MORE COLOR SCHEMES: YOU LIKE IT? IT'S YOURS.

> Immature artists imitate. Mature artists steal.
>
> Lionel Trilling

There are lots more color schemes that we'll get to later, in Chapter 7, but I can't talk about them until we've covered topics like color wheels, complementary colors, and other bits of color theory. Besides, that's the other 80 percent of the effort that we're not bothering with in this chapter. In the meantime, if you want to explore some other possibilities besides the three basic color schemes we've looked at, just open your eyes. They're all around you.

Most graphics programs include sample output or sample color designs. Use these color combinations as the starting point for designing your own graphics—

even when you're working in other programs and designing graphics from scratch. Start with one or two samples that look attractive on screen, and print them out. If they don't look good in printed form, keep trying until you find some that do. If all else fails, try printing some samples that don't look as good on screen. They may surprise you.

Be sure to mark each sample page you print, whether you like its looks or not, with any information that might affect the color. You'll want to include the type of ribbon, the name and version of the program, the version of printer driver, any program driver settings that affect color, and, of course, the names or settings for the colors themselves. Put the samples in a notebook or file folder for later reference.

Keep in mind that one of the most important issues that affects color is your individual printer. If you buy a new color printer, or print from more than one model of printer—with one at home, say, and one at the office—be sure to keep the samples from each printer clearly marked with the printer name. You will likely find some mixes of color work well on one printer but not the other. If you need to print the same files on both printers, you'll want to find color schemes that work well on both, even if they print with noticeably different colors.

You can get ideas for color schemes in lots of other places besides the samples from your graphics programs. Feel free to steal color schemes from posters, brochures, magazine adds, or fliers handed out on the street. Any time I see a color flier, I grab it and bring it home for my collection. When I'm looking for ideas, I browse through the collection. When you see something you hate, pay attention to that too. Sometimes you can learn more from what you don't like if you vow never to do the same thing.

When you see a color scheme you like in a printed format, don't fall into the trap of trying to match the colors exactly. That's a sure way to wind up bald from pulling out all your hair. Matching the colors is virtually impossible—for all the reasons we covered in Chapter 1 and others we haven't gotten to yet. Use the poster, flier, or whatever as a guide, sure. Try to get something that's close enough to the original for the colors to work well together, absolutely. But don't go crazy trying to get an exact match. Remember, the idea is to find an easy way to put together workable color schemes, not to set an impossible task for yourself. That would be what they call counterproductive.

BACKGROUNDS

> Every philosophy is tinged with the colouring of some secret imaginative background, which never emerges explicitly into its train of reasoning.
>
> Alfred North Whitehead
> *Science and the Modern World* (1926)

When we looked at warm and cool colors earlier, I pointed out that cool colors were a good choice for (way cool) backgrounds. Another rule of thumb for backgrounds is: Make sure they provide a good contrast to whatever colors you're using in the foreground.

A difference in hue—even the difference between warm and cool colors—isn't enough by itself to make colors stand apart. Yellow is warm and blue is cool, but a pale light yellow won't stand out as well against a pale light blue as it will against a darker, more fully saturated blue. This is more of an issue with thin lines and text than with large areas of color, but even with large areas, darkness and saturation make a difference. So, in addition to a different hue, you'll generally want another clear difference between background and foreground colors, with one of them darker, more fully saturated, or both. Or vice versa.

Make either the background or foreground dark, saturated, or both.

Good colors for backgrounds are: blue, red, green, and purple. (Yeah, I know. Red is a warm color and you're supposed to use warm colors for the foreground, but if it's a dark red, it works—particularly if you use small areas of bright yellow or white in the foreground for contrast. So go figure. These are only rules of thumb, guys.) You might also want to consider using a less saturated color in the background, or using a gradient fill that runs from full saturation to no saturation.

What works on paper doesn't always work on transparencies. With transparencies, you'll generally want to pay even more attention to getting highly contrasting colors. You'll also want to avoid thin lines in favor of thick lines, and use larger fonts than you might otherwise use.

And then there are transparencies.

The rules for transparency backgrounds vary too. Worse, they vary depending on the room where you'll be projecting the transparencies. The rule of thumb is that dark backgrounds work well in dark presentation rooms but may be too dark for a room with a lot of ambient light. Light backgrounds make a graphic easier to decipher when there's ambient light, but they tend to make the entire transparency look washed out. Good colors for backgrounds on transparencies are blues and neutral colors: black, gray, and brown.

Not so incidentally, the only way to see how well a transparency holds up to light is to project it. And the only way to see how it looks under given lighting conditions is to project it in those lighting conditions. But the best way to proof a transparency, as opposed to judge how well it will hold up when it's projected, is to hold it up to view it against a white background, like a piece of paper.

MAKING EDGES STAND OUT

> All our words from loose using have lost their edge.
>
> Ernest Hemingway
> *Death in the Afternoon*, ch. 7 (1932)

Most times when you have two colors next to each other, whether they're foreground colors against the background or two foreground colors, you want them to stand out from each other well enough so you can see a sharp edge. Simply having two hues won't usually do that for you. If the brightness and saturation are the same, you'll get an effect similar to what you see in Figure 2.14.

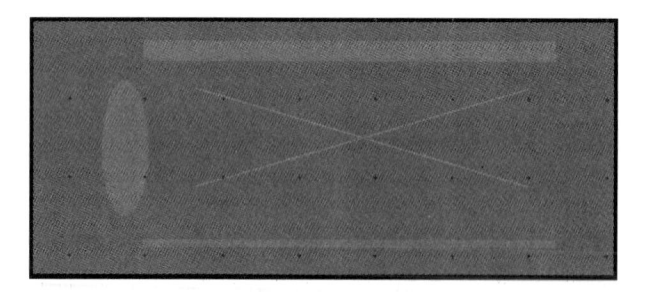

Figure 2.14 Even having different colors (or different shades of gray) doesn't guarantee that edges will stand out as sharp as they can be.

To be as clear as I can here, Figure 2.14 doesn't show precisely what I'm talking about because the two shades of gray differ in brightness. In fact, they differ only in brightness because the saturation for both is zero, and when saturation is zero, the hue doesn't matter. But the brightness level is close enough that you can get a sense of what you'd see with two different hues, but matching saturation and brightness.

The point is that the edges in Figure 2.14 aren't quite as sharp as they could be. One way to make the edges a lot sharper is to add an outline to each shape, which is what I've done in Figure 2.15. I've also changed the two hairline thin lines to black. Presto chango, suddenly the edges stand out so you can't miss them.

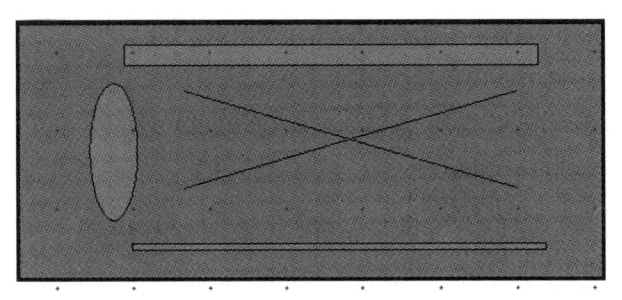

Figure 2.15 Add and outline, and suddenly the edges are a lot more obvious.

What's that, Tim? You say you have some business graphics programs that don't let you add outlines to the shapes? Well, that's not necessarily a problem. You can also make edges stand out as crystal clear by cranking up the difference in brightness. Take a look at Figure 2.16.

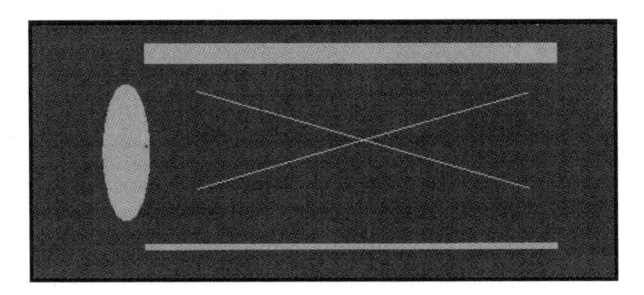

Figure 2.16 A big enough difference in brightness also makes the edges stand out.

I've gotten rid of the outline in Figure 2.16, but the edges stand out just as sharp as in Figure 2.15 and are far more obvious than in Figure 2.14. In this case, I made the background darker and the foreground lighter, but I could have changed only one or the other and gotten the same effect. It's only the difference between the colors that matters. Try it on your favorite graphics program and see. (But unless you have a monochrome monitor, use colors instead of shades of gray.) Start with two colors with the same saturation and darkness, and change the darkness only. Then go back to the starting colors and change the saturation only.

The moral here: To make sure the edges between two colors stand out, add an outline, or make sure the colors have noticeably different brightness levels, saturation levels, or both. In some programs, you won't be free to adjust brightness and saturation levels directly. But even if the only control you have is the option to pick colors from a list, you should be able to get the same effect as long as you have enough colors to choose from.

TEN RULES FOR TEXT AND COLOR

> What our eyes behold may well be the text of life but one's meditations on the text and the disclosures of these meditations are no less a part of the structure of reality.
>
> Wallace Stevens
> *The Necessary Angel,* "Three Academic Pieces," no. 1 (1951; first published 1947)

Text poses special problems for color graphics. On the one hand, you have to be able to see it well enough to read it. But no matter what colors you use, the relatively thin lines in text automatically make it harder to see than a larger object in the same color. Here is an assortment of tips for making text easier to read. Most of these apply to thin lines in graphics as well.

Lightness makes the biggest difference. Make sure there is a significant difference in lightness between the text and background. I'm not talking about the brightness levels in the HSB model, but lightness, which—in this context, at least—is slightly different.

Different hues have different levels of lightness. Yellow is a light color; blue and green are relatively dark colors. So even fully saturated, fully bright yellow text is reasonably readable against a fully saturated, fully bright blue or green background. If your graphics program lets you set the brightness level, you can set a lower brightness to make the blue or green darker, and the yellow text will be even more readable.

Saturation also affects lightness. At full brightness, zero saturation becomes white, and white is lighter than any hue. So at high levels of brightness, low levels of saturation give you lighter colors.

It's the overall differences in lightness between text and background, not just the difference in brightness as given in the HSB model, that matter. The greater the difference, the more readable the text. Nothing on this list is an ironclad absolute, but this rule comes closest.

Colors on colors can be hard to read. Shy away from colored text on a colored background. It's relatively easy to get away with breaking this rule. The problem isn't that colored text never works on a colored background, but that it's too easy to pick colors that don't work. If you're sure you know what you're doing, break this rule with abandon; otherwise, play it safe and avoid the problem.

White, black, and gray are good choices. If colored text on a colored background is best avoided, you don't need a course in formal logic to conclude that either the text or background will wind up white, black, or gray. Those are perfectly good choices, and you shouldn't be reluctant to use them.

Now blend in the rule that the most important issue for readability is the difference in brightness. The conclusion: the ideal choice for readability is white text on a dark-colored background, black text on a light-colored background, or colored text on a neutral background—white, black, or gray.

If you still want to use colored text on a colored background, avoid heavily saturated color backgrounds. It's not too hard to find a combination of colored text on a fully saturated color background that's still perfectly readable, but keep in mind that colors affect colors. A change in background color from one graphic to another, or one part of a graphic to another, can change the perception of the text color. And if you're using colors to carry part of the information, the apparent change in color can be confusing. The more saturated the background color, the more likely this is to be a problem, which leads to the next rule.

Don't forget: Colors on colors change colors.

When you're using colored text on a colored background, the best choice for the background is a pale color. If you want to minimize the effect of the background on the color, stay with the same hue, at a lower saturation and brightness. (This isn't the only choice for minimizing the effect of the background color, but it's the easiest.)

Consider a pale background.

If you have a lot of text, particularly on a series of graphics, shy away from fully saturated hues for the text. Fully saturated colors can be fatiguing to the eye, which makes the text harder to read.

Don't use fully saturated color for text.

Don't use blue for text. Small shapes and lines in blue are difficult to focus on, and that makes text in blue difficult to read. The only thing harder to read than blue text is blue text on a blue background, even with different levels of brightness. Don't take my word for it. Try it and see.

Blue is a bad idea.

Well, maybe there is one thing harder to read than blue text on a blue background: blue text on a red background. You've seen the effect with bright red and bright blue together, yes? The two colors next to each other make it difficult to focus on the image. You might want this effect sometimes, but not when you want people to be able to read the text. Don't use blue text on a red background.

Don't use blue on red.

Don't use red text on a blue background either. For the same reason. Some colors just don't go together.

Don't use red on blue either.

Don't get carried away with using different colors for different parts of your text—one for headings, one for bullets, one for highlighted words, one for a highlighted item in a list, and so on. The more colors you use, the harder the text is to read.

Be subtle.

GET IT RIGHT IN BLACK AND WHITE II: THE HANDOUT

> The world is not black and white. More like black and grey.
>
> Graham Greene

Almost everyone occasionally needs to hand out black and white copies of something created in color. For example, you may want to give out copies of the slides you used in a presentation, but you won't want to hand out actual color

82 *Chapter 2*

transparencies, and you probably won't want to bother printing them. It is much better to hand out copies churned out at the low page price of a black and white copier. Or you may have a gorgeous color graphic—either as a page by itself or as part of a full blown report—that you need to fax first, then follow up with the color version by pony express.

Color doesn't turn into black and white very well.

Now here's the problem: If you fax or copy a color graphic, you'll very often wind up with any number of colors coming out as the same shade of gray. That can make graphics essentially unreadable. Figure 2.17 shows what good job a copier can do to destroy readability.

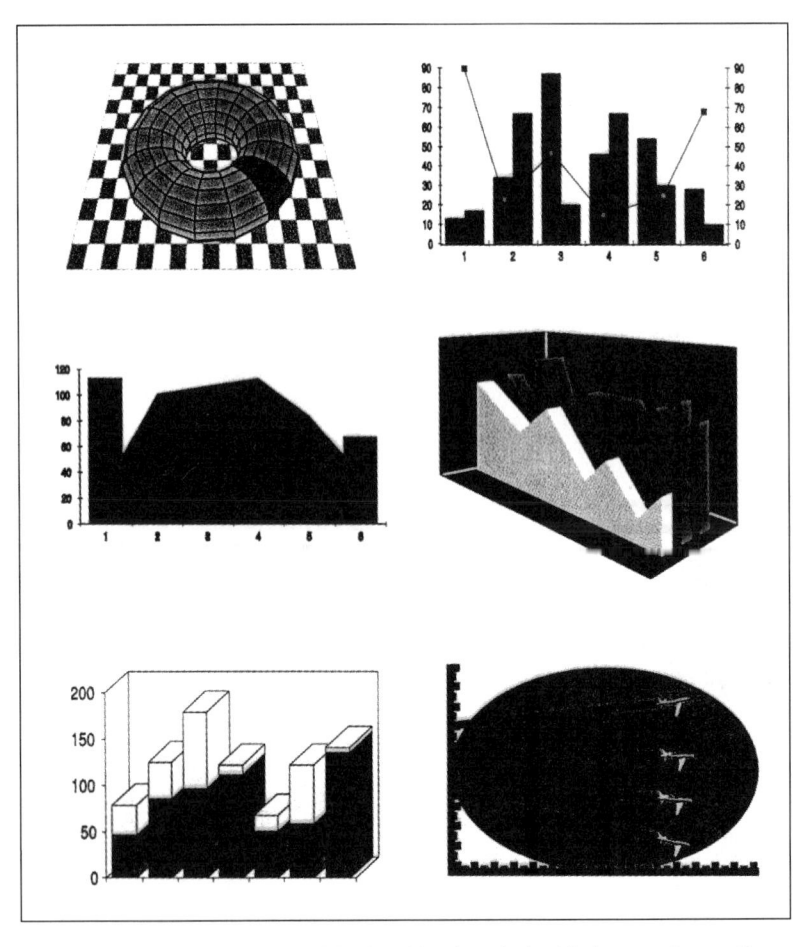

Figure 2.17 It's an ugly graphic, but I had to do it. All the graphs on the left have lost information in the process of copying a color page. All the graphs on the right still show the information they started with, but they're not particularly attractive.

Getting Pretty Good Color with Hardly Any Effort 83

I printed the original for Figure 2.17 on a Tektronix Phaser 340, which offers just about the best looking graphics output you can get on plain paper. The colors are vibrant and fully saturated, with next-door neighbors standing out from each other very nicely. But you'll have to take my word for that because you certainly can't see it in the copied version.

I've included an assortment of graphics in Figure 2.17 so you can see what happens with different color schemes and different kinds of graphics. The three graphics on the left side are affected enough by being copied to make them essentially useless. The three on the right are all readable, but pug ugly.

Going down the left hand side of the figure, the torus-shaped graph at the top—a variation on a pie chart—shows only two sections. The original has five—in brown, blue, green, orange, and red. Four of the five have melted together into a single light gray section.

The second graph down is a combined bar and area chart. You can see two bars—one at the extreme left and one on the extreme right. The others have disappeared into the lower of the two colored areas. Here again, two strikingly different colors—a reddish brown and a light blue—have turned into one.

The bottom chart on the left, finally, has four colors in each stacked bar, rather than the three you can see. In this case, green and blue have magically turned into the same near black.

Each of the three graphs on the right side of the figure also turn two or more strikingly different colors presto chango into nearly the same color.

In the top chart, both bars in each pair share the same dark gray, rather than being two distinct colors, as in the original, and the line graph gets lost in the background of the bars. But you can still see each bar in the chart, as well as the data points for the line graph, so you can still read the chart without problems.

In the middle chart, the middle and back slices melt into each other. But in the original (not in the version reproduced here), you can still make out the two separate areas, thanks to the lighter color for the top edges of the areas. The best that can be said of this one is that you can still read the chart, if you work at it.

In the bottom chart, the lines in the line graph aren't hard to spot in the original (although they disappear here). But you'd never guess that the gray oval behind the graph is a world map, with blue oceans and green continents. There's certainly nothing—on any of these graphs—that would strike you as well designed, interesting, or easy to interpret.

There are two kinds of lessons you can draw from Figure 2.17. The first is an understanding of the kind of graphic that can survive a copier or fax machine, however badly it winds up limping after the experience. But that would be the wrong lesson. A much better lesson is that you shouldn't make copies from your color output.

Don't make black and white copies of color graphics.

84 *Chapter 2*

Use Monochrome Masters for Your Monochrome Copies

> What's black and white and read all over?
>
> Children's riddle

The simple truth is that monochrome originals copy better than color originals. Figure 2.18 shows the same page of graphs as Figure 2.17. In this case, the figure shows what the graphs look like after copying, but this time, the master page was in black and white. This master page was also printed on the Phaser 340, at 600 by 300 dpi resolution.

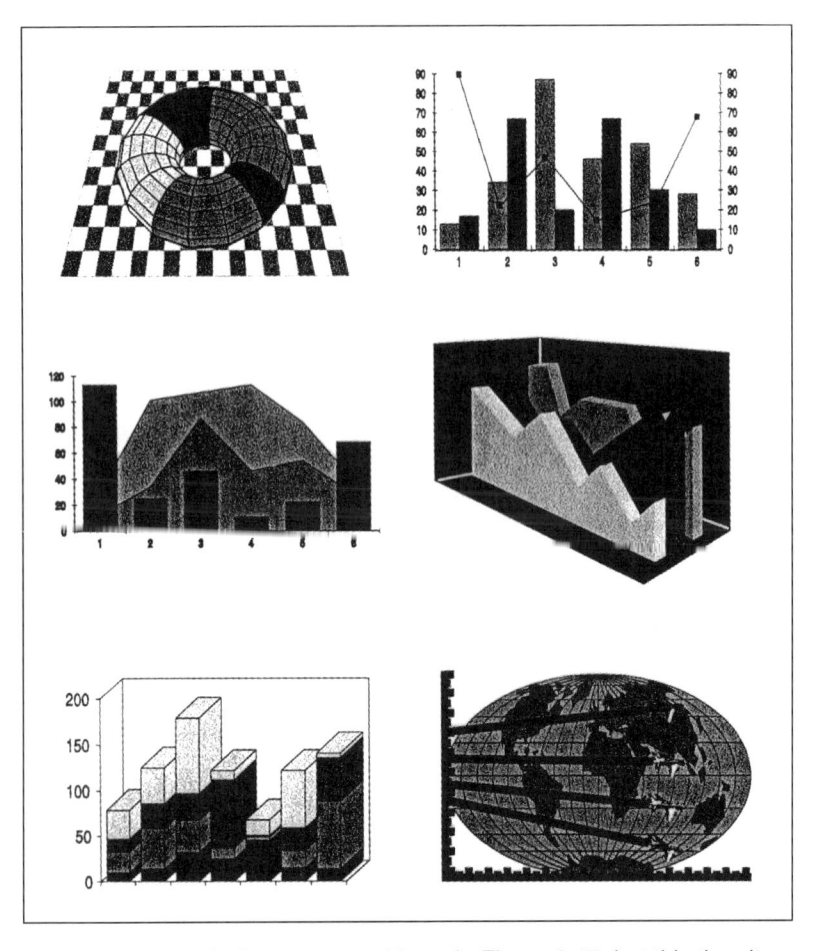

Figure 2.18 Here's the same graphic as in Figure 2.17, but this time it looks better because I trimmed its beard, gave it a shoeshine, and printed it in black and white before I copied it.

I'll say it again, in case you zipped past it: The figure shows what the *copies* look like. The original looks better (and you'll see the original shortly as well), but I thought it was fairer to use the copy since I'm comparing it to the copies of the color version. If you print monochrome originals to hand out—using your laser printer, say—instead of running off copies on a copier, your results should look better than the figure.

Whatever the limitations of handing out copies rather than original monochrome output, they still beat copies of a color original six ways from Sunday. If you compare Figure 2.18 with Figure 2.17, you'll see that it solves all of the problems in Figure 2.17. On the left side of Figure 2.18 at the top, the torus shows five distinct sections; the combination bar and area graph in the middle shows all the bars as well as both areas; and the 3-D stacked bar chart at the bottom shows four distinct sections for each bar.

On the right side, the graphs are all more readable and more attractive than those in Figure 2.17. In the top graph, each bar in each pair is shaded differently so you can see each one more easily. In addition, the line stands out against the bars so you can read the line graph more easily too. In the middle graph, the three areas stand out clearly from each other so they're easier to make out. In the bottom graph, not only can you see the global map, but the thick dark lines of the line chart stand out far better against the lighter background.

For some graphics, you can get this dramatic difference for black and white copies simply by printing in monochrome mode—a feature you'll find in most, but not all, printers. For other graphics, you may have to adjust colors slightly, or simply redefine colors as shades of gray to make sure they don't come out the same shade.

For these examples, I made no changes at all in the stacked bar graph, the combination bar and line graph, or the area graph. I changed at least one color in each of the other three graphs. The only graph that I absolutely had to change was the torus, which still lied by showing only three sections when I printed it in monochrome without any other changes. (Or, at least, three sections that were obvious enough to live through the copy step.) Except for the torus, the changes were aimed at improving the look of the graphs, not the readability. But even without those changes, the copies from the black and white master were much more attractive than the copies from the color master.

The point is simple enough: When you hand out black and white versions of your color pages, start with a monochrome original at the copier. If you have a few extra minutes, it's worth investing the time to spruce up the output so it will look even better in monochrome.

The Windows PostScript Printer driver version 3.5x has a check box in the Options dialog box labeled Color, as shown in Figure 2.19. (If you have a PostScript printer installed on your system, you can check the version easily enough. Go to the Windows Control Panel, choose Printers, highlight the name of the PostScript printer you have installed, and choose Setup. You can then choose About to see the driver version number, or simply choose Options to see the Options dialog box. Other versions of PostScript drivers offer a similar check box elsewhere.)

You would probably think that if you don't put an X in the Color check box, you'll get black and white output on your color printer, especially since the help file for the driver says so. You would, of course, be wrong. This option doesn't do diddley. More precisely, it works with programs like Microsoft Word, which take full advantage of the driver. But most high-end graphics programs—the kind you're most likely to use for color printing—do an end run around the driver, except for some basic communications with the printer. And programs that ignore the driver ignore the check box.

The good news is that most color printer drivers, whether PostScript drivers or not, let you print a color page in black and white by adding or removing an X from a check box (a different check box, that is) or by picking a monochrome or gray scale option from a pull-down list. For PostScript printers, this other check box or pull-down list controls whether you get color or black and white—no matter what you've done with the check box in the Options dialog box.

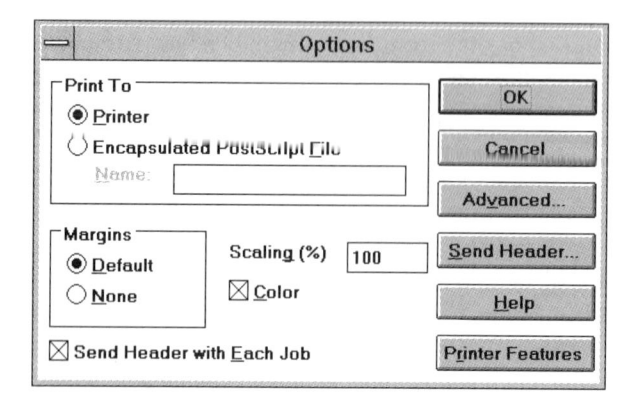

Figure 2.19 Notice the Color check box in this PostScript driver dialog box. Now forget about it. It doesn't do what it promises.

How to move a color page to black and white

To create a black and white version of your color pages, start with the finished color document, and either print it on a monochrome-only printer or set the driver for monochrome and print it on your color printer. (If your printer driver doesn't have a monochrome mode, your software might. That's okay too, as long as it uses shades of gray rather than crosshatch patterns for the different colors.)

If you have a choice of printers, you'll generally want to go for the higher resolution. You'll get better black and white output from a 600 dpi laser printer, for example, than from a 300 dpi thermal wax printer.

Got your black and white print? Good. Take a look at it and see if the colors came out in sufficiently different shades of gray. If you plan to use it as a master, rather than hand out originals, run the page through a copier and look at the copy. If you're happy with the result, you can stop here. Print out more originals to hand out, or make as many copies as you need.

If you're not happy with the result, you have two choices. One is to muck around with the original color file so you can use the same file for color and for black and white. The other is to make a copy of the file and modify it. If you take the second route, you'll have to maintain two files if you ever make changes in either. That's a bit of a pain, but if you can't change the colors on the original for whatever reason, it's the only option you've got.

Even if you're planning to change the original, you're best advised to make a copy first and work on it instead. You may decide midstream that you want to go back to the colors you started with, which won't be so easy if you've already saved the changed file under the same name. So work on the copy. When you're sure you're happy with it in color as well as in black and white, resave it under the original name.

Changing the colors to give you a better black and white version of the image is basically a matter of informed trial and error. The *trial and error* part means you have to keep adjusting the color and printing new test copies until you get it right. The *informed* part means that if you approach the changes with a little common sense, you can use the results of each test print to judge what your next change should be.

Begin by noting which colors came out looking the same and which came out looking different on the first black and white test print. You may be able to use exactly the same color scheme, changing what the colors apply to so that similar shades of gray are no longer next to each other. If you're using a program that doesn't give any control over changing colors—other than picking a different color from a limited list—this may be your best choice if you don't want to mess with the color scheme too much. If you're using a program that lets you tweak color to taste, however, there's a better approach.

You often don't have to pick radically different colors to get radically different results in black and white. The difference between the globe backgrounds in Figures 2.17 and 2.18, for example, is a relatively small change in hue and an even smaller change in saturation of the background. Similarly, the three

changed colors in the torus graphs in Figures 2.17 and 2.18 differ in brightness in one case; hue and saturation in another; and hue, saturation, and brightness in the third. But all three are recognizably similar colors in the color versions—a light green versus a darker green, a light cyan versus a darker cyan, and a light brown versus a darker brown. By changing the colors as little as possible, I've managed to solve the problem with the black and white version, while still giving the color version pretty much the same color scheme that it started with.

The key here: If the program you're using lets you adjust hue, saturation, and brightness, try small changes in colors first, make notes on the changed settings, and print out the results to see the effect. Once you've seen how much difference a given size change makes for a given color, you can make a better guess for how much to change it for the next test. Don't forget to print the modified image in color before you overwrite the original file. If you don't like what you see, you may want to go back to the original color version and try again.

Faxing Color Pages in Black and White

> In 1850 F. C. Bakewell, in London, invented a "copying telegraph," consisting of tinfoil wrapped around a rotating cylinder, upon which writing, added by a pen dipped in varnish, could be scanned by a contact carried by an endless screw . . . By 1964 over 40,000 simple drum scanner-recorders, known as Desk-Fax, were handling over 50,000,000 messages annually.
>
> *Encyclopaedia Britannica*, 15th Edition, Volume 18, page 73

Faxing brings up some additional issues, although the basics are mostly the same as for black and white handouts.

Yes, Arnold, I know that one choice is to fax your color pages on a color fax machine, but there's a minor problem: Will everyone in the class who has a color fax machine please raise your hand? I don't see many hands, Arnold. And even if you have a color fax machine on your end, you can't fax in color unless the other guy has one too. So let's stay with faxing in black and white. While we're at it, let's be clear that I'm only talking about faxing on Group 3 fax machines, which work on standard phone lines. Group 4 fax machines, which work over digital phone lines, are also relatively rare.

Faxing with a fax machine If you're going to print your pages first and fax them by running them through a stand-alone fax machine, the procedure for making sure the pages work in black and white is pretty much the same as that for handouts. Except where it's different.

One issue is that the quality of the fax is going to depend in large part on the quality of the image you start with just this side of the fax modem. Yes, Arnold, I mean fax modem, not fax machine. Even if you're using a fax machine, there's a fax modem in it, and what matters is the quality of the image after it's been scanned and before it gets to the modem. Once it gets to the phone line, you have no control over what happens. That means you'll want to use the copier feature on your fax machine, instead of using a real copier, for your test copies to give you a best-case version of the page after the fax machine scans it.

There are, however, a couple of complications to the scanning step:

First, almost all fax machines offer a choice of resolutions. At a minimum you can expect to find standard resolution (roughly 100 by 200 dpi), and fine (roughly 200 by 200 dpi). Some fax machines also offer a superfine mode (typically 300 by 300 or 400 by 400), but these higher resolutions are proprietary and won't generally work unless you have the same brand fax machine on both sides of the phone line. Unless you never use standard mode, run your test copies at standard resolution. If the copies are decipherable at 100 by 200 dpi, they'll be even better at 200 by 200 dpi. It doesn't necessarily work the other way.

Second, some fax machines offer a choice of modes. If you have a choice, you can expect to see two-level black and white (often called text) and gray scale (often called photo). The black and white choice scans images in just two gray levels, black and white. The gray scale choice scans images in shades of gray. Depending on your fax machine, you may find other choices too.

For obvious reasons, if your fax machine offers a gray scale mode, that's the one you want to use for scanning pages you've printed in shades of gray. If you have additional choices, you'll want to get familiar with them too. Some fax machines, for example, offer a compromise mode for pages that mix text and gray scale images.

Once you've settled on a resolution and mode for copying, you're back to the same trial-and-error steps as for handouts. Print out the page in black and white, run it through the fax copier, take a look at the results, change the colors, and print out again. When you're satisfied with the results, you're done. Fax and be happy.

The problem with faxing by fax machine is that it won't give you the best possible quality. Let me back up a bit to my comment that the quality of the fax depends in large part on the quality of the image you start with just this side of the fax modem.

When you fax by fax machine, you're starting with a second-generation image, printed out and then scanned in. The scanning step inevitably degrades the image. If you fax directly from your computer, you start with a first-generation image, and that means you automatically start with better image quality. A nice bonus is that for multipage faxes, you don't have to stand around making

Faxing from your computer

sure the pages feed into the fax machine correctly. Pages stored on a hard disk don't jam going through the feeder.

If you've never faxed from a computer

In case you're not familiar with fax programs, here's a quick rundown. Virtually every fax program that runs in Windows or on the Mac lets you send faxes from virtually any program by essentially printing from that program. In Windows, you can set the fax driver as your printer driver, and fax by giving the print command from any program. With Mac programs, you can typically either select the fax driver in the Chooser or define a hot key to bring up the fax dialog box on command. With either Windows or the Mac, you can then fill in the phone number, an optional cover page, and other details, before giving the actual command to send the fax.

If you have a fax modem and haven't tried faxing from your computer yet, you're missing out on one of life's great conveniences; it's better than cooking popcorn in a microwave oven. How convenient is it? Well, my wife, whose attitude toward computers is that she sees no point in learning how to do anything on the computer that I can do for her, thinks it's a Good Thing.

True story: I installed Delrina's WinFax Pro on my wife's computer months before she was willing to try it. Every time she needed to send a fax, she would print out a file, take it over to the fax scanner, and scan it in. Every time I suggested she try printing directly from the computer, she said she didn't have time to learn how. Finally, I coaxed her into letting me show her how to send a fax from disk. Now she tells her friends they should get a fax modem and software.

If you have a modem that you bought at all recently, it almost certainly includes a fax capability. If you have a fax modem, it almost certainly came with fax software. (Yes, Arnold, this time I'm talking about a modem that includes a fax capability and plugs into your computer.) If you haven't tried the software yet, now's a good time. Dust off the package, install the program, and see what it can do. Even poorly designed fax programs make life easier for faxing anything that starts out on your computer. The better designed programs are . . . well . . . better.

Testing pages when faxing from disk

One small problem with faxing color pages directly from disk is that the only way to find out what the pages look like is to fax them and see how they come out on the other end. If you try printing them on a printer, the levels of gray may be very different from what you'll see in the fax. If you have a fax machine handy, this shouldn't be much of a problem—unless your computer modem and fax machine are both on the same phone line.

> **If you don't have a handy fax machine or second computer you can fax to for test runs, you'll have to do something creative, like fax to a friend and get the pages back later. For most faxes, this isn't worth the effort. But if, for example, you run a clambake business, like a friend of mine, and regularly fax your brochures to potential customers, you'll want to make sure the brochures look as good as they can. More generally, for any pages that you're going to fax repeatedly and often, it's worth the effort to get them right.**

When you send a test fax from a fax program, check out the choices you have, if any. Fax programs, like fax machines, typically offer standard and fine resolution settings, and they may offer gray scale and other modes also. The same considerations apply for these settings when sending from disk as when sending from a fax machine.

If you're stuck in a situation where you can't easily run test prints, you can fall back on printing black and white test prints on your printer and hope the grays are the same as on the fax, or close enough. But when you send the fax, it's even more important that you check your resolution and mode choices, and use a gray scale mode if there is one.

One last issue is that the quality of the fax is going to depend partly on the fax machine on the other end. If you're faxing a page to someone with a laser-printer–based fax machine printing on plain paper at 300 dpi, the output on that end is going to look better than if you're faxing to someone with a thermal printer–based fax machine. There's not much you can do about that, but keep it in mind. If you worry about readability on a worst-case thermal fax machine, you can be sure your fax will be readable on the best-case plain paper machine. This rule holds true no matter what you're faxing, but it's more of an issue for gray scale or color images than for, say, text pages. If what you're sending is critical to your business—like my friend's clambake brochures—you may want to hunt up a thermal fax machine and send a test fax, just to make sure it's readable.

DIFFERENT PRINTERS PRINT DIFFERENT GRAYS ALSO

> I reverently believe that the Maker who made us all makes everything in New England but the weather. I don't know who makes that, but I think it must be raw apprentices in the weather-clerk's factory who experiment and learn how.... In the spring I have counted one hundred and thirty-six different kinds of weather inside of four-and-twenty hours.
>
> Mark Twain

I've mentioned several times that different models of printers will print the same file using noticeably different colors. They will also print with noticeably different shades of gray. I'm bringing this up now partly because it may affect how you print test prints for black and white handouts and faxes. If you have more than one printer handy, you may want to try printing a master on each printer before you start mucking around with the colors.

Another reason I'm bringing this up is that I want to drive home the fact that different printers print the same image differently. I can't show you that in color in this part of the book (although you'll find some examples in the color pages), but I can show it to you in black and white.

92 *Chapter 2*

Figure 2.20 is the original master I used for the copy in Figure 2.18. It's printed in 600 by 300 dpi resolution on the Tektronix Phaser 340. Figure 2.21 is the same file printed on a NEC SuperScript Color 3000, printed in 300 dpi resolution, using the printer's thermal dye mode.

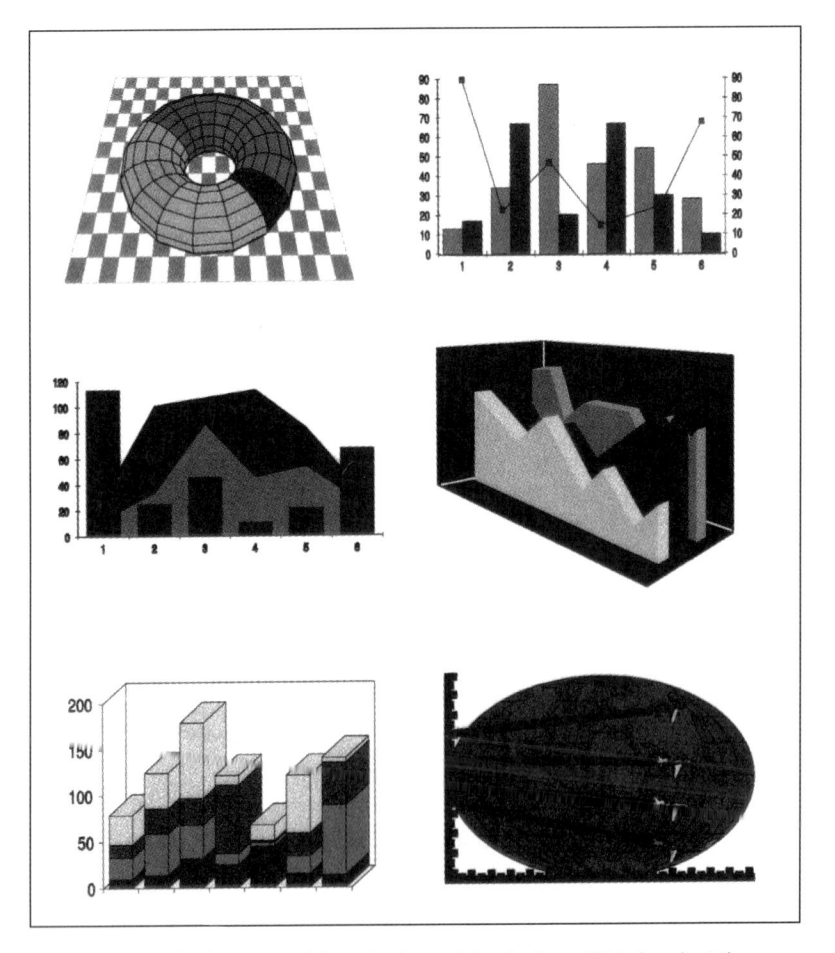

Figure 2.20 You've seen this set of graphics before. This is what the original looks like, without being filtered through a copying machine

If you take a quick glance at the figures, you'll see that almost every shade of gray is lighter in Figure 2.21 than in Figure 2.20, but that's not the only difference. Compare the bars in the combination bar and area graphs—the middle graphs on the left side—to the background in the 3-D area graphs—the middle graphs on the right side.

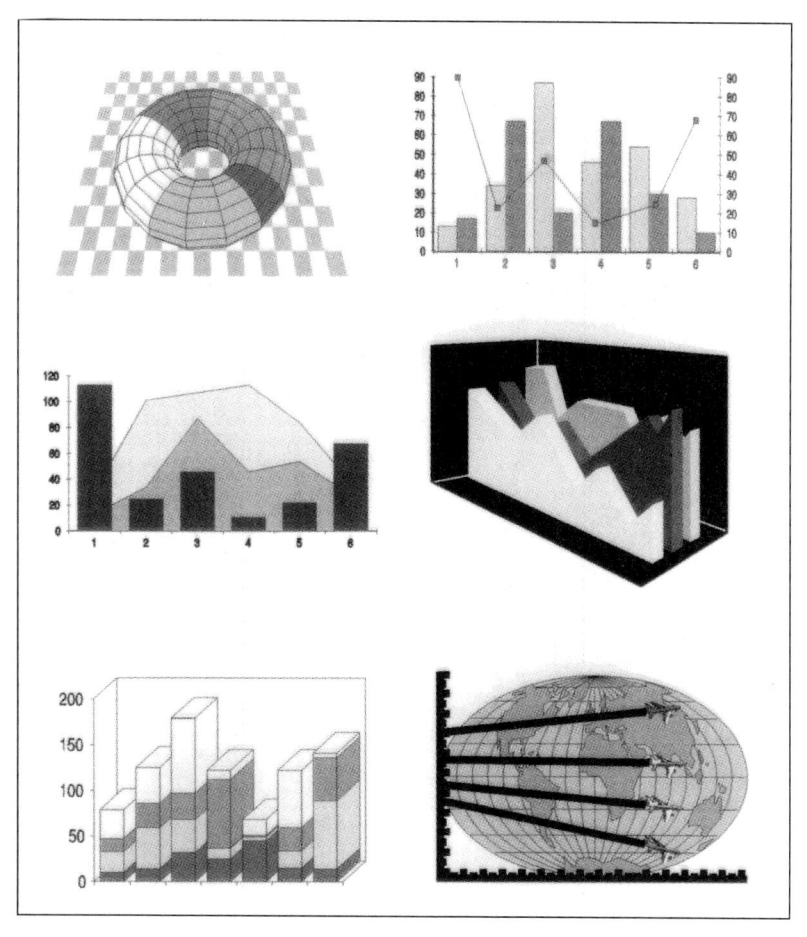

Figure 2.21 Here's the same set of graphics again, in different shades of gray. Same file, different printer.

In Figure 2.20, the bars in the one graph are almost the same black as the background in the other, while in Figure 2.21, they're distinctly different shades of gray. In this case, the lack of a shading difference in Figure 2.20 doesn't matter because the bars and area slices aren't next to each other.

Take a look at the middle area slices in the 3-D area graphs. The version in Figure 2.21 stands out a lot better because it's a distinctly different shade of gray. The version in Figure 2.20 disappears into the background in some places. In fact, the only reason the graph is readable in Figure 2.20 is because most of the middle slice stands out against the back slice, and the top edge of the middle slice is a slightly lighter shade. Switch the colors between the second and back slice, and the back slice will almost disappear.

You can spot some problems and other potential problems too. The torus in Figure 2.20 shows only three clearly different sections. Note too there's a section of the torus that's white in Figure 2.21 but a light gray in Figure 2.20. If you made one of the sections on either side of that section white, the two would melt into a single section in one case but still be distinct sections in the other. The same potential problem shows up in the bar chart on the bottom left of the two figures in the top section of the bars.

The moral is . . . The point is that just because a shade of gray page prints well on one printer is no reason to think it will print well on another printer. The practical meaning: If you have different printers at home and the office, you can spend hours making sure a page looks good on one printer and still not have the vaguest idea how it will look on the other. More important, the same lesson applies to color pages. Take this one to heart. It will save you a lot of grief.

3 Printers Aren't Monitors

> James Brown and Frank Sinatra are two different quantities in the universe. They represent two different experiences of the world.
>
> Imamu Amiri Baraka
> Interview in David Frost, *The Americans* (1970)

I don't suppose the statement that printers aren't monitors will come as much of a surprise to many people. Of course, I mean that not just in the trivial sense that one device draws its pictures in light on a screen, while the other paints a more permanent picture on paper. I also mean it in the more significant sense that there are differences in the images they draw. Even this shouldn't come as a surprise if you've read the first two chapters in this book. (And if you haven't, you should go back and read at least Chapter 1, which gives you the background you'll need to get the most out of this chapter.)

Printers and monitors not only use different technologies to draw their pictures, they use different color models and different routes to mixing colors. And that affects both the colors they get and the colors you see (which, as I pointed out in Chapter 1, are not always the same thing).

No, I'm not being mysterious here (or, at least, I'm not trying to be). Keep in mind that colors and lighting both affect colors. So the colors you see on a page depend on the lighting in the room. And for any given color in any given lighting, the color you see depends not just on the color you're looking at, but at the colors around it as well.

Picture this: You've just spent three hours being creative with a graphic or a scanned photo and your hand is cramping from all that mousing around. But you finally have just what you want on screen. Do you think that when you print the image you'd like the colors on the page to pretty well match what you see on screen? Would you expect a full-screen image to print a lot larger than a postage stamp and still take full advantage of the printer's resolution?

Did anybody answer, no? I didn't think so.

It sounds like a simple enough thing to ask—that printed output match the screen—but it's not. The reason it's not is that printers aren't monitors. Both are output devices, yes. Both plug into your computer, yes. Both come in versions that can produce color images, yes. But beyond that they have little in common. The better you understand the differences, the better you can compensate for them, and the fewer unpleasant surprises you'll run into when you give the command to print.

In this chapter and the next, we'll take a closer look at the differences between monitors and printers, starting with the differences in how they produce colors. More important, we'll take a look at how to minimize differences in the results. In Chapter 4, we'll look at some of the other issues besides differences in color.

THE PRIMARY ISSUE

> Anthropology is the science which tells us that people are the same the whole world over—except when they are different.
>
> Nancy Banks-Smith
> Quoted in *Guardian* (London, July 21, 1988)

Both monitors and printers create all the colors they're capable of by mixing just a few colors, called primary colors. As I discussed in Chapter 1, however, the primary colors for monitors are different from the primary colors for printers. Printer primaries are cyan, magenta, and yellow; monitor primaries are red, green, and blue.

Did someone ask if it would be easier to match screen and printer colors if both used the same primaries? Well, yes, it would, but you can't change primary colors on a whim. The choice of primaries is based on physics and biology. (Don't look so worried at the mention of physics, Tim; this is easy physics. Easy biology too.)

Light versus Ink

> Nature and nature's laws lay hid in night;
> God said Let Newton be! and all was light.
>
> Alexander Pope

Primary monitor colors Let's take the physics side of it first. There is a physical difference between mixing lights and mixing inks—or any other pigments. Figure 3.1, which you've seen before in Chapter 1, shows how the primary colors of light mix to form the secondary colors—yellow, cyan, and magenta—and how all three primaries mix to form white.

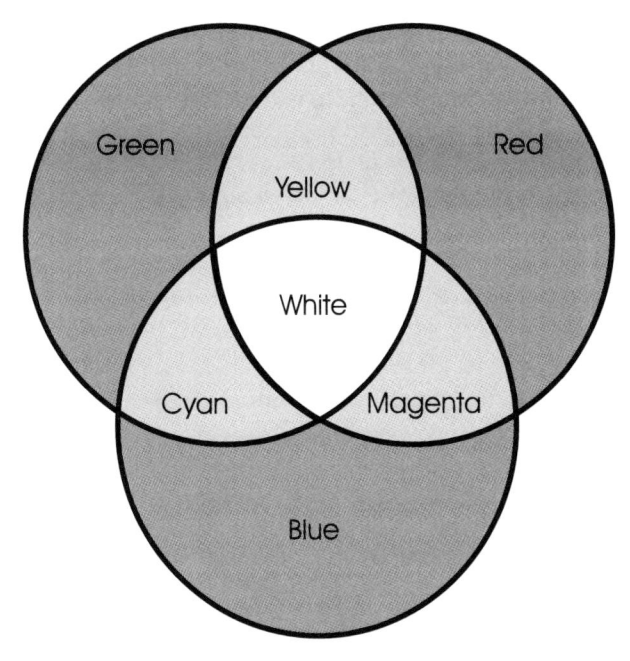

Figure 3.1 The three primary colors, in light, mix to form white.

If you're familiar with how these colors mix, you may take this for granted. But there are a couple of things in this figure that are surprising on some level, if you think about them. The first is that if you mix all three primary colors, you get white.

Yes, Arnold, I admit that's not too surprising once you know what Isaac Newton found out—that you can break white light into all the colors of the spectrum by shining it through a prism. But if it were so obvious that white light consisted of all the other colors of the spectrum, or that you could get white light by adding all the other colors together, it wouldn't have taken the genius of Isaac Newton to figure it out. Certainly someone would have thought of it a few thousand years—or at least a few hundred years—earlier.

Not convinced? Okay, go get some felt-tipped pens in red, green, and blue. Got 'em? Good. Try mixing the red, green, and blue inks on a page and tell me what color you wind up with. Now tell me again how obvious it is that red, green, and blue should add up to white when you mix them as light.

For those who don't have any felt-tip pens handy, Figure 3.2 shows what happens when you mix the primary printer colors—cyan, magenta, and yellow. Magenta and yellow mixed together turn into red; yellow and cyan turn into green; and cyan and magenta turn into blue.

See anything surprising here?

The primary printer colors

If you're not familiar with what cyan and magenta look like, you might want to check it out with your favorite graphics program since knowing what the colors are will help you follow what I'm talking about here. Describing colors is dangerous, because it's subject to argument, but I'd call cyan a light blue—verging on sky blue—with a turquoise tinge. Magenta is a purplish red. If you don't agree with these descriptions, take it as one more proof that colors are subjective.

Mix all three colors—cyan, magenta, and yellow, or red, green, and blue for that matter—with a printer and you get black. Or, at least, you get something close to black if you're mixing real inks. The actual color you wind up with depends on the colors you start with, which is why most printers add black to the cyan, magenta, and yellow—to make sure that blacks are really black.

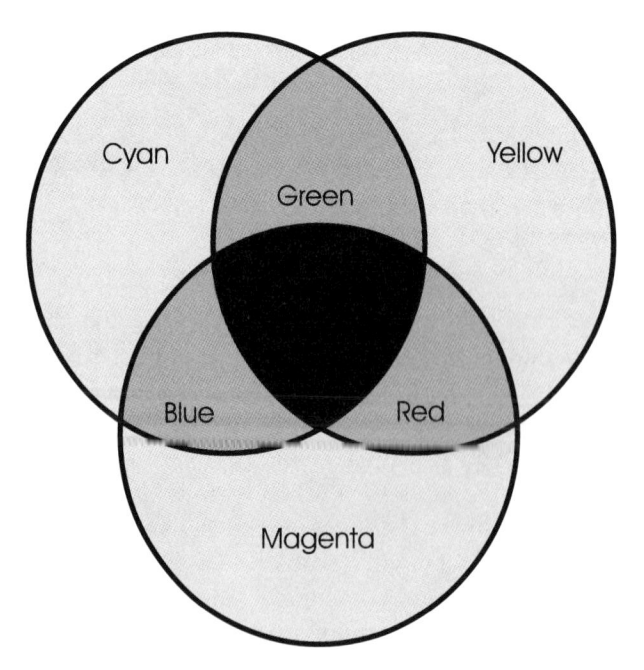

Figure 3.2 The three primary colors for printers mix to form black.

This is one of the big differences between painting with light on the screen and painting with pigment on the page. Mix colored lights, and you wind up with lighter, brighter colors. Mix colored inks, and you wind up with darker, duller colors.

That, in turn, means that if you design a printer to use deep dark red, green, and blue inks, you'll never get a bright yellow. You can get a mustard yellow, but never a fully saturated bright yellow. By starting out with cyan, magenta, and yellow, on the other hand, you can easily get a deep dark red, green, and blue. It works the other way too. If you design a cathode ray tube monitor to paint its pictures with cyan, magenta, and yellow light, you'll come up way short on red, green, and blue.

The second surprising, or at least interesting, thing about Figure 3.1—or Figure 3.2, for that matter—is that when you mix two colors together to get a third color, the third color doesn't necessarily seem to have anything in common with either color in the mix.

Second surprise

If I ask you to describe yellow, for example, I doubt you'd come up with greenish red. But if you look at Figure 3.1, you'll see that mixing green and red light will give you yellow. And if I ask you to describe red, I doubt you'd come up with yellowish magenta. But if you look at Figure 3.2, you'll see that mixing yellow and magenta inks will give you red. All of which brings us to the biology part of the equation (I promise to keep this short).

Greenish red and yellowish magenta

The Colors You See

> Let me look into a human eye; it is better than to gaze into sea or sky.
>
> Herman Melville.
> *Moby Dick* (1851)

The fact that colors get darker when you mix pigments but lighter and brighter when you mix light is based on a physical reality. Mixing rays of light means there's more light there, so it's brighter. Mixing pigments means the pigments are absorbing more light, so it's darker. But the colors you see when you mix colors have far less to do with physical reality than with what's going on in your eye and brain.

What's that, Mary? Oh, you learned in physics class that there is no physical reality to color. Well, that's true. It's also tough for most people to believe. Color seems to be part of whatever we're looking at—a blue sky, green grass, or red sunset. In reality, color is an internal experience—a sensation, like an itch or a burn or the pressure of a touch. The physical reality is the wavelength or wavelengths of light that reach the eye. Color is the sensation we've learned to associate with those wavelengths.

So what I should really say is that the colors you see depend completely on what's going on in your eye and brain as a reaction to the wavelengths of light that are reaching your eye. And you should keep that tucked away in the back of your mind. But when I talk about light, I'll still talk about colors most of the time because it's a lot more convenient to talk about red light and blue light than about *the wavelength we associate with red* and *the wavelength we associate with blue*.

Rods and cones

The human eye has two kinds of light-sensitive cells: rods and cones. (But you probably knew that already.) The cones are the key players for handling vision in daytime and other reasonably bright light. The rods are the key players in extremely low light levels to let you see at night. In relatively low level lighting, like dawn and dusk, both kinds of cells kick in.

Why you don't see color in the dark

Both rods and cones work by generating a nerve impulse when they absorb light. You don't see color in the dark (assuming it's light enough to see anything at all) because all rods react the same way to light. More precisely, they all have the same absorption spectrum, which is simply a measurement of how well the rods absorb each wavelength of light along the spectrum. That means any given wavelength of light that happens along is just as likely to be absorbed by one rod as by another.

Why you do see color when it's light

You *can* see colors in brighter light because all cones are *not* the same, which is to say, they don't have the same absorption spectrum. As it happens, there are three different types of cones, named red, green, and blue for the wavelengths of light they're best at absorbing. The color you see depends on which cones absorb the light in what proportions. And that, in turn, depends on the wavelength—or wavelengths—of the light.

Three kinds of cones equals seven million colors.

Now here's the really interesting question: If you have only three kinds of cones, how come you can see seven million or so colors? (Yes, Arnold, I really mean seven million, not the seventeen million colors some printers and video cards can produce.) The answer: Each color you see depends on a particular mixture of cones of each type absorbing some light.

> **File this under interesting, nonessential facts. Even seven million colors is more than most people can see because you lose the ability to distinguish colors as you get older, just as you lose some hearing. For the well-aged eye, the number of colors you can see drops down to two to three million. (And the old joke around print shops is that this explains why the more experienced pressmen find it so easy to match colors.) But even two or three million is still a lot more than you might expect from just three kinds of cones. And no matter how many colors you can distinguish, the reason you can see those colors is still the same: Each color you see depends on a particular mixture of cones of each type absorbing some light.**

Think of it as the three populations of cones taking a vote to decide what color you get to see. (The truth is a lot more complicated. In fact, your eyes don't even pass red, green, and blue signals to the brain. Instead, the neurons are wired in a way that converts the information from the eye into three signals: the level of brightness, the amount of red or green, and the amount of blue or yellow. But there's no reason to go into that here. The idea of three populations of cones taking a vote is a useful, if simplified, analogy.)

When you see a pure yellow light (as measured by its wavelength), your red, blue, and green cones absorb light in particular proportions, and you see yellow. When you see a combination of red and green (as measured by the wavelengths of the light), your red, blue, and green cones absorb light in the same proportions, and you see yellow once again. Basically the wavelengths in both cases feel the same to your visual system (which includes your cones but isn't limited to them), so your brain sees the same color.

Having all the colors you can see determined by just three kinds of cones has lots of implications. The most important for the moment is that having red, green, and blue cones explains why the primary colors—red, green, and blue—are enough to reproduce all the colors you can see, simply by varying the intensity and amount of each primary color in the mix.

The three kinds of cones also explain why the three primary colors for mixing light are red, green, and blue, and why we're stuck with those as the primary colors. A little less obvious is that having red, green, and blue as the primary colors for light explains why cyan, magenta, and yellow are the primary colors for printing. That has to do with the difference between mixing colors by adding color and mixing colors by subtracting color—a sort of color arithmetic.

Arithmetic for Colors

> Nobody before the Pythagoreans had thought that mathematical relations held the secret of the universe.
>
> Arthur Koestler
> *The Sleepwalkers* (1959)

When you mix colors of light, you're literally adding colors—or, more precisely, light of different wavelengths—together. Add red, green, and blue light in equal amounts, as shown in Figure 3.3, and they add up to white; add green and blue only, as shown in Figure 3.4, and they add up to cyan; and so on, as shown in Figures 3.5 and 3.6 That's why red, green, and blue are called additive primaries.

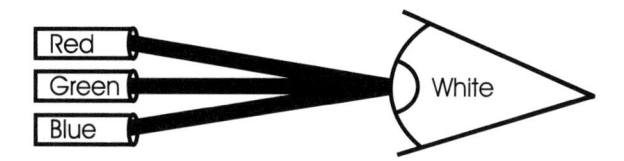

Figure 3.3 Red, green, and blue are additive primaries, because they get added together.

Figure 3.4 Add green and blue for cyan.

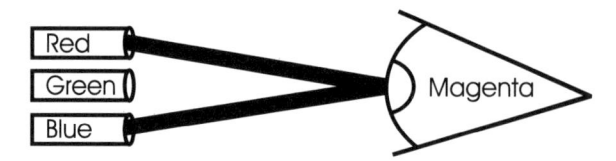

Figure 3.5 Add red and blue for magenta.

Figure 3.6 Add red and green for yellow.

When you mix colors of ink (or paint, or any other pigment), you're still seeing colors as mixtures of red, green, and blue light, but instead of adding colors together to get the mix, you're subtracting colors from reflected light, which is why cyan, magenta, and yellow are called subtractive primaries.

I see Mary and Tim both have hands raised. Mary first. You say you learned in physics class that the subtractive primaries are red, blue, and yellow? And, Tim, you learned the same thing in art class? That's not unusual. I learned it that way in physics class also. But it's wrong. It's a common mistake because it's easier to talk about red, blue, and yellow, which everyone's familiar with, than to try to describe cyan and magenta, which are just words to lots of people. Since you could describe magenta as a purplish red and cyan as a light blue, some people take the easy way out and call them red and blue. That doesn't make them red and blue.

There's another reason for the confusion also. Artists use something called a color wheel to help design color schemes. The primary colors on a color wheel are red, blue, and yellow, with secondary colors of orange, violet, and green. But the color wheel is something else entirely; it relates to color schemes, not color mixing. I'll talk about the color wheel in Chapter 7 under the general subject of how to create color schemes.

Back to the subtractive primaries. A cyan ink is cyan because it absorbs red light while reflecting blue and green light, as shown in Figure 3.7. And since blue and green add up to cyan, cyan is what you see.

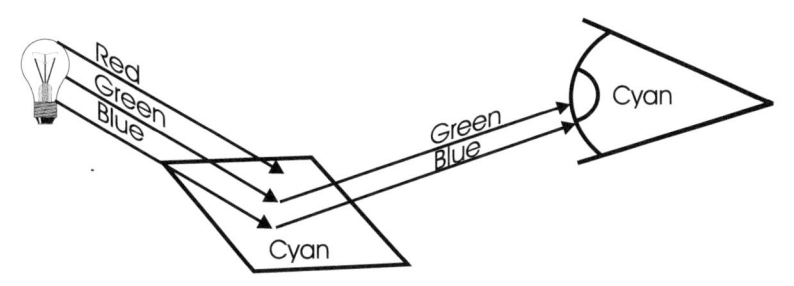

Figure 3.7 Subtractive primaries absorb light. Cyan absorbs red, leaving green and blue light.

What's that, Tim? Oh, you're wondering what happens to the other colors you start with in white light—the orange, yellow, indigo and violet that I conveniently left out of the figure. Well, obviously these get absorbed and reflected too, but that's irrelevant. Your cones know only about red, green, and blue, and they see other colors only in terms of red, green, and blue components— even when the only wavelength in the light is, say, all cyan, instead of a mixture of green and blue wavelengths. So from your eye's point of view, the only colors in white light *are* red, green, and blue.

You may be ahead of me here but I'll walk you through this anyway. Magenta and yellow work the same way. Magenta ink absorbs green, while reflecting red and blue, which add up to magenta, as shown in Figure 3.8.

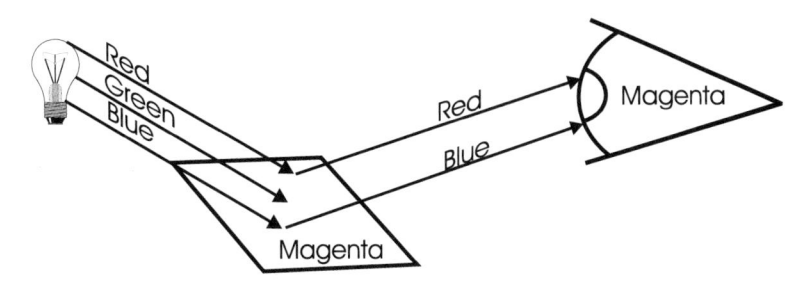

Figure 3.8 Magenta absorbs green, leaving red and blue light.

Yellow ink absorbs blue, leaving red and green, which add up to yellow, as shown in Figure 3.9.

104 *Chapter 3*

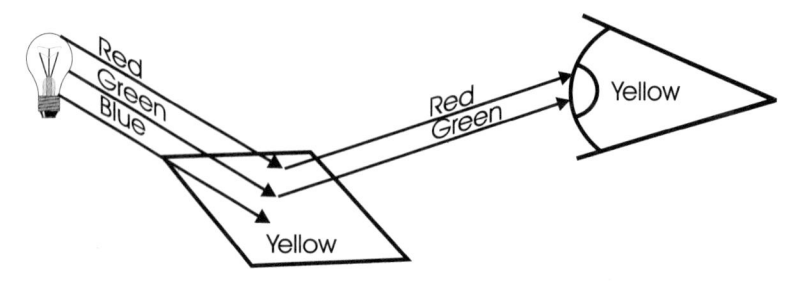

Figure 3.9 Yellow absorbs blue, leaving red and green light.

Combine two colors—yellow and magenta, say—and the combined inks each absorb some light, in this case, both green and blue, leaving red, as shown in Figure 3.10.

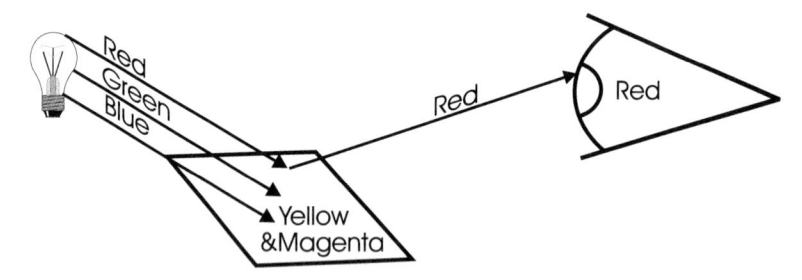

Figure 3.10 Combining two inks absorbs two colors; in this case yellow and magenta together absorb green and blue, which is why yellow and magenta mixed together are red.

When you combine all three color inks, as in Figure 3.11, the inks absorb all the colors of light, which is why you see black.

Figure 3.11 Combine all the subtractive primaries, and they absorb all the colors of light, leaving black.

A white page doesn't absorb any of the colors, so you see red, green, and blue together, adding up to white. (I'll spare you a figure on this one.)

And that, finally, is everything to need to know about additive and subtractive primaries and the differences between RGB and CMY or CMYK (that's red-green-blue, cyan-magenta-yellow, and cyan-magenta-yellow-black, in case you've forgotten). It may be more than you wanted to know, and it isn't everything there is to know, but it's everything you need to know.

You certainly know, at this point, why monitors are RGB devices, while printers are CMY devices. And you can impress your friends with the details. (Yes, Arnold, I mean *CMY* or *CMYK* devices, but that gets real clumsy real fast. So I'm going to conveniently ignore the black from now on except where it really matters.)

WHY COLORS DON'T—CAN'T—MATCH

> All of us failed to match our dreams of perfection. So I rate us on the basis of our splendid failure to do the impossible.
>
> William Faulkner
> Interview in *Writers at Work* (First Series, ed. by Malcolm Cowley, 1958)

If the only difference between color on monitors and color on printers were that monitors use RGB while printers use CMY, it might be hard to match colors between screen and paper, but it wouldn't be impossible. All you'd need would be software that could translate each color on the screen from some combination of red, green, and blue to the right combination of cyan, magenta, and yellow. Getting the translation right might be tricky, but it should certainly be doable.

So what's the problem? You guessed it: There are lots of other differences. High on the list is the simple fact that monitors can show you colors that printers can't print. And, to a lesser extent, printers can print colors that monitors can't show.

Let that sink in a bit.

I see Mary looking puzzled. What was that, Mary? Oh, you're thinking that if the red, green, and blue cones are the only way that the human eye sees color, then the three primary colors, in various combinations, should be enough to let us see all the colors there are. And it shouldn't matter whether we're using the additive primaries red, green, and blue or the subtractive primaries cyan, magenta, and yellow.

You're absolutely right, in principle. In practice, however, you're limited to using whatever colors you can get for the primaries—in the form of phosphors for cathode ray tubes and pigments for the ink, wax, or toner in printers. The actual colors you're using are what determine the colors you can get out of the device. To get every possible color, you'd have to start with fully saturated, monochromatic colors, right out of the spectrum.

Bet you can't print this one.

Whoops. There's one of those Humpty Dumpty words that shifts meaning when you're not looking. You probably figured out that monochromatic doesn't have anything to do with black and white in this case, or even with monochromatic color schemes. You may not have figured out just what it does mean. It's actually not referring to color at all, but to wavelength. If you start by shining white light through a prism to get a spectrum, and you aim the spectrum at a narrow slit, the light that makes it through the slit will all have the same wavelength, or, at least, a narrow range of wavelengths. That qualifies it as a pure, or monochromatic, color. You can produce a matching color by mixing two or three pure colors, but the mixed version isn't a pure color even though you can't tell the difference between the two by eye. The mixed version is . . . well, a mix of colors because it's a mix of wavelengths.

To get a pure color out of a phosphor, the phosphor would have to produce light of all one wavelength, rather than a mixture of wavelengths. To get a pure color reflecting off a pigment, it would have to absorb everything but one wavelength. The problem is that real phosphors and real pigments aren't monochromatic. They aren't fully saturated either. These two facts of life limit the colors you get from mixing the real-life primaries together.

Color Gamuts

> She runs the gamut of emotions from A to B.
>
> Dorothy Parker

There's an easy way to visualize the difference between the colors a printer can print and the colors a monitor can show, thanks to the kind of chart shown in Figure 3.12.

The chart in Figure 3.12 isn't something I just made up. It's part of a color specification system that's been around since 1931 and is an international standard. The system was developed by the Commission Internationale de L'Éclairage, which translates to . . . ummm . . . let me get my high school French book . . . ah, here it is . . . the International Commission on Lighting, or Illumination, depending on who you talk to. But most people just refer to the commission as the CIE and the color system as either the CIE system, or CIE color system. I'll talk about the CIE color system (just a little) in Chapter 6. For right now, all you need to know is that it's a standard.

Figure 3.12 takes the fully saturated colors of the spectrum and maps them to the outside of the horseshoe-shaped chart. Think of it as taking the spectrum and bending it into a horseshoe. The chart then closes off the bottom of the horseshoe with a straight line to tie the violet and red extremes of the spectrum together.

Printers Aren't Monitors **107**

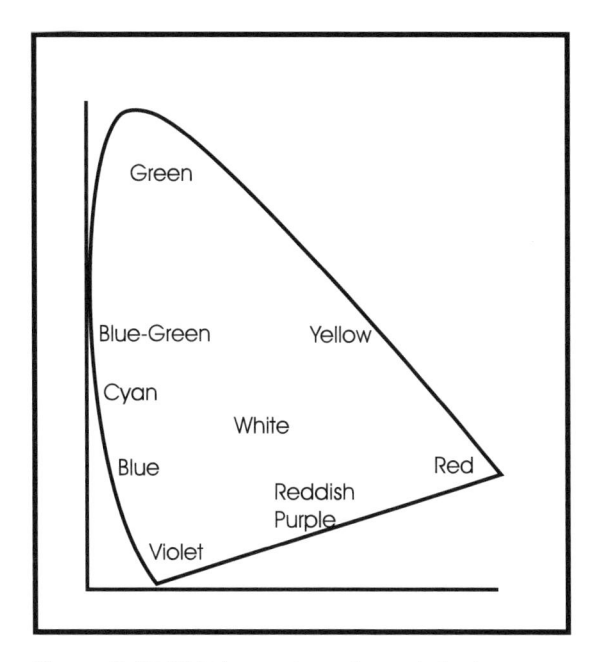

Figure 3.12 This horseshoe-shaped chart maps colors from full saturation on the outside line to white on the inside.

Here's an interesting little tidbit to amuse and amaze your friends. If you mix colors from the extreme red and violet ends of the spectrum, you can create purples that don't exist in the spectrum itself. Those purples—ranging from reddish purple to purplish red—lie along that straight line at the bottom of the horseshoe.

As you move inside the horseshoe, you move away from full saturation, starting at the horseshoe-shaped line and moving away from the line. Inside the horseshoe, the colors blend into each other, and blend into white as you reach zero saturation—with the white area about halfway between the blue and yellow extremes in the chart. Since the chart maps colors from their full saturation on the outside line to white, or zero saturation, on the inside, you can think of it as representing all the colors you can possibly see.

Don't take this description completely at face value. I've oversimplified it a bit to keep the explanation short and simple, but it's close enough for our purposes. Yes, Arnold? You really want to know the details? Okay, here they are for Arnold only. The chart is called a chromaticity diagram. What, you ask, is chromaticity? Well, I have one book that dares to explain it as a property, "defined by its chromaticity co-ordinates." Yeah, right. Here's a little better answer: Chromaticity is a somewhat arcane construct that takes both hue and

saturation into account. (The horseshoe-shaped area, taken as a whole, shows all hues at all saturations, starting with full saturation at the horseshoe and going to zero saturation at the white area.) Since you can define any color by hue, saturation, and brightness, you can also define any color by chromaticity and brightness. But none of this really matters for understanding the chart.

It's more useful to know that the vertical axis shows the percentage of green in the color and the horizontal axis shows the percentage of red. There's no need to show the percentage of blue, because after you subtract the percentage of green and percentage of red from 100 percent, whatever's left over is the percentage of blue.

It's also useful to know that there's a third dimension is missing from the chart. What you're looking at is a 2-D slice from a 3-D solid, where the third dimension is the lightness—or darkness, if you prefer. So everything I'm about to say, in treating this as a 2-D chart, is a simplification. But the concept is right, and the concept applies to the full 3-D solid.

One of the interesting things about the chart in Figure 3.12 is that if you find the coordinates for the phosphors you're using in your monitor's CRT and draw straight lines between the red, green, and blue points, the triangle you wind up with will show you the entire color gamut—or range of colors—for your monitor. Figure 3.13 shows a typical monitor's color gamut.

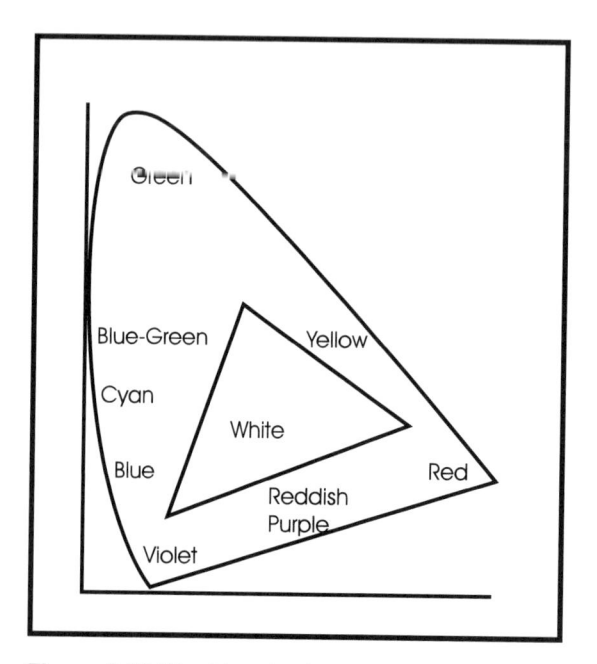

Figure 3.13 The triangle shows a typical color gamut for a cathode ray tube monitor.

You can also do pretty much the same thing for a printer. With a printer, however, you use six points because there are six colors (not including black and white) in the basic printer repertoire. You already know about cyan, yellow, and magenta. The other three are red, green, and blue.

How did red, green, and blue creep in here for a CMY device, you ask? Easy. Printers, unlike monitors, can print one dot over another to mix colors. So in addition to printing dots in cyan, yellow, and magenta, they can also print dots in red, green, and blue, by printing two colors on the same spot. When you plot all six points and draw the lines between them, you wind up with a lopsided hexagon that defines the range of colors the printer can print. Figure 3.14 shows a typical printer color gamut.

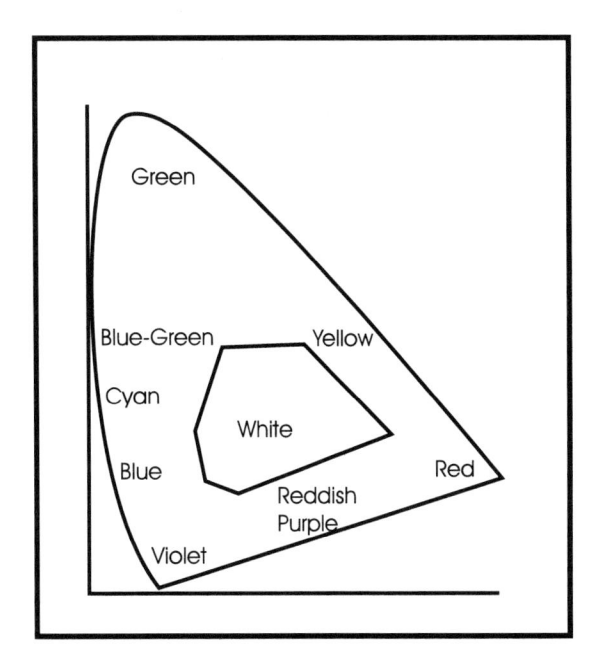

Figure 3.14 The lopsided hexagon shows a typical color gamut for a printer.

All of which finally brings us to the whole point of this exercise, which is to compare the color gamut for a monitor to the color gamut for a printer. Figure 3.15 does the dirty deed.

As you can see in Figure 3.15, there are colors in each color gamut that simply aren't in the other. In this particular case, which is fairly typical, the monitor offers more saturated greens, reds, and blues, while the printer offers more saturated cyans and blue-greens. More important, the monitor's color gamut is larger than the printer's. It includes the vast majority of colors in the printer's color gamut,

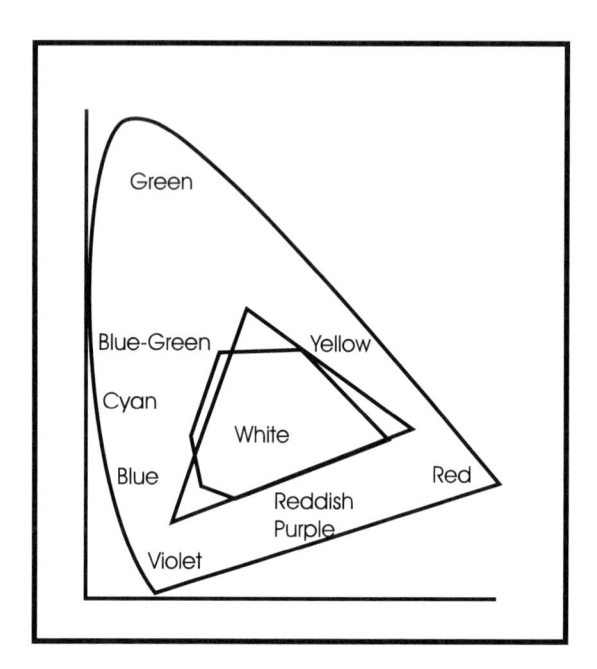

Figure 3.15 Comparing a printer color gamut to a monitor color gamut.

while the printer's color gamut is missing large chunks of colors from the monitor's color gamut.

I could throw in a couple of other details here, like: The gamuts vary with each printer and monitor. Or: The gamut for any given monitor will change as the monitor ages. Or: The gamut for any given printer will change if the colors in the dye, wax, ink, or whatever vary from one lot to the next. But the key point is that the mismatch will always be there. In particular, monitors are known for producing blues that printers can't touch—particularly light blues.

What the Different Color Gamuts Mean in Real Life

> Stand firm in your refusal to remain conscious during algebra. In real life, I assure you, there is no such thing as algebra.
>
> Fran Lebowitz
> *Social Studies*, "Tips for Teens" (1981)

These diagrams of color gamuts are all good and well, but they don't really tell you what you'll run into in real life, even though they'll help explain it once you run into it.

If you want to get a sense of how much the gamuts can vary for monitors, take a trip to any store that sells televisions, and set all the TVs to the same channel. Try as much as you like to adjust the colors to make them all match, you'll still wind up with noticeable differences. (That's assuming, of course, that you don't get kicked out of the store for messing with the merchandise. Don't tell 'em I sent you.) You'll even wind up with noticeable differences with two TVs built on the same assembly line.

Color gamuts for printers vary at least as much as color gamuts for monitors, because the variations in color printer technology—from ink jet to wax jet to thermal dye to thermal wax to laser—use a wide range of primary colors as their starting points. Even within a given technology and even for printers from a single manufacturer, if you compare the cyan, magenta, and yellow inks from two printers, at least one of the primary colors will usually be noticeably different.

Just for fun, I compared some color samples from a Hewlett-Packard DeskJet 560C and a Hewlett-Packard DeskJet 1200C. The yellow for the DeskJet 1200C was a little lighter, the cyan a little darker, and the magenta a little darker and a little more reddish. **Differences between printers**

These differences were exaggerated with the secondary colors. The green and red from the DeskJet 1200C were a little darker compared to the DeskJet 560C colors, while the blue was significantly darker. That makes good sense, since the cyan and magenta, which make up the blue, are both darker for the 1200C. There were also significant differences in hue, with the DeskJet 560C's red a touch orange compared to the 1200C's red, and the 560C's blue significantly more violet.

Whatever the differences between the two printers, however, they were nothing compared to the difference between either printer and the colors on screen. Cyan, magenta, and blue looked completely different on screen and on paper. Cyan on screen was a light, bright distant relative of the much darker and bluer version on paper. Magenta on screen was nearly violet, compared to the much redder, and slightly darker, printed version (from either printer), and the bright blue on screen turned into dark navy blue, with a touch of violet, on paper. **Differences between printers and monitors**

Green and yellow did a little better. Green kept its hue but was much darker on paper. Yellow was both darker on paper and a slightly different hue, a few notches toward orange. Red . . . well, red's a special case I'll talk about a little later.

Don't take my word for any of this. Try it yourself. Take your favorite graphics program (I used CorelDRAW for this one) and draw six squares that will each print at about one inch square, as in Figure 3.16. Then color each square with one of the primary or secondary colors as indicated in the figure, and print the page on whatever color printer you have handy. (But be sure that you turn off any color-matching features in your application program and printer driver before you run this test.) **A quick comparison of your monitor to your printer**

To be absolutely sure you're doing this right, you'll need a program that lets you see the settings for each color and change them if necessary, preferably using a CMYK model. CorelDRAW 5, for example, lets you set colors though the dialog box shown in Figure 3.17. The color in the figure is green.

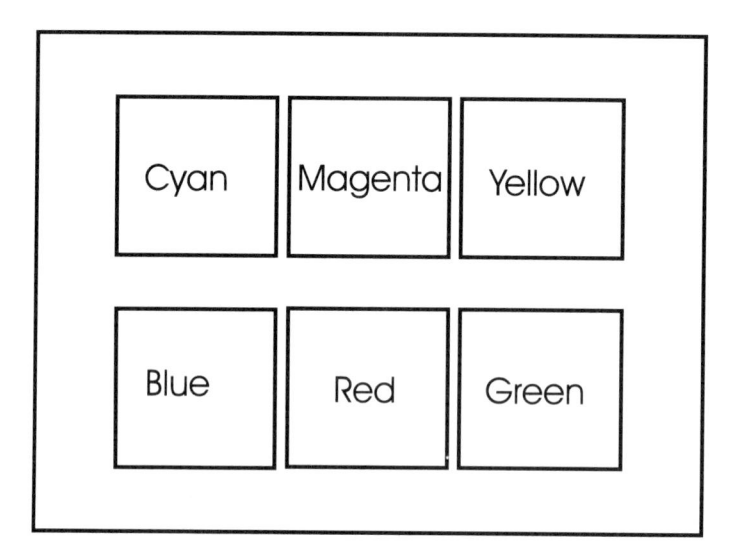

Figure 3.16 To get a quick reality check of the difference between colors on your screen and on your printer, print six squares as shown here—in cyan, magenta, yellow, blue , red, and green—and compare the screen to the printed version.

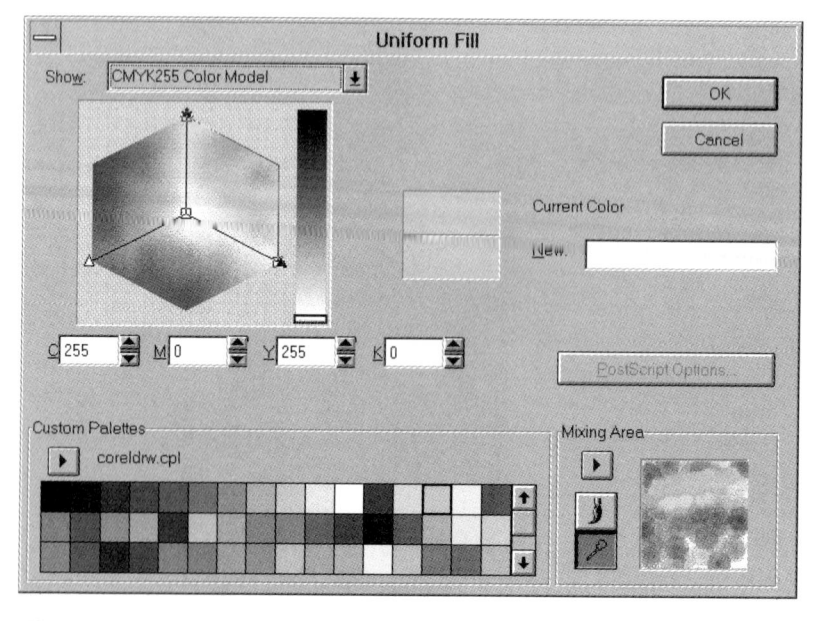

Figure 3.17 If you can set colors using numeric values for the CYMK model, with a scale that runs from 0 through 255, setting both cyan and yellow to 255 produces green.

Typically, the settings for a CMYK model will be on a scale of 0 through 100 or 0 through 255. Assuming a scale of 0 through 255, you'll want a 255 setting for cyan and 0 for the others to print cyan; 255 for yellow and 0 for the others to print yellow; and 255 for magenta and 0 for the others to print magenta. For blue, you'll want cyan and magenta both at 255, with a 0 setting for yellow and black. For red, you'll want magenta and yellow at 255 with 0 for blue and black. For green, you'll want cyan and yellow at 255 with 0 for magenta and black.

Some programs—including Windows 3.1 Paintbrush for example—will limit you to an RGB model. RGB models also typically offer settings of 0 through 255 for each color. To print red, green, or blue with an RGB model, set the color you want to 255 and the other two colors to 0. To print cyan, set both green and blue to 255 and red to 0. For magenta, set red and blue to 255, and green to 0. For yellow, set red and green to 255, and blue to 0.

With most programs, regardless of color model, you'll be able to pick each of the six colors from a predefined palette, much like the blocks of color in the misleadingly named Custom Palettes box at the bottom of Figure 3.17. Even so, you should check the settings for each color, if you can, to make sure they're what you think they are.

If you're using a program that doesn't offer this kind of fine-tuned numeric control over the colors, look for colors that the program labels blue, red, green, cyan, magenta, and yellow. These should be the right colors in virtually all—if not all—cases (though you should never underestimate the creativity of programmers who are convinced they have a better idea).

The exact colors you get will depend on your monitor and printer, but the comparison between the colors on screen and on paper should be similar to what I've described. These comments certainly apply not just to the two ink jet printers I've already mentioned, but to the Tektronix Phaser 340 wax jet and the FARGO Primera Pro in thermal dye mode, which I also ran this test on for comparison. The colors from each of these printers are significantly different from the colors for the two ink jet printers—or the colors from each other, for that matter. But the colors from all of the printers have more in common with each other than any of them has in common with the colors on a monitor.

A More Complete Comparison of Color Gamut

> Things are not as bad as they seem. They are worse.
>
> Bill Press

Of course, comparing the six primary and secondary colors doesn't show you the color gamuts directly. It merely shows you six points on the outside edge, which is to say, the most saturated versions of six hues at maximum brightness. But since these colors completely determine the color gamut for any given printer or monitor, any difference in these colors indicates a difference in color gamuts.

If your graphics program lets you designate colors by numeric settings in a color model, you can also see a more complete comparison of your printer and monitor color gamuts—or, more precisely, a comparison of the most saturated colors in those gamuts. Here again, you can print a sample of color patches and compare the printed version to the screen.

If you have a choice of models for setting the colors, the preferred choice for this sample is the HSB model (that's hue-saturation-brightness, in case you've forgotten) or something similar. Similar in this case means anything that lets you set hue with a single number. Figure 3.18 shows the CorelDRAW dialog box for setting colors once again, this time showing the settings for green in the HSB model.

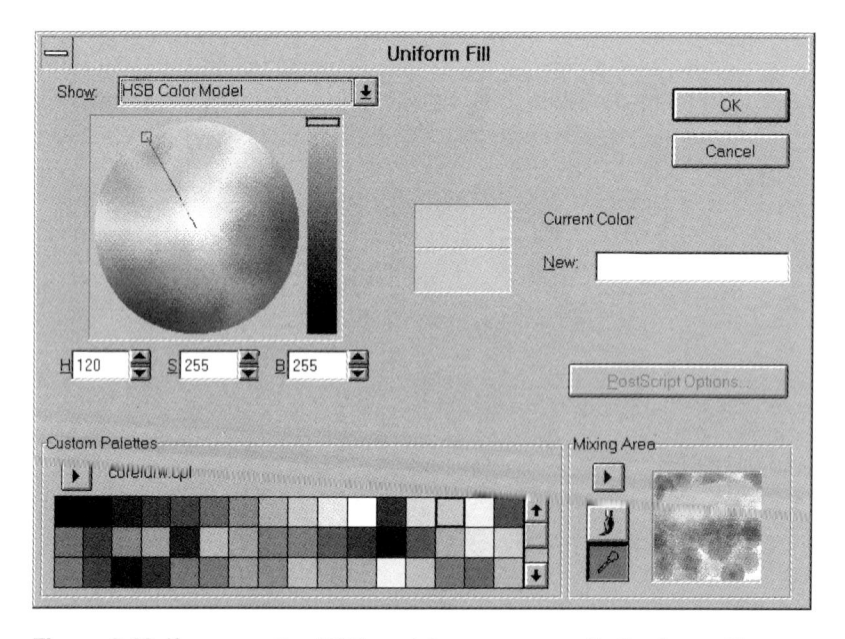

Figure 3.18 If you use the HSB model, you can specify the hue with a single setting, rather than mixing cyan, magenta, and yellow.

The advantage of the CMYK model—and the reason I suggested it for confirming the colors in the first sample—is that it lets you specify colors in terms of the amount of each primary printer color. That's important for the first sample because the results aren't meaningful unless you're sure you're looking at pure primary and secondary colors. An RGB model serves the same purpose, although it's one step removed, because you have to specify colors in terms of the primaries that a monitor uses. You can get the same results using an HSB model, but first you have to know that red is 0, yellow is 60, green is 120, and so on.

The advantage of the HSB model for printing a greater selection of hues is that it lets you set the hue with a single number. Instead of having to worry about how much of each primary to use for each step in color, you can pick an arbitrary size step and change the hue setting to match. You'll want to leave saturation and brightness at the highest levels, and keep them constant for all the colors.

As you can see in Figure 3.18, the HSB model arranges all the hues in a circle. Since a circle has 360 degrees, the range of settings for the hues is normally 0 through 360. (Actually, 0 and 360 give you the same hue, just as 0 seconds on a watch puts the seconds hand at the same place as 60 seconds.)

You can print color patches of all 360 hues, if you like, but you can get a good sampling by going in steps of 10—printing hue 0, 10, 20, 30, and so on. Even with steps of 10, you'll find that in some cases you'll be hard pressed to see any difference between neighboring hues. Besides, it takes only one-tenth the time to set up a page to print 36 hues as it does to set it up to print 360 hues.

If you set up six rows of six squares each, as in Figure 3.19, you can easily fit all 36 hues on one page with room to spare. You'll also conveniently start each row with one of the primary or secondary colors.

> **If the program you're using is limited to CMYK or RGB models, you can still set up a page with a range of hues, but it will take a little more work. With a CMYK color model, start at red by setting both magenta and yellow at maximum. Work your way to yellow by keeping yellow at maximum, but lowering the amount of magenta with each step. If the range of settings is 0 through 255, for example, and you want six steps between red and yellow, as in Figure 3.19, simply lower the setting for magenta by 42 or 43 for each step (255 divided by 6 is 42.5, so you'll want to alternate between steps of 42 and 43). Once you hit yellow, with the yellow setting at 255 and everything else at 0, start adding cyan, in increments of 42 and 43 for each step, until you hit green at a setting of 255 for both yellow and cyan. Next, lower the amount of yellow with each step until you hit cyan at a setting of 255 for cyan and 0 for everything else; add magenta with each step until you hit blue; lower the amount of cyan with each step until you hit magenta; and finish up by adding yellow with each step until you're one step short of red.**
>
> **With an RGB model the concept is the same; only the details are different. Start at red with red at maximum and everything else at 0. Add green with each step until you hit yellow at a maximum setting for both red and green, and then lower the amount of red until you hit green. Then add blue with each step until you hit cyan, and then lower the amount of green until you hit blue. Finally, add red with each step until you hit magenta, and then lower the amount of blue until you're one step short of red. Either of these strategies—using CMYK or RGB color models—will give you the same result as changing a simple hue setting.**

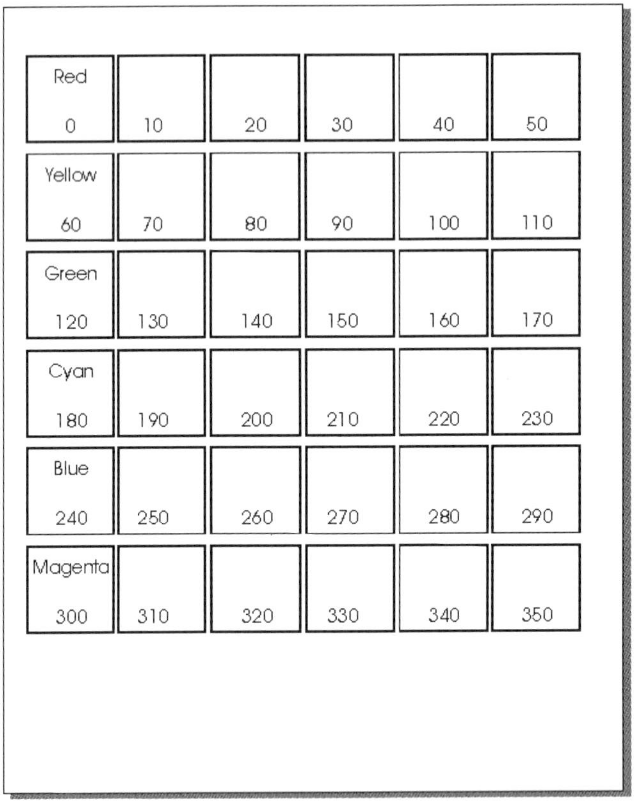

Red 0	10	20	30	40	50
Yellow 60	70	80	90	100	110
Green 120	130	140	150	160	170
Cyan 180	190	200	210	220	230
Blue 240	250	260	270	280	290
Magenta 300	310	320	330	340	350

Figure 3.19 You can get a good sampling of the entire range of hues with just 36 color patches. The numbers in this figure are the hue settings, assuming a range from 0 through 360.

Here again, the exact colors you get and the differences between the colors on your monitor and on your printer will vary depending on what monitor and printer you have. But there will be differences. I guarantee it.

The colors won't match between screen and printer. The first thing you'll probably notice is that few, if any, colors match between the screen and the printout. Even the degree of difference between colors won't match. Colors that look the same on screen often come out as different colors on the page, and colors that look different on screen come out the same on the page.

In my tests using a Tektronix 340, for example, the first three blocks on the first row are all red on screen and appear identical. But on the page, the first three blocks are clearly different from each other, and only the first block is red. The second is a robust orange. The third is a yellowish orange. There are equivalent differences for almost every block of color on the page, but I'll spare you the blow-by-blow details. You should see the the same sort of differences in your own samples.

A closer look should show that even though the colors don't match, the range of yellows, reds, and oranges is pretty much the same between the screen and the printed page. In my tests, for example, the first red block on the first row on the page pretty well matched the last block in the last row on the screen; the third block in the first row, which was yellowish orange on the page, closely matched the fourth block on the first row on screen; and the first block in the second row was yellow on both page and screen, though it was slightly darker on the page.

The important issue here for comparing color gamut is whether the range of colors match, not whether the colors match block for block. If the range of yellows and reds is pretty much the same, as in my tests, the gamut for yellows and reds matches. If the individual blocks don't match, it just means that the printer's idea of red or yellow isn't the same as the monitor's idea. The more formal way of saying this is that you're using device-dependent color, which simply means the color you get for any given setting will change from one printer or monitor to the next.

You should also find that the story is very different with blues, violets, and greens—with colors on screen that are completely different from the colors that get printed. In my tests, the blues, greens and violets on screen were all significantly brighter than anything on the page, and some were more saturated as well. With a little trial and error, I could make the screen colors match the page, by cranking down brightness and saturation as needed. But there is no way to make the colors on the page, which are already at maximum brightness and saturation, match colors on the screen that are brighter and more fully saturated.

And that's what the difference in color gamuts means in real life: You can't match screen colors that your printer can't print.

MORE REASONS WHY COLORS DON'T MATCH

> When angry, count four; when very angry, swear.
>
> Mark Twain
>
> *Pudd'nhead Wilson* (1894)

If the difference in color gamuts were the only thing working against matching colors between screen and page, it would be enough of a problem by itself. But if you look carefully at the output on your screen and printer, you'll find more stumbling blocks—and more reasons why color printers encourage lots of counting and some nasty language.

I've mentioned before that a white piece of paper isn't the same color as a white computer screen. You can prove this to yourself easily enough by loading Windows or some other program with a white background and holding a piece of paper up against the screen. Odds are that the paper's white will be noticeably darker than the screen white and slightly tinted as well—though you'll likely have trouble deciding what hue it's tinted in since it's so slight.

If your graphics program lets you adjust color by changing settings in a color model, and you want to while away a few minutes (or hours), you might try creating a square on the screen and then try to match it to the paper color. If you succeed, you'll be doing better than I can. With the paper and screen I'm using as I write this, the paper is tinted slightly in the yellow-orange range, at least in the yellow light I'm working in, with a saturation setting well under 10. But that's as close as I can come to pinning it down.

Paper white changes with the angle to the light.

This is actually an instructive exercise and well worth trying. One thing you should see as you struggle to match the paper color is that the color of the page changes if you change its angle relative to the light or lights in the room. Angle it one way, so it's getting the full effect of the overhead yellow light, and you'll see one color. Change the angle, so the page is ever so slightly in the shade, or getting a little more daylight from the window, and you'll see a slightly different color. This isn't something you would normally notice, because your eye and brain simply adjust to the difference. But when you're trying to match the screen color to the paper, the changes are more obvious.

Paper white changes with the color of the light.

Another interesting exercise is to change the lighting significantly mid-stream. If you're close to a window, try working with the shades drawn first. Then open the shades and turn off the overhead light while looking at the page. You should find that the color of the paper changes noticeably. In my tests, for example, the paper lost its yellowish tinge when I switched from yellowish fluorescent lights to daylight.

Screen white doesn't change with angle or light.

While you're at it, try the same two tests with your monitor. If the monitor's on a tilt and swivel stand, move it to the full extent of the swivel left and right and the tilt up and down. Unless you have a visible reflection on the screen at some angle, you shouldn't see any change in color at all.

Change the surrounding lighting, and you shouldn't see any change in screen color either. In both situations, the reason the screen behaves differently from the paper is the same: The paper color depends completely on reflected light, while the screen generates its own light.

Other colors change too.

Once you've proven to yourself that paper white changes with angle and lighting, you may want to try the same tests with colors. Not too surprisingly, what's true for white is true for other colors also—and for the same reason: The colors you see on paper depend on reflected light, while the colors you see on screen depend on the monitor generating its own light.

What the Differences Between Screen and Paper Mean in Real Life

> In real life, unlike in Shakespeare, the sweetness of the rose depends upon the name it bears. Things are not only what they are. They are, in very important respects, what they seem to be.
>
> Hubert H. Humphrey, 1966

These simple observations about the differences between screen and paper are the core reasons why matching colors precisely between screen and paper is ultimately impossible, even if you stay strictly with colors that are in both your printer and monitor color gamuts.

Earlier in this chapter, I talked about a comparison I made between colors on screen and on paper, using the primary and secondary colors red, green, blue, cyan, yellow, and magenta. I mentioned that cyan, magenta, and blue looked significantly different on screen than on paper, while green and yellow did a better, but far from perfect, job of matching. I also said that red was a special case that I'd talk about a little later. Well, now it's later.

Red is the only color in the batch that—for most of the printers I tested at least—was absolutely identical between screen and printed page.

Did I say *identical*? Well . . . sorta, kinda, maybe. Depending on what you mean.

Absolutely identical, because when I folded the paper through the block of red, to bring the red to an edge, and then I held that edge up against the red on the screen, the colors on screen and paper *were* identical. Or, at least, they were close enough so I wouldn't quibble about the differences.

Sorta, kinda, maybe, because how well the colors matched depended on the light that hit the paper, and reflected to my eye. When I held the paper flat against the screen, the red was a touch darker on paper than on the screen. When I held it at a slight angle, the match was perfect—or close to it. When I held it at a 90 degree angle to the screen, or stood so the paper was in my shadow, the red on paper was far darker than the red on screen—nowhere near a match. And when I turned off the overhead light and opened the window shades, the two colors were unquestionably different hues.

Depending on what you mean, because even in the light where the red on screen and red on printed page matched, they didn't *look* the same, except when I held the paper against the screen to compare them directly. The difference between page white and screen white was enough to make the same color look red on the screen but a reddish orange on the printed page.

Not so incidentally, don't think that this not-quite-matching match is something specific to red. You'll run into the same sort of quasi-match with any color that you can closely match between printer and screen. It's just that for this particular test, red happened to give a close match. And that let me make the comparison.

So did the colors match? Well, yes, in a very limited sense, under specific lighting conditions. But even then, they didn't look the same. And as Vice President Humphrey said (in an admittedly different context), things are not only what they are. They are, in very important respects, what they seem to be.

This comparison of a single color is a much simpler situation than you'll find with most images you print. Most images will include multiple colors, and each color can affect your perception of the other colors. But the basic lessons apply to any color image:

Lesson one: Since you can't reliably match colors between screen and printer, you can't know what an image will look like until you print it.

Lesson two: Since colors will change with changes in lighting, you can't know what printed colors will look like under any given lighting until you see them under that lighting.

Lesson three: Your perception of a color on paper is more important than whether the color actually matches the screen color. You can argue all you like that in my tests the red on paper matched the red on the screen for specific lighting conditions. But the version on paper still looks orange-red. So when getting a color right really matters, don't worry whether it matches the screen. Worry about what it looks like on paper. And if you generally use a less expensive paper for drafts than for final output, don't assume that the color will look the same on both kinds of paper. The only way to know how it will look on the more expensive paper is to print it on the more expensive paper.

COLOR (MIS)MATCHING

> "... you used an odd word earlier—odd to me, I mean ... 'Tonestapple,' or something like it."
> "Oh, 'tanstaafl.' Means 'There ain't no such thing as a free lunch.' And isn't," I added, pointing to a FREE LUNCH sign across room, "or these drinks would cost half as much."
>
> Robert A. Heinlein
> *The Moon Is a Harsh Mistress,* 1966

Why color matching is like a free lunch

Did someone ask about color matching—that magic marriage between screen and printer that some programs and some printers claim to offer? I've talked about color matching to several printer manufacturers, and I've suggested to them that color matching is a lot like a free lunch: There ain't no such thing. I've yet to find anyone who disagrees, including those who claim color-matching features for their printer drivers.

What most hardware and software companies mean when they talk about color matching is better understood as minimizing mismatches. And even then, the claim is best taken at something less than face value.

Logically, there are two basic steps in making screen and printer colors bear a passing resemblance to each other. First, you have to define the color capabilities of both screen and printer. And second, you have to translate the colors so they'll match each other. Before you can translate the colors, however, you have to decide whether to adjust the printer colors to more closely match the screen, or adjust the screen colors to more closely match the printer.

Matching the Printer to the Screen

> I've come close to matching the feeling of that night in 1944 in music, when I first heard Diz and Bird, but I've never got there. . . . I'm always looking for it, listening and feeling for it, though, trying to always feel it in and through the music I play everyday.
>
> Miles Davis
> *Miles: The Autobiography*, Prologue (1989)

Most color-matching schemes—particularly those you'll find in printer drivers—adjust the printer colors to match the screen. That's mostly because it's easier for a printer driver to change the commands that get sent to the printer than change the commands that get sent to the screen. (This is a bit of an understatement; printer drivers are designed to control printers, after all, not screens.)

The Tektronix Phaser 340 printer driver, for example, offers several choices for the Color Correction option shown in Figure 3.20, including None and Simulate Display.

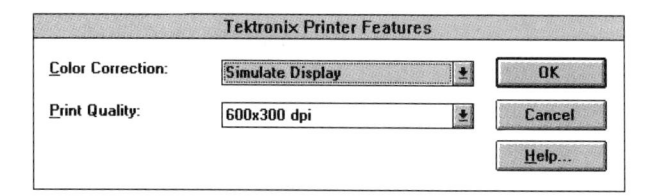

Figure 3.20 The Tektronix printer features include a Color Correction option, shown here set to Simulate Display.

I already described what the 36 color patches from Figure 3.19 looked like when I printed them on a Phaser 340 with color correction set to None. The range for reds, oranges, and yellows was similar between screen and printer, although individual patches didn't necessarily match. The range for blues, greens, and violets was noticeably different between screen and printer, with the colors on the page clearly different hues than the equivalents on the screen, and much darker as well.

When I printed with color correction set to Simulate Display, the match between screen and printer improved somewhat—with *somewhat* being the key word. Most patches in the red to orange to yellow range—which pretty well matched without color correction—were essentially unchanged, while patches in the violet to magenta range were a lot closer to the screen colors than in the first print sample.

Green, cyan, and blue patches, however, were still an obviously different hue compared to the equivalents on screen, and darker as well. Even so, they were a lot lighter than without color correction, and, once again, a closer match to the screen than the first print sample.

What about the monitor?

Missing from the Tektronix color correction feature is any attempt to define the color capabilities of the screen. Instead of trying to match particular monitors, and changing the color correction depending on the monitor, the Tektronix driver treats all monitors the same way. This simplification works reasonably well because the full range of differences among monitors isn't as great as the difference between any given monitor and the printer. However, some printer drivers try to offer somewhat more sophisticated matching by taking the monitor into account also.

The Canon BJC-600e driver, for example, offers a Print Color setting similar to the Tektronix color correction setting with choices for Grayscale, Color (which means no color correction), and Screen-Matched Color. The driver also tries to go one step further, to let you define a Monitor Type. The Canon driver offers a drop-down list with about a dozen brands of monitors to choose from, so the driver knows which monitor to match if you choose Screen-Matched Color.

In theory, the Canon BJC-600e driver should do a better job of matching the printed output to the screen than the Tektronix Phaser 340 driver, because it takes the monitor into account. As a practical matter, though, the difference between BJC-600e color output with and without the Screen-Matched Color setting is about the same as the difference between Phaser 340 output with and without the Simulate Display setting. And the failure to outdo the Tektronix printer isn't because the BJC-600e is an inexpensive ink jet printer that costs about one-tenth as much as the Phaser 340.

The problem that any printer has when it tries to match a monitor is that even within a given brand of monitors, and even within a given model, you'll find substantial variation from one to the next. So simply choosing a brand name off a list isn't likely to give you a close match between your monitor and the monitor the driver is basing its calculations on.

More important, the various factors I've discussed in this chapter, particularly differences in color gamut, put limits on how closely you can match the printer to the screen in any case. All the color-matching calculations in the world won't let you print colors that are outside the printer's color gamut.

Here's something else to keep in mind: Color-matching options don't necessarily give you the best color for all images. In my experience, you can generally get much more realistic colors for photos on the Tektronix Phaser 340, for example, by setting color correction to None rather than Simulate Display, even though the colors look fine on the monitor. There's no hard-and-fast rule about this, however. The best setting changes for each image. When you come right down to it, you just have to be familiar with your printer. If colors come out looking a little off, you'll want to experiment with different settings to see the effect. More important, keep notes about the best settings for different kinds of output, so you have a record of the best setting to use the next time you print the same kind of image.

Also be aware that a psychological match is sometimes better than a real match. Tektronix has run extensive tests that give the closest possible match between printer and screen, and found that people don't like it. Almost everyone will complain that a close match on paper to a light blue on screen is too pale, too washed out. People consistently prefer a more saturated version of the same hue. And it is this sort of psychological match that most printer manufacturers try for.

Matching the Screen to the Printer

> I think there ought to be a club in which preachers and journalists could come together and have the sentimentalism of the one matched with the cynicism of the other. That ought to bring them pretty close to the truth.
>
> Reinhold Niebuhr
> *Leaves from the Notebook of a Tamed Cynic* (1930), 1928 entry

If you noticed my choice of words earlier when I said that *most* color-matching schemes adjust the printer colors to match the screen, you've probably already figured out that some color-matching schemes work the other way around, trying to make the screen colors more closely match the colors at the printer.

If you think about it, adjusting the screen colors actually makes more sense than adjusting the printer colors. The color gamut for monitors is larger than the color gamut for printers. Even though each gamut has some colors that you won't find in the other, there are more colors that you can see on screen but can't print than there are colors you can print but can't see on screen.

If you have some way to adjust the screen colors, you can leave out all those blues and violets on screen that the printer can't print anyway. That gives you a better chance of seeing something on screen that approximates what you'll see at the printer. This is the route CorelDRAW 5 takes, with a sophisticated color manager that aims at making the screen colors more closely match the colors at the printer.

More precisely, for any given setting in whatever color model you're using, CorelDRAW modifies the colors you get on screen to match the capabilities of the printer. With unusual honesty, the CorelDRAW manuals and help screens don't generally talk about color matching. They talk about color management, color correction, and predictable color output, but they only rarely mention color matching.

Color management

Even if you don't use CorelDRAW and have no plans to, it's worth taking a look at the CorelDRAW color manager as an example of what's involved in trying to match printer and monitor—or trying to make the printed colors more predictable, as Corel prefers to put it. Figure 3.21 shows the CorelDRAW 5 System Color Profile dialog box, which is the starting point for CorelDRAW's color management feature. If you have CorelDRAW, you can open this dialog box by choosing File, Color Manager.

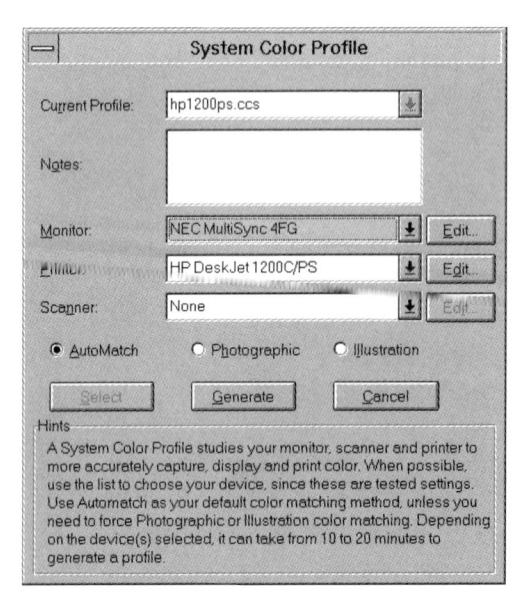

Figure 3.21 To use CorelDRAW's color management feature, you first have to define a system color profile.

If you're lucky, you'll find both your monitor and printer in the drop-down lists attached to the text boxes that are cleverly labeled Monitor and Printer. And note that unlike the choices in the Canon BJC-600e driver, these choices are for specific models of monitors and printers.

If your monitor and printer are on the lists, you can simply choose them, then choose the Generate button below the text boxes, enter a name for the file, and sit back and wait while CorelDRAW generates a color profile for your system. (You'll notice that there's also a Scanner text box in the figure with its own drop-down list, but let's ignore that for now. We'll talk about scanners in Chapter 8.)

Once CorelDRAW finishes crunching the numbers, you have to tell it to use the color profile it just created. If you choose View, Color Correction, you'll see a secondary menu with choices for None, Fast, Accurate, and Simulate Printer. The first three choices are mutually exclusive, with None giving you the fastest screen draw times but no color correction at all, and Accurate giving you the most accurate color. That's accurate in terms of what your printer will print, based on the system color profile—I'll discuss how accurate in a moment.

The Simulate Printer choice is an additional option. CorelDRAW will gray out the choice if you've chosen None, but it will be available if you've chosen Fast or Accurate. For the most accurate color rendition on screen, you'll want to choose Accurate and make sure there's a check next to Simulate Printer.

If you're using software that offers this sort of choice—between speed and color accuracy—don't take the program's word for it that the speed really changes. In my tests on a 66 MHz 486DX/2-based computer, there was no noticeable difference in screen drawing times in CorelDRAW whether I set color correction to None or to Accurate with Simulate Printer checked. That gives me no reason to ever set color correction to anything less accurate. If you see a noticeable difference in screen drawing times—with a different software package or a slower computer—you may want to set color correction to None, or the equivalent, while you're working on the layout for an image, but switch to Accurate with Simulate Printer, or the equivalent, when you're concentrating on the colors.

Of course, the point of this exercise is to make the screen colors match—make that *predict*—the colors that print. The good news is that the colors manage to match better with the color management feature than without it.

More precisely, using the same 36 color patches I used for testing the Tektronix and Canon color-matching features and using a NEC 4FG monitor and an HP 1200/C printer, the greens on screen were a little darker than without color correction but still not as dark as the printed versions. The blues and violets were much more in line with the printed versions, but still noticeably different hues. Reds, oranges, and yellows were essentially unchanged.

This general description makes CorelDRAW's color management sound roughly equivalent to the color matching in the Tektronix and Canon printer drivers. Overall, however, the CorelDRAW color manager did a better job of matching the screen colors to the printer than the printer drivers did in matching the printer colors to the screen.

More good news: Since printer colors have more in common with each other than any of them have with screen colors, the color profile for the HP 1200/C printer gave a closer match on screen even for output from other printers. That's fortunate, because CorelDRAW offers only a limited number of predefined printers to choose from in its System Color Profile dialog box. Similarly, you'll find only a limited number of monitors. But hold that thought for a moment.

The most intriguing result I wound up with is that I got the closest match between printer and screen by using both the color correction in the printer drivers and the color correction on screen. The match between the screen (which was color corrected for an HP 1200/C, remember) and the printed samples from the Canon and Tektronix printers (both of which used the color correction in their own drivers) was about equal for both printers, though each printer did a better job with different colors.

I then took the test one step further, by printing a sample on the HP 1200/C, with the HP DeskJet driver set to Match Screen. Interestingly, the HP 1200/C output was similar to the Canon BJC-600e output, but the output from the Canon printer did a slightly better job of matching the screen overall, even though the color correction on screen was set to match the HP printer.

The moral here is twofold: First, if you have color-matching features in both your printer driver and your software, try using both at once. You may well get a closer match between screen and printer than by using one choice or the other. Second, don't assume that you'll get the best color match between screen and printer by picking the right monitor and printer names from a predefined list. If you experiment, you may find a better match.

Also, if you experiment with different settings, be sure you note which colors the printer and screen do the best job of matching for any given combination of settings. If you're stuck with an image that's full of greens, say, you'll want to use settings that ensure the printer will come closest to the greens on the screen. If you're creating an image from scratch, you'll want to stay primarily with the colors that match most closely between printer and screen.

Now comes the hard part. If you're using a program with color management features similar to CorelDRAW's and your monitor or printer doesn't show up on the predefined lists, you may have the option of defining the color characteristics for your monitor and printer yourself. With CorelDRAW, for example, the Edit button to the right of the Monitor text box opens the Monitor Calibration dialog box shown in Figure 3.22. The Edit button to the right of the Printer text box opens the Printer Calibration dialog box shown in Figure 3.23.

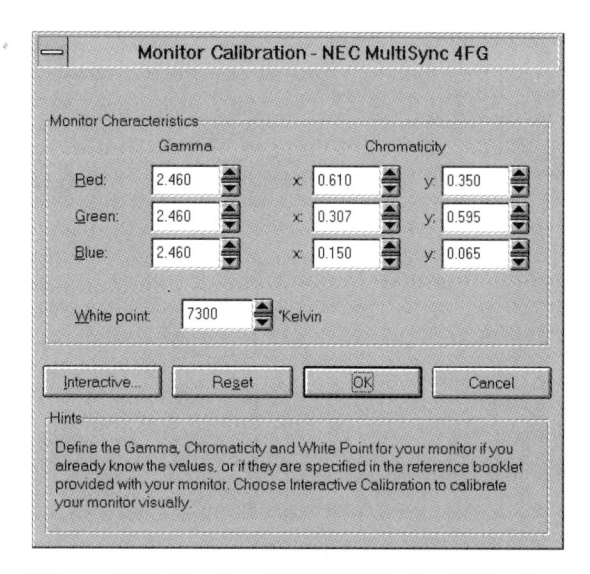

Figure 3.22 The CorelDRAW 5 Monitor Calibration dialog box lets you define the settings for your monitor, if you happen to know them.

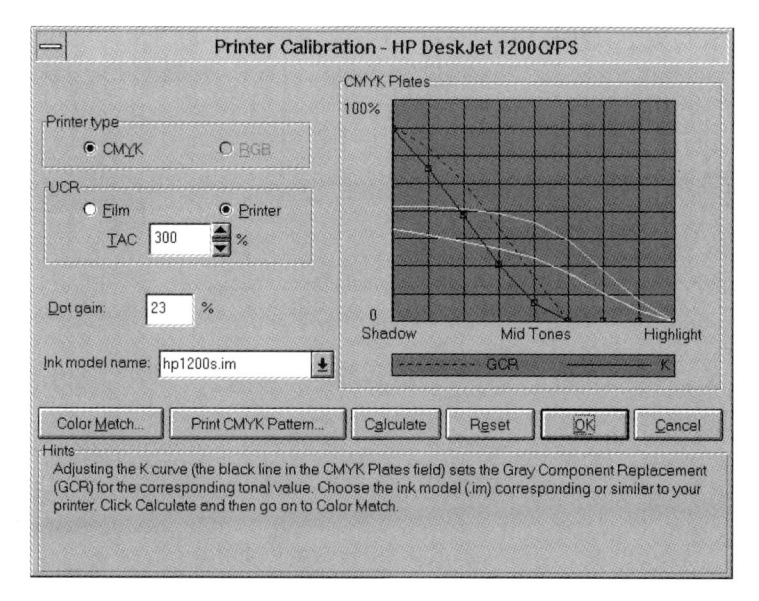

Figure 3.23 CorelDRAW's Printer Calibration dialog box lets you define the settings for your printer, if you happen to know them. Good luck.

Don't let it bother you if the dialog boxes in Figures 3.22 and 3.23 seem a little daunting, with numeric settings, a graph, and terms like gamma and TAC that you may not be familiar with. They *are* daunting, and that's precisely the point.

We'll come back to these dialog boxes and explain the less familiar terms in Chapter 6. For the moment, take my word for it that setting up the information for a printer and a monitor is a nontrivial task. And that's not a flaw in CorelDRAW, it's built into the nature of the task itself. That's why most color-matching schemes, in printer drivers and elsewhere, tend to ignore these details. Odds are you should ignore them too.

How Close a Match Do You Need?

> I love her too, but our neuroses just don't match.
>
> Arthur Miller
> *The Ride Down Mount Morgan*, act 1, 1991

The simple truth is that you'll never get an exact color match between screen and printer, at least not for all colors. (And I hope I've convinced you of that by now.) So the question is how close a match you need. Graphics professionals may need as close a match as technology can give them, and for them it may be worth the sweat and tears for every step closer they can get. But for most people, the point of diminishing returns comes at a very early stage in the process.

If your printer driver or graphics program offers a choice for matching the screen and printer, by all means try it out and see how well it works. If they both offer color-matching features, try both out separately and together. That much is certainly worth the effort. And if a color-matching feature lets you choose your monitor, printer, or both from a predefined list, then so much the better. Picking two names from two lists is hardly any work.

I already pointed out that you may get a better match by choosing some other printer or monitor off the list than the one you actually have. If you want to experiment with other settings, it's probably worth trying the settings for each printer that uses the same technology as yours. But even this isn't likely to improve the color match very much.

For most people, that's about as far as you'll want to go. The next step up is to try each monitor setting, and then, once you've found the best monitor option, try each printer setting. If you want to be exhaustive, you can work through every combination of printer and monitor to see which one will give you the best color match. I wouldn't bother with either of these approaches though. The improvement, if any, isn't likely to be enough to be worth the work.

If your monitor or printer isn't on the color matching list

If you have a color-matching feature that offers lists of monitors and printers, but your monitor and printer aren't on the list, you have to be creative in picking a setting. For the monitor, try another model from the same company, if you have

photo handy, hang around for Chapter 8, where I'll show you some samples of what I'm talking about.

Gamma correction goes beyond the limits of simple brightness and contrast adjustments by effectively changing the contrast in light areas differently than in dark areas. That lets you see the details in both light and dark areas—both the clouds in the sky and the individual trees in the treeline, for example, or, for a face that's lit from the side, both the well-lit side and the side that's in shadow.

Now you know just a little about gamma correction, but you don't even have to know that. All you have to know is how to follow the instructions at the top of the Monitor Tuning box in Figure 3.24. Use the slider bar to change the inner nested box until it matches the outer box. Figure 3.25 shows four settings for gamma and how they affect the inside box in the two nested boxes.

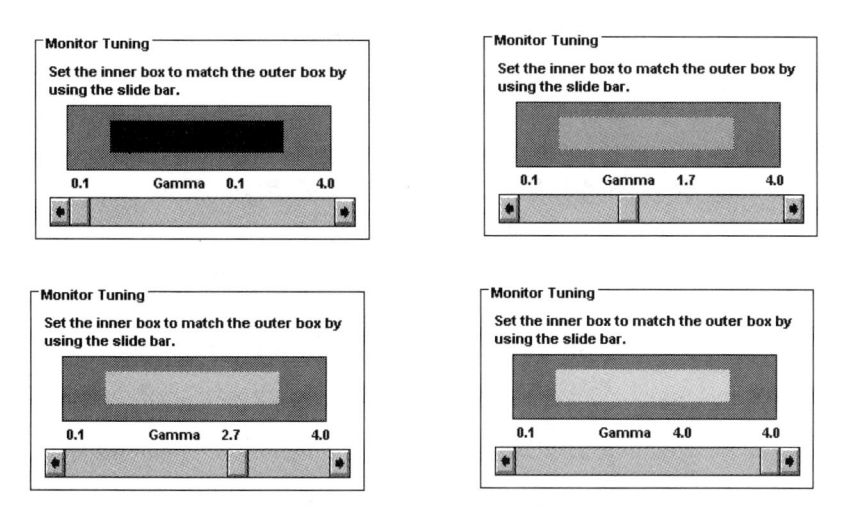

Figure 3.25 Change the setting on the Gamma setting bar, as shown here, and the inside box changes from dark to light. The trick is to find the setting where the inside box matches the outside.

Moving the slider bar to change the inside box is just as easy as it sounds. Matching the two boxes isn't. In fact, there are one or five things you need to know about matching the inside and outside boxes.

Rule one is that the best setting may not be what the program or driver thinks it is. In the NEC driver, for example, setting the monitor choice in the Color Matching box sets the gamma to a predefined level. Set the monitor to MultiSync, and the driver sets the gamma to 2.1, as shown in Figure 3.26. And since MultiSync monitors are NEC products, you'd probably think that a NEC printer driver would get that setting right. Well it does . . . sort of . . . with the emphasis on *sort of*.

Brightness and contrast affect gamma settings.

On my MultiSync monitor, with brightness and contrast set where I like them, I get the best match at a gamma of 1.9. But by playing with brightness and contrast controls, I can change the best setting to anywhere between about 1.7 and 2.6 if I stay with reasonable levels for brightness and contrast. I can also set the monitor so the best setting is as high as 3.0 if I make the screen a little darker than reasonable.

So rule two is that a predefined setting for a given monitor is likely to be a fair approximation of the right setting. But if you change the setting, you'll probably get a better match.

And rule three is that since the best setting depends on your brightness and contrast controls, you should either leave the controls alone or reset the gamma when you change brightness and contrast.

Getting it right

You should also be aware that there's a slight trick to getting the inside box to match the outside. Figure 3.26 is a screen capture of the nested boxes, zoomed in far enough so you can see the details of the fill in both boxes. (And also zoomed in far enough so the left and right sides of the outside box are lopped off.) As you can see in the figure, the outside box is a checkerboard of black and white squares; the inside box is a solid gray.

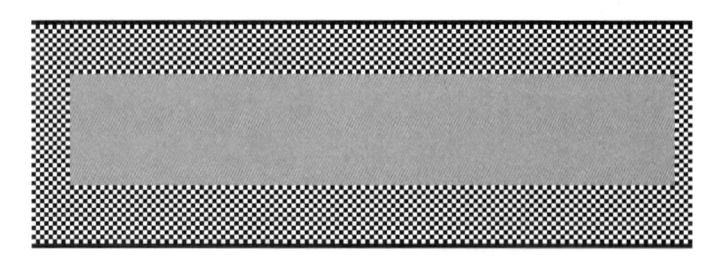

Figure 3.26 Holy checkerboard, Batman! Look at the closeup of the boxes you use for adjusting the gamma setting. Yes, Robin, you could play a mean game of checkers on the black and white squares in the outside box.

This difference in the fills is precisely what lets the driver calculate the gamma setting when you match the inside box to the outside, but it also makes it a little hard to decide when they match. What you need to do is trick your eye into seeing the outside box as a solid gray, instead of a checkerboard pattern, or even as tiny dots.

Turning checks into solids

I've heard suggestions that you should squint at the screen while you're adjusting the setting, but that's only worked for me late at night when I'm overtired and having trouble focusing my eyes anyway. The better choice is to back off from the screen. (And take off your glasses, if you wear them.)

Back off far enough, and the checkerboard will merge into gray. If you don't have a program handy to try this with, you can get the same effect with Figure 3.26.

Put this book down so you can see the figure, and step back several feet to see what I mean.

With a monitor, most people need to be four feet from the screen, or even farther, to hide the pattern entirely. With a little luck, your mouse or keyboard will reach that far. If not, get someone to help you. It's easier to decide between two settings, neither of which quite matches the outside box, if you can switch back and forth between them rapidly enough to see the difference. Don't depend on getting a close match by dragging the slide with the mouse. Drag it to get close to the right setting, but do your fine tuning with the keyboard or with the arrow buttons on the slider bar.

Typically, none of the settings will give an exact match. Instead, you'll wind up with two settings that bracket the exact match—one a little lighter, and one a little darker. If you can't decide which one is closer, pick either one and don't worry about it. At most, you'll be a little more off with one choice than the other, but you'll be a little off with either one.

Not so incidentally, you don't have to look very hard to find variations on the theme of matching two boxes on screen to adjust the gamma correction. I've seen versions with the two boxes side by side, versions that change the outside solid box to match the inside checked box, and versions with several sets of paired boxes that range from white to black. I've also seen versions that use pairs of red, green, and blue boxes instead of, or in addition to, gray. These typically let you match each pair of colored boxes separately. However, all these variations work essentially the same way as the NEC printer driver option, and all are easy enough to be worth taking the time to set them properly.

Variations to look for

But enough about color. Let's take a short break, class. When we resume, in Chapter 4, we'll take up some issues about monitors and printers that have nothing to do with color.

4 More Ways Printers and Monitors Don't Match

> Some facts should be suppressed, or, at least, a just sense of proportion should be observed in treating them.
>
> Sir Arthur Conan Doyle
> Sherlock Holmes, *The Sign of Four* (1890)

In Chapter 3, I concentrated on the whys and wherefores of the differences in color between printers and monitors. But I wouldn't want you to get the impression that color is the only difference you have to worry about. There's also a difference in resolutions, or, more precisely, in the number of dots per inch that printers and monitors have to work with.

Hand in hand with that is a difference in addressability, which is to say that there are more addressable points on the printed page than on the screen. Vastly more. A VGA display on a Windows system, for example, has a resolution of 640 by 480. Think about that. That's just 40 more dots across its entire width than a 600 dpi printer has in a single inch across and fewer dots in its entire height than that same 600-dpi printer has in a single inch down. These differences can lead to some unpleasant surprises.

In this chapter we'll take a look at these differences, and then take a more direct look at monitors themselves. Before we get to either of those topics, however, I have to talk a little about the nature of graphics.

THERE'S GRAPHICS, AND THEN THERE'S GRAPHICS

> When you come to a fork in the road, take it.
>
> Yogi Berra

Computer images come in just two varieties, although you may be under the impression that there are more than two since each variety goes by two or more names. Variety one is usually called *bitmapped* (or *bit mapped*), but you'll also hear it called raster graphics. Variety two is usually called *object-based* or *object-oriented*, but you'll also hear it called vector graphics or vector-object graphics.

A lot of people stumble over the idea of even two kinds of graphics, finding it hopelessly confusing—in large part because of the ever-changing names. Mention bitmaps, rasters, or object-oriented graphics in a group of reasonably intelligent computer users, and you'll see eyes glaze over and minds snap shut. However, the basic differences between the two kinds of graphics are straightforward. Honest. It's just the names that are hard to keep straight.

Pay attention. There'll be a quiz later.

Bitmaps Map Bits to a Grid

> **pointillism** (pwàn´tê-îz´em, point´l-îz´-) noun
> A postimpressionist school of painting exemplified by Georges Seurat and his followers in late 19th-century France, characterized by the application of paint in small dots and brush strokes.
> [French *pointillisme*, from *pointiller*, to paint small dots, stipple, from Old French *pointille*, engraved with small dots, from *point*, point, from Latin *púnctum*, from neuter past participle of *pungere*, to prick.]
>
> *The American Heritage Dictionary of the English Language*, Third Edition, Houghton Mifflin Company. 1992

> Dot's incredible!
>
> Anonymous James Joyce fan, 1995

Bitmapped graphics literally map bits to a grid, which should make the name easy to remember. Except . . . what does that that mean, you ask?

A bit is a pixel. Well, first of all, it helps to know that a bit is the same as a pixel, which is short for picture element, and is, by definition, the smallest element in a picture (or the smallest unit in an image if you're fussy about defining a phrase by using the same words as in the phrase).

So what does mapping bits to a grid mean? It means that the program keeps track of the image bit by bit—or dot by dot—just like a pointillist painting. If you draw a straight horizontal line, the program tracks it as a set of individual bits that are all in the same row (or rows, depending on how thick the line is). If you draw a circle or a curve, the program tracks it as individual bits that are arranged to form a circle or curve.

Sometimes you can even see the grid. Some programs will even show you the grid. Figure 4.1, for example, shows a small circle with a straight line in it that I drew in Windows Paintbrush. Figure 4.2 shows the same circle and straight line after I've zoomed in on it to work with individual bits on the grid.

More Ways Printers and Monitors Don't Match   **137**

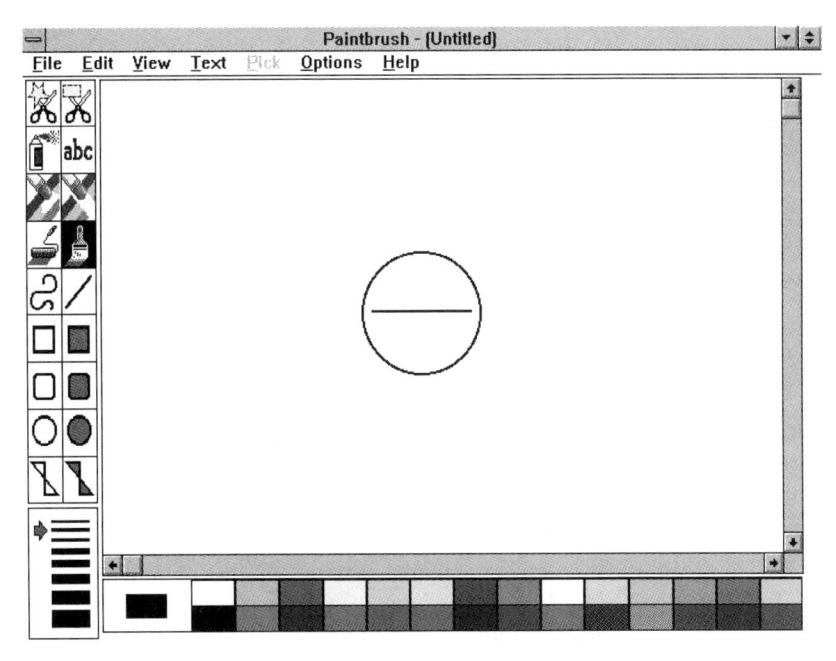

Figure 4.1 Paintbrush, as a bitmapped program, keeps track of this circle and straight line as bits mapped to a grid.

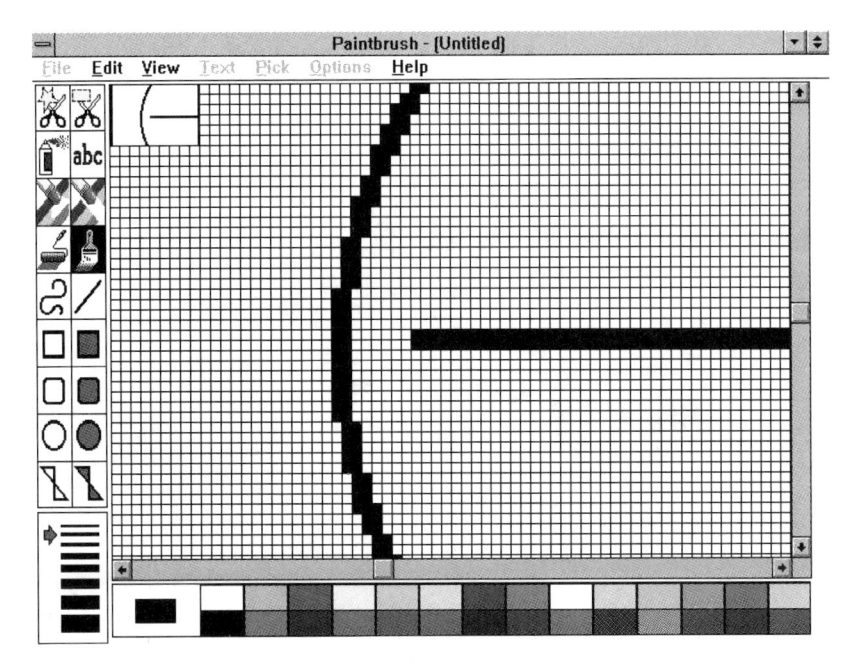

Figure 4.2 Here's a portion of the same circle and straight line as in Figure 4.1, but this time zoomed in, and with the grid showing, to make it easy to work with individual bits.

Paintbrush, if you're not familiar with it, is one of the programs that comes with Windows 3.1. Unless you've done something unusual to your installation, you should find it in the Accessories program group. If you've moved to Windows 95, you'll find an equivalent program called Paint. To open Paint, choose the Start button, then Programs, then Accessories. Paint should show up as one of the shortcuts on the Accessories menu.

As you can see in Figure 4.2, the lines in this particular image are two bits thick, and the circle is noticeably more jagged when you zoom in on it. Paintbrush lets you modify the image literally bit by bit, adding another row of bits to make the line thicker, or adding bits to the end of the line to make it longer. When you point to a cell on the grid and click the left mouse button, and Paintbrush will fill in a bit at that cell. Click the right mouse button, and Paintbrush will delete a bit if one's already there.

Paint programs use bitmaps.

In general, paint programs (think of them as pointillist paint programs to make this easy to remember) use bitmapped graphics. And any scanned image is necessarily scanned in as a bitmap. Photographs are always bitmaps, whether you scan them in or take them off a Photo CD. Figures 4.3 through 4.5, for example, show a photo at three zoom levels. You could easily miss the bitmapped nature of the image at the 100 percent size in Figure 4.3, but it's easy to see the bits in Figure 4.4 and impossible to miss in Figure 4.5.

Figure 4.3 At an unzoomed 100 percent size, you won't see any hint of the bitmapped nature of a photo.

Figure 4.4 Zoom in to 400 percent, and you'll begin to see some sense of the individual bits.

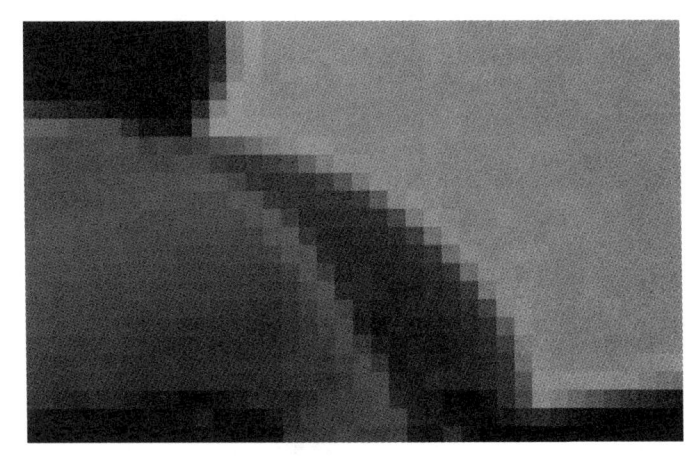

Figure 4.5 Zoom in to 1600 percent and bingo. If you don't see the individual bits here, go directly to an eye doctor and get a prescription for new glasses.

Object-Based Graphics Treat Graphics as Objects

> **object** (òb´jĭkt, -jĕkt´) noun
> Something perceptible by one or more of the senses, especially by vision or touch; a material thing.
>
> *The American Heritage Dictionary of the English Language,* Third Edition, Houghton Mifflin Company. 1992

Object is one of those all-purpose computer buzz words that changes meaning depending on which marketing department is trying to sell you something. Even the mainstream English meaning, as defined in the *American Heritage Dictionary*, is about as specific as *thing*—which was one of the first words I learned in French class, and which I leaned on heavily whenever I couldn't come up with the right word on exams. (*Tristan and Isolde then saw a thing*.) But object really does mean something, in both English and computerese, and object-oriented graphics in particular are something you should know about.

Object-oriented graphics programs get their name because they let you treat various pieces of the image as objects—literally a separate, complete ... uh ... thing. Each individual line, curve, circle, or whatever can be an object by itself, or you can select two or more objects and tell the program to group them together and treat the group as a single object.

In an object-oriented program, you can pick up an object and move it, and you can easily change size—either keeping everything in proportion or not. To pick up an object in most object-based graphics programs, you point to it with a mouse, click and hold the mouse button down while you drag the object, and then release the button to leave the object in its new position.

To resize an object in a typical object-oriented program, you first click on it so it shows handles (actually small black squares) as in Figure 4.6. You then grab a handle with the mouse by clicking and holding down the mouse button, drag the

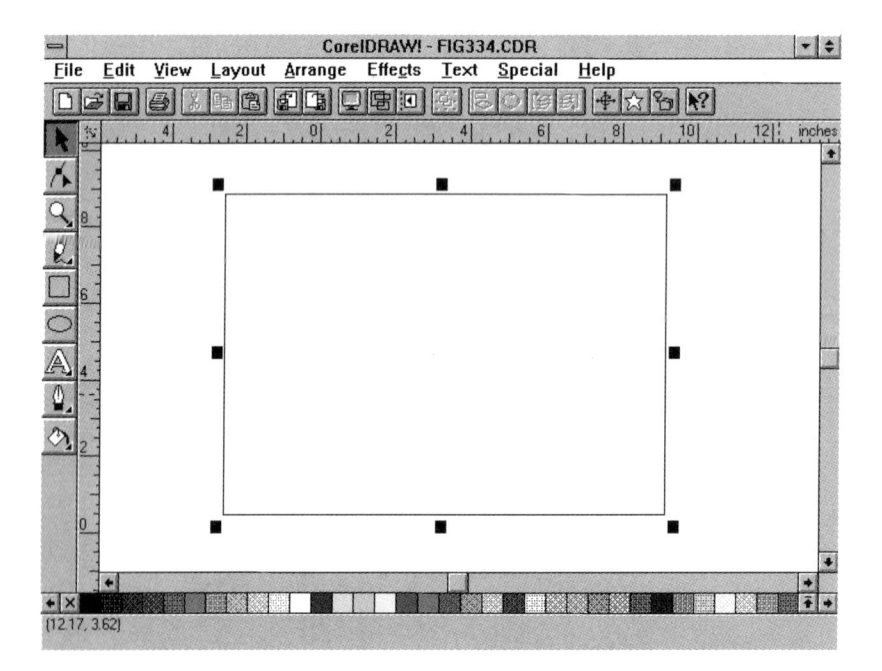

Figure 4.6 The black squares at each corner and on each side of this rectangle are handles that you can grab with the mouse to stretch or shrink the rectangle.

handle to its new position, and release the button. The program will stretch or shrink the object as appropriate.

Object-oriented programs don't want to know about bits. They keep track of lines, curves, and fills as mathematical formulas. And, for our purposes, that's the key difference from bitmapped graphics.

No bits here please.

If you draw a straight line, say, in an object-oriented program, the program knows where the line starts, where it stops, and how thick it's supposed to be. It fills in the line between the two end points, just like you or I might fill in a connect-the-dots puzzle with pen or pencil. If you want to extend the line, you don't add more bits. You simply move one of the end points. If you want to make it thicker, you don't add more bits either. You simply tell the program to make it thicker.

Object-oriented programs are usually called drawing programs to distinguish them from the bit-oriented paint programs. CorelDRAW, for example, is object oriented. So are the drawing features in Microsoft Word and Ami Pro. WordPerfect for Windows includes both object-oriented drawing tools and bitmapped paint tools in its repertoire.

Drawing programs use objects.

Figures 4.7 through 4.9 show a circle and straight line in CorelDRAW at three zoom levels. As you can see, even at the highest zoom level there's no more sense of individual bits than at the lowest zoom level, and no more jaggedness. In all three cases, the jaggedness of the curved line is limited by the screen resolution.

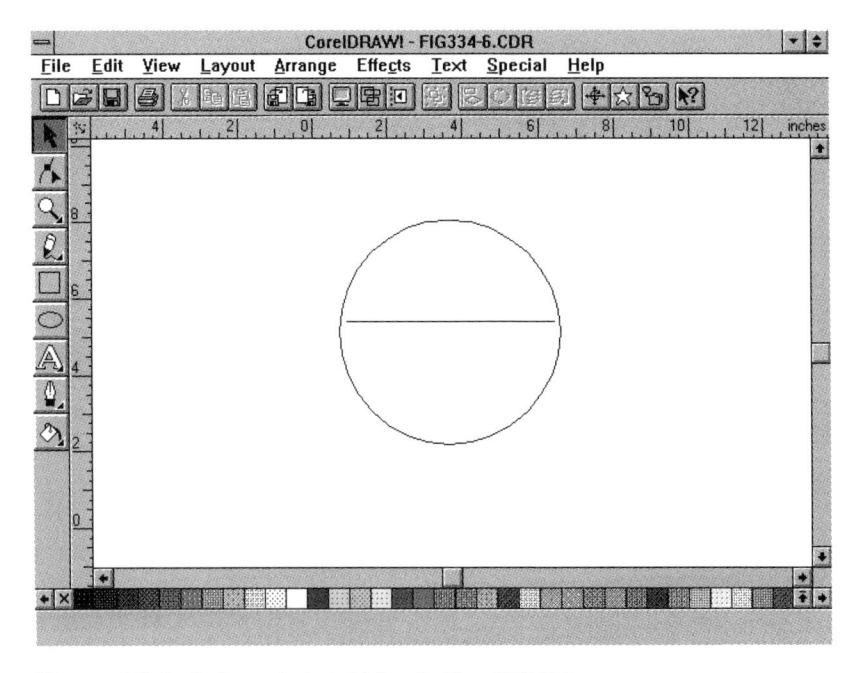

Figure 4.7 A circle and straight line in CorelDRAW.

142 Chapter 4

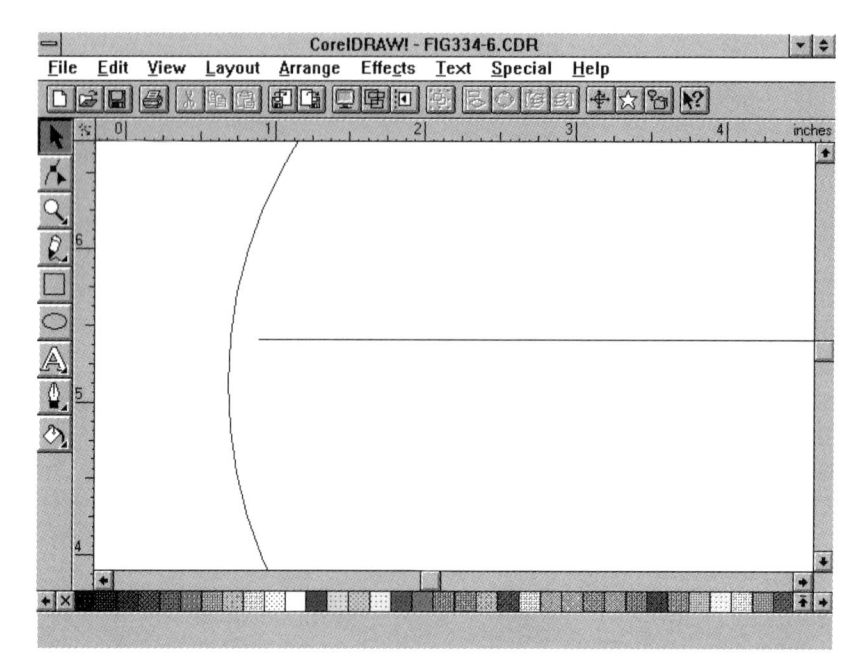

Figure 4.8 Zoom in on the drawing and you won't see bits.

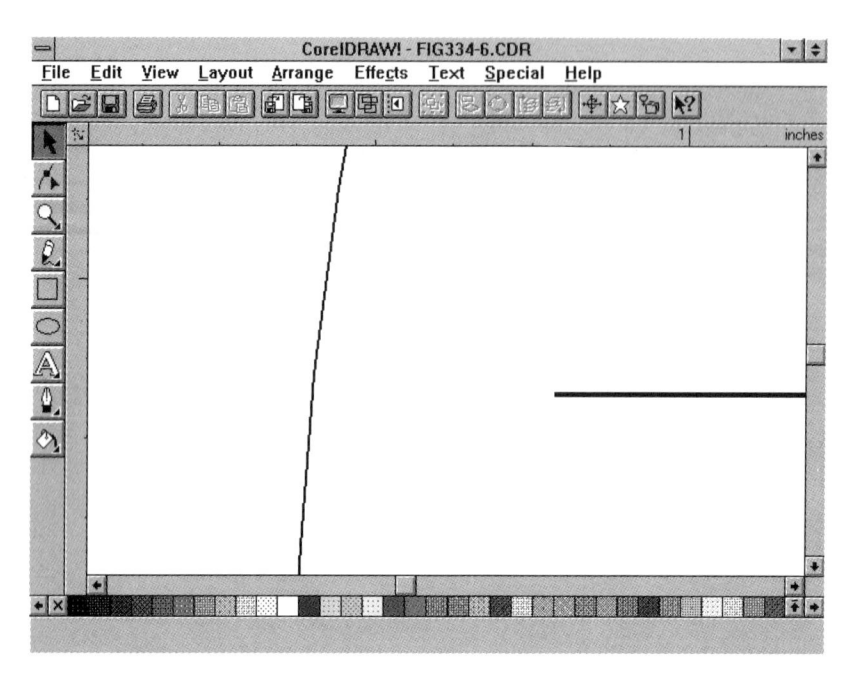

Figure 4.9 Zoom in still further, and still no bits. The jaggies in the curved line are limited by the resolution of the screen.

And there's the basic difference: Bitmapped graphics use bits; object-based graphics don't. Got it? Good.

Bitmapped Objects

> Ms. Peter's Law—Today if you're not confused you're just not thinking clearly.
>
> Irene Peter

Now that you've got the basic difference between bitmapped and object-based graphics solidly under your belt, I have to muddy the waters a bit. No, I'm not about to change the definitions on you. It's just that there are two issues that slightly blur the line between bitmapped and object-based graphics.

The first issue is relatively minor: You have to make a distinction between the way a program works with an object-based graphic—as a mathematical formula—and the way the program shows the graphic on screen or prints it at the printer.

Even objects print with dots.

Screens and printers use dots. So even an object-based graphic winds up as dots where the electron beam hits the phosphor or the toner hits the page. The essential difference between bitmapped and object-based graphics isn't how the graphic is displayed or printed, but how it's stored and manipulated by the program. A bitmap is stored as bits. An object gets translated to bits only when the program draws it on screen or at the printed page. It's stored as a mathematical formula.

The second issue that blurs the distinction between objects and bitmaps is that you can load a bitmapped image, such as a photo or a Paintbrush file, into an object-oriented graphics program, such as CorelDRAW.

Bitmapped images in object-oriented programs

At that point, you have something of a hybrid. The bitmapped image is still bitmapped in the sense that if you zoom in on it, you can see the individual bits (unless they're all the same color and bunched together in a solid mass). But it's also an object in the sense that the drawing program will treat the inserted photo or bitmapped file as one large object. You can stretch it just like any other object, but you won't be able to treat anything within it as a separate object.

How's that again?

Say you create a file with a square and a circle in Paintbrush and import the file into CorelDRAW. The entire file, including all the white space around the square and circle, will turn into a single object in CorelDRAW. You'll be able to stretch, shrink, or rotate it, including all the white space along with the square and circle. But you won't be able to, say, change the color of the fill in the circle, or stretch the square without stretching the circle also.

You'll get pretty much the same effect if you use OLE or an Insert picture command to insert a bitmapped graphic in, say, Word.

And then there's OLE. No Bull.

144 *Chapter 4*

> **Time out:** If OLE is just another TLA to you—that's Three Letter Acronym, in case *TLA* is also a TLA—the translation is Object Linking and Embedding. By either name, OLE lets you insert . . . uh . . . link or embed that is . . . all or part of one file into another file, using data files from any two applications that support OLE. You can, for example, insert all or part of a spreadsheet or a graphic file into a word processing document.
>
> The embedded (or linked) file (or partial file) gets treated as an object. (Well that makes sense. This is, after all, called *Object* Linking and Embedding. Be aware that an OLE object isn't the same thing as an object-based graphic. As I said before, *object* is one of those words that means whatever some company's marketing department wants it to mean. But there are still some similarities.) Getting treated as an object means that if you've inserted, say, a spreadsheet in a word processing document, you can stretch or shrink the spreadsheet, text and all, as a single object. And if you've inserted a graphic, you can stretch and shrink it as a single object also. The beauty of OLE, in case you've never used it, is that you can double click on the object to open the embedded or linked file in its original application and edit it as usual. But that's another subject entirely. The important point for our purposes is that you can insert a bitmapped graphic in, say, a word processing document, with OLE or without it, and find that the bitmap is suddenly an object.

What you wind up with, when you insert a bitmapped image in an object-oriented program or the equivalent, is a bitmapped image that you can treat like an object in some ways. But the image is still a bitmap in the most important respect: If you zoom in on it, you'll see the individual bits. The considerations for printing—which is, after all, what we're concerned with here—are the same as when printing from a bitmapped graphics program. All of which brings us back to the issue of the differences between monitors and printers.

Matching Dots

> riverrrun, past Eve and Adam's, from swerve of shore to bend of bay, brings us by a commodius vicus of recirculation back to Howth Castle and Environs.
>
> James Joyce
> First sentence in *Finnegans Wake*, 1939

Sometimes the shortest distance between two points is a circuitous route. I took the side trip into graphics programs to make sure you fully understood the difference between bitmaps and objects. Now you're ready to appreciate the problems in translating screen images into printed output.

I mentioned earlier that printers have lots more addressable points on the printed page than monitors have on the screen. Some basic arithmetic shows how many more. A VGA display, for example, has a resolution of 640 by 480. That's a total of 640 times 480, or 307,200 addressable dots on the entire screen. Even a high-resolution monitor, at 1280 by 1024, has only 1,310,720 dots on the screen.

Printers have more dots than screens.

A printed page, on the other hand, with 600 by 600 dots per inch, has 600 times 600, or 360,000 addressable dots *per inch*. For an 8½ by 11 inch page, with a one-half inch nonprintable area on the bottom margin, that comes out to . . . let's see . . . 600 times 600 times 8.5 times 10.5. That's 32,130,000 dots per page. Let's just round that off to 32 million. Even a 300 by 300 dpi printer comes out to 300 times 300 times 8.5 times 10.5, or about 8 million addressable dots.

The bottom line, for those who rushed through the last two paragraphs because they don't like numbers: You have about 300,000 addressable dots on a VGA screen, compared to about 8 million dots on a 300-dpi printer.

This difference in the number of dots doesn't much matter for object-based graphics. Whether you put an object-based line on the screen or the printer, the program has to convert the mathematical description of the line into the right number of bits. So if you've defined a line to be, say, 3 inches long, the program will make it 3 inches long at the printer.

With bitmapped graphics, on the other hand, the difference in the number of dots can create problems. Say you have a bitmapped graphic that fills a 640 by 480 VGA screen, and you want to print it on a 300-dpi printer. If the software (meaning some combination of the graphics program and printer driver) maps each dot on the screen to a single dot on the printer, you'll wind up with a printed graphic that's just 2.1 inches wide by 1.6 inches high. So instead of getting output that fills the page like the left side of Figure 4.10, which is what you were probably expecting, you'll get something like the right side.

Dot for dot

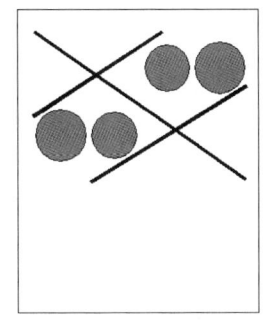

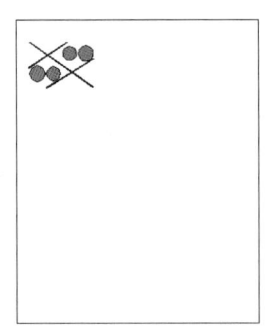

Figure 4.10 When a program prints one dot in a bitmapped image for each dot on the screen, a full screen image will shrink from what you were expecting, as shown on the left side, to a large postage stamp size, as shown on the right.

It gets worse.

If you have a 600-dpi printer, mapping one dot on screen to one dot on the printer will shrink the image even more, to about 1 inch by 0.8 inches, leaving you with something like the left side of Figure 4.11. If you have a 600 by 300 dpi printer, mapping dot for dot will not only shrink the graphic, but squash it too, like the right half of Figure 4.11.

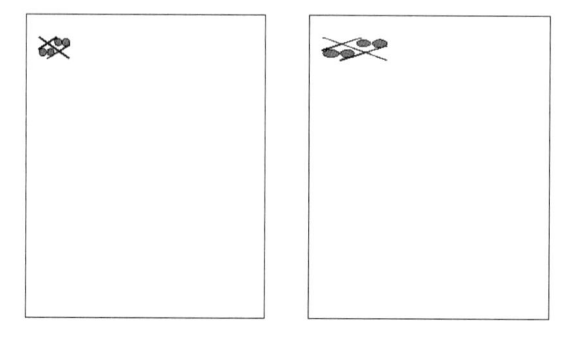

Figure 4.11 With a 600-dpi printer, the image can shrink even more, as shown on the left side of this figure. With a 600 by 300 dpi printer, the image can look like someone sat on it, as shown on the right.

There's another problem too. Even if you translate a full-screen image to the full width of the page, you won't take advantage of all the additional dots your printer can address. Suppose, for example, that you draw a diagonal line across the screen. If you enlarge it and add a grid to show you all the addressable points on the screen, it will look like Figure 4.12.

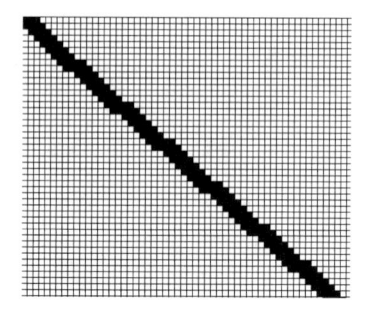

Figure 4.12 If you took a really close look at a diagonal line on screen, and added a grid to show you all the addressable points on the screen, it would look like this.

You'll notice a staircase effect along the edge of the line, which is known as the jaggies—or aliasing, if you want to be formal about it. Suppose you enlarge this line slightly and print it exactly as is, without adding any dots to fill in the jagged edge. If you took a close look at the line on the page and added a grid to show you all the addressable points on the page, it would look something like Figure 4.13.

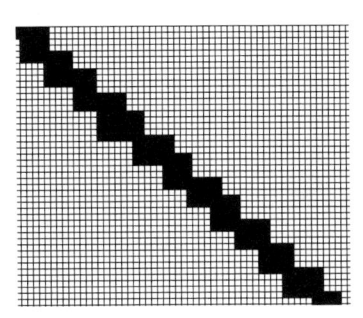

Figure 4.13 Scale a line up in size to print on a page but otherwise leave it as is, and you can wind up with easily visible aliasing on the edges.

To make this less theoretical, I used CorelDRAW to whip up the lines in Figure 4.14. As you can see, it's hard to miss the difference between the two.

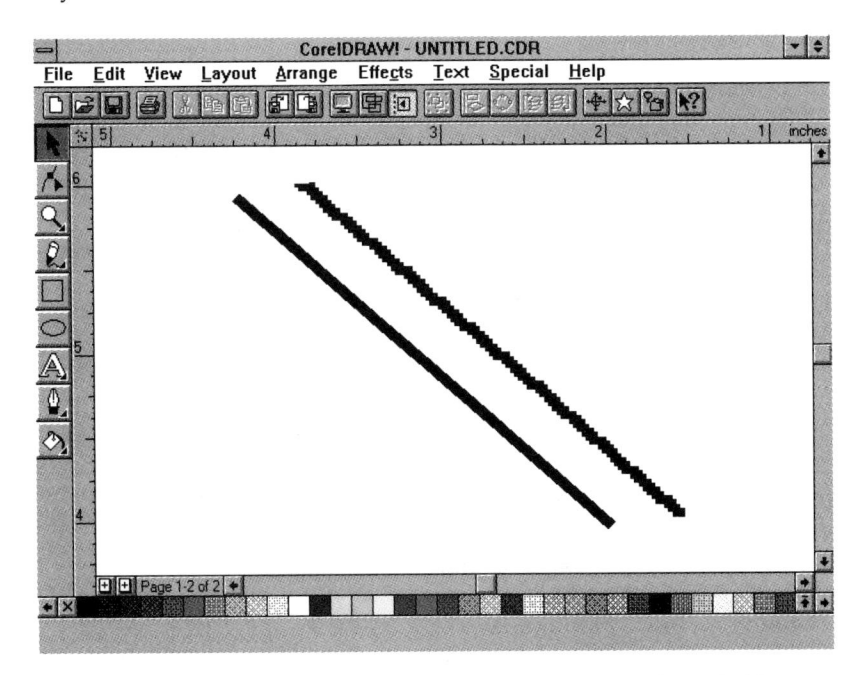

Figure 4.14 One of these lines is a bitmap that I simply enlarged without filling in the staircase gaps. The other line is an object that fills in the gaps.

Now for the quiz I promised earlier. (And you thought I forgot.) One of the lines in Figure 4.14 is a bitmap that I drew in Paintbrush, imported into CorelDRAW, and enlarged in the same way your software might enlarge a graphic going to a printer—without smoothing off the edges. The other line is an object that I drew in CorelDRAW, so that it takes full advantage of the available resolution. Which is the bitmap? (Hint: It's the ragged one. Anyone who hesitates answering needs new glasses.)

Dealing with Dots

> By trying we can easily learn to endure adversity. Another man's, I mean.
>
> Mark Twain
> *Following the Equator* (1897).

The good news about the problems you can run into when you print bitmapped images is that you won't necessarily run into them. The bad news is that if you do run into them, there isn't much you can do about it—other than learning to endure them or avoid them. More precisely, whether you can do anything about the problems depends almost entirely on the graphics program you're using. But even if you can do something about them, you may be better off not doing it.

When squash is in season

If you have a 600 by 300 dpi mode on your printer or a similar difference between vertical and horizontal resolution, you'll either run into the problem of squashed graphics, as shown in Figure 4.11, or you won't. But there's no easy way to predict it, because whether the problem will show up or not depends on both your graphics software and your printer driver.

I ran into the problem using the FARGO Primera Pro with Paintbrush, when I set Paintbrush to use printer resolution. But the problem disappeared when I cleared the X out of the Use Printer Resolution check box. I didn't run into the problem at all with the Tektronix 340 and Paintbrush. Neither printer had problems printing from Corel PHOTO-PAINT at 600 by 300 dpi with any settings in the program.

> **I'll amend that comment about predictability just a bit. If you have a PostScript printer, you won't run into squashed graphics, because one of the points of using PostScript is that it's device independent. Unless something gets terribly off course, you'll get the same size output no matter what PostScript printer you're using. With any other printer language, however, the statement stands. There's no easy way to predict what will happen.**

Since you can't predict whether a given printer, other than a PostScript printer, will have problems at enhanced resolution settings (for lack of a better term), your only choice is to test your printer with every program you use for printing graphics. The first time you print from any given program, limit the print run to one page. If that works without problems, feel free to start that 50-page run and go out to lunch. But don't go anywhere until you see that test page.

If you see squashed graphics, take a look at the settings in the program's Print or Print Options dialog box for choices that might affect the results. You've got to be creative here, since these might not always be obvious. I wouldn't have expected the choice Use Printer Resolution to make the difference between squashing graphics and not, but it did. If you can't find a setting in the program that will let you take full advantage of your printer's resolution, you'll have to change your printer settings to a standard resolution like 300 by 300 or 600 by 600 dpi. (If you don't know how to change the settings, don't worry about it. You will by the time you finish Chapter 9.)

Almost any bitmap graphics program—even lowly Paintbrush—will let you scale a bitmap to any size you like. That means you shouldn't have to print postage-stamp size graphics unless you want to. When you scale up the image to a larger size, however, you'll see jaggies.

Of pages and postage stamps

One solution is to create your bitmaps at a larger size to begin with. You'll find that just about any paint program will let you define an image size larger than 640 by 480. Unfortunately, it's hard to work with a graphic that you can't see all at once, so that's a less than ideal solution unless the program also lets you zoom out to see the whole image.

Another problem with large-size bitmapped graphics is that they take up a lot of room. Even white space in a bitmapped image has to be recorded as individual bits in the image. And each individual bit in the bitmapped image can need 24 bits (or more) in the file.

The problem with large bitmaps

Whoa there. We've just descended into a bit of jargon confusion. The bits we've been talking about until now are the bits in the image—the picture elements, or pixels. The bits in the file, on the other hand, make up the code that stores the information—the 1s and 0s, if you like to think of them that way, or the positive and negative magnetic domains on the disk. In a black and white image, it takes just one bit in the file to specify whether a given pixel is black or white, depending on whether the bit is 0 or 1. In a gray scale or color image, the number of bits per pixel depends on the number of colors or shades of gray. Two bits is enough to specify four colors—as 00, 01, 10, and 11. Four bits is enough for 16 colors, eight bits is enough for 256 colors, and 24 bits is enough for 16.7 million colors.

A 16-color, 640 by 480 image is roughly 150 kilobytes (640 times 480 times 4 bits per pixel, divided by 8 bits per byte). Double the width and height of the image, and you quadruple the size of the file to over 600 kilobytes. Make it a 256-color image, and you double the size again, to better than 1.2 megabytes. Go for an even larger size or more colors, and you're in the multi-megabyte range.

Bigger files not only take up more room on your hard disk, they take longer to load, take longer to save, and are more likely to force your system into swapping data from RAM to hard disk, generally slowing down whatever you're doing.

Given the way computers speed up with each new generation while prices keep dropping, multi-megabyte files may not matter by the turn of the century (which is 2001, by the way, not 2000). But for the moment, it's a strong argument for not getting carried away with making files too large.

> **Some bitmapped-based graphics programs offer another way to deal with jaggies to a limited extent. Adobe Photoshop and Corel PHOTO-PAINT, for example, are designed with photographs in mind, and they're filled with all sorts of so-called filters for enhancing images and for modifying them with special effects.**
>
> **The filters let you do everything from sharpen an image, to smooth edges, to make an image look like a reflection in a pool of rippling water. More important, the filters work just as well on bitmapped drawings as on photographs. And the smoothing filters can help minimize jagged edges. Even with programs that offer these features, however, you'll still see some jaggies when you scale the image up to match the page width.**

What all of this adds up to is that you've got to make compromises. If you want reasonably small files, you have to be satisfied with either small graphics with smooth edges or big graphics with jagged edges. If you insist on having big graphics with smooth edges, you'll also have to live with files that use up acres of valuable hard disk real estate. That's pretty much what you're stuck with—unless, of course, you use an object-oriented program in the first place.

Rasters and Vectors

> A wise man hears one word and understands two.
>
> Yiddish Proverb

Way back at the beginning of this discussion, when I first brought up the idea that graphics come in two basic varieties, I mentioned that bitmapped graphics are also called raster graphics and object-oriented graphics are also called vector graphics. Both terms are tied to display technology. You may find it easier to remember which is which if you know the difference between a raster display and a vector display.

Raster displays   The cathode ray tubes, or CRTs, in TVs and computer monitors draw their pictures with a set of lines that run across the screen, starting at the top of the screen and working their way down to the bottom. Within each line are some number of picture elements. Bits. This set of horizontal lines is called a raster, and any display that creates pictures this way is called a raster display—or a raster-scan display, since the horizontal lines are called scan lines.

The key point: Even when a raster display draws, say, a white vertical line on a black background, it's still drawing a full set of horizontal lines. It's just being choosy about which bits it turns on in each line by zapping the phosphors with the electron beam.

Vector displays

A few gadgets with CRTs don't work this way. Oscilloscopes are the ones you're most likely to be familiar with. Instead of constantly drawing scan lines from top to bottom, an oscilloscope aims its electron beam along the path of the line that it's drawing. When an oscilloscope draws a vertical line, the electron beam is actually following a vertical path. It's also drawing a continuous line. No bits. And any display that creates pictures this way is called a vector display.

You may remember vectors from high school math or physics. (I see Tim cringing in the back row at the mention of math. Bear with me a minute; this will be almost painless.) Vectors are variables with both size and direction. Tell someone to go two miles north, then three miles east and you've just given directions in the form of two vectors. You've probably also heard of pilots vectoring around a storm, meaning they've used vectors to go around a storm rather than following a path straight through it. (And aren't you glad about that if you're in the plane with them.)

The instructions for drawing lines on a vector display are likewise vectors. Start here, go so far in such and such direction, and you've got a line. More to the point, you have a line defined by a mathematical formula, and that's called . . . all together now . . . an object.

What this boils down to is that a raster display draws bitmapped images. In fact, a raster *is* a bitmap. And a vector display draws objects. If you're using an object-based graphics program, the image is stored and manipulated as an object, but it has to be rasterized—meaning it's converted to a bitmap—to show it on screen because computer monitors are raster displays.

That much is pretty easy, as long as you can remember which word goes with which kind of display. If you're on speaking terms with vectors, one way to keep them straight is to keep vectors in mind and simply recognize that vectors can describe objects. Raster displays are the other kind.

If your math or physics background is limited, you may find it easier to associate rasters with printers—even if you can't remember what a raster is—and work your way backward. Printers have to rasterize images before they can print them, and you'll occasionally run across references to this rasterization. Some printers have raster image processors, or RIPs, to handle the rasterization. Others let the computer do the work and then send the rasterized image to the printer.

If you can remember that printers use dots (that's not hard) and printers need to rasterize their images (only a little harder), you shouldn't have any trouble recognizing rasters as bitmaps. So raster displays use bitmaps, and vector displays are the other kind.

SOME MONITOR BASICS

> Good shot, bad luck and hell are the five basic words to be used in a game of tennis, though these, of course, can be slightly amplified.
>
> Virginia Graham
> *Say Please*, Ch. 8 (1949).

I can't close this chapter without talking a little bit about monitors themselves. Monitors come in different sizes, with different resolutions and different color capabilities. They also come in versions based on different technologies. And to get the most out of your color printer, you have to know at least a little about your monitor as well.

Throughout this chapter, and in the overview of monitors in Chapter 1, I've worked from the assumption that you're using a cathode ray tube–based monitor, or CRT for short. If you're using a desktop system, that's a pretty good bet, but if you're working on a notebook or other portable, you almost certainly have a liquid crystal display, better known as an LCD.

Both kinds of displays have more in common than they have differences, which means that most of what I've said about CRT displays applies to LCD displays as well. In particular, both use an RGB color model to mix colors. (I'll ignore monochrome displays here since you're probably not using a monochrome display if you have a color printer.) Despite the similarities, however, there are some practical differences between the two. I'll mention those differences as I talk about the variations on size, resolution, and color capabilities.

There are also several flavors of CRT technology that you ought to be aware of. All of these are simply variations on a theme, but some of the variations make a big difference. I'll bring these up as I go too. But what I'm concerned with here are practical issues: size, resolution, and color. I'm not particularly concerned with the technology, and there's no reason you should be either. You should find these comments helpful in understanding the limitations of your monitor. You may find them helpful in picking your next monitor as well.

A warning to Mac users: The details I'll be bringing in here are strictly from the DOS and Windows world. Don't let that throw you, however. The concepts apply just as well to a Mac.

Size: Bigger Is Better

> I *am* big. It's the pictures that got small.
>
> Norma Desmond
> *Sunset Boulevard,* by Billy Wilder, Charles Brackett, and D. M. Marsham, Jr., 1950

If you're working in color, you're probably working with graphics. And if you're working with graphics, the more you can see on screen at once and the more detail you can see, the easier the graphics are to work with. Getting more on screen at once is a matter of increased resolution, which we'll come back to a little later. Being able to see what you've got is a matter of size. In general, the bigger the screen, the better you can take advantage of higher resolutions.

As you may already know, if you've ever changed resolutions with a given CRT-based monitor, higher resolutions in a graphical environment like Windows, OS/2, or the Mac shrink the image on screen. That effectively provides more room to show information.

A given size square, for example, is defined as so many dots across and so many down. If you increase the resolution to fit more dots on the screen—at 800 across by 600 down, say, instead of VGA's standard 640 by 480—the dots that define the square take less area and the square shrinks. Move to a larger screen at the same resolution, and the same block of pixels will take more physical area than it did on the smaller screen, which gives you a physically larger square with the same number of dots.

That's only half of the equation. The other half is that when you switch to a higher resolution, you can fit more squares of the same size on the screen at once. If you stay with the same size screen, each of the squares will be smaller than the original. But if you move to a larger screen, the squares will grow to a larger size also, which lets you put more information on screen without making the smaller details too small to see.

What a Difference an Inch Makes

> You can observe a lot just by watching.
>
> Yogi Berra

Not too long ago, a friend asked my advice about buying a new computer, and when I gave it said, *Oh, but that's not what* Consumer Reports *said*. Actually, she said that in response to several of the suggestions I made, but the item of immediate interest was the monitor.

My advice was to get no less than a 15-inch monitor and to treat 14-inchers like undersize fish: Throw 'em back. But *Consumer Reports* doesn't (or at least didn't) agree. My friend gave me a copy of the article, and sure enough the article said, in no uncertain terms, that 15-inch monitors were a marketing gimmick with no advantages over a 14-inch monitor.

More precisely, the article said:

> For an IBM-compatible machine: Our tests indicate that you should choose a ... 14-inch monitor, capable of at least SuperVGA resolution ... Don't spend more for a 15-inch monitor; the size difference is mostly a marketing ploy.
>
> "How to Buy a Computer," *Consumer Reports*, November 1994

Well ... I promise not to give any advice on cars or refrigerators. But *Consumer Reports* would do well to listen to Yogi Berra's advice: You can observe a lot just by watching.

The advantage you gain from increasing screen size by even one inch—going from 14 to 15 inches—is greater than you might think. It's certainly greater than *Consumer Reports* thinks. The linear measurement of 14, 15, 17, or whatever inches is a kind of shorthand. The important measurement is the area available on screen.

How big is the monitor, really?

The actual display on a typical 14-inch monitor is roughly 9.8 by 7.4 inches, or—wait a second, let me grab my calculator ... ummm ... about 72 square inches. A typical 15-inch monitor is roughly 11.0 by 8.3 inches, or about 91 square inches. That comes out to 25 percent more area, or one-fourth again as much information if you adjust the resolution to keep the image at the same size.

What size monitor do you need?

This difference doesn't matter much if you're using a DOS program that uses text mode. It matters a whole lot if you're using a graphical interface like Windows. Your preferred choice of resolution for any size monitor depends on your eyesight and your tolerance for small-size images. But the rule of thumb in the DOS world is that a 14-inch monitor is acceptable for standard VGA resolution at 640 by 480 and marginal for SuperVGA at 800 by 600. A 15-inch monitor is a good choice for 800 by 600 and marginal at the next standard step up—at 1024 by 768.

If you move up to a 17-inch monitor, the display jumps to roughly 12.4 by 9.3 inches, or 115 square inches. That comes out to 28 percent more area than a 15-inch monitor, or 60 percent more than a 14-inch monitor. Move up to 21 inches—which is about the largest monitor that can fit comfortably on a desktop and is the preferred size for graphics professionals—and the display jumps to 15.75 by 11.8 inches, or 186 square inches. That's 60 percent more than a 17-inch monitor and 100 percent more than a 15-inch monitor.

As a practical matter, a 17-inch monitor is a good choice for 1024 by 768 and a marginal choice at 1280 by 1024. A 21-inch monitor is ideal for 1280 by 1024 and usable at 1600 by 1200 for the professional graphic artist who won't be satisfied with anything less.

When I use a 15-inch monitor with Windows, I compromise by setting Windows to 1024 by 768 resolution, but choosing the video driver with large rather than small fonts. (A video driver, if you're not familiar with the term, is just the piece of software that gives the video card its marching orders.) With a 17-inch monitor, I use 1280 by 1024 resolution, but again, using large rather than small fonts.

These settings let me see more graphics on the screen at once but make the text a little larger and a little easier to read than it would otherwise be. Your graphics card should offer a choice of drivers with large and small fonts for each resolution it can manage. Depending on the card, you should be able to change the drivers either through the standard Windows Setup choices or a separate video setup utility.

One other note just to avoid confusion: All these comments assume that a given monitor can work at the resolution you want, which isn't necessarily true. It's entirely possible to find a 17-inch monitor that doesn't offer 1280 by 1024 resolution or a 21-inch monitor that doesn't offer 1600 by 1200. You need to check the available resolutions for each individual monitor.

And as long as we're on the subject of monitor resolution, stay away from interlaced resolutions. Interlacing is a technique for drawing each screen image in two passes, painting every other line on the first pass, and filling in the blank lines on the second pass. Interlacing lets inexpensive monitors reach higher resolutions, but it also leads to a noticeable flicker that makes a bottle of aspirin a required accessory. The highest resolution you want to use on any given monitor is its highest *non*-interlaced resolution. Interlacing is a Bad Thing.

There's another issue about resolution and size also. Namely, resolution is limited by dot pitch.

How big are those dots

Figure 4.15 should look familiar. You've seen it before, in Chapter 1. The circles represent the phosphor dots on a monitor screen, in red, green, and blue.

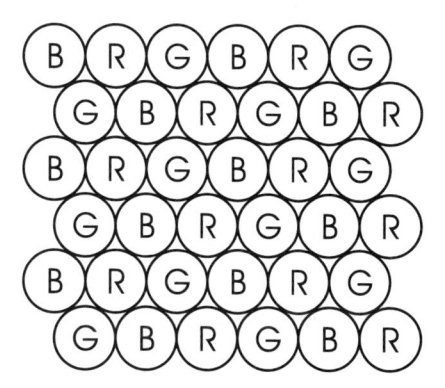

Figure 4.15 We've been here before: Most monitors paint their pictures with phosphor dots in red, green, and blue.

One of the differences between monitors is the size dot that they use. You probably already know that better monitors have smaller dot pitches. And you may know that dot pitch is not the same as dot size. But the two are related, so that a smaller dot pitch means a smaller dot size. (Okay, since you asked, you measure dot size as the diameter of the dot. You measure dot pitch as the distance from the center of a dot to the center of the next dot down that's the same color, two rows below.)

Dot pitch is given in millimeters. If you have a halfway decent monitor, at anything smaller than 21 inches, its dot pitch should be 0.28 mm or less. If you're lucky enough to have a 21-inch monitor, the dot pitch should be 0.31 mm or less. Larger dot pitches tend to produce fuzzy lines, particularly at higher resolutions.

As it happens, the size of the phosphor dots isn't necessarily the same as the size of the dots the monitor uses to build pixels—let's call them spots for the moment. Figure 4.16 shows how a monitor can use more than one dot of a given color to build a larger spot. This ability to use more than one phosphor dot for each color within a pixel is why monitors can use more than one resolution, while still filling the whole screen.

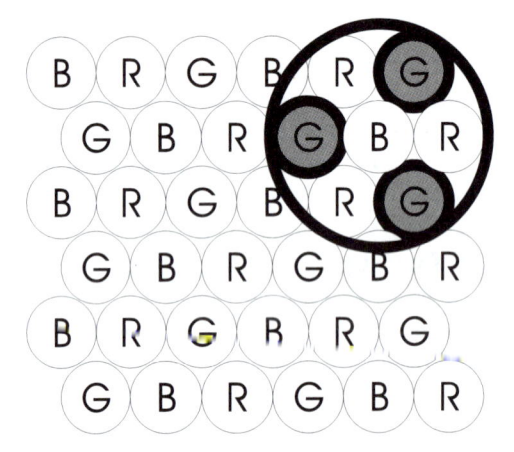

Figure 4.16 Monitors typically use more than one phosphor dot for each individual color within the triad of colors that builds a pixel.

But here's the interesting part: Although this trick lets the monitor use lower resolutions with more phosphor dots per color spot, the size of the dot puts a lower limit on the size spot, which can't, or at least shouldn't, be anything less than a single phosphor dot. That puts an upper limit on the resolution the monitor can handle. Quite simply, if you have fewer dots of each color across or down than there are pixels for a given resolution, you'll wind up with fuzzy edges, no matter how fine a resolution the electron guns are capable of.

Even with a 0.26 mm dot pitch, which is available in only a few monitors, this limits a 15-inch monitor to 1024 by 768 resolution and a 17-inch monitor to 1280 by 1024. You can find 15-inch monitors that claim 1280 by 1024 resolution and 17-inch monitors that claim 1600 by 1200 resolution, but you shouldn't take these claims too seriously. You certainly won't want to use those monitors at these resolutions.

If you happen to have a monitor that uses a Trinitron or Trinitron-style tube, you may find it interesting to know that strictly speaking, Trinitron tubes don't have a dot pitch. Instead of circular dots, the Trinitron mask consists of vertical stripes, with the vertical dot size determined by the width of the electron beam. Even so, the same general concept applies to Trinitron tubes.

The moral here is simple enough: Bigger is better. If you want to see a larger portion of your graphics on screen as you work with them and you want to see the detail also, you need a large monitor. For those of us who aren't professional artists, a 17-inch monitor is the practical (read: affordable) compromise. A 15-inch monitor is the absolute minimum for any graphics work, whether you use color or not.

There's another issue that also makes a 15-inch monitor a much better choice than a 14-inch monitor. You may never have noticed, but monitor displays come in four distinct shapes: spherical section, cylindrical section, flat, and flat square. And shape matters.

Shape matters too

Spherical section monitors used to be the only choice. The screens on these CRTs are literally a small section of a sphere, with the screen visibly curved in both vertical and horizontal directions.

Spherical, cylindrical, flat, and flat square

Cylindrical shape screens are curved like a soup can—flat in the vertical direction, but curved in the horizontal direction.

Truly flat screens are flat in both directions.

Flat square screens are neither flat nor square (much like the mad monk Rasputin, who was neither mad, nor a monk, nor was his name Rasputin). In truth, they're shaped like a section of a sphere, just like spherical-shaped screens. With flat square screens, however, the sphere is larger by an order of magnitude, and that's enough to make the display look flat.

The shape of the display has a significant effect on what you see on screen. With a spherical section display, the image is a little like a picture painted on a beach ball, and is visibly distorted in both horizontal and vertical directions, particularly near the edges. A cylindrical shape—which you'll find primarily in Sony Trinitron tubes—distorts the image a little less—like a picture painted on the side of a can.

Images on flat tubes—which use Zenith's Flat Tension Mask—actually look slightly concave, though you'll find you can get used to flat screens quickly enough. Images on flat square CRTs look flat.

Here's the kicker: Most 15-inch monitors (as well as most 17- and 21-inch monitors) use flat square CRTs. Most 14-inch monitors (as well as most 16-, 19-, and 20-inch monitors, if you can find any) use spherical section CRTs. And that's another good reason to treat a 15-inch monitor as a minimum.

The next time you buy a system, don't even consider a 14-inch choice. If you're currently stuck with a 14-incher, consider moving up. And if your budget can stretch to a 17-inch monitor, you'll find it well worth the investment. You may even thank me for suggesting it. (My friend who started out with the *Consumer Reports* article did.)

Einstein calculated that a ruler would shrink if you got it moving fast enough. Monitor size shrinks without moving the monitor at all. A 14-inch monitor usually measures about 13 inches from bezel corner to bezel corner. (The bezel is that plastic frame around the outside of the CRT.) A 15-inch monitor usually measures about 14 inches, and a 17-inch monitor usually measures about 16 inches.

Contrary to what you may have heard from those whose fantasies take a sinister turn, this is not a conspiracy to defraud you. The 14-, 15-, and 17-inch sizes are actually the diagonal measurements for the cathode ray tube, itself. The visible part of the CRT is typically an inch less than the full size because of the bezel that frames the outside of the screen. The maximum picture size for most CRTs is also about an inch less than CRT size.

Now comes the interesting part: I've seen some monitors where the bezels hide less of the CRT, so that a 14-inch monitor may measure as much as 13.8 inches from bezel corner to bezel corner. The picture size, however, depends on the CRT, not the bezel, so it will still typically measure roughly 13 inches. I haven't seen an equivalent situation in larger monitors, but that may just mean I haven't seen it, not that it doesn't exist.

The rule of thumb is that the corner-to-corner measurement on the picture size will be about an inch less than the corner-to-corner measurement for the CRT itself. More important, you should avoid monitors with unusually large bezel-to-bezel measurements for the CRT size. The overly large visible area generally results in a distracting, wide black band around the picture.

Size and LCDs

> Oh, well. Never mind.
>
> Gilda Radner as Emily Letella
> "Saturday Night Live"

Almost none of these comments about size apply to LCDs, which is something you need to know if your only computer is a notebook.

LCDs have a reputation of being hard to read compared to CRTs, and it's a well-earned reputation. (Trust me on this. Until recently, the standard joke, when someone was proudly showing off his or her new notebook, was to ask, *Is it on yet?* And it wasn't all that much of a joke.) But assuming you have high enough brightness and contrast—and almost all new LCDs qualify today—LCDs are actually inherently easier to read than CRTs.

LCDs use a very different technology from CRTs to draw their pictures. At the risk of oversimplifying a bit, color LCDs consist essentially of a light in back of a collection of sharply defined square cells. Each cell functions as a shutter to let light through or not. (More precisely, the molecules of liquid crystal line up to let light through or block the light, but we don't need that level of detail here.) Each pixel on the screen consists of a triad of one red, one green, and one blue cell.

How LCDs work

This difference in how LCDs draw their pictures compared to CRTs makes a tremendous difference in what the pictures look like. Assuming you have high enough brightness and contrast, once again, the sharply defined cells give text characters and graphics much crisper edges than you can get from a CRT by aiming an electron beam at a phosphor. That makes any given image more readable than the same size image on a CRT, just as text on a printed page is more readable than the same size text, as measured by a ruler, on a CRT.

Another important difference is that the diagonal measurement for an LCD screen is also the actual picture size, not an inch bigger. That means an 11-inch LCD offers the same size image as a 12-inch CRT.

LCDs get measured differently.

So where a 14-inch CRT monitor is the minimum acceptable for VGA's 640 by 480 resolution, an LCD can manage acceptably at just 9.5 inches. For SuperVGA's 800 by 600 resolution, a 10.3-inch LCD is generally as readable as a 15-inch CRT. And for 1024 by 768 resolution, a 12-inch or larger LCD should be a match for a 17-inch CRT.

Not so incidentally, there's another important difference between LCDs and CRTs. If you switch resolutions on a desktop monitor (assuming your monitor can handle multiple resolutions), the overall image size stays essentially the same, while the individual elements—like icons or text characters—change size. Go to a higher resolution, and individual elements get smaller. Go to a lower resolution, and they get larger. CRTs can manage this trick because they can aim the electron beams to hit either more or fewer phosphor dots for each pixel.

You can't do that with LCDs because of their design, with one red, one green, and one blue cell for each pixel. It's not too hard to extrapolate to a larger image size in DOS text mode to take advantage of the full screen at lower resolutions. The system can use a different set of characters and adjust the spacing between lines to fill out the screen. But with a graphical environment like Windows, adjusting the image size is essentially impossible.

Try mapping a 640 by 480 image onto an LCD with the right number of cells for 800 by 600 pixels, and you'll be forced into making some pixels two cells wide or two cells high while others are one cell wide and high. That would make some lines in individual text characters, for example, fatter than others, which would make the text harder to read. LCDs deal with this problem by using just 640 by 480 of an 800 by 600 display and leaving a black frame of unused cells around the image. If you switch to a higher resolution, the size of the individual elements stays the same. You just see more of them, and the image itself gets larger.

Colors: More Is Better (Usually)

> Mere colour, unspoiled by meaning, and unallied with definite form, can speak to the soul in a thousand different ways.
>
> Oscar Wilde
> Gilbert, in "The Critic as Artist," pt. 2 (published in *Intentions*, 1891).

Whether you're using an LCD or CRT, you also have a choice in the number of colors—a choice that's particularly important if you want the colors on screen to bear some vague relationship to the colors that come out of your printer. If your screen can show only 16 colors, for example—which is what you get in the standard Windows VGA driver—it has to fake any additional colors by dithering. And dithering doesn't work as well on a screen as it does on a printer. The relatively few addressable dots per inch make the dithering patterns much more obvious. Figure 4.17, for example, shows two dithering patterns from a screen set for 16 colors.

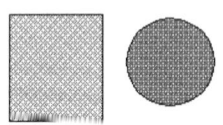

Figure 4.17 Dithering patterns like these on screen are much more obvious than dithering patterns on a printer.

Color depth, color resolution

As you may have already found out the hard way, the number of colors is another area where you can get sandbagged by people who use different names for the same thing. Depending on who you talk to, the number of colors goes by any of several names: Color depth, color resolution, and even, occasionally, number of colors. They all mean the same thing.

The depth in color depth is analogous to depth on the bench in your favorite sports team. If there's a lot there (colors or good players) you've got more depth.

Color resolution gets its name from what amounts to an optical illusion. If you look at a photograph on screen (or in printed output for that matter) at a given resolution but two different color depths, you'll see the one with more colors as having better resolution.

The real difference is that the version with fewer colors breaks up shapes with dithering patterns and with bands of distinctly different colors, rather than showing colors shade gradually into each other. The effect is that the version with fewer colors looks like a lower resolution.

Number of colors is pretty obvious, but it gets less obvious real quick when someone says something like, *You can set the video to anything from 256 colors to 24-bit color.*

Say what?

I've already mentioned that the number of colors you get depends on the number of bits per pixel. For a monochrome screen without any shades of gray, you need only one bit, to determine if the pixel should be on or off. For color or gray scale images, the number of bits determines how many colors you can define or how many shades of gray. Two bits combine in just four ways:

Colors and bits (not kibbles and bits)

```
00
01
10
11
```

This lets you assign one color, or one shade of gray, to each of the four codes. In other words, *two-bit color* is an alternate pronunciation for *four colors*. (Which means a four-color capability is two-bit color, in both senses of the phrase.)

Four bits give you 16 combinations, or codes:

```
0000    0100    1000    1100
0001    0101    1001    1101
0010    0110    1010    1110
0011    0111    1011    1111
```

That means four bits lets you assign one color or shade of gray to each of the 16 codes. So four-bit color means the same thing as 16 colors.

And so on.

You can easily figure out how many colors you can get from any given number of bits. Start out with two colors for one bit, and then double the number of colors for each additional bit. To make it even easier, Table 4.1 lists the number of bits and number of colors for various color depths.

All of the entries in Table 4.1 are for color depths that I've seen recently in printers, video displays, or both. But the most common levels of color depth by far are: 8-bit, which gives you 256 colors; 16-bit, which gives 65,536 colors; and 24-bit, which gives 16,777,216 colors. Of course, no one talks about 65,536 colors, much less 16,777,216 colors. It's too unwieldy.

Common color levels

That's why most people, once they get beyond 256 colors, talk about the number of bits, rather than the number of colors. And those few who talk about the number of colors usually round them off. You may recognize 65,536 as 64K, or

64 times 1024. That's why you'll see the number of colors for 16-bit color given as 64K or 64,000 at least as often as 65,000. (I've never seen it rounded to 66,000, which is the way I learned how to round numbers in elementary school.)

Table 4.1 This chart will help you convert between number of bits and number of colors.

Number of bits	Number of colors
1	2
4	16
8	256
12	4096
14	16,384
15	32,768
16	65,536
18	262,144
24	16,777,216

Figure 4.18 Well, *almost* nobody talks about 16,777,216 colors.

Instead of 16,777,216 colors, you'll see references to 16 million (very common), 17 million (a close second), 16.7 million (also common), or 16.8 million colors (correct, but almost never used).

What Color Depth Means

> You'll never really know what I mean and I'll never know exactly what you mean.
>
> Mike Nichols

Now you can talk about colors and bits with abandon, but you also need to know what the different color depths translate to as a practical matter on the screen.

How many colors can you see on screen?

First, let's head off a possible source of confusion. People often talk about a given color depth in terms of the number of colors you can see on the screen at once. But that's not precisely right.

Here's a quick quiz:

1. How many pixels do you have on a screen whose resolution is 640 by 480?
   Hint: It's the same as the number of addressable dots.
   Answer: 640 times 480, or 307,200

2. So even if you make every dot a different color, how many colors can you see at once on a screen?
   Hint: You can't see more colors than you've got dots.
   Answer: 307,200

3. Okay, how many colors can you see at once on a high-resolution screen with 1280 by 1024 resolution?
   Hint: 1280 times 1024 is 1,310,720
   Answer: You can figure this one out yourself.

So if you're talking about a color depth of, say, 16 colors, 256 colors, or even 65,000 colors, the color depth also tells you the maximum number of colors you can see on screen at once. When you get to more colors than you have pixels on screen, however, the color depth tells you how many different colors your system can keep track of at once, not how many colors it will show you at once.

This is a subtle, but important, distinction. Even though 19-bit color—with more than 500,000 colors available—can keep track of more colors than a VGA screen can show at once, it may not include all the colors you need for any given picture, particularly a photograph. At a 19-bit color depth, you'll still be missing some of the colors you need to show a smooth transition of flesh tones on a face that's partly in shadow, for example. The issue is not just how many colors you have available, but whether you have all the colors you need.

All of which brings us to the question, How many colors do you need?

How many colors do you need?

For simple graphics, meaning anything limited to blocks of solid colors—as with Figures 4.19 through 4.21—even 16 colors should be enough to serve your needs, as long as you aren't particular about which colors you use.

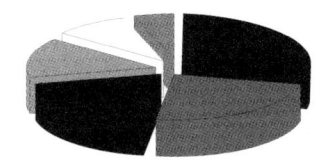

Figure 4.19 This business graphic can't possibly use more than six colors—one for each pie wedge—plus a seventh color if you want to add one for the background.

164 *Chapter 4*

Figure 4.20 Even this cartoon-level drawing qualifies as a simple graphic. It's colored here with just six shades of gray and would work just fine with six colors.

Figure 4.21 These fantastical figures need just three colors each. That makes them a lot easier to color than to build. (And if you manage to build one in your basement workshop, let me know.)

Banding and dithering

For somewhat more sophisticated graphics, like the one in Figure 4.22, with gradient fills that gradually change from one color (or shade of gray) to another, 16 colors won't do. Depending on the software you're using, you'll wind up with bands of dithering patterns, as in Figure 4.23, or simply bands of noticeably different shades, as in Figure 4.24. If you work much with this kind of sophisticated graphic, 256 colors is the minimum you'll want.

Things get a little trickier at higher color depths (and not just because *higher . . . depths* sounds like an oxymoron). At 32K colors, a.k.a. 15-bit color (see how the jargon works), you have more than enough colors for any graphic you can think of and enough so some scanned photos will have a true photorealistic quality. However, a large number of photos at 32K color will have at least some posterization.

Figure 4.22 For sophisticated graphics that include gradient fills like the background in this one, you need at least 256 colors.

Figure 4.23 If you limit yourself to 16 colors on screen, you may have to live with dithering patterns, rather than gradually changing colors, for gradient fills on screen.

Figure 4.24 Too few colors can also show as obvious bands of different colors or shades, rather than a gradual change in colors.

Posterization

Posterization, in case you're not familiar with the term, is an artistic effect that can make a photo like the one in Figure 4.25 look almost like a drawing, as shown in Figure 4.26.

Figure 4.25 This picture is obviously a photo. Compare it to the version in Figure 4.26.

Figure 4.26 This posterized version of the same photo as in Figure 4.25 looks like it might be a drawing rather than a photo.

The way you get from Figure 4.25 to Figure 4.26 is by limiting the number of colors—or the number of shades of gray—in the picture. Limiting the colors or shades of gray eliminates subtle shading.

Eliminating shading, in turn, has two effects. It eliminates the clues that tell your eye when you're looking at a three-dimensional surface, and it leaves abrupt changes in colors or shades that are appropriate for comic book art, but not for photorealistic images. The result, as with the jet in Figure 4.26, is that three-dimensional surfaces look flat, and the shading looks artificial, as with a comic book.

While posterization has it's place as an eye-catching effect, it's not something you generally want when you're trying to work with photorealistic images. If you have too few colors available, however, slight posterization will often creep in, as in Figure 4.27. Typically, the posterization will show in only part of the picture, as in the figure. If you see any posterization at all, you'll most often see it in skies that vary greatly in brightness, as in Figure 4.27, or in skin tones.

Figure 4.27 This picture is slightly posterized, an effect that shows primarily in the sky, with abrupt changes of color—or shade of gray.

Move from 32K colors to 64K colors, a.k.a. 16-bit color, and a much lower percentage of photos will show posterization. In fact, the percentage of photos that show any posterization will keep dropping with each additional step up the bit ladder until you hit 24 bits, or 16.7 million colors. At 24 bits, you can fill in enough shades on any photo to fool the human eye into seeing photorealistic, continuous color—assuming you map the shades of color appropriately.

Not so incidentally, just to confuse the issue of color depth a little further, some people talk about deep color or high color, meaning at least 16-bit color but less than 24-bit color. Deep and high are usually opposites—mountains are high and oceans are deep, right?—but in this case they mean the same

thing; namely, enough colors so a high percentage of scanned photos will show with photorealistic color. Even more people talk about true color as an alternate pronunciation for 24-bit color. True color in this case means enough colors so any photo looks like it's truly supposed to look.

Pick a Card

> I am sorry I have not learnt to play at cards. It is very useful in life.
>
> Samuel Johnson
> Quoted in James Boswell, *Tour of the Hebrides,* 21 Nov. 1773 (1785)

Unless you have an ancient computer, with one of the early color standards for PCs (read: CGA or EGA, and count yourself lucky if you've never heard of those standards), your monitor should be able to handle any color depth you throw at it. What determines the color depth is your video card. (Well... in some cases the video electronics may be built in to your motherboard, but I'll use video card to mean the video electronics, wherever they happen to be.)

There's a lot more to say about video cards than we'll cover here. The key issue, for our purposes, is how many colors they can handle at what resolutions. You may find it useful to know that the answer depends primarily on how much memory is on the card. If you want greater resolution or color depth than you currently have, you may be able to get it by adding memory to the card. At the very least, you'll want to keep the issue of memory in mind the next time you buy a video card.

Table 4.2 shows the maximum number of colors you can squeeze into various amounts of memory at the four most common resolutions.

Table 4.2 This chart shows the maximum number of colors you can get at various resolutions with any given amount of memory. But don't count on these numbers.

Amount of Memory on Card	Resolution			
	640 × 480	800 × 600	1024 × 768	1280 × 1024
512 kilobytes	8192 colors	256 colors	32 colors	8 colors
1 megabyte	16.7 million colors	131,072 colors	1024 colors	64 colors
2 megabytes	16.7 million colors	16.7 million colors	2 million colors	4096 colors
4 megabytes	16.7 million colors	16.7 million colors	16.7 million colors	16.7 million colors

There's a catch here. Just because you have enough memory on the card for a given number of colors at a given resolution doesn't mean the card will come with a driver for that number of colors (or even that the card offers that particular resolution, but that's another issue entirely). For example, a half megabyte of memory, a.k.a. 512 kilobytes, is enough for 8192 colors at 640 by 480, but I wouldn't bet the ranch on finding a video card that comes with drivers for 8192 colors. With a 512K video card, I'd be surprised to find drivers for more than 256 colors.

Table 4.3 shows the maximum color depth you'll typically get after you take the drivers into account.

Table 4.3 This chart shows the typical maximum number of colors you can reasonably expect for various amounts of memory on a video card.

Amount of Memory on Card	Resolution			
	640 × 480	800 × 600	1024 × 768	1280 × 1024
512 kilobytes	256 colors	256 colors	16 colors	8 colors
1 megabyte	16.7 million colors	65,000 colors	256 colors	16 colors
2 megabytes	16.7 million colors	16.7 million colors	65,000 colors	256 colors
4 megabytes	16.7 million colors	16.7 million colors	16.7 million colors	16.7 million colors

Don't forget that whatever color depth you wind up using, you have to match the resolution the video card puts out with the resolution your monitor can handle.

Did someone ask how I came up with these tables? Well, if you didn't ask, skip this tip. But if you want to know how I got the numbers, read on. If you can handle simple arithmetic, it's easy to find out the amount of memory you need on your video card for any given resolution and color depth. Just multiply the horizontal resolution, vertical resolution, and color depth. A 640 by 480 picture has 640 times 480, or 307,200 pixels. (This number should be looking familiar by now. The number of pixels is also the number of addressable dots, which we've visited more than once.) If the color depth is 256 colors, or 8 bits, you need 8 bits of data for each pixel to completely describe the picture.

That's 8 bits times 307,200 pixels, or a total of . . . umm . . . (Where's the rain man when you need him?) . . . 2,456,600 bits of data. Divide that by 8 to get the number of bytes, at 8 bits per byte, and you're back at 307,200 bytes of data for the image. Memory for video cards typically comes in half-megabyte or megabyte chunks. So a video card with half a megabyte is easily enough for a 640 by 480 by 256-color image.

At 1280 by 1024 resolution, in contrast, you have 1,310,720 pixels. Multiply that by 24 for 24-bit color, then divide by 8 to the get the number of bytes, and you wind up with 3,932,160 bytes of data. (Don't trust me; do the math.) And that's why you need 3.9 megabytes or more of memory on the video card for 24-bit color at 1280 by 1024 resolution.

Speed matters

One or two other points about video cards are worth passing mention here. If you plan to work with 24-bit color, or even 16-bit color, you have a lot of data to push around inside your computer—roughly ten times as much data for a 1280 by 1024 by 24-bit image as for a 640 by 480 by 256 color image. That makes speed, which is always important, all the more important at higher resolutions and greater color depths.

The next time you buy a video card, you might want to get video RAM, or VRAM, on the card instead of plain old garden-variety DRAM. Even better is WRAM, but, as I write this, it still isn't widely available. There's no need, for our purposes, to go into the technical differences between these three kinds of RAM. All you have to know is that VRAM is faster and more expensive than DRAM, while WRAM is faster and less expensive than VRAM, but still more expensive than DRAM. The faster part makes it worth the more expensive part if you plan to use higher color depths.

You're also well advised to look for local bus video, which means your video runs at the speed of the central processing unit in your system rather than the slower bus speed that most cards are stuck with. (If you're not familiar enough with hardware to know what that means, don't worry about it. All you really need to know is that local bus video paints pictures on the screen faster.)

If your desktop PC uses a local bus—which usually means a PCI bus for Pentium systems or a VESA local bus, a.k.a. VLB, for 486 systems—it probably came with a local bus video card. If you replace it, make sure you replace it with another local bus card.

Hint: It helps to know what kind of bus you have first. Check your manuals or call the manufacturer if you're not sure. And, by the way, lots of portable computers these days have their own versions of local bus video. Next time you buy a portable, you may want to look for that feature.

And that's about it, for our purposes, for video cards.

Designer Monitors

>Oh, sir, there's one more thing . . .
>
>Peter Falk, as Columbo

There's one last point I'd like to mention about monitors. Nokia, a company that makes great monitors, recently got the brilliant idea of making some monitors in designer colors—red, white, blue, green, and gray—instead of the usual off-white. The thought was that the colors would spruce up office decor and bring a touch of fashionable design to computers.

I've seen some reviewers compliment Nokia on this step forward in monitor design. I strongly suspect these people don't work with color graphics or color output. For those of us who do, the colored monitors are definitely not a Good Thing. They are a Bad Thing.

Forget the fact that nobody's making matching computers in red, white, blue, green, and gray.

Forget the fact that nobody's making matching keyboards either.

Forget the fact that without matching keyboards and computers, a colored monitor will stand out like a sore thumb, detracting from your office decor rather than adding to it. None of that matters. (But take a look at Figure 4.28, to see what I mean about sore thumbs.)

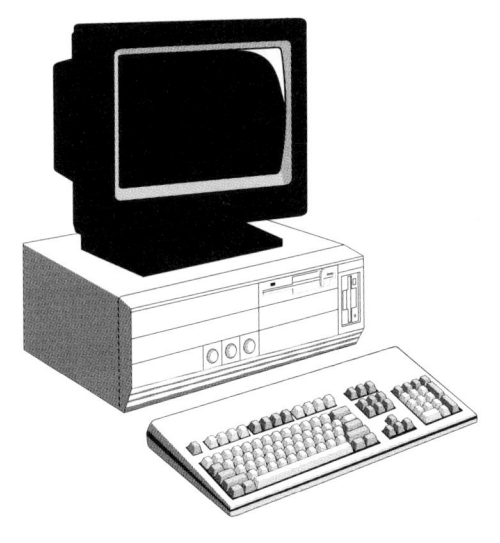

Figure 4.28 Accent colors on a colored monitor don't work without matching colors for the computer and keyboard.

What matters is that the colored bezel around the screen—that plastic piece that frames the monitor—is going to affect the colors you see. I've had a chance to play with the red version of the monitor, and I'm here to tell you, it ain't pretty.

Colored bezels affect the screen.

If you've read this book straight through from the beginning, you already know that a surrounding color affects the perception of colors. With the red Nokia monitor, the red bezel brings out the reds, makes light yellow seem much yellower, and makes Windows white a distinct off-white. Also, the dark outline of the red bezel detracts a bit from the image because of the sharp contrast between the bright screen and bezel, rather than the usual gentle fading from bright screen to not so bright on the periphery.

Don't take my word for this. Go get some red construction paper—that's about the right color—and cut out some strips that are just wide enough to cover the bezel on your monitor. Tape them together as a frame so you can easily pick the whole frame up or put it back down as a unit. Then try looking at a graphic on screen, first with the red frame and then without it. For the greatest effect, try closing your eyes as you add or remove the frame. This little experiment should be enough to convince you that colored monitors are a Bad Idea. But if you need further convincing, try the same experiment with some other colors.

The moral here is simple enough. If you're going to play with colors on the screen, don't mess with a colored monitor. Off-white may be dull to look at, but it works.

Any questions? No? Then let's get back to talking about printers. Next chapter, please.

5 Pick Your Poison

> One of the most common disrupters of marital bliss is the choice of where to spend a vacation. What this country needs is an ocean in the mountains.
>
> Paul Sweeney

The problem with having lots of choices available—whether they're for vacations or printers—is that you have to make a choice. A vacation at the ocean has a different attraction than a vacation in the mountains, and neither of them has much in common with a theater tour in London or New York.

The various choices in printers have their own attractions too. But even if you've already made your choice, or someone's made one for you, it helps to know as much as you can about the technology you're using.

The better you understand what goes on under the hood—uh, printer cover—the easier it is to predict how well your printer will handle any given kind of output. More generally, it's often useful to know what you can expect from any given technology—especially if you have the chance to beg, borrow, or plead your way into printing on someone else's printer.

In this chapter, we'll take a second pass at the different kinds of color printers—bangers, spitters, zappers, and heaters. (That's dot matrix, ink jet and wax jet, thermal wax and thermal dye, and lasers, if you've forgotten.) We'll cover some of the same territory as the section about printers in Chapter 1, but we'll cover it from a different perspective. We'll also explore each kind of printer a little more deeply and poke our noses into some of the darker corners.

So put on your spelunking gear, and check the batteries in your flashlight. Here we go.

COLOR PRINTERS: THE EXPERT'S TOUR

> An expert is a man who has made all the mistakes which can be made in a very narrow field.
>
> Niels Bohr
> Quoted in Alan Mackay, *The Harvest of a Quiet Eye* (1977)

Don't let this come as a shock, but the expert I have in mind for the expert's tour is you. If you've read the first four chapters of this book, you should have picked up enough about color and about printers to have a fair amount of expertise by now. If you've tried printing in color, you've probably made enough of your own mistakes to learn quite a bit more.

No bangers   So as one expert to another (I've certainly made enough mistakes to learn something), let's agree to ignore dot matrix printers. We don't need no bangers 'round here, for all the reasons I gave in Chapter 1. And with that out of the way, let's start with some general observations about paper, which is one of the more important issues for any printer.

Paper

> Whoever wants to know the heart and mind of America had better learn baseball, the rules and realities of the game.
>
> Jacques Barzun
> Quoted in Michael Novak, *The Joy of Sports*, pt. 1 (1976)

> Whoever wants to know how to use color printers had better learn about paper.
>
> Anonymous printer maven

Paper comes in all kinds of varieties—in different sizes, weights, and colors, and with and without special coatings. You can sort them all, however, into five broad categories: Plain paper, premium plain paper, ink jet and thermal wax paper, glossy paper, and thermal dye transfer paper. And like the Y in vowels there's a sometimes sixth category: transparencies.

Plain paper   Plain paper, for our purposes, is the kind of paper you might use in a copier or a typewriter. Most often, this means white, 20-pound weight copy paper, but it can include just about any kind of paper, in any color, from 20- to 25-pound weight, including cotton bond papers. Most envelopes and labels qualify as plain paper too.

By the way, here's something to file away under generally useless facts: Paper weight is the actual weight of 500 sheets of mill size paper of a given . . . uh . . . weight. That's equivalent to 2000 sheets of the same paper in letter size. So 2000 letter-size sheets of 20-pound weight paper—that's four packages of 500 sheets each—weighs 20 pounds. The heavier weight the paper, the more elegant it seems, up to a certain point. A 28-pound weight is elegant. A 50-pound weight is about right for a business card. An 80-pound weight is a good choice for a booklet cover. Then again, a 24- or 25-pound weight may be the most your printer's designed to handle.

Premium plain paper, which you could argue is a subcategory of plain paper, is any kind of general purpose special paper. (Does that sound like an oxymoron?) By *general purpose* I mean that it's not fine-tuned for a particular printer or brand of printers. By *special*, I mean it offers something different from plain old copy paper. Laser paper falls in this category. So do heavy-weight papers at 28-pound weight and heavier—including, say, sheets of business cards.

Premium plain paper

Ink jet and thermal wax papers are special-purpose papers—or a category of special-purpose papers—for (surprise) ink jet and thermal wax transfer printers. Don't think that papers for the two kinds of printers are interchangeable, though. They're not. I've lumped them together because they share the same general features. In both cases, the key difference from plain paper is a smooth surface on one side that accepts ink from ink jet printers or wax from thermal wax transfer printers better than plain paper can manage.

Ink jet and thermal wax paper

There was a time, not too long ago, when both ink jet and thermal wax papers were coated on one side. The typical coating was clay and was so obviously different from plain paper that you could spot the coating instantly. But most thermal wax papers today aren't coated. They're simply made to be smoother than plain paper. Coatings for current ink jet printers are also much less obvious and not necessarily made from clay—though clay is still the most common choice.

With today's papers, either kind of paper—thermal wax or ink jet paper—typically looks and feels much like plain paper. The paper may be a little heavier or lighter weight than copy paper, and it's usually a little shinier but not by much.

More precisely, coated paper for ink jets typically has a slightly heavier weight than 20-pound-weight copy paper, and a slightly smoother feel on the printing side. Paper for thermal wax printers may be either heavier or lighter than copy paper and typically has a slight shininess on both sides.

This relatively minor difference between the look and feel of plain paper and special-purpose thermal wax or ink jet paper is a Good Thing. It means that the paper doesn't call attention to itself. It's also an occasional pain. The problem is that the coatings on ink jet papers and the smooth size of thermal wax paper are so subtle these days that on some papers it's nearly impossible to tell which side to print on.

Impossible, that is, until you print.

When you print on the coated side with an ink jet printer, the inks aren't absorbed as much, so colors are more vibrant than on the uncoated side. You'll also get a noticeably larger color gamut printing with an ink jet printer on coated paper rather than on plain paper.

When you print on the smoother side of the paper with a thermal wax transfer printer, the wax sticks better than with the less smooth side—and much better than with standard paper. Print on the wrong side, or use the wrong paper, and you'll see dropouts—white spots on the page where there should be color. (The spots are called dropouts because the printer tried to put some wax there, but, like an unwilling student, the wax dropped out.) Print on the right side (as opposed to the wrong side, not the left side), and you'll see solid areas solidly filled in, wall to wall.

Some manufacturers are kind enough to mark the box the ink jet or thermal wax paper comes in with the message *print on this side*. **Then all you have to do is figure out whether the print side goes up or down in the paper bin. But if the box isn't marked or you lose track of which side is which after you've taken the paper out of the box, you've got a problem if you can't tell the difference.**

Sometimes the simplest way to find out which side is which is to print on both and compare the result. Mark the top side of the top three pages on a stack. Then take the top two pages, turn one over so it's facing the other way, and print the same color image on each page. You should see a significant difference, particularly if you have areas on the page with solid blocks of color. Once you know whether to print on the marked side or unmarked side, you can load the rest of the paper the right way. And keep in mind that plain paper has a right side for printing also, so you may want to try this same trick even with plain paper for printers that use plain paper. The difference won't be as dramatic as with ink jet or thermal wax paper, but every little bit helps.

One other trick you might want to try for determining which side to print on is one I mentioned in Chapter 2: You can rub each side of the paper against your lip. (And, as I said before, watch out for paper cuts.) Your lips are much more sensitive than your fingertips and should do a better job of spotting the smooth side.

Because ink jet and thermal wax papers are each designed to work with specific inks or specific wax ribbons, you should generally buy the papers your printer's manufacturer recommends. You'll usually find the name of the recommended paper somewhere in the printer manual, and it usually has the printer manufacturer's name on it. Expect it to be relatively expensive.

In a pinch, however, you may be able to use other printer's papers, particularly with ink jet printers. I've printed on Hewlett-Packard paper with a Canon printer and gotten noticeably better output than printing on plain paper.

This trick doesn't work as well with thermal wax transfer printers because issues like different temperature printheads and physically different waxes make thermal wax printers pickier about the paper they print on. Just to prove the point, I tried printing with a NEC Color SuperScript 3000 in thermal wax transfer mode using FARGO paper. The results were much better than with plain paper but not good.

If you try using plain paper with most thermal wax printers, you'll get enough white specks to make the image look like a television screen filled with snow. The NEC printer did a much better job with the FARGO thermal wax paper, but only in comparison, reducing the blizzard of white specks you'd expect on plain paper to lightly falling snow.

A second category of special paper, for ink jets only, is glossy paper. Actually, glossy paper also has a coating on one side of the paper, if you want to get nit-picky about it. Did someone say that makes it a coated paper too? Well, maybe so, but no one calls it that. (No one ever said that marketing departments are overly logical in picking names for their products.) If you ask for coated paper, it's not likely that anyone will hand you glossy paper instead, and if they did, you'd know it immediately.

Glossy paper

Unlike coated paper (by which I mean the nonglossy stuff), glossy paper is easy to spot, and it's easy to tell which side to print on. Although the coating on coated paper isn't obvious enough to draw attention to itself, the coating on glossy paper is . . . well . . . glossy. (No points for guessing that one.) It's also a heavier weight and feels different to the touch. All that makes it pretty hard to miss.

As a general rule, glossy paper will give you the best possible output from an ink jet printer, assuming you're using the specific glossy paper that's meant for the printer. The paper, ink, and the way the printer lays the ink down are all fine-tuned for each other so the printer can strut its stuff. Colors tend to be even more vibrant than on coated paper, and the color gamut is larger as well.

With at least one printer (I'm thinking of the Epson Stylus Color, but there may be others by the time you read this), you can even use a higher resolution on glossy paper than on other kinds of paper. The result can give you something very close to photographic quality output.

As with coated paper, glossy paper is designed for specific printers with specific inks. Unlike coated paper, however, glossy paper tends to be fussy about being matched up with the right printer and ink. If you try to use one manufacturer's glossy paper with another manufacturer's printer, you'll likely be disappointed with the results. As with coated paper, you'll usually find the name of the recommended paper somewhere in the printer manual, and the paper usually has the printer manufacturer's name on it.

> Even though the glossy paper for any given ink jet printer will usually give you the best possible image, glossy paper isn't always the paper of choice. Coated paper is often the best compromise between a high-quality image and paper that can mix with standard copier paper without standing out as too obviously different. Coated paper is also a lot easier on your budget. Coated ink jet paper is typically about ten cents a sheet. Glossy paper is often as much as a dollar a sheet.

Thermal dye transfer paper

Thermal dye transfer printers are the only kinds of printers that absolutely must use their own, special-purpose paper for all printers under all conditions. The paper is much heavier weight than plain paper and sports a shiny polyester coating on one side to absorb the dye. Yeah, I know; that makes it both coated and glossy. But since this is the only choice for thermal dye printers, coated and glossy are just descriptions, not names for identifying the paper.

Between the heavy weight and the polyester coating, thermal dye paper looks and feels very much like glossy photo paper. That's often appropriate, and even desirable, since thermal dye transfer printers do their most impressive work with photos. It also means that there's no way you'll ever mistake thermal dye paper for plain paper.

And sometimes Y— transparencies

Transparencies aren't paper. Not in any way, shape, or form. But sometimes it's convenient to lump them in with paper, in some wider, generic sense. For example, you might want to say *Ink jet printers let you use any of several papers, including plain paper, coated paper, glossy paper, and transparencies*. So sometimes when I refer to paper, I'll use it as shorthand for *paper plus transparencies*. (Yeah, the technically correct phrase would be *print media*, as in: *Ink jet printers can use any of several print media*. But somehow I can't bring myself to use the term.)

Be aware that even though all transparencies look essentially alike, they aren't. Well, sure, if you've seen though one transparency, you've pretty much seen through them all, but that doesn't mean that your printer can treat one transparency just like another.

As a general rule, you'll want to get the specific transparencies your printer manufacturer recommends. For one thing, different kinds of printers, and different models of printers, each need their own special coatings on the transparencies for the ink or dye to stick. Also, some printers depend on special markings on the transparencies to tell them that they're printing on a transparency instead of paper.

Once again, you should find the name of the recommended transparencies somewhere in the printer manual, and it will usually have the printer manufacturer's name on it. Expect transparencies to be expensive, particularly for thermal dye transfer printers.

The Importance of Plain Paper

> Do not conceive that fine clothes make fine men, any more than fine feathers make fine birds. A plain, genteel dress is more admired, obtains more credit in the eyes of the judicious and sensible.
>
> George Washington

Now that we have those definitions out of the way, let's talk a little bit about the paper you print on. For most people and most purposes, the ideal printer will print on plain paper.

One reason for using plain paper is simply to save money. Special-purpose papers, particularly the paper for thermal dye transfer printers, can be expensive. But a more important reason for some people is that plain paper lets you use the same paper for your color pages as for your black and white pages.

Of course, if the only time you ever print in color is for pages that stand by themselves, like party invitations, this isn't an issue. But if you need to mix color pages in with black and white text, you'll find that sticking individual pages of heavy-weight or glossy paper between plain paper pages draws attention to the paper itself, which can be distracting.

Whether you're printing a report for a client, a term paper for school, or a newsletter for your homeowner's association, the finished product will generally feel more professional if all the pages have the same weight and feel. The main exception to this rule is that you can usually get away with heavier weight paper for the color images if you have a separate section of color images—like the color section in this book.

There's another benefit to plain paper too. It not only lets you use the same paper for color images as for text, but it lets you mix color on the same page as text. If you want to include a color graphic that's not big enough to need a page of its own, you can stick it on the page with text around it. The result will look a lot more professional than having a separate page with a small color image and lots of blank space around it. **Mixing color images with text**

Did someone ask why you couldn't do the same thing with a printer that uses a special, heavy-weight paper? Well, you can. But again, the paper would stand out as different, and the text would look a little different from the way it looks on plain paper too. Here again, the differences are likely to be distracting, and the finished product simply wouldn't look as professional.

The advantages of printing color images on plain paper are even greater if you can print your black and white pages with the same printer as part of the same print job. **One printer fits all.**

If you're using a different printer for color and for black and white, you have to print color pages separately from black and white pages, and then collate them.

If you're printing both on one printer that can bounce back and forth between color and monochrome, you can just insert your color images along with your text in your newsletter, report, or whatever, and then give the command to print. Everything gets put together at the printer, and all you have to do is retrieve the finished product from the output bin.

Did someone mumble that you can print black and white pages on any printer?

Well . . . if you want to get nit-picky about it, Yes, that's true. You can use any color printer for black and white also. The only problem is that if you're using, say, a ribbon-based thermal wax printer, you'll have to wait longer than I'd consider reasonable for each page, while the printer goes through all of the colors on the ribbon. You'll also have to pay for all the colored ribbon that you didn't use.

Let's get practical.
If you want a printer that's practical both for black and white and for color, you need one that can bypass colors when it doesn't need them. That way, if everything on the page is black, the printer won't have to waste any time rolling through cyan, magenta, and yellow ribbon panels that it's not using. And you won't have to waste any money paying for inks (or wax, or dye, or whatnot) that never got anywhere near the paper.

And that, conveniently enough, takes us to the spitters, starting with ink jet printers, which are one of the obvious choices for printing on plain paper.

INK JET PRINTERS

The palest ink is better than the best memory.

Chinese proverb

Ink jet printers offer three key strengths: They don't cost as much as other kinds of color printers, they can print on plain paper, and they let you use the same printer for printing in color and in black and white. Some offer other strengths as well. But before we get into that, let's be clear that not all ink jet printers are created equal.

Virtually all color ink jet printers today fall into one of two categories. Some happily print in color or black and white depending only on what you send to the printer. Others are nasty curmudgeons that are stuck in one mode or the other until you change ink cartridges.

The difference between the two groups is how many different color inks the printer can hold at once. Printers that can easily switch back and forth have room for all four colors—cyan, yellow, magenta, and black—either in four separate cartridges or in one cartridge for black ink and one for the three colored inks. Either version is a four-color printer.

Printers in the curmudgeon group have room for either a black cartridge or a color cartridge with cyan, yellow, and magenta, but they don't have room for both cartridges at the same time. I'll call these three-color printers, for lack of a better term. (Crippled, would be another possibility, but I wouldn't want to prejudice you against them. Not too much, anyway.)

The advantage of three-color printers is that they tend to be cheaper than four-color printers, by which I mean less expensive, not necessarily chintzy. Their disadvantage is that at any given moment, they're set up as either monochrome printers or color printers. To change them from one to another, you have to change cartridges.

Three-color printers

That means you can't, for example, put a color page in the middle of a monochrome document and expect it to print in color. Instead, you're in the same pickle as if you had two printers—one for color and one for black and white. You have to print all the monochrome pages in one print run, print the color pages in another, and collate the two by hand.

Three-color ink jet printers are also poor choices for printing both black text and color on the same page. They can print a composite black, by combining all three inks, but as I've pointed out elsewhere in this book, composite black tends to be off-black. And it wastes a lot of ink.

The advantage of four-color printers is that they're true switch hitters, jumping back and forth between color and monochrome as quickly as your computer can send a command. Printing a color page in the middle of a black and white document is a snap, and printing a color image in the middle of a black and white page is no big deal either.

Four-color printers

The disadvantage of four-color ink jets is that they are more expensive than their three-color cousins. The last time I looked, however, (which was two days ago, as I write this) the least expensive four-color printers were only about $20 more than the most expensive three-color printers. Keep that in mind the next time you buy an ink jet printer.

Here's something to file under disclaimers: These comments about color ink jet printers falling into two groups is a general rule, not a universal law. They apply to almost any, if not any, color ink jet printer you can buy today, but not to every color ink jet printer ever made.

Some older members of this breed use only three inks: cyan, yellow, and magenta. And the only way they can produce black is to use all three inks. Other dinosaur jets offer four colors of ink, but were designed strictly with color printing in mind and are so slow that you wouldn't want to use them for black text. Printers from either category are decidedly bad choices for printing anything but color, and most of them weren't so good at color either. Now that you know to watch out for these at garage sales, I'll ignore them. Just don't assume that every color ink jet printer you see is automatically useful for black and white printing also.

So much for what's good about ink jet printers. Now for the bad and the occasionally ugly.

When the Ink Drops Meet the Page

> If I've learned anything in my seventy years, it's that nothing's as good or as bad as it appears.
>
> Bushrod H. Campbell

Watch an ink jet printer do its thing, and you'll immediately see that this breed spray paints the page in bands. The printhead moves across the page, the printer advances the paper, and then the printhead moves across the page again for the next band.

Another kind of banding

The inevitable result is that the printed output often shows visible bands across the page. I'm not talking about the sort of bands you get from not having enough colors available for a gradient fill. That gives you a distinctly different color or different shade in each band. I'm talking about lines of a lighter or darker color or even lines of white running across the image, as in Figure 5.1. The lines break the image into bands even within a solid block of otherwise consistent color.

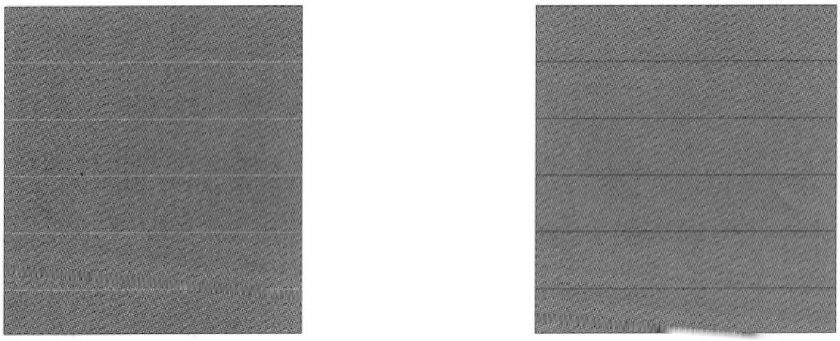

Figure 5.1 Ink jet output is often broken up into bands with light lines, as on the left, or dark lines, as on the right.

Some printers show bands like this from the day you take them out of the box until the day you move on to something better. But most printers let you get rid of the bands at least under some conditions.

Why you get bands

In general, you'll see dark lines separating bands when the printhead overlaps the bands just a bit. The thin dark line shows where you have extra ink on the page because of the overlap. You'll see light lines when the printhead leaves a little gap between bands or when there's a clogged nozzle so the ink can't get to the page. Let's ignore clogged nozzles for a moment, however.

One reason you might get visible bands is because of misregistration.

Say again?

Registration isn't just what you do when you sign up for voting. It also refers to the alignment of different parts of an image. When you create an image by assembling different pieces, like the individual bands the printhead spray paints, each piece has to be aligned properly, or registered. If the registration is off, the bands may overlap or have gaps between them.

Some ink jet printers offer a registration test pattern that lets you pick the best alignment out of a choice of alignments for the printhead. You run the test and pick the alignment that shows the least banding—ideally none.

If you see banding when you first get your hands on a printer and you've already ruled out clogged nozzles, your first step should be to go directly to your manual and look up registration test, test print, alignment test, printhead test, test patterns, and any other variation you can think of, until you find the test or are convinced that your printer doesn't offer it. Run the test if it's available, and set the printer for the right registration before you try other solutions.

Misregistration can also crop up on some printers when the printhead is printing both left to right and right to left, as in Figure 5.2. Much better for eliminating bands is to print each band left to right, move the printhead back to the left side, and then print the next band left to right again, as in Figure 5.3. The only reason for not printing this way is that it takes longer, since the printhead has to move over each band twice—once to get to the starting position and once to print.

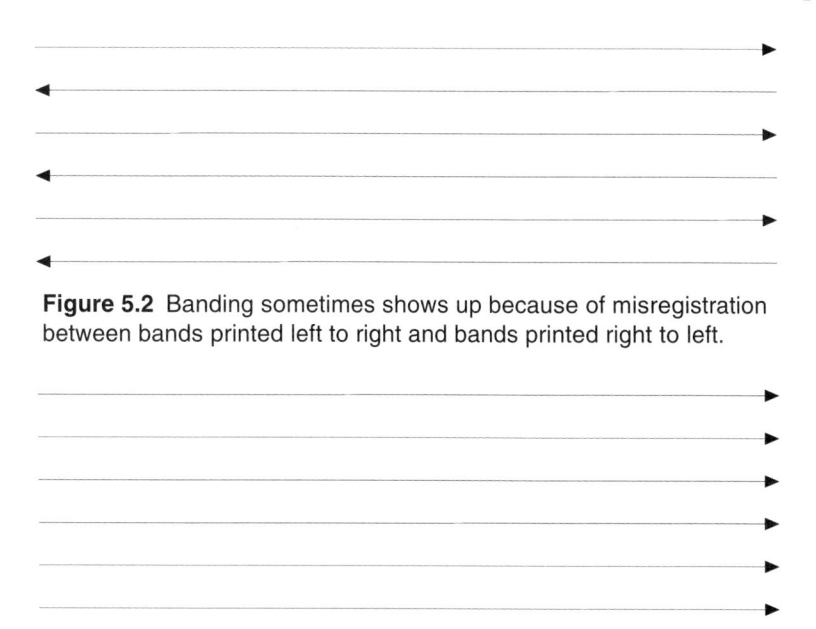

Figure 5.2 Banding sometimes shows up because of misregistration between bands printed left to right and bands printed right to left.

Figure 5.3 Banding is less likely when the printer prints all the bands from left to right, although this slows the printer down a bit.

Printing in both directions, as in Figure 5.2, is called bidirectional printing. Printing in one direction, as in Figure 5.3, is called unidirectional printing.

Now comes the hard part.

If changing from bidirectional printing to unidirectional printing can make bands disappear, you don't need me to point out that you should try setting the printer for unidirectional printing to see if the bands go away.

No. That's wasn't the hard part. The hard part is finding out how to set the printer for unidirectional printing.

In the bad old days, when printer manuals were filled with indecipherable jargon, the settings for unidirectional and bidirectional printing were easy to find in the manual and easy to change on the printer. All you had to do was look up unidirectional or bidirectional in the manual's index, and then change a switch or a menu setting.

No more.

Most printer manufacturers have gone out of their way today to make both their manuals and their printer settings more "user friendly," if you'll pardon the expression. I put *user friendly* in quotes partly because it's one of the uglier phrases in technobabble and partly because it often means oversimplifying things to the point where you can't find out what you need to know.

What sort of oversimplification, you ask? Try this: Most ink jet printers have settings to let you adjust how the printer will print on different kinds of paper. You set the printer for plain paper, transparencies, coated paper, glossy paper, or whatnot and the printer will adjust how it prints to match.

If you're working in an environment like Windows or on the Mac, you should find choices for the various settings in the printer's driver. If you're working from a DOS program, you can typically set the paper type with buttons on the printer itself.

In theory, the adjustment can be almost anything—the amount of ink the printer sprays on the page, the speed it moves the printhead across the page, a change in the proportion of dots in each primary color, a change from unidirectional to bidirectional printing, and so on.

Unfortunately, you won't generally find this information in printer manuals. And knowing what one printer does doesn't tell you anything about another printer, since different printers often have different choices in paper types. Worse, even when the choices have the same names, two printers picked at random are likely to make different adjustments for any given paper type—even if the two printers are from the same manufacturer.

Pick up the typical ink jet printer manual today, and you'll find a clearly written, heavily illustrated, easy-to-read introduction to your printer. But odds are you won't find any details about its various print modes or any mention of unidirectional or bidirectional printing, much less any indication of how to set the printer for one or the other.

This doesn't mean that you can't set it though.

Sometimes, as with some printers from Canon, the setting for unidirectional versus bidirectional simply goes by another name. According to Canon, in fact, that's the only—I repeat, *only*—difference between the plain paper setting and the coated paper setting for some of its printers, including the BJC-600e. Coated paper, for Canon, is simply an alternate pronunciation for unidirectional printing. Plain paper is an alternate pronunciation for bidirectional printing.

Unidirectional and bidirectional: Alternate pronunciations

The logic behind this seems to be that if you're printing on plain paper, you probably don't care all that much about how the output looks, so you might as well use bidirectional printing. But if you're printing on coated paper, you must care, so you should use unidirectional printing.

The flaw in the logic is that even when you're printing on plain paper, you may very well care what the output looks like. If you do, you'll want to set the printer for unidirectional printing . . . uh, I mean coated paper . . . even though you're printing on plain paper.

In other printers, the setting for unidirectional and bidirectional is mixed in with other settings. Hewlett-Packard, for example, ties the unidirectional and bidirectional feature to its print quality settings—fast, normal, and presentation—at least with the DeskJet 560C. (HP also stresses that identical settings do different things for each of its printers.)

In fast mode with plain paper, the 560C is strictly bidirectional. In normal mode and presentation mode, it uses something HP calls smart bidirectional printing, which means it's bidirectional where there's a gap in the image, as with lines of text, but unidirectional otherwise.

There now, isn't that much easier to understand than unidirectional and bidirectional? Yeah, right. (I mean: Yeah, write—to printer manufacturers that do this sort of oversimplification. Tell them you'd rather have the information you need to really use the printer.)

Be aware that apparently simple changes in settings can change several features at once, and that a given setting may interact with other settings. For the 560C, for example, changing between fast, normal, and presentation modes not only sets the printer for bidirectional or smart directional, it changes resolution and something that HP calls shingling.

Picture the page as an extended checkerboard, with one checkerboard square for each dot. In shingling, the printer fills the black squares on one pass and the red squares on a second pass. It also overlaps bands, by filling the red squares in one band, with the top half of the print nozzles, at the same time it's filling in the black squares in the next band, with the bottom half of the print nozzles. That's two-pass shingling. Four-pass shingling is similar, but the printer fills in every fourth square on the first pass and comes back three more times to fill in the missing dots. This interlacing of bands also helps minimize banding.

> If you set a 560C for plain paper, fast and normal modes don't use shingling, but presentation mode uses two-pass shingling. Set the printer for HP LX JetSeries paper, and normal mode uses two-pass shingling while presentation mode uses four-pass shingling. You probably won't want to use the LX settings for plain paper, however, since HP says that also changes the amount of ink the printer puts on the page. But none of this applies to any other printer, including other HP printers, since every printer is different.
>
> The point is, you won't usually know what the printer settings are doing unless you call the manufacturer and bug tech support for the information. Then, while you're waiting on hold, you might try printing some samples using different printer settings. If you can see the current band the printhead is working on, as you can with some printers, you may be able to tell whether it's printing bidirectionally or unidirectionally in each mode. (Try opening the printer cover during printing so you can see the printhead and the paper.) Other differences in printing are harder to spot, but if you use the same paper for each mode, you can certainly see what effect each one has on the output.

Once you've figured out how to make your printer print unidirectionally, you can try it out to see if the bands disappear. If the output doesn't look any better, then printing bidirectionally isn't your problem. If the bands still show but not as much, it's only part of the problem.

Nozzles and Drops

> From a drop of water a logician could infer the possibility of an Atlantic or a Niagara without having seen or heard of one or the other.
>
> Sir Arthur Conan Doyle
> Sherlock Holmes, in *A Study in Scarlet*, pt. 1, ch. 2 (1887)

If the ink from ink jet printers went on dry and didn't spread at all, you'd be pretty much stuck with whatever bands you happen to get after adjusting the registration and switching to unidirectional printing. But the ink doesn't go on dry, and it does spread, mostly by being absorbed into the paper.

If you could actually see what's going on at the printhead during printing, you would see that the ink gets sprayed from a relatively large number of individual nozzles—typically a few dozen but sometimes hundreds in the more expensive members of the breed. If you could also slow things down enough to see details, you would see that the ink comes out as individual drops, with each drop carefully controlled and aimed at the page.

Now comes the fun part, when the ink hits the paper.

If a given piece of paper absorbs ink too well (compared to what the printer design expects) or not well enough, you can wind up with two bands overlapping to form a dark line, or not meeting up properly to form a light-colored line or even a white line.

And that's another way you can get bands.

Now here's the good news: All of this means you can usually affect the bands—and sometimes make them disappear—by changing the paper you're using. If one of the differences between paper settings for your printer is how much ink gets sprayed on the page, you can also affect bands by telling the printer that you're using a different kind of paper.

Beating the bands

Changing paper usually gives you the best shot at getting rid of the bands, particularly if the printer manufacturer sells its own special-purpose paper and the printer offers a setting specifically for that paper.

Using special paper

The problem that any ink jet printer has with printing on plain paper is that there are so many different kinds of plain paper. Even for any given weight or type of paper, you'll find variations from one brand to another. And that means that the plain paper setting on your ink jet printer may not be right for any given plain paper that you pick at random.

The flip side of that record is that manufacturers can fine-tune ink jet printers to particular papers. So if you use paper that's specifically recommended for the printer, and you set the printer for that paper, you're likely to see bands magically melt away. (And don't forget the more vibrant colors and larger color gamut that I've already mentioned.)

The problem with special papers is that they cost more than plain paper. Before you spend the extra money, you might want to experiment a bit with other brands of plain paper or premium plain paper. Simply changing brands can make the banding better or worse.

I've found that with a Canon BJC-600e set for printing on plain paper, for example, I get less obvious bands with Staples copy paper than with some other paper I've tried. Hammermill laser paper does even better; the bands are still there, but they're subtle enough so you could easily miss them.

Using different plain paper

Don't try to generalize from this example. With a Hewlett-Packard DeskJet 560C set for printing on plain paper, I get band-free output on the same Staples copy paper that shows bands with the Canon printer. That doesn't mean that the HP 560C is a better printer, though. The HP DeskJet 1200C, which is unquestionably a better printer than the 560C, also winds up with bands on the Staples paper. You have to experiment on a case-by-case basis.

You might also want to experiment with setting the printer for different types of paper without actually changing paper, even if you have no idea what the printer is doing differently with the different settings.

With the Canon BJC-600e, for example, I've found that if I set the printer for glossy paper when I print on the Staples copy paper, the bands all but disappear. Unfortunately that's at the cost of blues and greens getting noticeably darker

Using different settings for the printer

because the printer sprays extra ink on the page when it's set for glossy paper, and the plain paper absorbs the ink.

If I use the Hammermill laser paper, however, and set the printer for glossy paper, the bands disappear without any change in color. If I set the printer for coated paper, which is the same as the plain paper setting but with unidirectional printing, the bands disappear on both kinds of paper, without changing the colors on either.

> **Pretty cool way to avoid buying the more expensive paper, huh? But don't expect miracles from either of these tricks. Just consider them experiments worth trying. Keep in mind that if you switch to a mode that uses more ink, you're still paying more per page for the ink. On the other hand, you'd have to use that same extra ink with the special-purpose paper anyway, so you're still saving the price of the more expensive paper—or at least the difference between the expensive paper and the paper you're using.**

Clogged Nozzles

> We sensed the devil in the machine and we were right.
>
> Oswald Spengler

Once you've figured out the right paper and settings to make banding disappear, or at least keep it to a minimum, you shouldn't see bands show up again—unless, of course, a nozzle gets clogged by a piece of dust, an air bubble, or dried ink. Nozzles get clogged all by themselves, particularly if you haven't printed for more than a few days. It's part of the joy of ink jet printing.

If you suddenly see banding where there was none before and you haven't dropped your printer lately to knock the printhead out of alignment, it's probably time to clean the nozzles. If you don't know which nozzles need cleaning, you should find that the printer can help you out. Most, if not all, ink jet printers offer a self-test that will show you if any nozzles are clogged, and if so, which colors they affect.

> **The way you run the self-test varies from one printer to another. You should find directions for running the self-test in your manual, or, if you're lucky, on the printer itself. If they're not on the printer, you may want make a copy of the instructions and paste them on the printer for future reference. Manuals are too easy to misplace. If the instructions are on the printer, you'll always know where to find them.**

Looking for clogs (not shoes) The self-test output is also different on different printers, but it typically includes four solid blocks of colors—in cyan, yellow, magenta, and black—as well as a set of thin horizontal lines in each of the four ink colors. Each set of lines is typically similar to the set of lines in Figure 5.4.

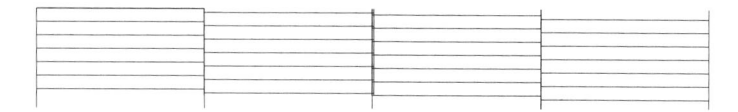

Figure 5.4 The self-test for checking for clogged nozzles in ink jet printers usually looks something like this.

If the self-test includes solid blocks of color and you have a clogged nozzle, it should show as a thin white streak in one of the blocks, but the clog will be even easier to spot in the horizontal lines. Since the printer draws each line with a single nozzle, a clog will show as a missing line. Either way—with a white streak or a missing line—you'll not only know you have a clogged nozzle, but you'll know which color is clogged.

Knowing which color or colors are clogged is important. You can often tell when you have a clogged nozzle, based on normal output, because you'll see streaks of the wrong colors where one of the inks didn't make it to the page. But if you're not sure which color is missing, your only choice is to clean all the nozzles. That wastes ink for the colors that don't have a problem. If you know which color is missing, you can clean the nozzles for that color only.

With some printers, cleaning the nozzles means giving a command through the front panel. With other printers, you'll find a plunger that you pump manually to clean the nozzles. In either case, you should be able to clean the nozzles for just those colors that have a problem.

All this should seem simple enough. And it is. In theory. In practice, however, you'll occasionally run into some Weird Stuff.

It's not quite as simple as it sounds.

A case in point: While I've been writing this chapter, I've been running tests so I can talk about things I'm actually looking at. I started out by firing up a Canon BJC-600e that I haven't used in several weeks, and I printed a test page that included blocks of cyan, magenta, yellow, blue, red, and green.

The first page came out with slight banding—with light-colored lines—on the cyan, blue, and green blocks. This was a dead giveaway that there was a clogged nozzle for cyan, so I ran the cleaning routine on cyan.

This should have solved the problem, right?

Well, that's what I thought, but when I printed the test page again, I wound up with even more bands—separated by light lines again—in cyan, blue, and green.

The problem that wouldn't quit

So I ran the cleaning routine on cyan again, and this time the lines separating the bands came out almost white. This was not progress. Or it was progress in the wrong direction.

I was already familiar enough with the Canon printer to know that the output on plain paper looks better if the printer's set for coated paper. So I decided I might as well try it that way to see what would happen. (I was grasping at straws.) At the same time, I set the driver to use the printer's so-called Color mode rather than its Color Advisor mode, which is something we don't need to go into here, except to say that it takes an extra step to print with the Color Advisor. Understand that I didn't think that turning off the Color Advisor would do anything; I was just getting tired of running through that extra step.

So I printed the page again and . . . you guessed it . . . even without cleaning the nozzles again, the test page came out with no banding.

Then, for the kicker, I set the driver back to plain paper and back to the Color Advisor mode and tried one more time—just to see if either of those settings had made the difference.

I wound up with the least banding I've ever seen from this printer using this particular paper and this printer setting. And the printer's been working without problems ever since.

What happened?

Beats me. There could have been a speck of dust or a blob of dried ink that refused to come out during cleaning but came out later when I was printing. Or maybe not. But it doesn't really matter what happened. The point is that Weird Stuff does happen. And you need to keep your eye out for streaks showing up or getting worse in ink jet output, even after you've printed a test page and checked the results.

The rule of thumb for keeping your eye out for banding and streaks is to always check the first few pages you print after not having printed in color for more than a day. That holds true even if the first page looks okay. As my little story shows, the banding can get worse with each additional page, at least until it starts getting better. If you haven't printed in color in several days, it's also a good idea to run the printer's self-test first. It doesn't cost anywhere near as much ink or time as having to reprint a page of color graphics because of banding or streaks.

Once you've printed several pages in a single session, clogs are more likely to go away than get worse. If you resort to cleaning, be aware that sometimes you need to run the cleaning cycle five to ten times to get rid of clogs. If you still have a problem after 10 times, you probably have a bad printhead or are out of ink (possibly because you just ran the head-cleaning routine 10 times).

Keep an eye on the output.   There's another reason to keep a careful eye on your output also, at least with some printers. Some ink jet printers have sensors that tell them when they've run out of one color of ink. The printer may continue printing a while after running out, until it realizes that it has run out, but once it gets the message, it will stop and wait for you to replace the cartridge.

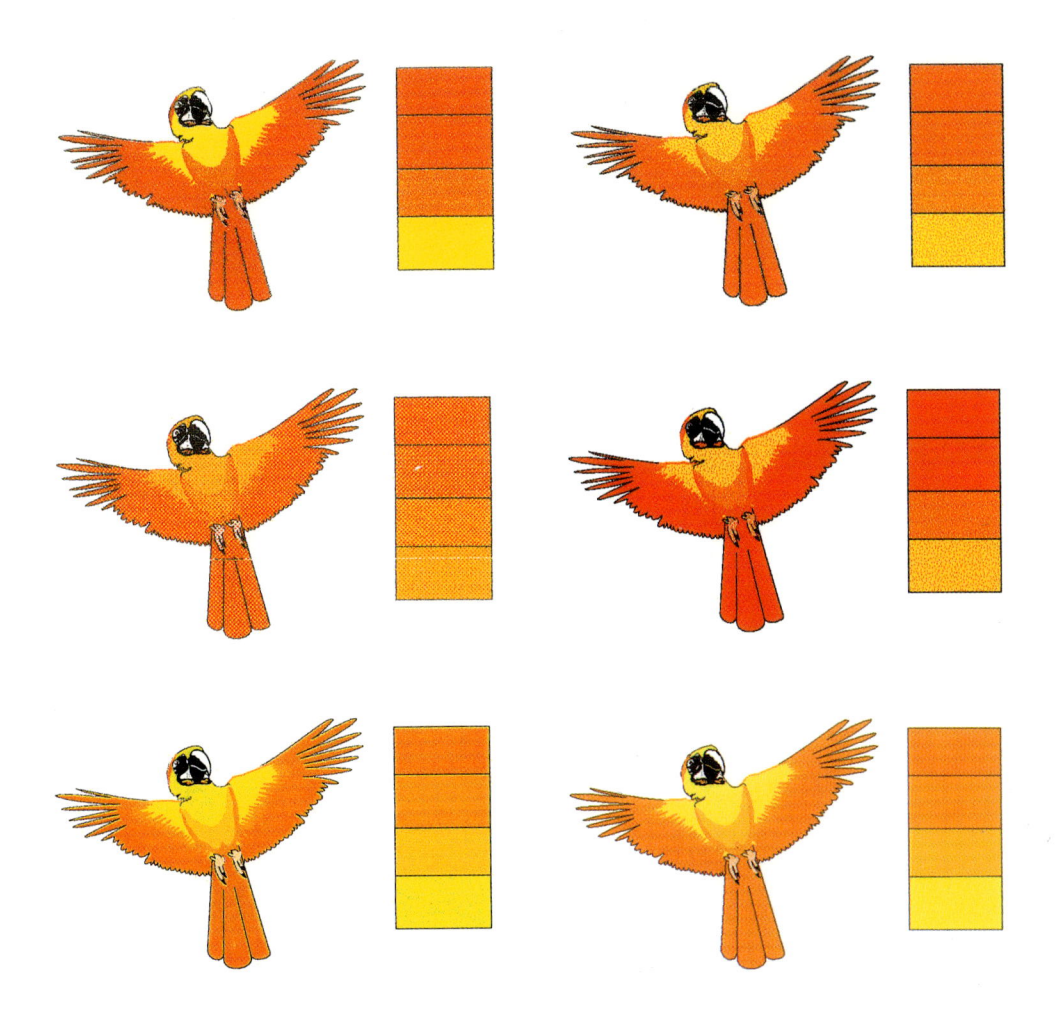

How many colors can you see here? (Warning: That's a trick question.) You're looking at six copies of one file printed on five different printers—including one printer in two modes.

Lesson one: None of the printers match any of the others for all four colors. The Hewlett-Packard DeskJet 1200C/PS, in PCL mode at the top left and PostScript mode at the top right, doesn't even match itself.

Lesson two: Colors that are different on screen can turn into the same color on paper—particularly when you're using a monochrome color scheme with a single hue but variations in brightness and saturation. Only the Apple Color LaserWriter 12/600 PS parrot, at the bottom left, shows four distinct colors. The NEC SuperScript Color 3000 parrot at the bottom right also (barely) shows four colors on the original, but the two darkest oranges are so close that the distinction can easily be lost in later generations, like the version on this page. None of these parrots show as much difference on paper between the two darkest oranges as you can see on screen.

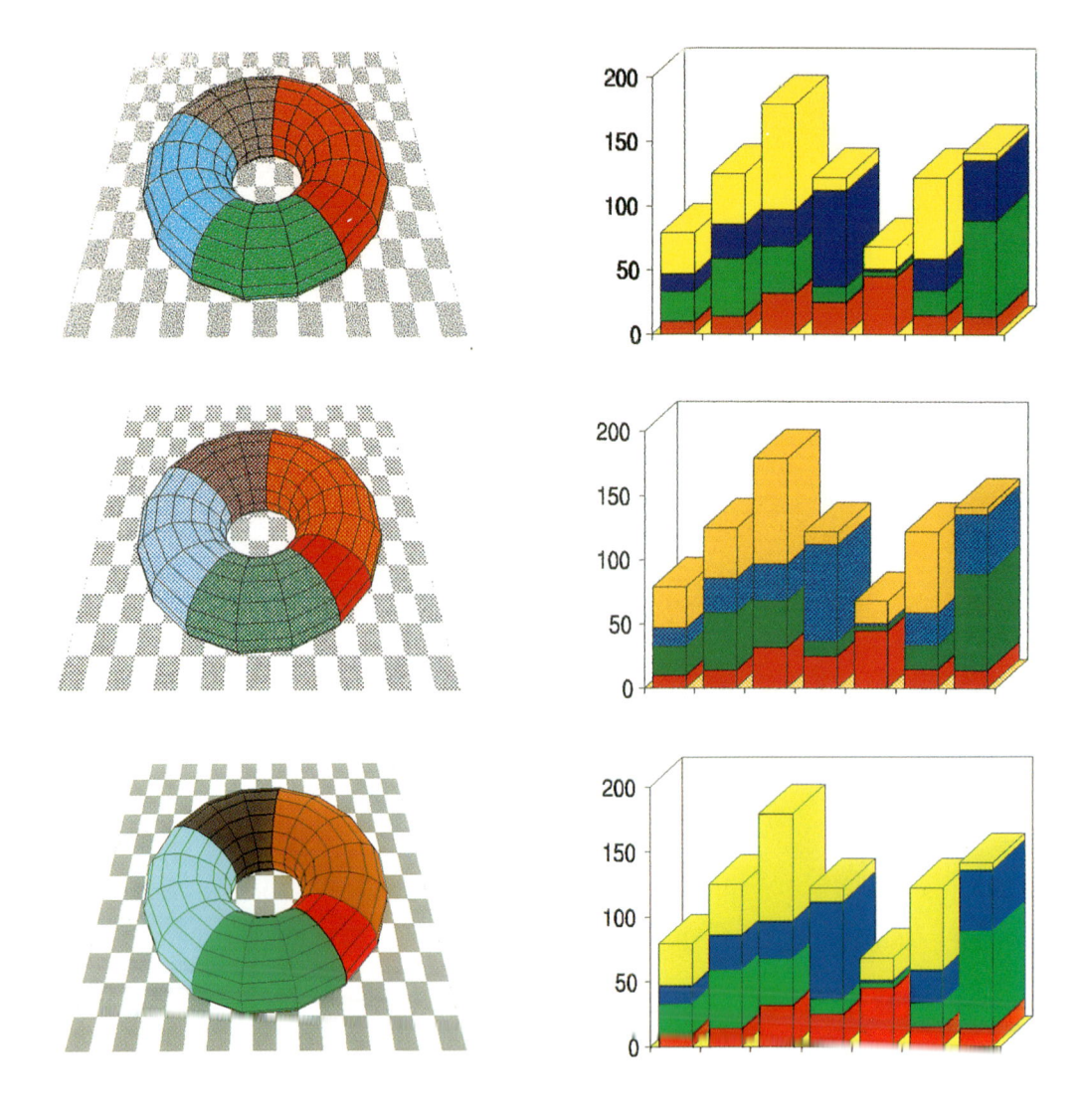

The difference in color from one printer to another can be enough to make a graphic work or not. Each pair of graphics on this page and the next was printed from the same file, but on a different printer. A quick glance should be enough to convince you that there are differences in color, but take a close look and you'll see some other problems too.

The two top graphs on this page were printed on an HP 1200 in PCL mode. Notice that the red wedge in the torus nearly disappears into the orange.

The Canon BJC 600e torus in the middle doesn't have that problem, but the bar chart colors are a little muddy. The green and blue in particular don't stand out as separate colors as clearly as they should, which makes the chart a little hard read.

The charts from the FARGO Primera Pro at the bottom don't have readability problems.

2

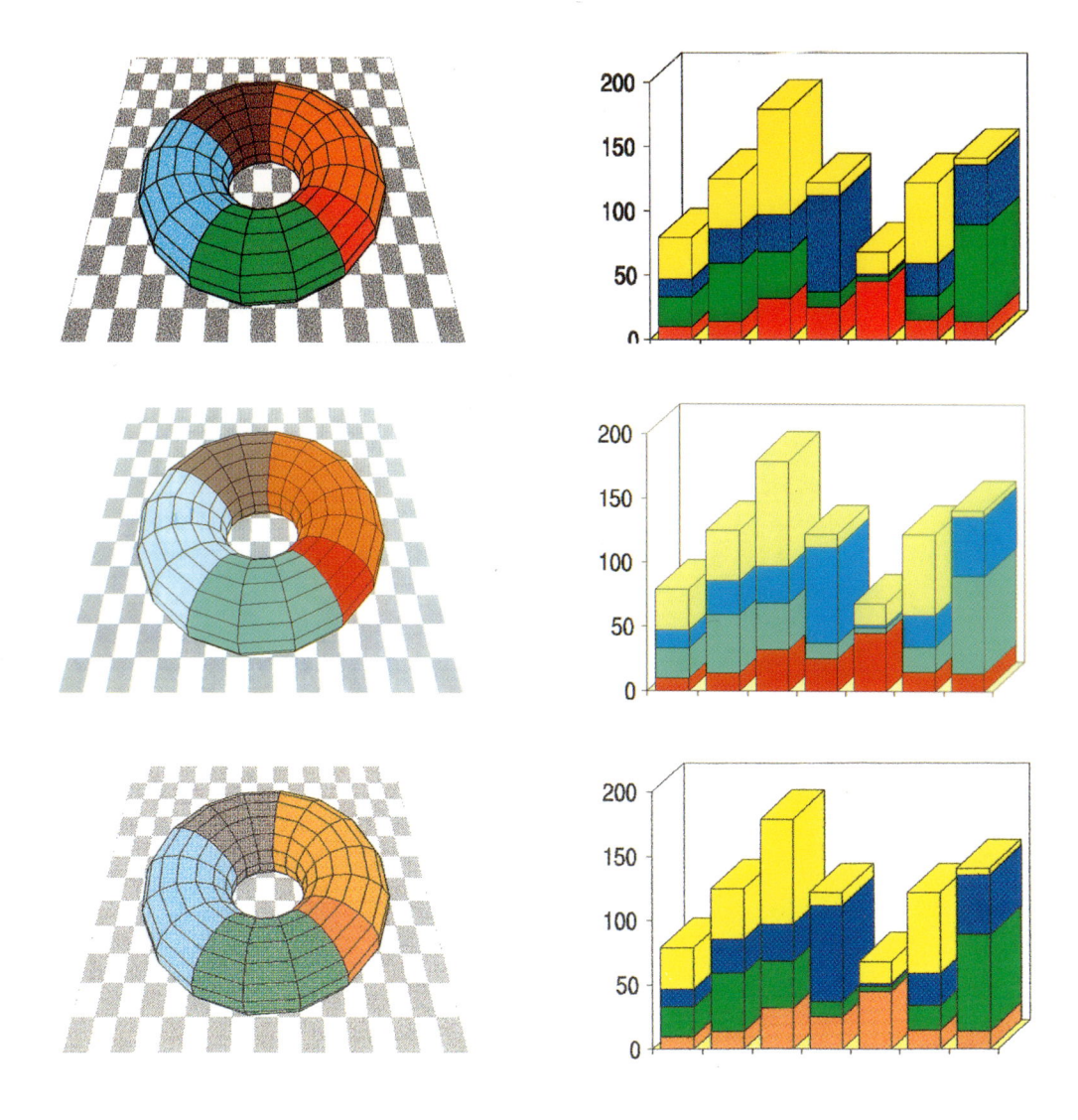

The two graphs at the top of this page were printed on a Tektronix 340, and stand out from all the others because of the fully saturated colors that are typical of wax jet technology. The middle two graphs are the NEC 3000's handiwork.

The bottom graphs on this page were printed on the HP 560C. With these particular files, the colors from the 560C work better together than the colors from the HP 1200 at the top of the facing page. That's because they're a little less saturated. Here again, the lesson is that just because you can print highly saturated colors doesn't mean you have to every time.

Even the color matching feature in PostScript Level 2 won't make the colors from different printers match. And just in case you think it will, this page is meant to disillusion you.

These three pairs of graphs were printed on PostScript Level 2 printers that were set to match color across printers. While the colors in these tori do a better job of matching each other than with printers in general, there are still obvious differences, particularly with the greens, which vary from a dark green in the top torus to a blue green in the bottom torus. And notice that the red in the top torus is hard to distinguish from the orange.

Differences between the combined bar and area graphs are more dramatic, with the bars varying from dark brown to reddish brown and the two shades of blue varying from very different to nearly the same. The moral: Don't expect colors to match if you print the same file on different printers. (And certainly don't expect the colors to match your screen.)

Most printers don't even necessarily match themselves.

In case you still have any fantasies about matching colors between printers or between your printer and screen, here's a final chance to wake up to reality.

Both graphics in each pair on this page were printed on the same printer from the same file. The differences in color are pretty obvious. I got that difference by setting the printer (a Tektronix 340) for different modes—*vivid color* in one case and *simulate display* in the other (although neither version matches the screen very well).

So colors don't match between screen and printer, or between one printer and another, and sometimes not even between a printer and itself.

What a difference a dot makes. Or sometimes not.

Thermal dye printers do the best job for photos, and the Tektronix 440 is one of the best of the breed. If you see any difference between this and a photo you're probably kidding yourself. The resolution is 300 dpi, but you don't see any dots because thermal dye printers don't mix color by dithering.

A good color laser printer comes in at a close second to thermal dye printers. But notice that there is a little less sense of three dimensionality, because there's a little less gradation in colors. The difference is easiest to see in the left-most green pepper. The resolution here is 600 dpi.

The best wax jet printers are a close match for the best laser printers, but all other things being equal, resolution will make a difference. The resolution here is 600 by 300, and it shows as a still more flattened effect, fewer highlights, and a slight graininess in the yellows and yellow greens.

Thermal wax printers are usually a bad choice for photos. This sample, printed at 300 dpi without any techniques to hide dithering, shows why. You can see dithering patterns and posterization—a sharp change in colors that should change gradually. The large pepper that goes from top to bottom about a third of the way from the left, for example, shows three distinct vertical stripes—in green, orange, and red.

Most ink jet printers aren't a good choice for photos either, and those few that are do their best work on special paper. But a few do a credible job on standard paper. The resolution here is 300 dpi, with enhancement techniques to hide the dithering patterns. Compare this to the thermal dye sample at the top of the facing page, however, and you'll see that a lot is missing here.

This is a more typical example of how ink jet printers handle photos—with graininess, posterization, and relatively unsaturated colors. The dithering patterns are less obvious here than in the thermal wax sample at the top of the page, largely because of a slightly higher resolution at 360 dpi.

These samples teach a simple lesson: Dots per inch is only a small part of the story.

This is some
sample text.
It may be a
touch brown.

This is some
sample text.
But it's black
here. Always.

This is some
sample text.
And it's black
here too.

Blacker blacks isn't a great motto for laundry detergent, but it's a great one printers, particularly ribbon-based printers.

    The samples on this page all come from the same thermal wax printer, but different ribbons.

    The top gray scale bar and the left-most graphic and text were printed with a three-color ribbon; the middle bar, graphic, and text with a four-color ribbon; and the bottom bar, right-most graphic, and text with a monochrome ribbon. The difference between the three-color and four-color ribbon is subtle but real. Take a look at the lighter shades of gray in particular, which are browner with the three-color ribbon than with the four-color ribbon.

    The difference between both color ribbons and the monochrome ribbon is more obvious, with even the four-color ribbon somewhat brown compared to the monochrome. That's because the printer is still using cyan, magenta, and yellow, as well as black, to print black and gray. The slightest misalignment of the paper on any pass through the printer translates to an off-black. So if you want the blackest blacks and the purest grays, use a monochrome ribbon. But if there's some color in the image as well, a four-color ribbon will usually give you better blacks and grays than a three-color ribbon.

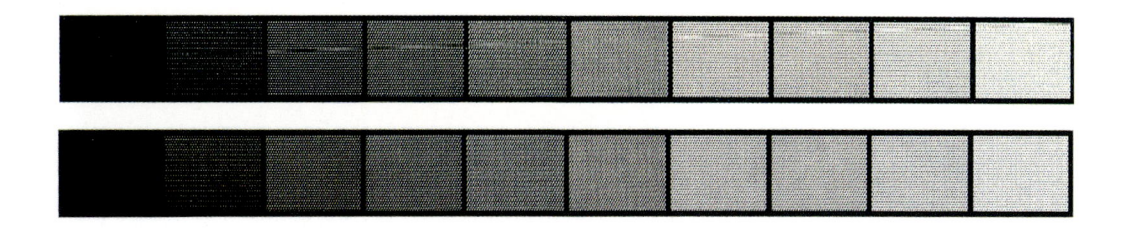

This is some
sample text.
It may be a
touch brown.

This is some
sample text.
But it's black
here. Always.

There's an exception to every rule. A case in point: The top gray scale bar and the left-most graphic and text were printed with the same three-color ribbon used on the facing page, and the bottom bar and right-most graphic and text were printed on the same four-color ribbon.

Because the slightest difference in alignment will make a difference in color, sometimes a three-color ribbon will print blacker blacks than a four- color ribbon, even on the same printer. But even though the blackest blacks from a three-color ribbon may be blacker than the brownest blacks from a four-color ribbon, the four-color ribbon will still print with blacker blacks more often.

Notice also that even on the off-black output from the four color ribbon sample, the text is fully black. That's because the text, unlike graphics, is printed solely from the black panel on the four-color ribbon, so there's no possibility of misalignment.

Colors change with changes in context.

The two filled-in orange circles are obviously different colors, with the left-most circle a darker orange than the one on the right. Except—you guessed it—they're both the same color.

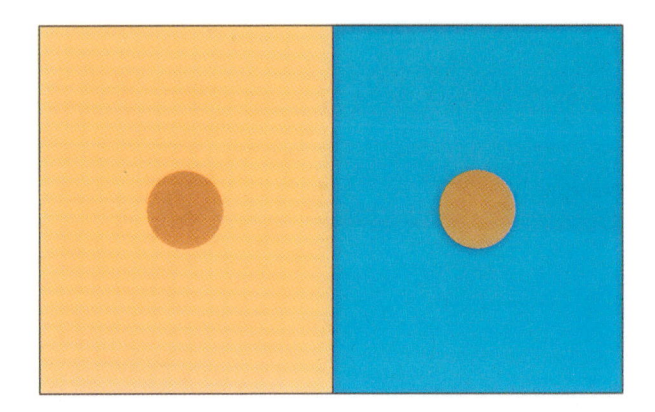

The green squares are both the same color. But when you surround green in a sea of blue, it brings out the yellow. Surround the same green with yellow and it brings out the blue.

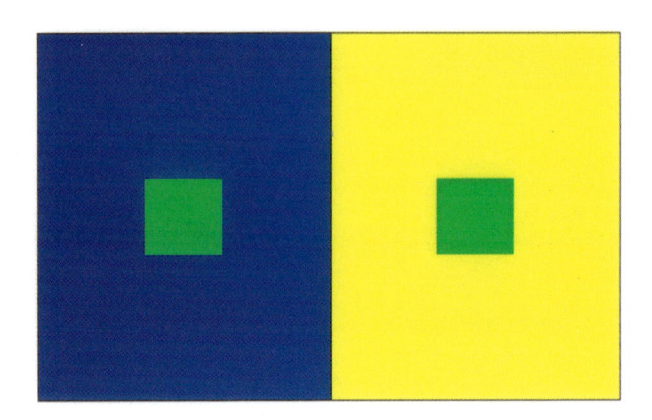

Surrounding colors can even make you see colors that aren't there. The lines on the left have an obvious gold tinge, and the lines on the right have a slightly bluish tinge compared to the block of gray below. But both sets of lines are actually 40 percent gray, exactly the same as the block of gray. (Adapted from Jackson, MacDonald, and Freeman, *Computer Generated Color*.)

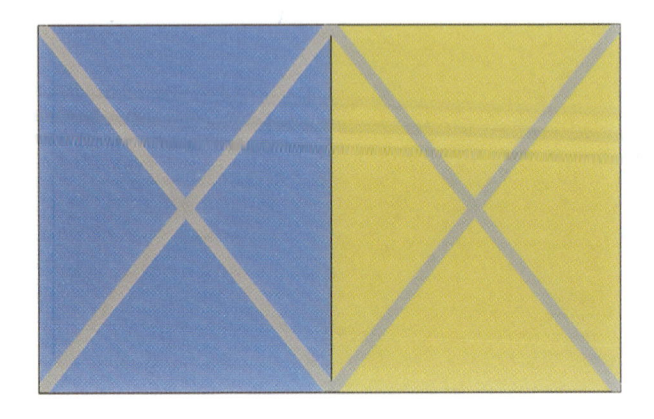

10

Here again, the filled-in circles are the same color on both sides of the figure, even though there is a dramatic, apparent difference between them.

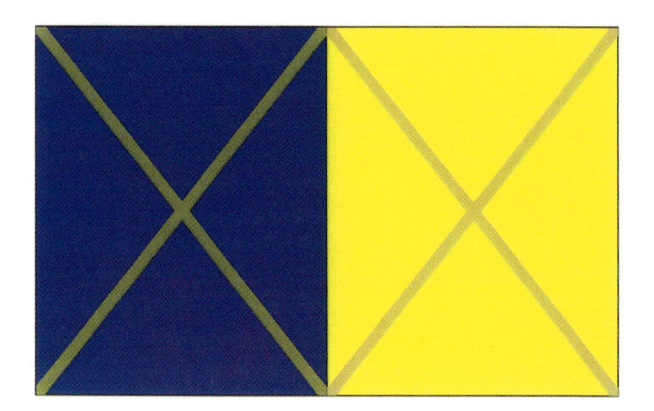

At last, you say, *a color that looks the same surrounded by two different colors.* Wrong. The colors look the same because they're two different colors, as shown in strips below this caption. The lesson: If the same color can look different when surrounded by different colors, different colors can look the same.

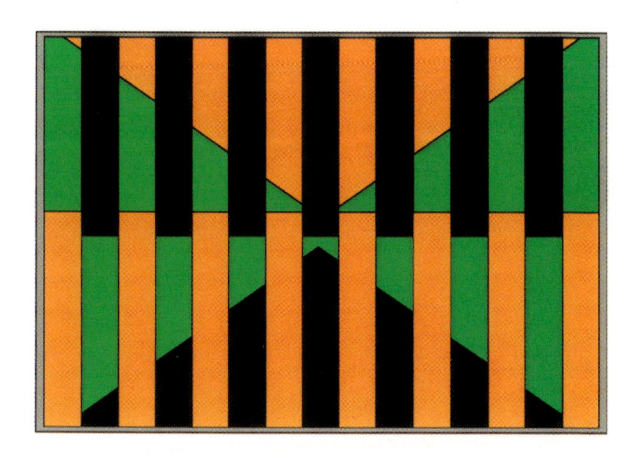

The effect of surrounding colors isn't limited to the simple case where one color is completely surrounded by another. It also shows up in more complex situations. The green in this figure is the same throughout, but where it's surrounded mostly by orange it looks different than where it's surrounded mostly by black. (Adapted from Jackson, MacDonald, and Freeman, *Computer Generated Color.*)

11

Small areas of color tend to look less saturated than larger areas. All the colors for any given shape on this page—circle, square, triangle, or rotated square—are the same. But if you look at the page from arm's length or farther, you'll probably see one or more of the colors in the small areas as distinctly less saturated than the same color in the large area. At least most people will see a difference in most lighting conditions, though different people will see the effect more easily with different colors.

    This tendency to see smaller areas as less saturated is why choosing a paint for your living room based on a one-inch square patch doesn't always give you the color you expect.

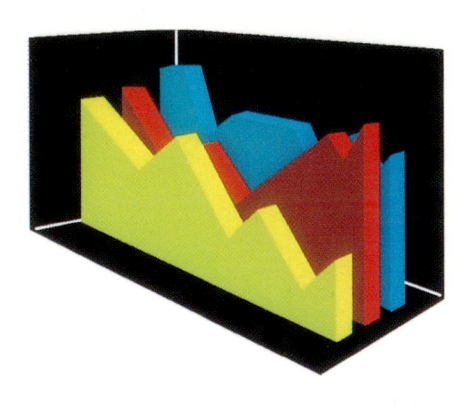

The colors you see often depend on the colors you expect to see. Your brain has no hesitation about seeing the middle slice of this 3D chart as red, with top and right surfaces well lighted, and the front surface in shadow. . . .

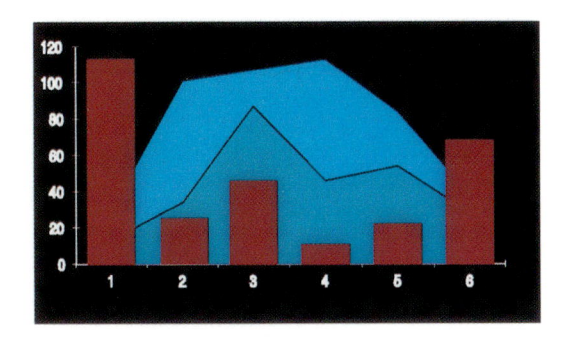

. . . But if you cover the top chart so that you're not influenced by it while you're looking at this one, there's no question that the same color in this combined area and bar chart is a reddish brown—and more brown than red.

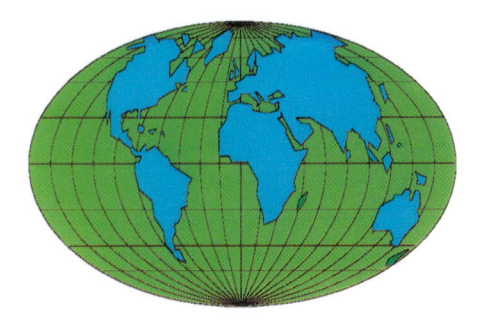

There are any number of color schemes in nature that you should keep in mind when choosing colors. People expect to see blue for oceans and green (or brown) for land—not the other way around. You can sometimes use a "wrong" color effectively for its surprise value, but going against natural color schemes is more likely to be a stumbling block to getting your message across.

There are also cultural assumptions to keep in mind—like using red for *stop* and green for *go*. Here again, going against cultural assumptions is likely to be a stumbling block to getting your message across.

Different hues aren't enough to make the foreground stand out from the background. All the colors in this graphic share similar saturation and brightness levels (on the page, not necessarily according to the graphics program). That makes edges—and even entire lines—fade into the background.

One way to make edges stand out sharp and clear is to add black outlines to colored areas, and use black or white, depending on the background, for thin lines and text.

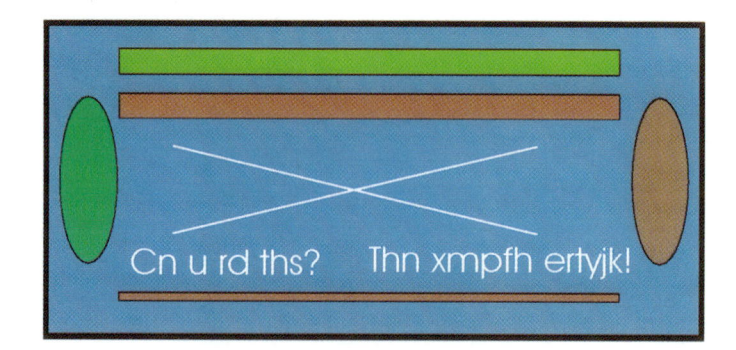

Another way to make edges stand out is to vary the saturation between background and foreground. The foreground graphics and text are the same here as in the top sample on this page. The background is the same hue and brightness, but it's less saturated.

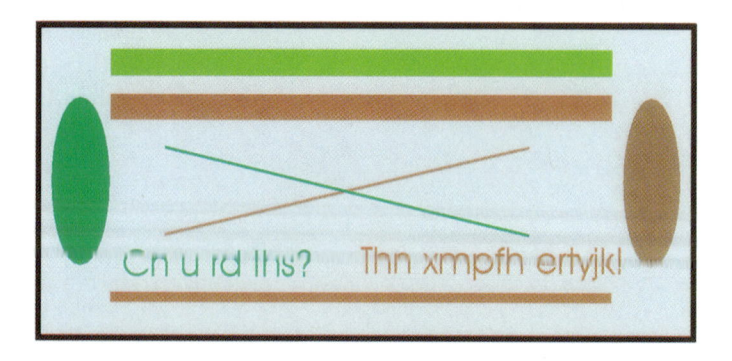

Yet another way to make edges stand out is to vary the brightness. All the colors here are the same hues and saturation levels as in the top sample, but the background is darker and all the foreground colors are brighter, which makes a big difference in brightness levels.

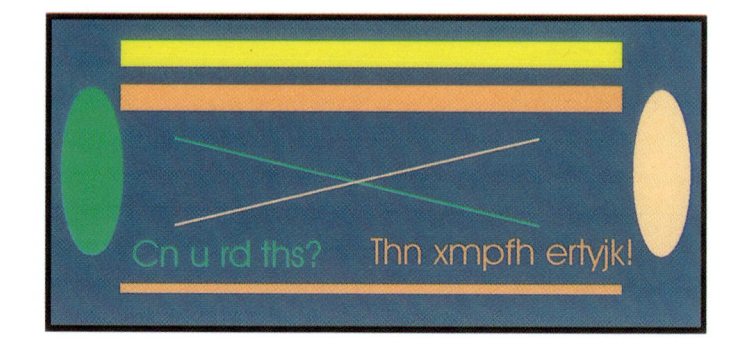

Blue Cyan Green Yellow Red Magenta Purple Brown Black White	Blue Cyan Green Yellow Red Magenta Purple Brown Black White	Blue Cyan Green Yellow Red Magenta Purple Brown Black White	Pick the wrong colors, and colored text can be almost unreadable with colored backgrounds. For maximum readability, use a neutral color for text (black, white, or gray) against a colored background . . .
			. . . or use colored text against a neutral background
Blue Cyan Green Yellow Red Magenta Purple Brown Black White	Blue Cyan Green Yellow Red Magenta Purple Brown Black White	Blue Cyan Green Yellow Red Magenta Purple Brown Black White	Using a low brightness level for the background while keeping the text color at maximum brightness will increase the contrast between text and background, making the text easier (but not necessarily easy) to read.
Blue Cyan Green Yellow Red Magenta Purple Brown Black White	Blue Cyan Green Yellow Red Magenta Purple Brown Black White	Blue Cyan Green Yellow Red Magenta Purple Brown Black White	Another way to improve readability is to use a pale color for the background. Background colors with low saturation levels have the additional advantage of having the least effect on perception of the text color, particularly if the text and background are the same hue, or complimentary hues.

Here are two typical ways to show the 12 basic hues in the color wheel.

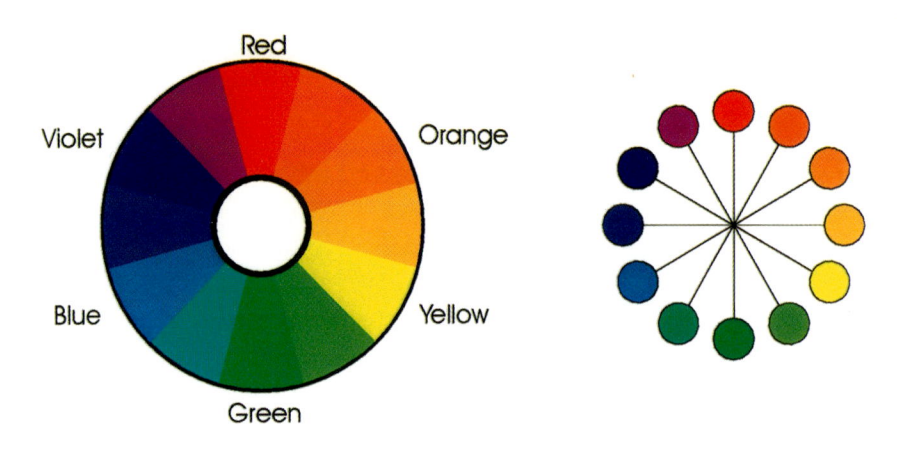

From left to right, here are the primary, secondary, and tertiary colors on the color wheel.

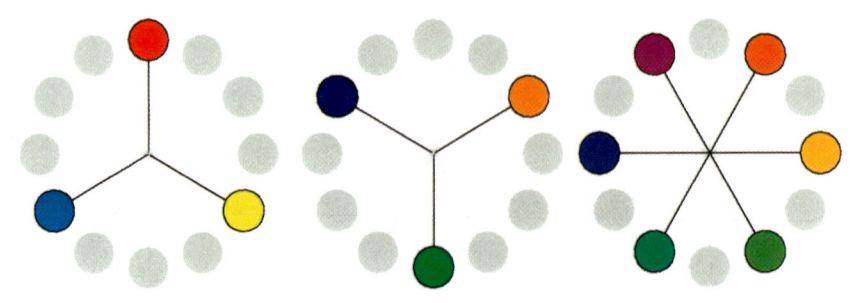

Complementary colors lie directly opposite each other on the color wheel.

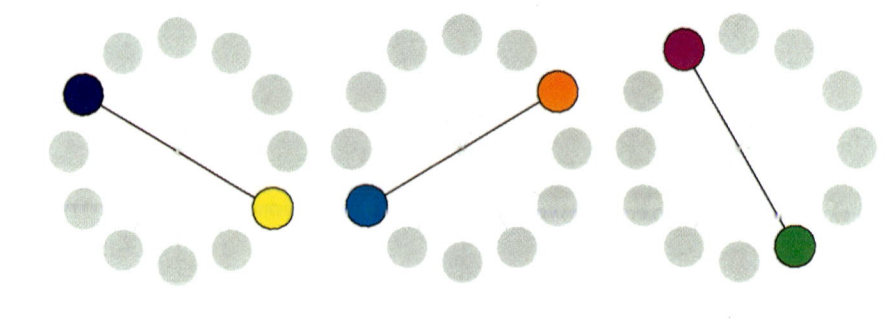

Split complements include a given color plus the two colors to either side of the first color's complement.

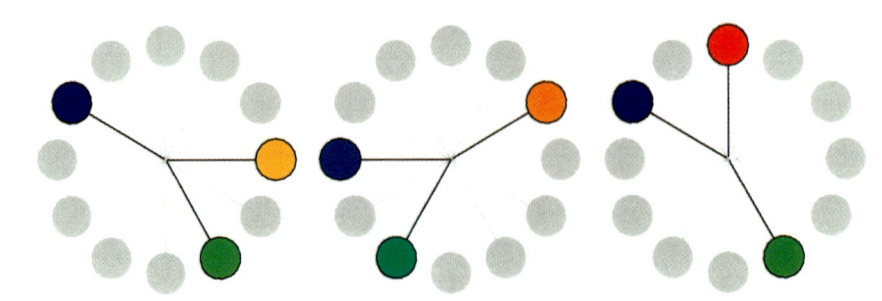

16

Unfortunately, not all printers include ink sensors. If you have a printer without a sensor, it won't know when it's run out of ink. Instead it will go merrily on its way, printing out page after page minus the missing color.

This is a good way to waste a lot of ink.

The moral: Make sure you know whether your printer includes ink sensors. And unless it does, stay around and glance at the output every so often any time you're printing more than one or two color pages.

While I'm on the subject of running out of ink, here's another tidbit to keep in mind. As I've already pointed out, some ink jet printers use a separate cartridge for each color. Others use just two cartridges—one for black and one for the three colored inks.

Three-color cartridges

As a group, the dual-cartridge printers are less expensive than the four-cartridge printers, but there's substantial overlap in price. If you have the choice, the dual-cartridge approach is best avoided.

Having one cartridge for three colors normally means that when you run out of one color of ink, you have to toss the cartridge, even though there may be lots of ink left for the other two colors. You'll want to keep this in mind the next time you buy an ink jet printer. But if you're already stuck with a dual-cartridge printer, there's a way around the problem.

Cartridge Refills

> Find a need and fill it.
>
> Ruth Stafford Peale

If you check out your friendly neighborhood office supply store, you should find ink cartridge refill kits. (If not, go to a different store.) The refill kits are mostly for printers that have a three-in-one cartridge for the color inks. Not only do they let you easily refill one color if you run out, but the refill costs a lot less than buying a new cartridge.

One potential issue with refill kits is that messing with ink refills can be . . . well . . . messy. One of the best features of cartridges is precisely that you don't have to deal with the ink directly to fill some container in the printer—the way you had to in the bad old days before cartridges. If you start refilling cartridges, don't be surprised if you wind up wearing some of the ink.

Yuck

> **If you go the refill route, pick up a box of nonsterile latex examination gloves—the kind your local vampire uses when he or she draws blood. You can find them in many large drug stores, but if you have trouble finding them, ask your doctor where he or she gets them. They're great to have around for all kinds of messy jobs, and they're cheap protection against getting ink up to your elbows.**

Be forewarned also that you can refill a cartridge only a limited number of times. I've heard two to three times suggested as the maximum, but I've also heard it called optimistic. I can't speak from personal experience on this one, because I refuse to use refill kits.

Whatever the limit, it's especially true of cartridges like the ones for Hewlett-Packard printers, which include the nozzles. The whole point of the HP cartridge design is that you get to minimize potential problems with clogging by replacing the nozzles when you replace the cartridge. Leave the cartridge in too long, and you're asking for problems, by going beyond the life expectancy for the nozzles.

There's another issue too. Manufacturers are continually improving their inks, and the printheads are fine-tuned for the ink they use. If you buy ink from a third party—and you have to with a refill kit, since the printer manufacturers don't sell them—you may wind up with something that meets older specifications, rather than matching the manufacturer's current inks. That, in turn, may mean that it smears more, clogs nozzles more often, or has a wider variation in color from one ink cartridge to the next.

More yuck

In the worst case, age, the wrong ink, or a combination of the two can wind up blowing out a nozzle and getting ink all over the inside of your printer. If that happens, you have a full-scale mess on your hands. (And you've probably voided the warranty.)

The moral here: If you decide to use refill kits, tread carefully. If you run out of one color while you still have plenty of the other two colors, you might want to refill that one color one time. But I, for one, would think long and hard before refilling the same cartridge a second time.

How Good Does It Look?

> The word good has many meanings. For example, if a man were to shoot his grandmother at a range of five hundred yards, I should call him a good shot, but not necessarily a good man.
>
> G. K. Chesterton

You may have noticed back at the beginning of this section on ink jet printers that I didn't include output quality as one of the strengths for the breed. That's because it's not. Or, at least, not usually.

To be fair, some ink jet printers manage to print some reasonably good-looking output. Others are far from it. In fact, the range of output quality is greater for ink jets than for any other kind of color printer. It also varies tremendously with what kind of image you're printing and the kind of paper you're printing on.

Graphics

Most ink jet printers can do a reasonably good job, or better, with graphics on plain paper. In the worst case, colors can be somewhat dull, as I mentioned in

Chapter 1, but they're more often vibrant and fully saturated. And the tendency for the ink drops to spread helps hide dithering patterns. That doesn't mean that the dithering patterns disappear altogether, but they'll usually be less obvious than identical dithering patterns on, say, a thermal wax printer at the same resolution.

You'll often see banding in gradient fills on ink jet output, with visibly different color or dithering patterns in each band. And, of course, there's the possibility of banding from dark or light lines where there's an overlap or gap in the path of the printhead.

So in the worst case, you'll get somewhat dull colors, visible dithering, banding in gradient fills, and dark or light lines dividing the image into visible bands: Not a pretty sight. But in the best case you'll get vibrant colors, barely visible dithering on some colors, and no bands of any kind: Something you can be proud of. No matter how good or bad the output looks on plain paper, you'll usually get noticeable improvements, with more vivid colors, if you use coated or glossy paper.

Photos

Photos on plain paper are another story altogether. You can sum it up with three rules.

Rule one is: Most ink jet printers are not designed for printing photorealistic output.

Rule two is: Those few ink jet printers that boast high quality photorealistic output do their best work on special paper.

Rule three is: Keep rule one firmly in mind.

Dithering patterns are more likely to show up in photos than in graphics because the continuous tones in photos just about guarantee that you'll need dithered colors. Some printers offer a choice that randomizes the dithering and turns repeating tile patterns into random dots, but the dithering still shows up as a graininess in the photo.

Bands separated by dark and light lines are also just as likely to show up in a photo, although they'll often look more like smudges or streaks. The kind of banding you get in gradient fills turns into posterization in photos, with sudden shifts in colors that are supposed to change gradually.

The flattening effect

Colors in photos will usually be slightly posterized, dulled down, or both. You'll probably notice this less as a loss in color than as a flattening effect on three-dimensional objects. A close-up shot of, say, an apple, (the fruit, not the computer) will look less round—less three dimensional—than it will in the original photo.

What's actually happening is that in real life subtle changes in color indicate three dimensionality, because the colors are intimately related to the way light bounces off the apple at any given point. So your brain has learned to interpret color changes as indicating shape. And if you look at a close-up photo of an apple, you'll get a sense of three dimensionality just from the changes in color. If the output is missing some intermediate colors, you'll see the apple as being flatter.

Some photos are flatter than others

You don't have to take my word for this. The color section in this book includes a close-up photo of an assortment of colored peppers as printed by various printers. The flattening effect is fairly obvious for the ink jet samples.

The flattening effect will be more of an issue for some photos than others. Print a picture of a bowl of fruit that fills the frame, for example, and the flattening will be pretty obvious. Use the same printer to print a long shot of a runner jumping a hurdle, and you may not notice any flattening at all, particularly if the runner is in focus and the background is out of focus.

The difference in effect comes from the difference in what your brain expects to see. In some real-life situations, you'll see less three-dimensional shading than in others, so you simply don't need as much subtle shading on the page for the photo to look realistic. If the background in the photo is out of focus, your brain will get other three-dimensional cues from the differences in foreground and background. Those cues may make up for the lack of shading.

The point is that a given ink jet printer can easily give you something that approaches photographic quality with one photo and not with another. Of three photos I printed on a Canon BJC-600e, for example, one could pass for a photograph from about four feet away, one is so posterized that it looks more like a painting than a photograph even from a distance, and one falls between the two extremes. At normal reading distance, the dithering in all three photos is impossible to miss. Even without reading glasses.

More generally, in the worst case you'll get visible dithering, obvious posterization, and dark or light lines dividing the image into visible bands. In the best case you'll get barely visible dithering, a slight flattening effect, no bands of any kind, and a chance at something that approaches photographic quality for at least some photos. As with graphics, you'll often get significantly better quality if you use coated or glossy paper.

Transparencies

Transparencies have traditionally been a weak area for ink jet printers. More printers than not have simply had a hard time producing colors that were saturated enough to hold up to an overhead projector. That's still true for some printers, but it's changed for others, thanks to a combination of improved ink formulation and transparencies designed for specific printers.

Some of today's ink jet printers are very much in the same league as thermal wax transfer printers, which is traditionally the technology of choice for transparencies. Others aren't even playing the right game. The only way to find out how well a given ink jet printer does on transparencies is to try it. If transparencies are important to you, that's something to keep in mind for your next ink jet printer—whether you happened to luck out with your current printer or not.

Ink jet printers also have another problem with transparencies. Most ink jet ink tends to smear when it gets wet. If you're giving a presentation by handling the transparencies directly, you may smear the ink if your hands are sweaty. And even if the ink doesn't actually smear, it may still show up on your fingers. The easy way around this problem is to keep the transparencies in plastic sleeves and slap the whole thing, sleeve and all, on the overhead projector.

WAX JET PRINTERS

> The difference between the right word and the almost right word is the difference between lightning and the lightning bug.
>
> Mark Twain

Wax jet printers (a.k.a. solid ink printers) are two notches up from ink jet printers in price—the intermediate step being thermal wax transfer printers, which are generally more expensive than even the most expensive ink jet printer.

Even so, wax jet printers are so similar to ink jet printers in how they work that some people lump them together with ink jets. After all, the primary distinction between the two is that wax jets spray liquid wax instead of liquid ink, and the wax dries by cooling instead of evaporation. But the difference between ink and wax on the printed page is... well... not as dramatic as the difference between Twain's lightning and a lightning bug. But pretty dramatic.

The difference between ink and wax is the difference between looking at a distant mountain through a slightly dirty picture window and looking at the same mountain through an open window on a crisp autumn day. And that's giving the ink jet the benefit of the doubt.

One of the strengths for wax jets is that they can print gorgeous output on any kind of paper that can make it through the printer. Literally. Tektronix sells one wax jet printer—the Phaser IIIi—that prints on paper towels, sandpaper, and taco shells.

Oh, yes. It also prints on plain paper.

This particular printer can show off like that because of unusual paper-handling features that don't choke on sandpaper and other assorted oddities. But the part about printing on anything that can make it through the printer applies to any wax jet.

Wax jets can manage that trick because wax, unlike ink, doesn't get absorbed by the paper or whatever else it lands on. If you sliced a sponge thin enough to make it through the printer, even the sponge wouldn't absorb it. And because the wax all stays on the surface of the... umm... target, it keeps its edges and color.

On almost any surface, and certainly on anything smooth enough to pass for paper, colors stay vibrant, edges and thin lines stay crisp and clean, and details are as sharp as you would expect from a laser printer with the same resolution. Photos tend to show dithering patterns, but for the best printers in this category, they'll pass for photographic quality at arm's length.

Classic wax jet

Actually, there are two kinds of wax jet printers. One kind—which I'll call a classic wax jet because it's been around longer—works just like an ink jet printer. The printhead sprays the ink directly on the paper, one band at a time. This classic approach to wax jet printing has the same kind of banding problem as ink jet printers. It also has a problem with transparencies, though not for the same reason as ink jet printers.

With wax jets, the problem with transparencies is that because the drops of wax cool quickly, they dry in a semi-spherical shape. This doesn't matter for printing on paper, but with transparencies, each drop acts as a tiny lens that affects the projected image. Some classic wax jet designs try to solve this problem by squeezing the transparency between rollers to flatten the dots. The fix works, after a fashion, but classic wax jets are still a poor choice for printing transparencies.

They're also a poor choice for black and white printing, even though you might expect otherwise. Any wax jet is a four-color printer, with four different colored waxes. That means, in theory, that you can use them for printing all your monochrome output. But even with nothing but black text on the page, classic wax jets are so slow that it's simply not practical to use them as a workhorse monochrome printer.

Classic wax jet printers have always been a niche product. They're of particular interest to artists who want to see what colors will look like when they're printed on a specific colored paper. But anyone who doesn't need that capability, as well as anyone who needs transparencies, has tended to go with other high-end printers—particularly thermal wax printers, which not only can print transparencies but cost less too.

New fangled wax jet

The second kind of wax jet printer is so recent that at this writing there's only one member of the breed—the Tektronix Phaser 340 (unless you count the Phaser 340 Plus, which is really just an upgrade of the 340). But it works so well that it deserves some imitation—the sincerest form of flattery.

This newest incarnation of wax jet doesn't spray wax on the paper. Instead, it sprays the wax on a drum and then transfers it by rolling the drum against the paper—much as an offset printer transfers ink from drum to paper or a laser printer transfers toner.

Using a drum eliminates banding, since the image isn't sprayed on the page in bands. It also eliminates the lensing effect on transparencies, since the drum flattens the wax drops even as it puts them on the paper. As a bonus, print speed goes up enough to make monochrome printing a reasonable possibility.

This new approach to wax jets is of much wider interest than the classic approach. The price is still higher than for the most expensive ink jets, or even for thermal wax printers, but it's low enough to match the low end of color laser prices. More important, the print speeds are in the same ballpark as color laser speeds also.

More advantages for the new fangled approach

With color images, a drum-based wax jet is often faster than a laser. And although it's noticeably slower than laser for monochrome, at this writing, it's faster than most ink jet printers. You might not want to use one of the current generation of these drum-based wax jets for all your monochrome output, but you could if you needed to.

It is also worth mentioning that the care and feeding of both kinds of wax jets are roughly equivalent to what's needed for an ink jet printer. Or, more precisely, the mechanics of care and feeding are the same, but there's less of it. Instead of ink cartridges, you load sticks or blocks of wax, but the wax is as easy to load as ink cartridges, maybe easier, and you don't have to load it as often.

One minor problem is that if you turn off the printer overnight, you'll have to wait 15 to 30 minutes for the wax to melt each morning. But the printer will give you plenty of warning for loading the next ink stick before it runs out.

Most important, if you happen to be in the market for a color laser printer, you should be considering a drum-based wax jet as an alternative. The price is about the same, the output quality is as good or better, and adding ink sticks every so often is a lot easier than dealing with toner, developer, and other laser consumables that we'll be getting to shortly.

COLOR LASER PRINTERS

> One shining quality lends a lustre to another, or hides some glaring defect.
>
> William Hazlitt
> "Characteristics," no. 162 (first published anonymously in 1823; repr. in *Complete Works*, vol. 9, ed. P. P. Howe, 1932)

Quick quiz: What do you think of when I say laser quality?

Probably something positive, like: *It must really look good.*

Or, if you're a spiritual Vulcan: *Crisp, clean edges for graphics and text, solid areas in graphics solidly filled in, photos showing dithered patterns, but only as appropriate for the resolution—whether it's 300, 600, 1200, or better.*

Now, what do you think of when I say color laser printers?

Probably something more positive than they deserve.

We're all so used to treating laser printers as the best possible choice in the world of black and white, that when we try to describe really good looking output, the phrase *laser quality* leaps to mind. But in the world of color, laser quality doesn't measure up. It's not that laser printers necessarily do a terrible job with color—although some do—it's just that they don't do all that great a job either.

Here's the good news.

The strong points for color lasers are that they print on plain paper, they can mix color and monochrome in a single print job or on a single page, and, in some cases at least, they can print black and white output at the same kind of speed you're used to from monochrome lasers. Prices are the same as for wax jets—two steps up from ink jet printers, or one step up from thermal wax.

And now the bad news

As I said in Chapter 1, output quality from color lasers varies all over the map. Most color laser printers today offer 600 dpi resolution or 300 by 1200, either of which all but eliminates visible dithering patterns in graphics. In most cases, you'll see fully saturated, vibrant colors, though some printers offer more vibrant colors than others. The best-case graphics I've seen from lasers combine both of these good points without any important flaws.

The worst-case graphics for printers that offer 600 dpi keep both good points, but show banding in gradient fills and a tendency to add dark colored lines, white lines, or both along the edges of filled areas. On some images, the dark or white lines are hardly noticeable. On others, they leave you with an out-of-focus effect that makes the output all but useless.

For worst-case graphics at 300 dpi, add visible dithering patterns to the banding and lines, and for older printers, expect somewhat duller color. Whatever the output quality, it generally holds up well on transparencies.

Scanned photos from color laser printers can look almost photorealistic from arm's length, but even at 600 dpi you can generally expect to see dithering as a noticeable graininess at normal reading distance. Don't be surprised if you see posterization as well. At 300 dpi, dithering stands out sharp and clear.

Monochrome output is worth special mention, because you probably expect it to match the output you're used to from monochrome lasers. In some cases it will. But in other cases, characters and thin lines will be a little less crisp and clean than you would get from a monochrome laser at the same resolution.

Be aware also that most color laser output has a noticeable shine to it, even for black text. In the worst case, this can be distracting. In the best case, it's hardly noticeable—and then only if you look for it.

Bilevel and Multilevel Printers

> The only thing on the level is mountain climbing.
>
> Eddie Quinn

I mentioned in Chapter 1 that some color laser printers combine dithering with continuous tones, and I promised to explain what that meant the next time I got around to lasers. Well, here we are, so here we go.

Most printers, including most laser printers, are strictly bilevel, which means they either put a dot of a given color on the page or they don't. There are no intermediate levels between full on and full off. That's why they have to use dithering to get any color beyond the basic eight: cyan, magenta, yellow, black, red (magenta mixed with yellow in a single dot), green (cyan mixed with yellow), blue (cyan mixed with magenta), and white (no dot).

Bilevel printers

True continuous tone printers—the kind that print with 16.7 million colors without dithering—are multilevel printers. Instead of each primary color being limited to full on or full off for each dot, they can adjust the intensity of each color, with some number of gray levels, or color levels if you prefer, between full on and full off.

Multilevel printers

More precisely, multilevel printers can adjust the intensity for each color in 256 steps. What's more, for each dot on the page, they can mix any available level of cyan with any available level of magenta and any available level of yellow. That's where the 16.7 million colors come from: 256 choices of cyan times 256 choices of magenta times 256 choices of yellow. That comes out to 16,777,216 colors, if you don't happen to have a calculator handy. Conveniently enough, that's the same number of colors that you can define with 24-bit color.

As you may have already guessed, there's no reason why a printer can't have more than two levels for each color but less than 256. Each additional level means less need for dithering. To understand why, you need to look at dithering more closely than we have so far.

Here's fair warning: We're about to get hip deep in arithmetic. So if you don't like numbers, be prepared to skim over the next page or so and just pick out the conclusions. Or you can just skip to the paragraph that's marked "Resolution versus colors" in the margin. There's no reason why you have to know the details if you don't want to. But if you're a detail kind of guy (or gal), put on your hip waders, and follow me through.

Way back in Chapter 1, I described dithering as mixing colors by laying dots down in patterns, using some number of dots to create each picture element, or pixel. I also pointed out that the number of dots and the arrangement of dots were up for grabs.

More about dithering

The most straightforward arrangement for the dots is a matrix, or cell, arranged in a square of so many dots by so many—four by four, five by five, six by six, and so on. The larger the cell, the more dots you have to play with, so the more colors you can create—or fake—with the dithered pattern. If you're using a monochrome printer and a two by two cell, for example, you can create five levels of dithered gray, with 0, 1, 2, 3, or 4 black dots, as shown in Figure 5.5.

Similarly, if you're using a monochrome printer and a four-by-four cell, you can create 17 levels of dithered gray—because you can use anything from 0 through 16 dots. More generally, you can fake as many shades of gray as you have dots in the cell plus one, for no dots. (The cell, by the way, is called a halftone cell, and the technique of tricking the eye and brain into seeing gray from a mix of black and white spots is called halftoning.)

Figure 5.5 The number of dithered colors or shades of gray depends on how many dots you use to create each dithered pixel. A matrix of two dots by two dots gives you five possible shades of gray.

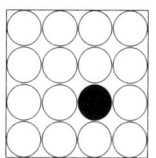

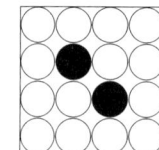

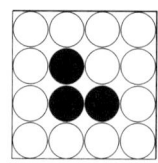

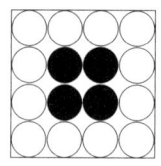

Figure 5.6 With a four-by-four cell, you have 16 dots to play with, for 17 dithered shades of gray.

If you're dithering with colors instead of gray, the same principle applies, but the numbers change. This gets a little tricky, so read carefully:

For any given size cell, you actually have a separate cell for each color—cyan, magenta, and yellow—with the three color cells essentially printing on top of each other. And that means you have as many levels available for each color as you would have for a single color on a monochrome printer. With a four-by-four cell, you have 17 levels of cyan *and* 17 levels of magenta *and* 17 levels of yellow. You can mix these 17 levels of each color together in any combination making the total possible number of colors 17 times 17 times 17, or 4913.

If the logic behind this calculation isn't immediately obvious (and it probably isn't if you haven't been in an advanced algebra class lately), think of this way: You can combine each level of cyan with any of 17 levels of magenta. So the total number of combinations of cyan and magenta is 17 times 17, or 289. You can also combine each of these 289 combinations of cyan and magenta with any of the 17 levels of yellow. So the total number of combinations of cyan, magenta, and yellow is 289 times 17. Which, last I looked, is the same thing as 17 times 17 times 17.

The other thing you need to understand about dithering is that, for photographs at least, each cell becomes a single dot in the printed image—or a single *spot* if you want to keep a clear distinction between the individual printer dots and the individual cells. (And you should. It helps avoid confusion.)

So the larger the cell, the lower the effective resolution. That's why you can easily see spots (not printer dots) in a photo printed on a 300-dpi monochrome laser printer.

If you use a five-by-five cell on a 300-dpi printer, the effective resolution is no longer 300 dpi, but 60 spots per inch—300 dots per inch divided by 5 dots per spot. More generally, the effective resolution for most desktop printers after dithering is typically 60 to 75 spots per inch (or spi).

This is one case where a picture is worth far more than the proverbial thousand words. Figure 5.7 shows two versions of the same photo. Both were printed at 300 dpi, but the one on the left was printed at 60 spots per inch—5 dots to a cell. The one on the right was printed at 30 spots per inch—10 dots to a cell. The jump in cell size is extreme enough so the difference in effective resolution is pretty hard to miss.

Figure 5.7 This photo is printed at 300 dots per inch on both left and right, but at 60 spots per inch on the left, and only 30 spots per inch on the right.

With graphics, the situation is a touch more complex, since both text and edges in line drawings can still take advantage of the printer resolution. However, the granularity of spots in dithered colors is still based on the size of the cell. Figure 5.8 shows both effects, with the same graphic printed at 60 spots per inch on the left and 30 spots per inch on the right. Notice that the text and lines look the same in both cases, although the size of the spots is dramatically different.

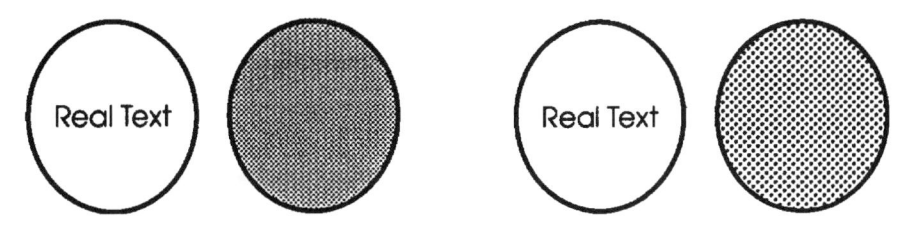

Figure 5.8 This graphic is also printed at 300 dots per inch on both left and right, but at 60 spots per inch on the left, and only 30 spots per inch on the right.

Resolution versus colors

Strip away the details, and you're left with one central point about dithering. You can get more colors by using bigger cells, but then you get lower effective resolution; or you can get higher effective resolution by using a smaller cell size, but then you get fewer colors.

Did someone ask for a concrete example? Okay. At 600 dpi, a five-by-five cell gives you 17,576 colors with an effective 120 spi (that's spots per inch) resolution. A six-by-six cell gives you 50,653 colors but only a 100-spi effective resolution.

Back to multilevel printers

All of which brings us back, finally, to multilevel printers. For any given size cell, each additional level of intensity means you can get more colors from a given size cell. Or, if you prefer, you can use smaller cells to give you a higher effective resolution and get the same number of colors.

> **I see Arnold is back in the room and asking for details. Okay, for those enquiring minds who want to know (the rest of you can skip this), each additional level of intensity increases the variations for each primary color by the number of dots in the cell. If you have 16 dots per cell with a bilevel printer, you have 16 variations plus 1. With three levels of intensity, you have 16 more variations available, or 2 times 16 plus 1. With four levels of intensity, you have 16 more variations available, or 3 times 16 plus 1. So for any given level of intensity, you have 1 less than the number of levels available times 16 variations. Plus 1.**
>
> **You can translate this into a general formula. To get the number of shades for each primary color, multiply the number of dots in the cell times the total number of levels minus 1, then add 1 to the result (for a cell with no dots). To get the total number of colors, take the number for each primary color and cube it. For those who prefer a formula that looks like a formula, this translates to:**

$$\{[(\text{number of dots per cell}) \times (\text{number of levels} -1)] + 1\}^3$$

In theory, multilevel printers—including printers that are short of true continuous tone printing—can print photos that are much closer to true photographic quality than what you'll get from bilevel printers. This is usually true in practice also, but not always. In my experience, some graphics and photos look better at bilevel 600 dpi than at multilevel 600 dpi on the same printer.

> **If you have a multilevel printer that lets you set it for multilevel or bilevel, the best strategy is to try the multilevel setting first for any given output. If it's anything less than impressive, try printing again at the bilevel setting.**

Trying to switch between bilevel and multilevel

One tiny little complication is that you won't necessarily be able to set the printer to bilevel. The Apple Color LaserWriter 12/600 PS, for example, doesn't give you the choice. (Apple's concept of making things simple, unfortunately, is to give you as few choices as possible.)

Even for printers that you can switch between bilevel and multilevel, finding the right settings isn't always easy. I ranted earlier about ink jet manufacturers hiding the commands for unidirectional and bidirectional printing behind such uninformative names as plain paper and coated paper. Laser printer manufacturers are guilty of the same sort of effort to protect you from useful information.

The Tektronix Phaser 540 driver, for example, gives you a choice between Fast, Standard, and Enhanced. With a little luck, you may be able to figure out that Fast is multilevel 300 dpi, Standard is bilevel 600 dpi, and Enhanced is multilevel 600 dpi. But I wouldn't bet on it. If you don't know what the settings mean, call the manufacturer and ask. (Hey, if enough people bother them, maybe they'll start supplying the information with the printers. Stranger things have happened.)

One final warning: Some marketing departments have a tendency to call multilevel color laser printers continuous tone printers, even though they're not. Any time you hear the term continuous tone applied to anything besides a thermal dye transfer printer, be skeptical. If the printer does any dithering at all, it ain't continuous tone. It's multilevel.

Care and feeding

> ". . . never trust machinery more complicated than a knife and fork."
>
> Robert A. Heinlein
> Jubal Harshaw in *Stranger in a Strange Land,* ch. 16 (1961)

One of the other illusions you probably have about color laser printers is that they're easy to set up and maintain. Well, if you're used to monochrome lasers, it's an easy mistake to make.

Laser printers in general use one of two approaches to toner: mono-component toner, a.k.a. single-component toner, or dual-component toner, with separate toner and developer. For our purposes, there's no reason to worry about the differences in how the two approaches work, except to mention that mono-component toner has several advantages, including more even coverage of solid areas on the page and better formed text characters, with crisper, cleaner edges.

On a monochrome printer, mono-component toner also means you have only one toner cartridge to install, and occasionally replace, instead of worrying about both toner and developer. (Although you don't have to replace developer anywhere near as often as toner.) Even with toner plus developer, however, you don't generally have to mess with a monochrome printer very often.

On a color laser printer, you need toner for each color, so the difference between a mono-component toner and a dual-component toner is the difference between four toner cartridges and four sets of toner plus developer. But even with mono-component toner, a color laser printer can be a bit of a chore to maintain, with four toner cartridges each running out on their own schedule.

Also be aware that toner isn't the only consumable you have to replace in color laser printers. Most, but not all, of these printers also need fuser oil replaced every now and then. The fuser oil typically goes in a plastic bottle inside the printer. And if you're unlucky enough to spill any, you'll be treated to a slippery puddle of silicon-based oil.

I don't want to draw too nasty a picture here. Even in the worst case—with fuser oil bottles and badly designed toner cartridges that may spill a little toner if you're not careful—maintaining a color laser printer is only a minor chore. But just in case you're considering buying a color laser printer, you should be aware that it's more of a chore to take care of than a typical monochrome laser printer. As I pointed out when I was talking about wax jets, if you're considering a color laser printer, you should be considering a wax jet also, since it has most of the same strengths and is a lot easier to maintain.

THERMAL WAX AND THERMAL DYE

> I have yet to see any problem, however complicated, which, when you looked at it in the right way, did not become still more complicated.
>
> Poul Anderson
> *New Scientist* (London, 25 Sept. 1969)

I've lumped thermal wax and thermal dye transfer printers together because they have even more in common than ink jet and wax jet printers. Ink jet and wax jets are both spitters, but you can't get one printer to spit both ink and wax. Thermal wax and thermal dye printers are not only both heaters, but they're so much alike that you can get one printer to do both jobs, working with either dye or wax ribbons.

All of which means that there are three different kinds of heaters: thermal wax, thermal dye, and dual mode printers. For our purposes, I'll lump all three into a single category I just made up and call them ribbon printers.

The vast majority of ribbon printers—all but one that I know of—are page printers. (And I've already said everything I need to about the one exception, in the section on thermal wax printers in Chapter 1.) For page printers, each ribbon panel is big enough to cover an entire page. The printer prints a full page of each color, one color at a time, with a separate pass for each color panel.

Ribbon panels don't necessarily match the paper size. Some printers can handle more than one size paper and let you use a single ribbon for all the sizes. This isn't always a good idea, however, since the ribbon is a major part of the cost per page. With dye ribbons in particular, a larger ribbon than you need can waste a lot of ribbon and cash. In general, you'll want to use the right size ribbon for the paper you're printing on, unless your printer has only one size ribbon.

Big margins

Whatever paper size you're using, you can generally expect large margins with ribbon printers. There's a reason for those margins. Color printers have to put each dot of color in exactly the right spot in relation to the other colors, because the human eye is really good at noticing even a small misalignment, or misregistration. Depending on how bad the registration, you may see the image as blurry, or you may simply see an edge of one color peeking out from the side of each shape on the page.

This need for precise registration is a potential killer problem for ribbon-based printers, because they print in three or four passes—printing a full page in one color, sucking the page back in, printing a second color, and so on. The solution is to make a large chunk of the paper off limits for printing. That gives the printer lots of room to grab and hold onto the paper to guarantee precise registration. It also leaves big margins.

The problem with big margins, of course, is that they limit the size of the image you can put on any given piece of paper. Most ribbon printers solve that problem by letting you print on a larger page than you need. Some ribbon printers, for example, offer a slightly larger size page—8½ by 12 inches, say—often complete with a perforated tear-off strip so you still wind up with a letter-size page when you're done. Others lack the perforations. But what the hey, you can always resort to scissors.

Thermal wax

Thermal wax printers are generally good choices for graphics, with vibrant colors and crisp clean edges. At 300 dpi, expect to see equally crisp, clean dithering patterns.

Some printers offer more sophisticated dithering schemes that help hide the patterns. At 600 by 300 dpi or better, the combination of the more sophisticated dithering and higher resolution makes dithering patterns much more subtle, to the point where photos begin to approach photographic quality. As I've already mentioned, thermal wax printers are a good choice for transparencies, with saturated colors that stand up well to a projector.

As I also mentioned earlier, the paper for most thermal wax printers is noticeably shiny and typically about the same weight as copy paper, although it's sometimes a little lighter or heavier. If you'd rather print on plain paper, you'll find that some thermal wax printers offer a special ribbon that can do the job. The ribbon has an extra panel that lays down its own coating on the paper first. The image goes on top of the coating.

You may find it useful to know that printing on plain paper usually costs the same as printing on special purpose thermal wax paper, to within a few cents. The plain paper saves you money, but the special ribbon costs more per image, which wipes out the savings.

As I suggested earlier, thermal wax printers are the next step up from ink jets in price. Most cost more than even the most expensive ink jet, but you can find a few slower members of the breed for under $1000, including dual mode printers.

Thermal dye

Thermal dye printers offer unquestionably the best-looking color output of any technology. For a start, you won't see any dithering, because thermal dye printers don't dither. These are continuous tone printers, which can make any dot on the page any color. And that means you get the full 16.7 million colors you need for true color without losing any of the printer's resolution.

> **That's important. I'll say it again a different way, just to make sure you didn't miss it: As I discussed earlier in this chapter, whenever you create colors with dithering, you have a tradeoff between resolution and the number of colors you get. The bigger the dithering cell, the more colors you can have, and the less resolution. But with a continuous tone printer, you don't dither, which means you don't have to trade away anything. You get your full 16.7 million colors, *and* your full 300 dpi (or whatever) resolution also.**

Throw in fully saturated, vibrant colors for graphics along with true continuous tones for photos, and you wind up with impeccable graphics and photographic quality photos. Some early thermal dye printers had problems with edges in graphics and text, because the dye diffusing into the polyester coating would tend to spread, but that problem has been solved for several years now. Any current model of thermal dye printer offers reasonably crisp edges for text and graphics. Both graphic and photographic output look just as good on transparencies as on paper.

The worst-looking thermal dye output has a tendency for dark areas to turn a shiny black if you look from the wrong angle. But head on, it still looks pretty good. Photos, in the worst case, lose some detail in shadows. But unless you have the original to compare to, you probably won't notice the loss. The best looking output matches the original photo point for point. The heavy-weight, polyester-coated paper even makes the printout look like a glossy photo.

One minor problem with thermal dye output is that the colors can fade. But, then, that happens to photographs too. Also be aware that if you put the page in a vinyl sleeve for protection, the dyes can migrate from the page to the vinyl. The solution: Don't try to protect the page in a vinyl sleeve.

Thermal dye output is the most expensive for any technology, with a typical cost—between the ribbon and special paper—of $2 to $3 for a letter-size page. Transparencies are even more expensive, which is why very few people use thermal dye printers for transparencies, even though they can often outdo transparencies from any other kind of printer.

As a group, thermal dye printers are not only the most expensive color printers to run, they're also the most expensive you can buy. But if you're willing to cut a few corners, you can find some dual mode printers for the price of an ink jet.

Dual mode printers

Printers that lead a double life come in two basic flavors—low end and high end. Either kind can switch between thermal wax and thermal dye in just a little longer than it takes to say Shazam.

The low-end printers can cost under $1000—about as much as a middling good ink jet. They're aimed at people who want good looking output only occasionally and are willing to wait around for it. They also let you save money by printing less expensive thermal wax output when you don't need thermal dye quality. If you print a lot of graphics, however, you'll find these printers can be maddeningly slow.

Typically, low-end dual mode printers keep their price down by leaving out network capability as well as some other expensive hardware; namely, the built-in processor and RAM that most thermal wax and thermal dye printers use to process, or rasterize, the image. Instead, they depend on your computer to do the processing.

High-end dual mode printers are meant for graphic artists who can use the thermal wax mode for drafts and the thermal dye mode for final output. Since the thermal wax mode can save several dollars for each page, the idea is that a graphic arts shop with lots of output can save thousands of dollars by using the draft mode.

Did someone say they don't believe you can save enough to make that big a difference? Do the math. A letter-size thermal dye page typically costs about $2 or more, while a thermal wax page costs $.50 or less. That's a $1.50 difference for each page. For 11- by 17-inch tabloid-size output, which is pretty typical for graphic artists, the difference is closer to $6.

Print as few as ten letter-size thermal wax pages a day, and you get a $15 saving every day. Five working days each week translates to $75 a week. With 52 weeks a year (no vacations for the printer), that comes out to a substantial $3900 a year. For ten tabloid-size pages a day, the difference jumps to a whopping $15,600 savings a year. That's enough to give some graphic artist a pretty good raise. There's a catch though.

In my experience, dual mode printers work best if you use one mode most of the time and switch to the other only occasionally. If you continually switch back and forth, you'll quickly get tired of the chore, and you'll waste a lot of pages from dust that gets into the printer when you change ribbons. As I've mentioned elsewhere (some things bear repeating), when you change ribbons, make sure you clean the printhead.

And here's a suggestion to chew on: If you change ribbons often enough so it becomes annoying, forget the dual mode route and get one printer for each mode. You can afford it with all the money you save on those inexpensive thermal wax prints. (Oh well, there goes the raise.)

WHAT LANGUAGE DOES IT SPEAK?

> We have really everything in common with America nowadays, except, of course, language.
>
> Oscar Wilde
> *The Canterville Ghost,* Ch. 1 (1887)

Some printer issues apply to any printer, no matter what technology it uses. Language is at the top of the list.

In Chapter 1, I mentioned four categories of printer languages: PostScript, PCL, operating-system specific, and other. (Actually, I said the ever-popular other, but the truth is, it's becoming less popular all the time.) In any case, I said all that needs to be said about other languages in the printer language section in Chapter 1. So I'll just mention that you're most likely to find other languages in ink jet printers. I'm going to otherwise ignore them here.

PCL

> For more than forty years I have been speaking prose without knowing it.
>
> Molière

If you have a monochrome laser printer, PCL is the language you've most likely been using for it, whether you know it or not. PCL, short for printer control language, is the umbrella term for Hewlett-Packard's . . . umm . . . printer control language—or printer command set. I say "umbrella term" because there are so many variations that you can't tell the language without a scorecard. (And that's not including inadvertent variations from other manufacturers who are using PCL but didn't quite get it right.)

In one variation or another, PCL is the most common language for color ink jets, and you'll also find it in some wax jets, lasers, and thermal wax printers.

Versions, versions, everywhere The reason there are so many variations is simply that HP (that's Hewlett-Packard) seems to come up with a new version of PCL with every new printer. Some of the new versions include such significant additions that HP bumps up the level to a new number, which is why you'll find a PCL 3, PCL 4, and PCL 5. (Versions before PCL 3 have been lost in the haze of pre-history. I've been looking at HP printers for over a decade, and I don't recall ever seeing one with a version number lower than 3.)

Other changes—like the boost from 300 dpi to 600 by 300 dpi—are so slight that HP doesn't even bother to acknowledge them with a change in name. In between are some variations like PCL 5C, which is the color version of PCL 5. (There is no PCL 3C, although there is a color version of PCL 3. Go figure.)

I'm not going to detail all the variations here, but there are some major dialects you ought to know about. The time may come when you have to use a given printer with a program or operating system that you don't have a driver for. If you know which version of PCL your printer uses, you may be able to make do with a driver for another printer that uses the same level PCL, or a lower level.

Each level of PCL is a superset of all lower levels, so that PCL 4 has all the features of PCL 3 and PCL 5 has all the features of PCL 4. If you use a driver for a lower PCL level than your printer offers, you won't be able to take advantage of all the features in your printer, but you'll still be able to print. If you use a driver with the same level PCL but a slightly different version of that level, once again you should be able to print, though not necessarily take advantage of all the printer's features.

HP describes the various levels of PCL by the applications they're meant for. PCL 1, for example, has print and space functions, which simply means it can print text and spaces and could just as easily describe a typewriter. It was designed for individual users who needed little more than the ability to type text. PCL 2, for electronic data processing and transactions, offers the same features for multiple users printing on the same printer.

Level 1: Print and Space; Level 5: Office publishing; Level 6, household furnishings

But we don't care about those two levels—unless you want to impress your friends and win bar bets. (And now you know why they've faded into the dust.)

PCL level 3 was the first version meant for word processing and office document production. This version was in the original LaserJet. You'll also find it in most ink jet printers that use PCL.

PCL 3

PCL level 4 adds page formatting features, like the ability to download fonts and print in landscape mode, as well as compression to take better advantage of the memory in the printer. This one first showed up in the LaserJet Series II.

PCL 4

> **HP never sold a color printer with PCL 4 in it, and most printers that go beyond PCL level 3 today jump right over level 4 to PCL 5. That means you won't find many color printers that use PCL 4. However, you may trip across some older printers from manufacturers other than HP that use a modified version of PCL 4 with their own color commands added. Brother, for example, used to sell some color printers in this category. Don't expect these printers to print the right colors with any drivers but their own. If you have the opportunity to buy one of these older printers at a corporate garage sale, make sure you get the drivers to go with it.**

PCL level 5, finally, adds what HP calls office publishing features, including scaleable fonts (which means you can scale fonts to any size you like) and more compression modes. It also incorporates HP-GL/2, the Graphics Language HP uses in its plotters. (That's in addition to the PCL graphics commands.) Level 5 first showed up in the LaserJet III and in an enhanced version, sometimes called Enhanced PCL 5 and sometimes called PCL 5e, in the LaserJet 4.

PCL 5

PCL 5C

PCL 5C, the color version of PCL 5, is a relative newcomer. It first showed up in HP's DeskJet 1200C, and you can generally find it in HP's high-end DeskJet printers, with model numbers 1200 and up. You can also find it in HP's Color LaserJet and in a few wax jets and lasers from other manufacturers. As I already mentioned, there is no PCL 3C, as such, but most ink jet printers that use PCL use PCL 3 with color commands added. HP just didn't bother giving the color version its own name.

> Be aware also that a few color printers offer PCL for black and white printing only. It seems that some government purchasing guidelines insist on PCL compatibility for lasers and other high-end printers, even though most applications are more likely to use PostScript. (Where's Al Gore's reinventing government initiative when you really need it?)
>
> At least one manufacturer gets around that minor problem by adding a monochrome version of PCL. Nobody in his or her right mind would ever use it, but it gets the printer the needed check mark on the feature list and lets people buy the printer. So if you're trying to print in color in PCL mode and all you get is black and white, take a closer look at the printer's specifications. There may be a reason for it.

And Everything Not PCL

> There is no such thing as an ugly language. Today I hear every language as if it were the only one, and when I hear of one that is dying, it overwhelms me as though it were the death of the earth.
>
> Elias Canetti
> *The Secret Heart of the Clock: Notes, Aphorisms, Fragments 1973–1985, "1976" (1991)*

Compared to the variations on PCL, the variations on other printer languages are simplicity itself.

PostScript
PostScript is by far the leading choice for all color printers other than ink jets, and you'll find it on a few ink jets also. The advantage of PostScript—and the reason for its popularity in high-end printers—is that it aims at what's called device independence.

Device independence is just another way of saying that if I print something on one printer, it should look the same as if I print it on another. Fonts should look the same, lines and pages should break in the same place, graphics should print at the same size regardless of printer resolution, colors should match, and so on.

If your reaction to that is, *Well, of course they should,* then you clearly have never tried printing a file on two printers that use some other language, or languages, other than PostScript.

Figures 5.9 and 5.10 show the same text formatted for two different printers—the HP LaserJet 4 and the HP DeskJet 1200C.

> The first words spoken on the moon, as most people remember them, were, "That's one small step for man, one giant leap for mankind." Neil Armstrong maintains that what he said was, "That's one small step for a man, one giant leap for mankind." The difference between what he said and what the world heard is probably accounted for by his pronouncing a as uh. So it came out as "foruh man," and the a was lost. But neither of those is really what stays in my mind as the first words on the moon. For me, the first words were, "Houston, Tranquillity Base here. The Eagle has landed."

Figure 5.9 This text is formatted for the Hewlett-Packard LaserJet 4.

> The first words spoken on the moon, as most people remember them, were, "That's one small step for man, one giant leap for mankind." Neil Armstrong maintains that what he said was, "That's one small step for a man, one giant leap for mankind." The difference between what he said and what the world heard is probably accounted for by his pronouncing a as uh. So it came out as "foruh man," and the a was lost. But neither of those is really what stays in my mind as the first words on the moon. For me, the first words were, "Houston, Tranquillity Base here. The Eagle has landed."

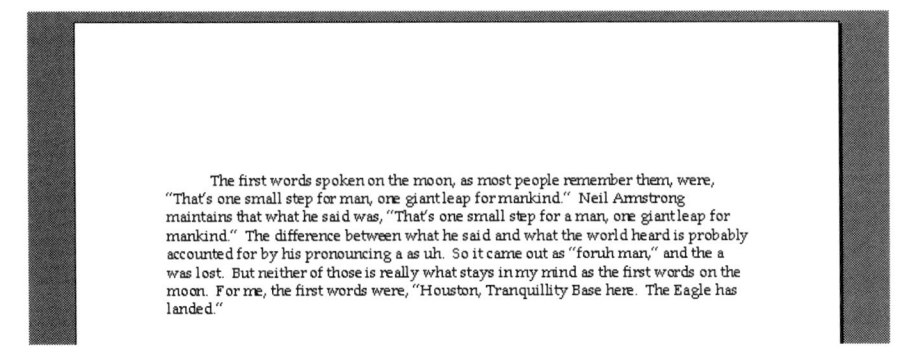

Figure 5.10 Here's the same text as in Figure 5.9, but this time formatted for the HP DeskJet 1200C.

Notice that the lines break in a different place in Figure 5.9 than in Figure 5.10, starting with the second line, which ends with the word *maintains* in Figure 5.9, but with *Armstrong* in Figure 5.10. Notice also that the difference in line breaks translates into an extra line in Figure 5.10. Extra lines like this on even one paragraph on a page can make pages break at a different line and can even change the number of pages in a document. And this is with two printers that claim to use the same language—PCL 5. This is precisely the sort of variation that PostScript is designed to do away with.

This particular problem, with changes in line breaks and page breaks, grows primarily out of differences in fonts from one printer to the next. Even two fonts that look almost identical can have a slightly different width for some characters, or slightly different spacing, so that one font fits more characters into a line than the other.

Even the same font can wind up with different spacing on different printers—or on the same printer set to different resolutions. The TrueType fonts in Windows, for example, will give you different line breaks if you print them at 600 dpi instead of 300 dpi on the same printer.

That's why device independence is PostScript's big claim to fame. If you use a given PostScript font (a.k.a. Adobe Type 1 font) on two different PostScript printers, the line breaks will match, even at different resolutions.

PostScript's device independence has made it the language of choice among the desktop publishing crowd and among graphic artists. Because professional print shops also use PostScript on their printers, you can actually print a PostScript file on a desktop printer and get a close approximation to what you'll see on final output after you send the file to a print shop.

The only noteworthy variations on PostScript are two levels—Level 1 and Level 2 (catchy names, yes?). As I mentioned in Chapter 1, one of the key features in PostScript Level 2 is an attempt to maintain color consistency among printers. So it shouldn't be too surprising that most current color PostScript printers use PostScript Level 2. If you get your hands on an older color PostScript printer, however, don't be surprised if it uses Level 1.

Not so incidentally, most printer manufacturers use Adobe PostScript—Adobe being the home of PostScript in the same way HP is the home of PCL. However, you can find an assortment of PostScript clones as well. As with most clones, these work just like the original the vast majority of the time, but you will occasionally run across some minor differences. These shouldn't be an issue if you use the printer with a driver that came with it. They may be an issue if you try using a non-Adobe printer with an Adobe PostScript driver.

GDI and dumb printers

I mentioned in Chapter 1 that Windows GDI printers use the Windows graphical device interface as a printer language—the same GDI that Windows uses for putting images on the screen. I also mentioned that there are equivalent printers (or even the same printers with different connectors and software) for other environments like the Mac. What I didn't mention is that GDI printers and their equivalents are dumb printers.

What's a dumb printer, you ask? It's a printer that doesn't have much in it besides the printer mechanism itself. Instead of rasterizing the image—converting it to printable form—it lets the computer do the rasterizing (through Windows in the case of GDI printers) and then send the rasterized image to the printer. Think of it this way: Printers are usually considered a peripheral gadget for computers. Dumb printers turn your computer into a peripheral for the printer.

By definition, a dumb printer doesn't process the image in any way. Most printers that work with a page at a time—which includes virtually all laser, wax jet, thermal wax, and thermal dye printers—include a processor and memory to let them process the image before printing. Even most dot matrix printers do some processing, setting a font to wide or condensed, for example. So it's noteworthy when a printer leaves these features out altogether.

The advantage to dumb printers is that the printer doesn't need its own processor or memory, which helps keep the price down. That's why GDI, and its equivalents in other operating systems, often goes hand in hand with low-cost versions of technologies that are usually in more expensive printers, namely thermal wax and thermal dye.

The chief disadvantage of this approach is that it ties up your computer while it's rasterizing the image. How long you have to wait will depend on your computer. The faster your system, the faster it will process any given image. Of course, that can still take quite a while. Print a complex image in thermal dye mode, which is inherently slow to begin with, and you should plan on a coffee break, no matter how fast your computer is.

A second disadvantage of GDI printers in particular is that they can't print from DOS programs. But, of course, this is only an issue if you have a DOS program that you need to print from. If you never venture out of Windows—or, at least, never need to print except from Windows programs—this isn't a problem.

> **Not so incidentally, low-end GDI printers (and their equivalents in other environments) aren't the only dumb printers out there. At least one high-end color printer I know of (at $18,500 I'd say it's pretty high end) works essentially the same way, doing all its work with software at the computer. And it's not even a GDI printer. It uses PostScript. There are also plenty of examples in the monochrome world of dumb printers that use PostScript and PCL. What all these printers have in common is that they tie up your computer while they're rasterizing the image. Some people think dumb printers are the wave of the future. Others think they're just dumb. (I come down on the just dumb side, for most printing needs at least.) The argument for dumb printers is that as computers get more powerful, they can spare some power to take over printing tasks. Maybe so. But up to now, every time computers have ratcheted up to the next power level, a new generation of software has come along to keep them busy.**

PRINTER SIZE—PAPER SIZE

> Size is not grandeur . . .
>
> Thomas H. Huxley

> Regardless of what you might accomplish in life, the size of your funeral is still going to be determined by the weather.
>
> Lewis Grizzard

Printer size—or, more precisely, the size paper a printer can handle—is another issue that cuts across the different technologies. All but a handful of printers fall in one of two size categories: A size, a.k.a. letter size, or B size, a.k.a. tabloid size. A-size paper is 8½ by 11 inches; B-size paper is 17 by 11 inches. That's wide enough to show two letter-size pages at once, which is useful for large graphics or for letting you see facing pages together for desktop publishing output.

A size and B size refer roughly to the largest paper size the printer can handle, but the emphasis is on *roughly,* and the categories are a little broader than the names imply. Most A-size printers, for example, can also handle legal size, at 8½ by 14 inches, and virtually all can print on A3-size paper, the European letter-size standard. Many A-size printers can handle the slightly oversize pages I mentioned earlier—with tear-off strips to give a ribbon-based printer something to hold onto for good registration, while letting it print on most of an 8½- by 11-inch page. Similar variation shows up with B-size printers.

It's an origami bird! It's a paper airplane! It's Super A and B!

There's also a super A size and super B size as subcategories within A and B size. There is no standard paper size for either of these. The definition for super A size is simply that the paper is bigger than A size in both dimensions—9½ by 12, for example, will do just as well as 10 by 13. The definition for super B size is similarly vague—bigger than 11 by 17 in both dimensions.

The implication of either super size is that you can print images as large as a standard page size, and preferably larger—a minimum 8½ by 11 inches for A size or 11 by 17 inches with B size. These full A- or B-size images are called full bleed images, or just full bleeds, because the image bleeds off the edge of an A-size or B-size page. The ability to print full bleeds is useful mainly for publishing or graphics, where you sometimes absolutely require a page-size image or even a little larger. If you can't think of why you'd need that large an image, don't worry about it; you don't need it. But if you do need a larger than usual image for any reason, a super size printer is the way to get it.

I have to rush in with a hedge here and point out that I've seen some super A-size printers that can't print an A-size full bleed, though they print larger images than you can get on the same printer with A-size paper. I've also seen super B-size printers that can't print a B-size full bleed. But any B-size printer should be able to print an A-size full bleed.

You can find both A- and B-size color printers for just about any technology. The exception is laser printers, which are, at this writing, limited to A size. There aren't even any super A-size color lasers.

One other note on size is that there is a third category: The oddball size. I've seen an occasional small size thermal dye printer (well, two of them anyway) designed specifically to print snapshot output on, for example, 4 inch by 5½ inch paper. These printers tend to be less expensive than their A-size cousins, and they certainly cost less per image because they use smaller paper and

less ribbon. If you're looking to print snapshots from, say, photos you scan into your computer, and you don't need to print anything larger, these may be just what you're looking for.

TWO BUYING TIPS

> Money couldn't buy friends, but you got a better class of enemy.
>
> Spike Milligan
> *Puckoon,* Ch. 6 (1963)

Most of the information in this chapter is useful both for using color printers and for the next time you go out to buy one. It seems appropriate to finish up the chapter with two quick buying tips.

Color printers can be expensive to run, with prices up to several dollars per page. So when you go to buy a color printer, you'll want to keep the price per page in mind.

Price per page

Calculating the price for a ribbon-based printer is easy enough—as long as you don't get sidetracked by the overall price of the ribbon itself. First find out the actual price per ribbon—not the list price, but the price you'll actually be paying. And don't overlook the possibility of buying several ribbons at once to save some money on each ribbon. Once you've got the price, divide the total price per ribbon by the number of prints per ribbon to give you the price per image, which is what you're interested in.

For ribbon-based printers, it's easy.

Unless you're using a ribbon that prints on plain paper, the paper is also a significant part of the price, so find out how much the paper costs and calculate the cost per page. Add the price of the ribbon to the price of the paper, and you have the cost per printed page. If you plan to print on different kinds of paper, including transparencies, or use different kinds of ribbons—three-color and four-color ribbons, for example—you'll probably want to calculate the cost per page for each combination you're likely to use.

Calculating the price per page for ink jets, wax jets, and lasers is much harder. In fact, it's essentially impossible without getting your hands on the printer and running tests—something no one outside of a testing lab is likely to do. But you should at least understand why it's impossible, and why you can't trust the manufacturers' claims.

For everything else, it's impossible.

With a ribbon-based printer, you know exactly how much ribbon you'll use on each page, namely, one panel of each color. So it's easy to calculate how much it costs per page. But when you spray ink or wax, or you fuse toner to the page, the amount of ink, wax, or toner on any given page is going to change depending on the image you're using.

We're behind you 400 percent.

Printer manufacturers deal with this lack of predictability by giving prices for some percentage of coverage of the page—10 percent, 25 percent, or whatever. But there's a problem here.

The maximum total coverage you can have with a CMYK color printer isn't 100 percent. It's 400 percent, which means covering 100 percent of the page with each of the four colors.

Of course, you wouldn't do that.

If you cover the entire page with cyan, magenta, and yellow (a total 300 percent coverage), you'll have a page of what's called composite black, because it's a composite of three colors. But you would never use the full 300 percent, even if you wanted a black page, because you could get a better black by using black and covering the page with a mere 100 percent coverage. So the maximum coverage you would ever reasonably use in a real image would be something less than 300 percent. Way less.

The same logic applies to CMY printers, but the maximum possible coverage would be 300 percent.

So when a printer manufacturer claims a certain price per page for, say, 10 percent coverage, it's not at all clear what that means. It's somewhere between a true 10 percent (meaning a 10 percent coverage with a single color) and a true 30 percent (meaning a 10 percent coverage with each of three colors).

Now here's the kicker. The true percentage of coverage for any claimed percentage is completely up to the manufacturer. And since different manufacturers use different scales for coming up with answers, you can't compare the answers from one manufacturer to the next without taking enough salt to worry about raising your blood pressure.

Be aware also that claimed price per page for printers that use plain paper doesn't include the price of the paper, which stays the same from one printer to the next. Also, with laser printers, some manufacturers include other consumables like fuser oil, and the fuser itself, while others don't. Again, this is completely up to the manufacturer. There are no standards.

The moral is simple: Don't take manufacturers' claims of price per page too seriously for ink jets, wax jets, or lasers.

And When You Buy . . .

> Never buy what you do not want because it is cheap; it will be dear [costly] to you.
>
> Thomas Jefferson

Finally, when it comes to choosing which printer to get, there are, to borrow from the old real estate joke, three important considerations: your application, your application, and your application.

There is a wide spread in color printer prices from under $500 to well over $10,000. And there's a spread in price per page also. But the real bottom line is whether the image itself will suit your needs. An inexpensive printer with a low cost per page may sound like a great idea. But if it doesn't produce acceptable output, it's a waste of money.

Concentrate first on finding the printers that can do the kind of printing you need and then consider price. When you go shopping, bring along some representative files to test on the printers. The samples the manufacturers provide are designed to show the printers off to their best advantage. You want to know how the printer will do on the kind of files you print.

6 A Bit of Color

> Color, which is the poet's wealth, is so expensive that most take to mere outline sketches and become men of science.
>
> Henry David Thoreau

> The rays are not colored.
>
> Isaac Newton

Understanding the capabilities of your printer is all good and well, but if you really want to get the most out of a color printer, you also have to understand some basics about color itself. I've covered a lot of the basics already—in Chapters 1 and 3—because without them I couldn't have explained things like color gamuts. In this chapter I'll take a closer look.

Let's start with some ground rules. I'm going to assume you've already read Chapters 1 and 3 and are familiar with color models, color spaces, and color matching in a general way (as opposed to being familiar with them in a major way, I suppose, or even a sergeant major way). If you haven't read them yet, now would be a good time. You'll get more out of this chapter if you do.

You should also be forewarned that this is the most technical chapter in this book. That doesn't mean it's hard to understand, but it goes deeper into some areas than you may want to go. You'll find suggestions sprinkled throughout the chapter for sections you may want to skip. Don't worry about missing something if you do. There's nothing later that builds on anything I'm suggesting that you skip here.

In fact, you may want to skip this entire chapter, or at least skip over it and come back to it later, when you're dying to get into the more advanced issues. But I'd recommend that you at least skim it so you know what's in here and where to find the more advanced stuff when you're ready for it.

That's the only warning (or forewarning) you get. So put on your rose-colored glasses, and let's move on.

COLOR MODELS REVISITED

> I hate flowers—I paint them because they're cheaper than models and they don't move.
>
> Georgia O'Keeffe
> *New York Herald Tribune* (April 18, 1954)

> I can't work without a model.
>
> Vincent Van Gogh
> Letter, Oct. 1888 (published in *The Complete Letters of Vincent Van Gogh,* vol. 3, no. B19, 1958)

If you've learned nothing else about color models up to now, you've probably learned at least that they're meant as convenient ways to describe color. The RGB model describes colors in terms of red, green, and blue components. The CMYK model describes them in terms of cyan, magenta, yellow, and black. And so on.

These particular models have some important limitations. At the top of the list is that the color you get with any given setting varies from one monitor or printer to the next. This much cyan, that much magenta, and a dash of yellow will give you one color on one printer and a visibly different color on another. (The same problem shows up with levels of red, green, and blue on different monitors.) The problem is that the colors you get on a printer using a CMYK model depend on the precise color of the inks you start with.

What you need, if you're going to try for reasonably predictable color for different printers, is some way to describe colors that doesn't change with each printer. In theory, you want a completely objective way to describe color—a color space that you can use to designate any color you want. Then you can worry about coming up with a translation scheme to match the individual printer to the designated color.

The stumbling block is the completely objective way to describe color. Since different people perceive colors differently, there really ain't no such animal.

There is, however, something that comes close—a semi-objective way to describe colors, called the CIE standards, which I mentioned briefly in Chapter 3. All you really have to know about them, besides the name and the fact that they don't vary the way CMYK and RGB colors vary from one printer or monitor to the next, is that PostScript Level 2 uses them as the basis for its color description. And that's where PostScript gets its claim on being able to match colors across printers.

If you're satisfied with that explanation, feel free to skip over the next section. It's there for enquiring minds, who want to know.

CIE Standards

> There is certainly no absolute standard of beauty. That precisely is what makes its pursuit so interesting.
>
> John Kenneth Galbraith
> *New York Times Magazine* (Oct. 9, 1960).

Color, like beauty, has no absolute standard—no objective, unarguable scale to measure it against and declare, Yes, I know exactly what color this is.

Did somebody ask about using wavelengths as an objective measurement? Well, it sounds like a good idea. Unfortunately, it doesn't quite work.

Getting the wavelengths is easy enough. You can measure all the wavelengths, a.k.a. the spectrum, of a beam of light or reflected light with a gadget called a spectrophotometer. (And that's a six-syllable word you should feel free to forget immediately, unless you want to impress your friends.) The problem is that the information isn't particularly useful. **Measuring wavelengths**

In Chapter 1, I brought up the jacket and pants problem—the pieces that match under the fluorescent light in the store but magically turn into different colors the first time you wear them in daylight. **The jacket and pants problem, revisited**

The reason for the jacket and pants problem is that the two pieces—the jacket and pants—reflect different wavelengths of light differently, which is another way of saying that they have different spectrums. (That's spectra for people who think English should use Latin forms, but my dictionary says spectrums is okay.)

Under one color light, each spectrum happens to produce a mix of wavelengths that you wind up perceiving as the same color. So even though the two spectrums are different, they look the same.

Change the color of light—from fluorescent, say, to incandescent or daylight—and the spectrums for the two pieces change—but in different ways, since the two pieces reflect different wavelengths differently. Once again, the two spectrums are different, but now they mix in ways that look different also. Presto chango, you've got two different colors.

The formal name for the jacket and pants problem, by the way, is metamerism. And the two colors that play now-you-see-a-match-and-now-you-don't are metamers, or metameric pairs. (There's another term you can bore your friends with). But the point is that metamers can have widely different spectrums even when they match, which is to say that wavelengths, by themselves, don't tell you what you need to know for building an objective—or even semi-objective—color model. **Metamers**

If you read Chapter 3, you had a quick introduction to the CIE chromaticity diagram in Figure 6.1, which describes colors in terms of their . . . ummm . . . ahhh . . . chromaticity.

222 *Chapter 6*

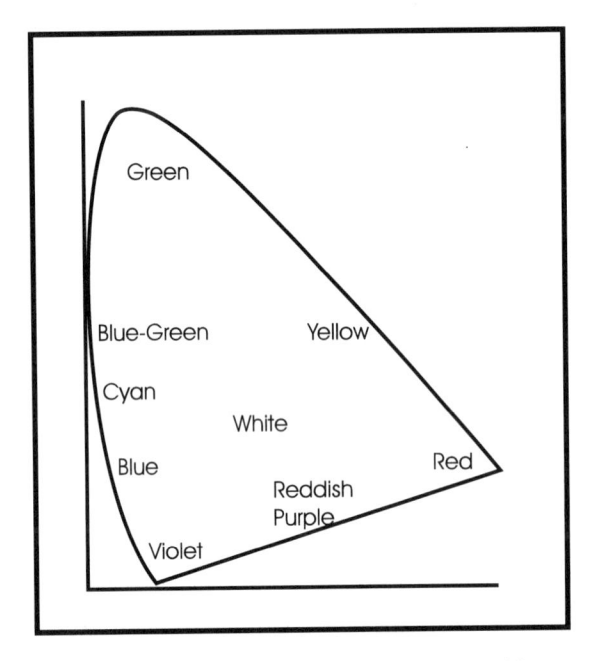

Figure 6.1 This CIE chromaticity diagram, with pure colors from the spectrum mapped to the outside of the horseshoe.

Chromaticity (which you may not remember, since I whizzed past it as fast as I could get away with in Chapter 3) takes both hue and saturation into account. The diagram maps the pure, fully saturated hues of the visible spectrum to the horseshoe-shaped line. As you move inside the horseshoe, toward the white area, you move to zero saturation.

So the position of any individual color on this chart depends on both hue and saturation—or chromaticity. And since you can define any color by hue, saturation, and brightness, you can, as I pointed out in Chapter 3, also define any color by chromaticity and brightness.

Here's something to file under things you don't really need to know but may find interesting (or may want to skip). The chromaticity diagram in Figure 6.1 uses the spectrum of a colored object to predict what the color will look like. The CIE scheme divides the visible spectrum into three components, which it calls red, green, and blue, although each chunk covers a much wider range of the spectrum than the names indicate. I'll call them red, green, and blue chunks here, to keep a clear distinction between parts of the spectrum and the actual colors you see.

The chart graphs the percentage of the red chunk on the horizontal axis and the percentage of the green chunk on the vertical axis. (The percentage of blue

chunk of the spectrum is whatever is left over.) So by looking at the spectrum of a particular color in a given light, you can tell what the color will look like. The intersection of 33.3% red chunk and 33.3% green chunk, for example, is dead center in the white area of the chart. Be aware, however, that other mixtures of colors also produce white.

The CIE equations that lie behind the diagram are based on a hypothetical average person, the CIE Standard Observer. This mythical Standard Observer is a mathematical average (with 2.4 children and 0.9 cars, no doubt) based on real color-matching experiments with real people. Individuals may still disagree whether two given colors match, but the hypothetical average is as close to a truly objective description of color as you can get.

Incidentally, the original chromaticity diagram was introduced in 1931, and it has some limitations of its own. But there's no need to go into those here. I'll simply mention that the CIE has since recommended other standards to address those limitations. You can usually recognize them by the *CIE* in the names, as in the CIE 1976 UCS Chromaticity diagram (now there's a mouthful), the CIELUV color space, and the CIELAB color space (sometimes given simply as the L*a*b* color space). But all of these build on the 1931 diagram, rather than replace it, and you don't need to know any more about them than that.

Other Color Models

> Heroism has no model.
>
> Louis Antoine Leon de Saint-Just

Before we leave color models entirely, I need to mention a few odds and ends, just so you won't get overly confused if you run into them elsewhere. Most important, is that the color models I've discussed in this book—RGB, CMYK, HSB, (that's hue, saturation, and brightness, if you've forgotten), and the various flavors of CIE—aren't the only color models out there. So don't be too surprised if you run into others.

One of the better known models that I've completely ignored is the Munsell color system, which was created by Albert Munsell. I see Tim, our resident artist, nodding in agreement. That's because the Munsell system is well known among artists, and Tim's probably run into it in an art class. — **The Munsell color system**

Munsell was an artist, and the Munsell system is designed from an artist's perspective. There's no point in going into the details here—you don't need to understand the model to work with printers. But it is worth mentioning that the Munsell system has its own terminology that you may run into occasionally.

The Munsell system describes each color by hue, value, and chroma, or HVC, and is sometimes called the HVC model. Hue means the same as hue in the HSB — **Hue, value, chroma** model, and value means the same thing as brightness in the HSB model. Chroma is similar to saturation, and you'll often see it defined as being the same. But it's actually a slightly different concept.

I won't get into the difference here, because you don't need to know it. You may find it helpful to recognize the term when you see it, however, which is why I brought it up. (And if you really want to know the difference between saturation and chroma, you'll find a short explanation under *chroma* in the Glossary.)

HSV, HLS, HSL

Two other models you may run across are HSV (hue, saturation, value) and HSL (hue, saturation, lightness), which is also known as HLS. The underlying concepts for these models are the same as for the HSB model. Hue and saturation mean the same thing in all three models. Brightness, lightness, and value are all measures of lightness and darkness.

The important thing to understand about the HSV and HSL models is that even though they are similar to the HSB model in concept, they're different in some particulars. They have different mathematical descriptions, which is another way of saying that their color spaces are each a different geometric shape. The good news is that there's no reason to go any deeper than this nodding acquaintance with these models.

COLOR MATCHING REVISITED

> There are strange flowers of reason to match each error of the senses.
>
> Louis Aragon
> Paris Peasant, "Preface to a Modern Mythology" (1926)

I spent a large part of Chapter 3 talking about color matching—or mismatching—between the screen and printer. I also promised to come back to some of the more advanced issues that I ignored then. If you don't want to know anything about those advanced issues, feel free to skip this entire section and fast forward to Chapter 7. This section is here for the two or three people out there who want to go the extra step to get a closer match between screen and printer.

Even if you fall in that group, this information isn't going to help much unless you use a program that offers advanced color management. There aren't many. I'll use CorelDRAW in my example, because it offers one of the more advanced color management features available. If you understand the choices in CorelDRAW, you should be able to make sense out of any program with an equivalent or lesser capability.

Calibrating a Monitor

> Everything is complicated; if that were not so, life and poetry and everything else would be a bore.
>
> Wallace Stevens
> Letter, 1935 (published in *Letters of Wallace Stevens,* no. 336, ed. by Holly Stevens, 1967)

In Chapter 3, I gave you a quick peek at the CorelDRAW 5 dialog boxes for calibrating the monitor and printer, and I begged off explaining them. (Which was a really good idea.) But I promised to come back to them to later. (Which may not have been quite as good an idea.) Well, here it is later. What I plan to do is take you on a quick tour of the dialog boxes so you'll understand the terms. You may still have trouble filling in the numbers, but at least you'll know what the numbers are for and how to fudge them.

Let's tackle the Monitor Calibration dialog box first.

As I pointed out in Chapter 3, both of the calibration dialog boxes are a little daunting. The Monitor Calibration dialog box, shown in Figure 6.2, is filled with terms whose meaning isn't immediately obvious. And if you don't know what the terms mean, there's not much chance you can figure out what numbers to fill in. (The Printer Calibration dialog box is even worse, but let's take one at a time.)

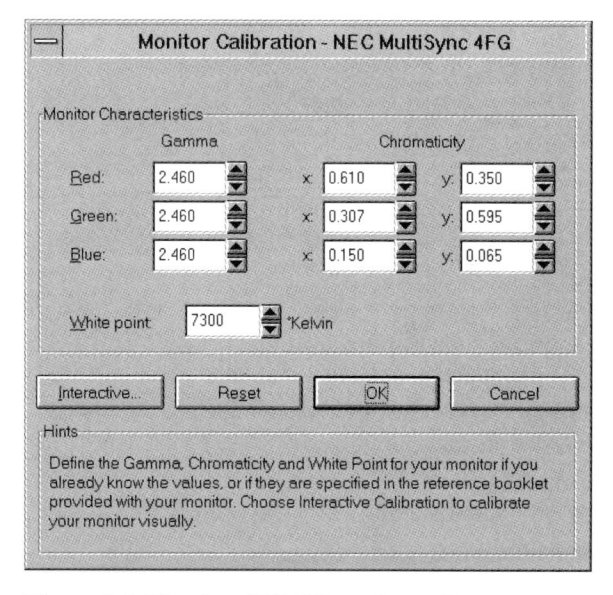

Figure 6.2 The CorelDRAW monitor calibration dialog box lets you define settings for your monitor, to help match colors between monitor and printer.

Chromaticity

As you can see in the figure, you need to fill in three kinds of settings to define the monitor characteristics: gamma for red, green, and blue; chromaticity for red, green, and blue; and white point. Let's start with chromaticity.

Everybody here remembers the CIE chromaticity diagram, right? I mentioned it earlier in this chapter, in a section I invited you to skip over. But even if you skipped the section, you should remember the chart, however vaguely, from Chapter 3, where I brought it up so I could explain color gamuts for monitors and printers. Well here it is again, in Figure 6.3.

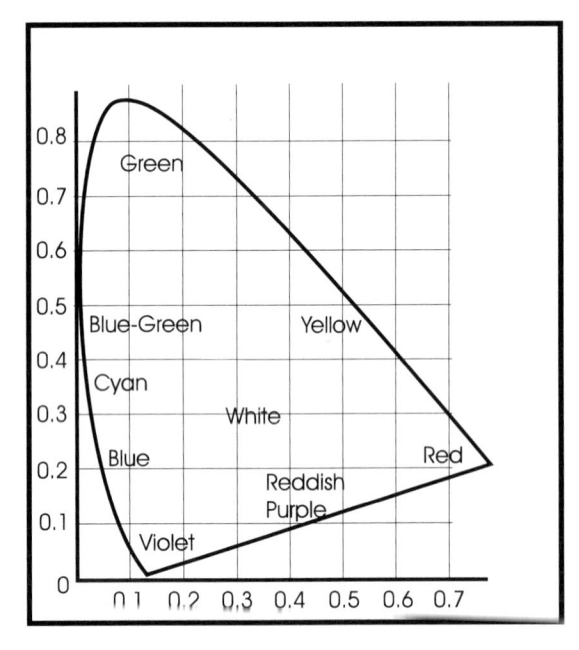

Figure 6.3 The CIE chromaticity diagram, with labels on the axes this time.

The horseshoe shape should look familiar. Fully saturated colors in the visible spectrum lie on the horseshoe outline itself, with less saturated colors on the inside. I've also added a grid in this version to show the values on the x and y axes. (That's x for the horizontal axis and y for the vertical, for those of you who haven't been in a math class lately.)

Now I have to repeat something from the section on the CIE standards that I invited you to skip over. If you read that section, it won't hurt to read these two paragraphs again, especially since I'm going to add more information. If you skipped over it, you can't afford to miss this little nugget, since it explains the values on the axes.

What the numbers mean

The CIE scheme divides the visible spectrum into three components. These usually go by the names red, green, and blue, although each chunk covers a much wider range of the spectrum than the names indicate. As I said before, I'll call them red, green, and blue chunks, to keep a clear distinction between parts of the spectrum and actual colors.

The CIE chromaticity chart graphs the percentage of the red chunk on the horizontal, or x, axis, as a number between 0 and 1, so that 0.1 is 10 percent, 0.2 is 20 percent, and so on. The percentage of the green chunk goes on the vertical, or y, axis, also as a number between 0 and 1. The percentage of blue chunk isn't ignored. It's whatever is left over after you subtract the percentage of red chunk and the percentage of green chunk from 1.

As you probably remember from Chapter 3, you can define the color gamut for a monitor by finding the coordinates for the phosphors in the monitor. You then draw straight lines between the red, green, and blue points to get a triangle that includes all the colors the monitor can produce.

You may be ahead of me by now. The coordinates for each of those points—red, green, and blue—are given as the percentage of red on the x axis and the percentage of green on the y axis.

Now go back and take a look at the chromaticity settings in the CorelDRAW Monitor Dialog box, and you'll see that for each color, you have two numbers between 0 and 1. And the numbers are labeled x and y.

If you use the numbers in Figure 6.2 as coordinates in the chart from Figure 6.3, and then connect the dots, you'll get the color gamut shown in Figure 6.4. (Or something close to it. I did this by hand.)

The point is that what CorelDRAW is asking for is for you to define the color gamut for the monitor.

There's good news and bad news about these numbers.

The bad news is that this is not the sort of number that you'll usually find in your monitor's manual. If you're lucky, the program you're using will have a sample profile for the model monitor you're using, with the numbers already in it. Otherwise, you'll typically have to call the manufacturer to get these numbers.

The good news is that because the numbers depend on the phosphors, they're essentially identical from one monitor to the next for any given brand and model. That means you don't have to do anything special to find the right numbers for your monitor as opposed to some mythical specification for the model. Unfortunately, the same can't be said for the gamma and white point settings. But that's getting ahead of myself. Let's talk about what those settings are first.

Gamma

We talked about gamma a little in Chapter 3 also. I mentioned then that the ideal gamma setting adjusts both brightness and contrast in a way that brings out details better in both light and dark areas. Well that explains what it *does*, but it doesn't explain what gamma *is*. Fortunately, you don't need to know what gamma is, because it's not something you have to deal with directly.

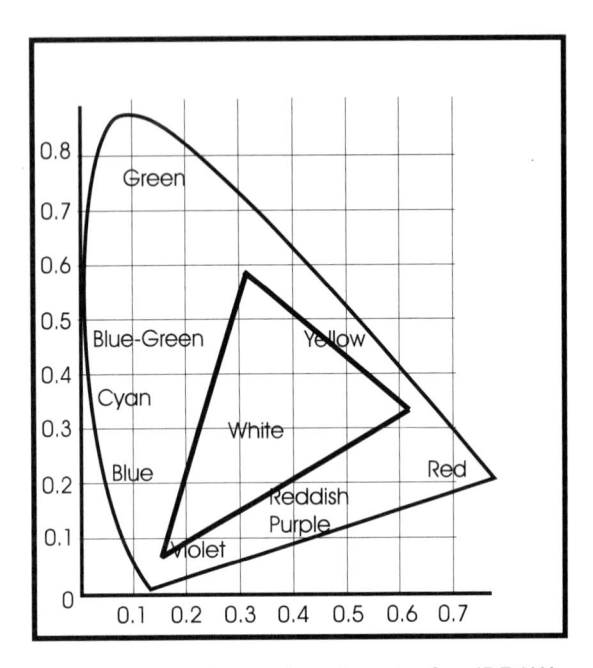

Figure 6.4 Map the numbers from the CorelDRAW Monitor Calibration dialog box on the CIE chromaticity chart, and voilà. You get the color gamut for the monitor.

I see Arnold's here, and wants to know what gamma correction really is. So here it is, for Arnold only. The rest of you can skip this note.

Gamma means something different for different technologies. It's different for photography, for example, than for monitors. For a monitor, gamma is a relationship between the drive voltage of an electron gun and the level of luminance (that's brightness to you and me) at the screen. When a program wants to create a pixel of a given color on screen, it has to control the brightness, or intensity, of the red, green, and blue dots in that pixel. That's basic. But it doesn't control the intensity directly. It controls the drive voltage for each electron gun, and it's the drive voltage that determines the intensity for each dot.

The problem is that the drive voltage and intensity don't have a simple straight-line relationship. If they did, increasing the drive voltage by equal steps would always increase the intensity by equal steps. But it doesn't. Increasing the voltage by a given amount at low intensity increases the intensity only a little. Increasing voltage by the same amount at high intensity increases intensity a lot. So if you make a graph of luminance on the vertical axis against voltage on the horizontal axis, you'll get a curved line. Worse, you can get a different curve for each electron beam. That makes it hard for a program to calculate the right drive voltage to use to get any given level of intensity for each electron beam.

That's where gamma correction comes in. If you graph the log of the luminance against the log of the drive voltage, you'll get a straight line. (Oh, goody. Logarithms.) The gamma is the slope of that line. Once you tell a program the gamma correction for each electron beam, it can calculate intensities, and give you the right colors. Or you can simply match the patches and not worry about why it works. So much, for now, for gamma.

Just match the patch.

I already mentioned the bad news about gamma—it varies from one monitor to the next, even for the same brand and model. In fact, it varies for any given monitor over its lifetime, as it ages.

The good news is that just about any program that asks you to set gamma will give you a way to determine gamma by eye. Typically this means you get a slider control and two patches of gray, or two patches each of red, green, and blue, and you adjust the control for each pair until the two patches match. (This is something I'm assuming you still remember from Chapter 3.) If you can match the patches, you don't need to know anything else about gamma. End of discussion.

White point

According to CorelDRAW's help file, the white point setting defines the color temperature of your monitor in creating white. Uh-huh. And now you probably know just as much as you did before.

This one isn't too hard to explain. Physicists have an ideal that they call a blackbody, which is so good at absorbing light that it doesn't reflect any light at all. Soot is a pretty close approximation to a blackbody. That's why it's black.

If you heat a blackbody enough so it starts to glow, the only light you see coming from it is the light that it's putting out. Since the color of glow changes with temperature—starting as red hot when it's relatively cool and working its way up to white hot—the color of the blackbody is also an indication of its temperature. And since the only light coming from the blackbody is the light that it's radiating, all blackbody radiators are the same color at any given temperature.

Now turn that around. Since you always get a given color at a given temperature, you can specify a color by giving the temperature it goes with. That's a color temperature. And that's why the white point on the CorelDRAW screen is in degrees Kelvin. The white point is the color temperature you get with all the electron guns at full intensity.

Just as with gamma, the color temperature for white varies from one monitor to the next, even for the same brand and model. It also changes as the monitor ages. But as with gamma, any program that lets you set the white point will usually let you adjust it by eye.

Just to make this a little more concrete, take a look at Figure 6.5, which shows CorelDRAW 5's Interactive Monitor Calibration dialog box. (You get there by choosing the Interactive button in the Monitor Calibration dialog box, unless you're using CorelDRAW 6 in Windows 95. CorelDRAW 6 doesn't bother with the dialog box shown in Figure 6.2. If you choose to calibrate your monitor, the program goes through a color wizard to take you directly to a slightly modified version of the dialog box in Figure 6.5.)

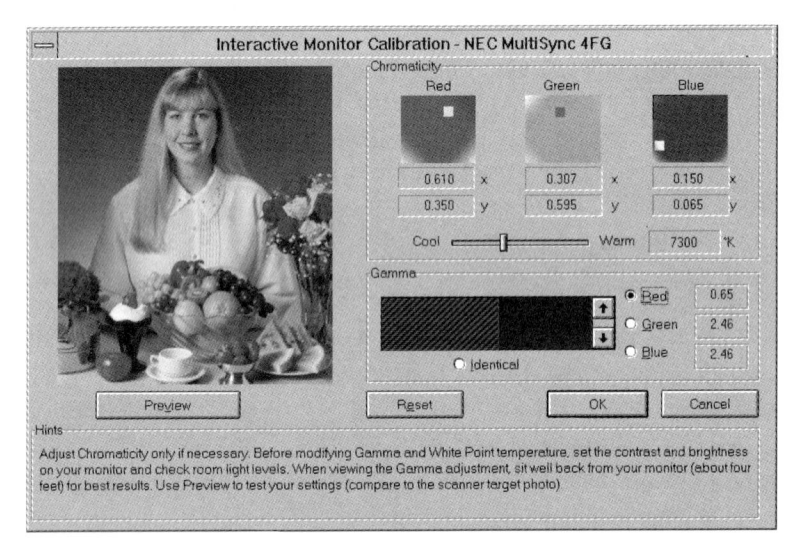

Figure 6.5 CorelDRAW's interactive calibration screen makes life a lot easier if you want to try for a better color match between screen and printer.

Equivalent features in other programs are likely to be different in detail, but they'll share a few similarities. In particular, notice the Gamma box. To make it easy to see the different blocks in the figure, I've set them to be extremely different. To make them match, you click on the up and down arrows to the right of the two blocks.

You can also see option buttons for Red, Green, and Blue to the right of the arrows. These let you adjust the settings for each color separately. The button under the two blocks, labeled Identical, lets you adjust all three colors to the same setting, using gray. If you have a program that gives you the choice between setting each color separately or setting them all at once, stay with the separate settings.

Setting the white point

Just above the Gamma box in the figure, you'll notice a slider that goes from cool to warm. That's the white point setting.

Here's the strategy for calibrating a monitor in any program that gives you all of these choices:

First, if the program comes with sample files for your model monitor, don't mess with the chromaticity settings. If it doesn't come with files for your

monitor, get the settings from the manufacturer, plug them in as numbers, and don't mess with the settings after that.

Second, get the gamma right. If you have the choice between setting everything at once, or setting red, green, and blue separately, set them separately.

Third, once you have the chromaticity and gamma settings right, you can play with the white point settings. CorelDRAW makes this fairly easy by giving you a sample picture on the left side of the dialog box and a matching photo tucked into the manual. If you get the photo out, you can compare it to the screen and simply experiment with different color temperature settings until you get a match. With CorelDRAW, by the way, you have to choose the Preview button after each adjustment to see the effect of the change. If you have a program that lets you set the color temperature for white, but doesn't give you a photo on screen and off to compare, fall back on calling the monitor manufacturer, and asking what to use. You won't get the precisely right setting for your monitor, but the manufacturer's guess will probably be better than yours.

One other point about calibrating a monitor: Unless your video card and driver use at least 32,000 colors (15-bit color, if you prefer), and preferably 64,000 (16-bit color) or more, you won't benefit much from previewing the image on screen. But if you're concerned enough with colors to care about matching colors, you ought to be running at least 64K colors anyway, so that shouldn't be a problem.

I should also mention that there's at least one other setting for monitor calibration, which you'll find in CorelDRAW 6 if nowhere else. The color manager in CorelDRAW 6 adds an ambient light setting, which you can set to low, medium, high, or to a custom setting. You should do just fine picking from the low, medium, and high choices—and usually medium or high, depending on how bright it is around your monitor. Low is for people who work with the lights off.

So much for monitor calibration. Now on to the printer.

Calibrating a Printer

> Men occasionally stumble over the truth, but most of them pick themselves up and hurry off as if nothing happened.
>
> Winston Churchill

The first thing you need to know about calibrating a printer is that there are radically different approaches to calibration. They range all the way from piece-of-cake easy to don't-try-this-at-home-kids hard.

At the easy side of the range, a few high-end printers come with software for calibrating the printer itself. The software typically comes with samples of some sort, and it lets you print out pages so you can match the printouts to samples by eye. You then tell the software which part of the printout matches which sample.

The easy way

The hard way

The software tells the printer, and the printer stores the settings. And just like that, you get better-looking colors.

At the hard side of the range are programs like CorelDRAW 5, which lets you build a profile that CorelDRAW can use to override what the printer wants to do. (In CorelDRAW, you'll find an option in the Print dialog box to use the printer profile or not.)

CorelDRAW 5 comes with over two dozen printer profiles, including some generic choices. If you start with one of the profiles that comes with the package, it's easy enough to tweak it for your individual printer. If you start from scratch, however, you have to print samples and measure the colors in those samples with something called a colorimeter. What's that, you ask? Don't worry about it. If you have to ask, you probably don't have one sitting around and probably don't want one. And that pretty much leaves you with tweaking the generic profiles.

In between these two extremes is an approach like the one in CorelDRAW 6. CorelDRAW 6 lets you use a scanner, if you have one, to scan a sample image that comes with the package. You can then print the scanned image, compare the printout to the original by eye, and adjust the printer based on what you see. If you don't have a scanner, you're back to relying on tweaking generic profiles.

Let's take the hard way.

Given the wide variety of approaches to calibrating a printer, I'll use CorelDRAW 5 for an example precisely because it's a tough one. If you understand the calibration choices CorelDRAW 5 gives you, as shown in Figure 6.6, you shouldn't have any trouble understanding an easier or less complete approach. Be forewarned that I'm not going to explain anything in much depth here; I'm just going to breeze through the choices and explain what they are.

Starting on the upper left of the dialog box, the first issue is to define your printer type as CMYK or RGB. This doesn't mean what you probably think it means.

Why a CMYK printer can be RGB

Just because your printer prints with cyan, magenta, yellow, and black doesn't make it a CMYK printer. At least, not from your software's point of view. Not if the software is trying to manage color. What your software cares about is whether the printer takes its orders in terms of CMYK, CMY, or RGB color models. Lots of printers, or printer drivers, take orders as RGB and do the conversion to CMYK themselves.

If the printer or driver wants CMYK, it's a CMYK printer. Otherwise it's an RGB printer. Even if it wants its orders in CMY, it's an RGB printer. (Yes, you read that right. And no, it's not really an RGB printer, but that's what CorelDRAW 5 calls it. If there ain't no K, it ain't CMYK. It's RGB.)

If you're lucky, the software's option names, help files, or both will do a better job of explaining this than CorelDRAW 5 manages. CorelDRAW 6, for one, does a better job. The RGB option is renamed to: 3 and 4 inks (RGB, CMY and some CMYK printers). The CMYK option is renamed to: 4 inks (CMYK printers). Even better, the program includes a test page you can print to tell you which option to

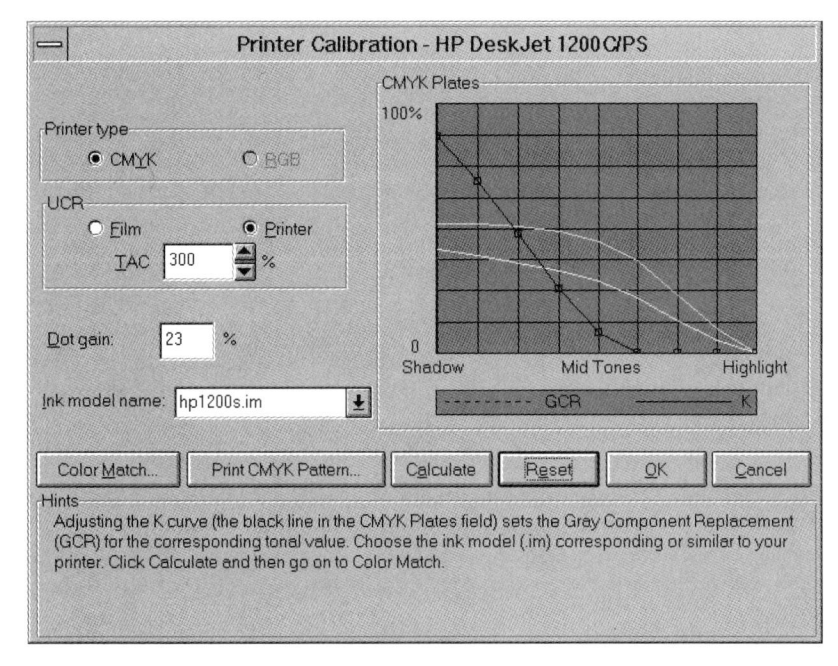

Figure 6.6 The CorelDRAW Printer Calibration dialog box lets you define settings for your printer to help match colors between monitor and printer.

choose. With CorelDRAW 5, you have to guess, call the printer manufacturer, or check with Corel.

While you're waiting for the answer, the rule of thumb is that most ink jet printers are RGB and most others are CMYK. Except for the exceptions, of course. The HP DeskJet 1200C, for example, is RGB in PCL mode, but CMYK in PostScript mode.

If you got to this dialog box (or an equivalent in another program) by picking your printer from a list, just accept the printer type the program offers.

The reason this option matters is that the most important other options in the dialog box deal with how to handle the black ink. If you pick RGB, those other options go away, and you get a much simpler dialog box (which we'll come back to later).

Next down, in the UCR box, is the choice between Film and Printer. It's not too hard to guess which one you want for a printer, yes? (Film is for output devices that create slides on film.) The more important item here is the text box labeled TAC.

This puts us in the land of too many TLAs (three-letter acronyms). UCR stands for undercolor removal. Basically, it's a technique for replacing the combi-

Getting TACky

nation of cyan, magenta, and yellow inks in neutral, or hueless, areas with black. But there's no reason you have to know that. The important TLA here is TAC, which stands for total area coverage. Worry about the total area coverage; let the program worry about how that translates to undercolor removal.

Quick question: What's the maximum percentage of ink coverage you can have on a page? (Warning: It's a trick question.)

Time's up. What's your answer? Did you say 100 percent?

Bzzzzz.

Wrong. (I *told* you it was a trick question.)

Why 100 percent isn't 100 percent. Each color ink can cover up to 100 percent of the page. But with four inks to work with, the color coverage can go up to 400 percent—100 percent for each ink.

Of course, 400 percent coverage is overkill since 100 percent black plus any amount of cyan, magenta, and yellow will still be black. And aside from wasting ink, 400 percent coverage simply doesn't look all that good. So what this entry is looking for is the maximum total ink coverage to use.

Corel suggests that most printers support a practical maximum of 300 percent coverage, with the best looking output somewhere between 260 and 280 percent. On the other hand, some of the printer profiles that come with CorelDRAW go as high as 340 or as low as 220. Corel also suggests you ask the printer manufacturer what setting it recommends. Good idea. When you ask, be aware that the best setting can change depending on the paper you're using, so ask about the specific papers you use.

Next down in Figure 6.6 are Dot Gain and ink model name. Don't bother with these. Just accept the entries the program gives you for the printer or generic type of printer you chose when you opened the dialog box. I'll just mention in passing that dot gain refers to the tendency for halftone dots to grow larger than their intended size.

And now for that graph . . . The right side of the page is the really scary part, with the mostly indecipherable graph, shown again in Figure 6.7, so you don't have to turn back a page to see it.

If you have CorelDRAW 5, you'll find you can grab any of the little black boxes on the black line and you can change the shape of the line by moving the boxes up or down. Just click on a box with the left mouse button, hold the button down while you move the line, and set the new position by releasing the button. If you then choose the Calculate button at the bottom of the dialog box, CorelDRAW will recalculate the cyan, magenta, and yellow lines in the graph.

Of course that doesn't explain what the graph is about. And it doesn't explain the GCR at the bottom of the graph—another TLA.

GCR is short for gray component replacement, which is a variation on undercolor removal. But instead of applying only to neutral colors, GCR looks for the gray component in other colors.

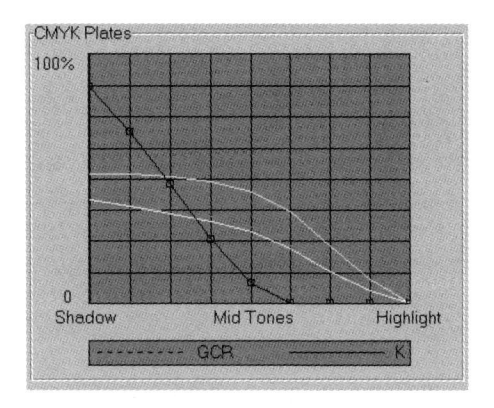

Figure 6.7 Here's the graph again from the CorelDRAW Printer Calibration dialog box.

The idea of a gray component in colors is simple enough. Since equal parts of cyan, magenta, and yellow add up to gray or black, depending on the saturation, any color that includes all three inks consists of a gray component, plus extra parts of one or two of the primary colors.

> **If you prefer seeing things in terms of numbers, try these: A setting of, say, 10 for cyan, 10 for magenta, 10 for yellow, and 0 for black in the CMYK model gives you a light gray. A setting of 10 for cyan, 10 for magenta, 75 for yellow, and 0 for black gives a somewhat dark yellow. More important, it's indistinguishable from a setting of 0 for cyan and magenta, 65 for yellow, and 10 for black. That's the gray component. Don't take my word for this. if you have a program that lets you define colors in the CMYK model, try it for yourself.**

Adjusting the curve for the black is another issue altogether. If you like, you can try changing it by trial and error to find the setting that looks best for your printer. But you're best advised to simply accept the settings the program gives you, based on the printer you chose when you opened the dialog box.

I promised to come back to the simplified dialog box you'll see if you choose RGB for printer type. To see how simplified, take a look at Figure 6.8.

And then there's them RGB printers

The only choice you have in this dialog box is to pick an RGB file—unless you want to print samples and measure them with equipment you probably don't have. Here again, you're best off accepting the file the program suggests, even if it's just a generic file. If you insist on a better match than that, you probably shouldn't be using an ink jet printer in any case.

And that, finally, covers everything you'll probably ever want to know about printer calibration—and maybe a bit more. In Chapter 7 we'll move on to the issue of using color.

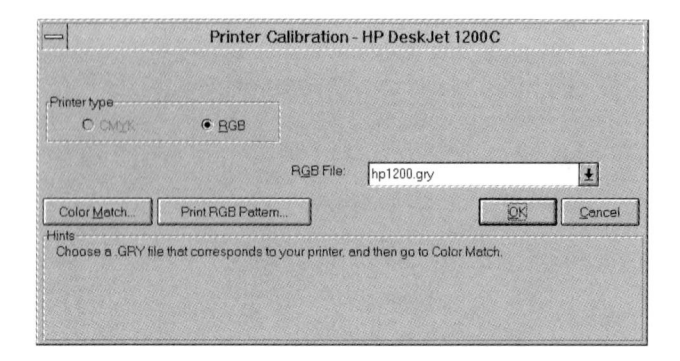

Figure 6.8 The CorelDRAW 5 Printer Calibration dialog box for RGB printers.

7 Making Color Work

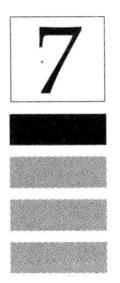

> The painter of the future will be a colorist such as there has never been.
>
> Vincent Van Gogh

Any artist can come up with a seemingly unlimited number of rules of thumb about using colors and creating color schemes. The rest of us react to these colors just the way we're supposed to, but often without being fully aware of our reaction. Part of what artists have going for them is an understanding of color harmony—some basic principles that serve as good starting points for color design no matter how talented, or untalented, you happen to be.

The main point of this chapter is to give you some background for designing your own color schemes. Don't get me wrong; I'm not going to try to teach you everything you need to know about using color in one short chapter. (And I'm certainly not going to try it when the only examples I can give are in black and white.) But I am going to give you hints about where to start experimenting with color on your own, and some rules of thumb for using color.

Before we can get to those, we have to talk a little bit about color theory—or, more precisely, the theory of color harmony. (Which, thankfully, sounds more formal and complicated than it is. It's much easier than, say, music theory.) When we're done with talking about color schemes, we'll round out the chapter with a short discussion of things you probably don't need to know. (What's that, you ask? Stay tuned and find out.)

So let's start with what you have to know to understand how to use color. Let's start with some theory.

COLOR (HARMONY) THEORY

> Let us work without theorizing.
>
> Voltaire
> Martin, in *Candide*, Ch. 30 (1759)

> Frankly, these days, without a theory to go with it, I can't see a painting.
>
> Tom Wolfe
> *The Painted Word*, Ch. 1 (1975)

One of the most useful starting points for choosing colors is the color wheel, shown in black and white in Figure 7.1. Since we're working in black and white here, you'll have to use your imagination to fill in the colors to match the labels. (Or you can sneak a look at the same color wheel on the last page in the color section in this book.) But even a black and white color wheel is useful, as long as the names for the colors are nearby.

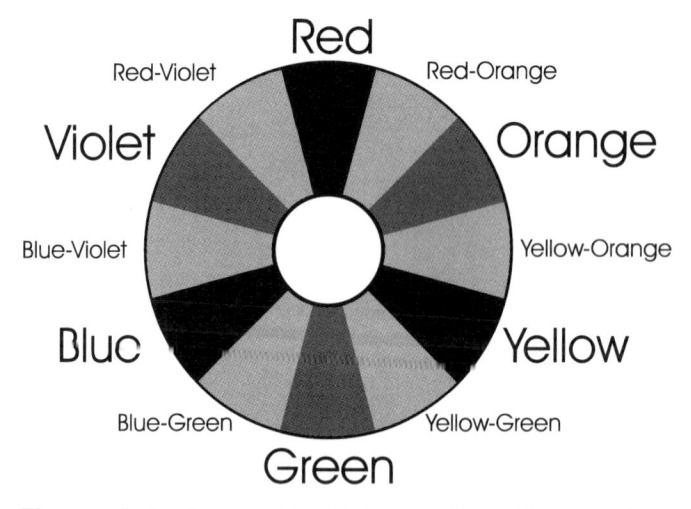

Figure 7.1 A color wheel, in black and white, with the twelve basic colors.

Variations on the color wheel

The first thing you need to know is that there are all sorts of variations on this color wheel. You can, for example, find versions that are the mirror image of Figure 7.1. Instead of going clockwise from red, to red-orange, to orange, the colors run counter-clockwise though the same colors. And there's no reason why red has to be in the 12 o'clock position. Pick up any book at random that discusses the color wheel, and you may find some other color at the top.

Whatever color is at the top, however, and whether the colors run in the same direction as in the figure or are a mirror image, the colors are always in the same order.

The second thing you need to know is that the color wheel in Figure 7.1 is somewhat simplified compared to some other versions. A full-blown color wheel has the same twelve wedges, with each wedge a single hue, but with each wedge also divided into slices of varying tints (the fully saturated hue with white added) and shades (the fully saturated hue with black added). So each wedge looks something like Figure 7.2. I'll ignore these variations here, but you should be aware that they exist.

A color wheel can be more complex.

Figure 7.2 Each wedge in a color wheel can show slices of different tints and shades, all with the same hue.

By the way, you can keep shades and tints straight by remembering that things look darker in the shade, so you get shades of colors by adding black. Tint is the other one.

The third thing you need to know is that artists talk funny. What's that mean, you ask? Well, read on.

The Artist's Vocabulary

> After all, when you come right down to it, how many people speak the same language even when they speak the same language?
>
> Russell Hoban
> Boaz-Jachin, in *The Lion of Boaz-Jachin and Jachin-Boaz,* Ch. 27 (1973)

When artists talk about color, they use most of the same words that the computer world uses. But they don't always mean the same thing.

The idea of tints and shades is one example. When you're talking about computers or printers, you can talk about shades of gray or shades of color—PostScript defines 256 shades for any given hue at any given saturation. But with

CMYK printers, every variation on lightness is a shade. There are no tints. After all, there isn't any white ink to add, just black. (Although moving toward lower saturation at maximum brightness—which means moving toward white—is the equivalent of adding white.)

There's even more room for confusion when you start talking about the colors themselves. To artists, the primary colors are blue, red, and yellow. I've seen comments in computer books that dismiss this as semantics and insist that artists really mean cyan, magenta, and yellow. People who say that haven't taken a close enough look at a color wheel.

As you can see in Figure 7.1 and more easily in the slightly different version of the color wheel in Figure 7.3, the blue, red, and yellow are spaced evenly around the wheel, forming an equilateral triangle.

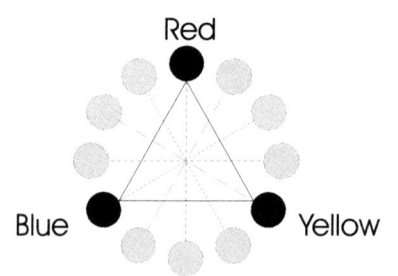

Figure 7.3 The primary colors on a color wheel.

The spacing between colors matters because it's the basis for all the rules for using the color wheel to put together a color scheme. We'll get to the details shortly. Right now, just take my word for it that if you don't have an equilateral triangle, everything else gets thrown off.

If you get your hands on a color wheel, you'll see that the colors in those positions are truly blue, red, and yellow. The red and blue may not be quite the same colors that a print shop would call red and blue, but they're a lot closer to a print shop's red and blue than they are to magenta and cyan.

Magenta (or the closest thing to it) would be one step counterclockwise from red, and cyan (or the closest thing to it) would be one step counterclockwise from blue. If you try drawing the triangle between those two positions and yellow, it won't be an equilateral triangle. Instead, you'll have four steps between yellow and red and only two steps between yellow and blue.

The secondary colors for an artist don't match anything we've talked about up to now either. Each secondary color—violet, orange, and green—is half-way between two primary colors, as shown in Figure 7.4. The three secondary colors form their own equilateral triangle. Here again, these colors are definitely orange, violet, and green—not red, green, and blue masquerading under different names.

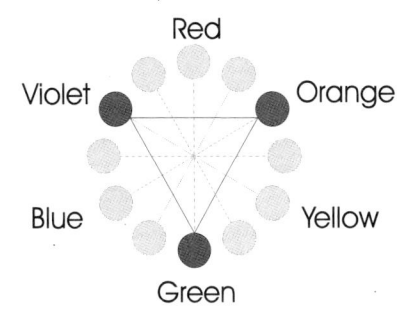

Figure 7.4 The secondary colors on a color wheel fall midway between the primary colors.

Artists also talk about tertiary colors—the other six colors on the color wheel. Each tertiary color sits between a primary and secondary color, as shown in Figure 7.5. They get their names from the colors to either side: red-orange, yellow-orange, yellow-green, blue-green, blue-violet, and red-violet.

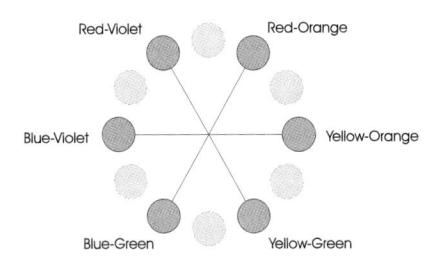

Figure 7.5 Each of the tertiary colors on a color wheel falls between a primary and secondary color.

The last piece of vocabulary you need to learn right now is complementary colors. The complement to any given color on the color wheel is the color directly opposite. So, as you can see in Figure 7.6, red and green are complements, red-orange and blue-green are compliments, and so on.

Not so incidentally, complementary colors aren't just some arbitrary accident of where the colors happen to fall on the color wheel. The colors are at those positions for a reason.

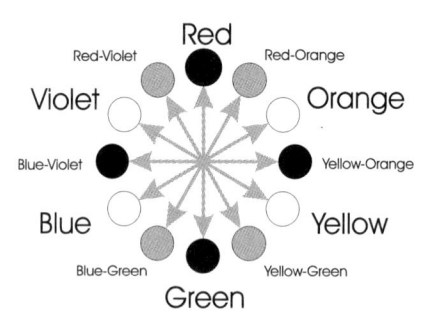

Figure 7.6 Complementary colors lie directly opposite each other on the color wheel.

If you stare at a small block of color against a white background for 30 seconds or more (preferably more), and then shift your gaze to a neutral background (like a blank white page or a block of gray), you'll see an afterimage of the color you were staring at. However, the afterimage isn't the same color as the original. The color you see in the afterimage is the complementary color. If you try staring at a small red circle, for example, the afterimage will be green. If you try the same thing with a green circle, the afterimage will be red.

With light, complementary colors add up to white—just as red, green, and blue lights add up to white. This is where the headache starts, when you realize that red and green are complementary colors on the artists wheel, but that red and green light adds up to yellow, not white. With light, red and cyan (or blue-green) add up to white. This is a contradiction that you just have to live with: Complementary colors on the color wheel are not the same as complementary colors of light. Like I said before, artists talk funny.

COLOR SCHEMES

> Artists can color the sky red because they know it's blue. Those of us who aren't artists must color things the way they really are or people might think we're stupid.
>
> Jules Feiffer

Now comes the payoff for working your way through the color wheel: Using a color wheel to come up with colors that work well together. There are thousands of color schemes you can put together from a color wheel, but they're all based on a few simple rules. Most of the rules talk about using two, three, or four colors. You can extend them by using different shades and tints of a given hue (to use the color wheel terminology), but keep in mind, as I pointed out in Chapter 2, that staying with only a few colors in graphics is generally more effective than using too many colors: Less is more.

The first thing you'll want to do is pick the main color for the graphic, then pick other colors that work with it. The basic rule is that you can find harmonious pairs of colors nearby, or at 60, 90, 120, or 180 degrees apart on the color wheel. And each of these angles gives you a whole set of color schemes to work from.

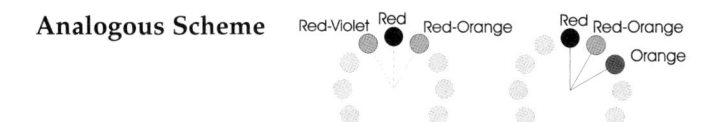

Analogous Scheme

An analogous scheme uses any three adjacent hues on the color wheel. Using nearby hues offers a subtle harmony, because the colors are close together. But you'll generally want to vary the saturation and brightness for each hue (or tint and shade of each hue, if you prefer). If you put two next-door neighbors together using the same saturation and brightness, they will tend to clash rather than complement each other.

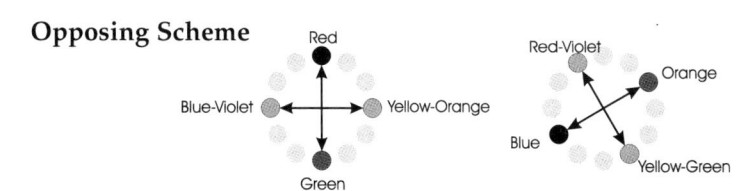

Opposing Scheme

Opposing colors, at 90 degrees apart, give you color schemes with both harmony and contrast. Red and yellow-orange, for example, are close enough to harmonize with each other, but far enough apart to give a sense of subtle contrast.

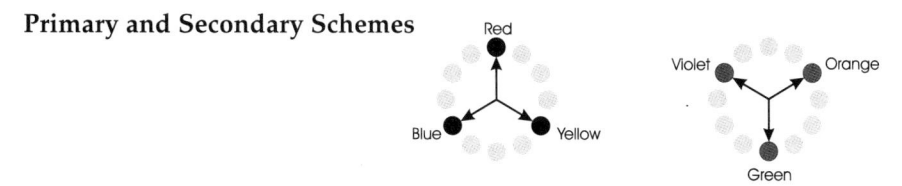

Primary and Secondary Schemes

The primary and secondary schemes each use colors that are 120 degrees apart on the color wheel—the primary colors red, blue, and yellow, or the secondary colors violet, orange and green. In this case, you can use any two of the colors in each scheme or all three. (Red, blue, and yellow work pretty well for Superman.)

Use these schemes with the hues at full saturation when you want the colors to stand out as boldly contrasting, or with less than full saturation for a less bold, but still contrasting color scheme. The secondary scheme is a little more interesting to the eye than the primary scheme, because it's used less often.

Tertiary Triad Scheme

You get two choices for a tertiary triad scheme (now there's a mouthful)—red-violet, yellow-orange, and blue-green; or red-orange, yellow-green, and blue-violet. As you can see, these are variations on the same theme as the primary and secondary schemes, with three colors 120 degrees apart. And as with the primary and secondary schemes, you can use any two of the colors in each scheme or all three.

Here again, use these schemes with the hues at full saturation when you want the colors to stand out as boldly contrasting, or with less than full saturation for a less bold, but still contrasting color scheme. Be aware that the red-orange, yellow-green, blue-violet combination has much the same feel as the primary color scheme. The red-violet, yellow-orange, blue-green combination has a more distinctive feel of its own.

Complementary Scheme

For real contrast, pick any two complementary hues—red and green, blue and orange, and so on, at 180 degrees apart.

Conventional wisdom, for those who aren't sure of their color sense, is that complementary schemes are better avoided. The colors can literally appear to vibrate when they're next to each other, making the edges between them hard to focus on. But if you vary the saturation or brightness of the colors, you can still come up with a harmonious, highly contrasting, color scheme.

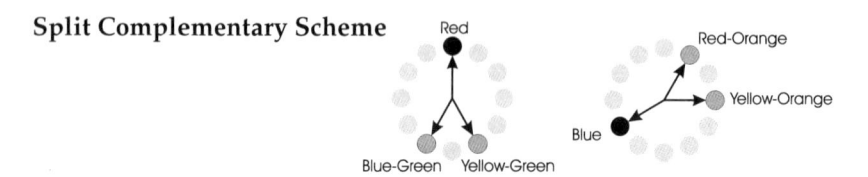

Split Complementary Scheme

At 60 degrees apart, you can use pairs of hues like blue-green and yellow-green, or red-orange and yellow-orange. If you want three colors, a split complementary scheme uses a hue plus the two hues to either side of the complement to that hue—giving you combinations like red, blue-green, and yellow-green, or blue, red-orange, and yellow-orange. The two nearby hues offer a pleasing harmony, and both contrast nicely with the third hue.

Other Color Schemes

> Why do two colors, put one next to the other, sing? Can one really explain this? No.
>
> Pablo Picasso
> *Arts de France,* no. 6 (Paris; 1946; tr. in Dore Ashton, *Picasso on Art,* 1972).

The color schemes you can find on a color wheel should be enough to get you started with any graphic you need to color, but there are some other color schemes you'll find useful at times also.

Warm and Cool Color Schemes

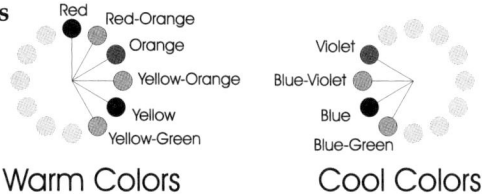

Warm Colors   **Cool Colors**

Among the two or three color schemes I suggested in Chapter 2 was one that uses warm colors for the foreground in graphics and cool colors for the background. The suggestion grows from the fact that warm colors—red, orange, yellow, and yellowish green—tend to stand out, while cool colors—blue-green, blue, and violet—tend to recede. (Green and magenta, as you may recall, can come out looking warm or cool, depending on what's around them. Stick them in the middle of warm colors, and they'll look cool. Throw them in with cool colors and they'll look warm.)

There's also another possibility for warm and cool colors—two possibilities actually—which I haven't mentioned yet. Instead of combining warm and cool colors together, you can build a color scheme exclusively from warm colors or exclusively from cool colors.

Coloring a graphic with nothing but reds, oranges, and yellows or nothing but blues, cyans, and violets can make it so eye-catching that you can't ignore it. As a general rule, though, it's easier to come up with an attractive color scheme with warm colors than with cool colors, since warm colors are inherently . . . well, warm. And inviting.

Monochromatic Scheme

We covered monochromatic schemes in Chapter 2. I mention them here only so you'll have everything in one place. A monochromatic scheme uses only one hue, with different shades and tints (in color wheel vocabulary), or different levels of brightness and saturation.

Keep in mind that settings for a given hue that look different on screen may not look different at the printer. As I pointed out in Chapter 2, it pays to create a test page for any given hue, with blocks of color using different saturation and lightness settings, along with some text to identify the settings for each block. Once you print the test page, you can use it for reference later. (And once you create it, don't delete the file from your disk. You'll need it again as the printed page ages and the colors fade.)

Achromatic Scheme

Don't overlook the possibility for an achromatic color scheme, a.k.a. shades of gray. Obviously, this isn't what you bought your color printer for, but there are times when an achromatic scheme—black and white printing—can be more visually interesting than color. Sometimes it will simply be more appropriate since colors may be distracting. Take a look, for example, at Figure 7.7, which uses shades of gray to dramatic effect.

Figure 7.7 Sometimes you don't want color.

Adding color to this graphic will take something away from the image and make it less dramatic. That's why some photographers shoot in black and white only. That's also why Woody Allen, among others, not only insists on making some films in black and white, but objects to colorizing old black and white movies. The moral: Don't use color just because you have a color printer handy.

Colors of the Rainbow

One other color scheme I mentioned in Chapter 2 was colors of the rainbow, for graphics like the one in Figure 7.8 where you can use a color scale—or in this case a gray scale—as a visual indication of a value.

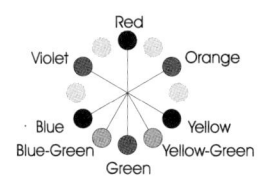

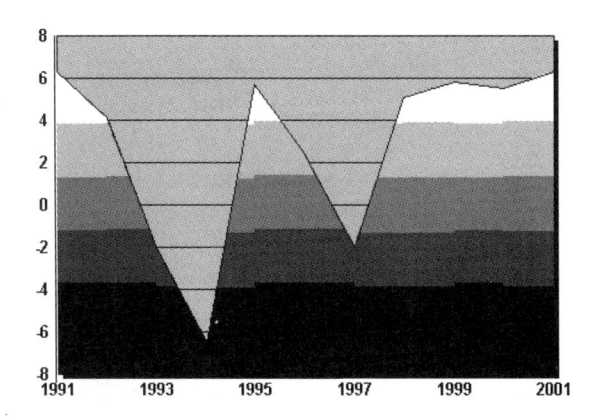

Figure 7.8 This graph shows how even a simple line graph can benefit from a color scale (or gray scale in this case).

If the graph in the figure looks familiar, it's because it's the same one I used in Chapter 2 to make the same point. The gray scale makes it easy to see the rough value of any point on the line without having to look over at the vertical axis.

One of the reasons this scale works is because the range from black to white is intuitively obvious; no one has to think about it to see that the lighter the shade, the higher the value. The rainbow provides a similarly easy-to-understand color scale, since anyone who has ever mixed paint knows that red fades into orange, orange into yellow, yellow into yellow-green, and so on. The reason for bringing this up again is that there are any number of other color scales you can use.

The most obvious alternative to a rainbow scale is part of the rainbow, but broken down into smaller steps. Instead of using red, orange, yellow, green, blue, and violet, you might use red, red-orange, orange, orange-yellow, yellow, and yellow-green. The smaller steps make it even easier to visualize the progression. **A partial rainbow**

Another possibility is to use a single hue, but vary saturation and darkness. You might start with a somewhat dark version of the color at full saturation, for example; work your way up to full brightness in, say, three steps; and then lower the saturation over two or three more steps. The overall effect will be similar to the gray scale in Figure 7.8, but in color. **A single hue**

Still another variation is a temperature scale. You can, for example, go from a brownish gray for cold, to dark brown, then dark red, bright red, orange, yellow, and, finally, white, for white hot. **A temperature scale**

Choosing a color scale

Feel free to invent your own scale. Color scales work best when the logic behind the scale is tied to the graphic it's in. If you're showing a graph of the high temperatures over July and August in New York and Boston, a temperature scale is a better choice than a rainbow. If you're showing the temperatures in February and March, you might want to use a scale with cool, instead of warm, colors. If the temperatures run the entire year, you might want to develop a scale that starts with cool colors, uses a neutral brown in the middle, and then switches to warm colors for higher temperatures.

Be creative.

PSYCHOLOGY OF COLOR

> What beautiful thoughts can be made out of forms and colors.
>
> Paul Gauguin

Somewhere early on in this chapter, before I launched into color schemes themselves, I mentioned that you'll want to start by picking the main color you're working with, and then design a color scheme around it. Let's go back to that first step.

Everyone responds to colors, and everyone has some psychological associations with colors. In fact, if you hook someone up to various gadgets that measure things like blood pressure, heart rate, and galvanic skin response (that's a measure of the electrical resistance of the skin), and then show them various colors, you'll see physiological reactions. No kidding. People have actually done research on this.

Blood pressure increases more when people look at red than at white, and more when they look at white than at blue. Longer wavelengths—the warm colors—get a bigger reaction from both blood pressure and galvanic skin response than shorter wavelengths—the cool colors. Heart rates can also change with changes in color, but there's no clear pattern, which suggests that the effect of a color on your pulse depends on your individual associations with that color.

Don't take these physiological reactions too seriously, though. They may be real, but research also shows that they go away very quickly. The more important reactions to color are psychological.

The third from the last page of the color section of this book shows three simple examples of how using colors with the wrong associations can get in the way of understanding. Take a look now, before I talk about the examples. The point is to look at them without knowing what you're about to see. Go ahead, I'll wait here till you're done . . .

Welcome back. Did you find the right page? If you did, you probably found that the green stop sign took just a touch longer to make sense out of than it usually takes for a red stop sign, yes? And the same should be true of both the red go sign, and the globe with green water and blue land. What I've done in all

three cases is not only use unexpected colors, but colors that you probably associate with the exact opposite of what I'm using them for. Red means stop, not go. Green means go, not stop. And when you're talking about a globe, it's the water that's blue and the land that's green; not the other way around.

That's part of what the psychology of color is about: using colors the way people expect them to be used. Unless, of course, you're trying for a particular reaction based on the surprise of using colors the wrong way. But that would also be taking advantage of the psychology of colors to get the reaction you want. (Although it would actually be the reverse psychology of colors, I suppose.)

The tricky part about the psychology of color is that the associations people have with color varies. Red for stop and green for go are probably as widespread as the infernal combustion engine. But most associations aren't that widespread. They vary from one culture to another, from one group to another within a given culture, from person to person within a group, and even from one context to another for any given person.

In Western culture, white is the color for purity and joy—and the usual color for a bride. Red is the right color for a sexy sports car and for the intriguing lady in red. In some Eastern cultures, I'm told, white is the color for death and mourning. And in those cultures, I suppose it would not be a good sign for the marriage if the bride wears white instead of the traditional red.

Within the U.S., corporate financial types think of blue as a good, reliable, corporate color (IBM, a.k.a. big blue, trades on that in its company logo.) Red is a Bad Thing, since it's what happens to your balance sheet when you're not making a profit. But health care workers think of red as healthy, and blue as the color of death (at which point you lose that healthy red glow). A code blue in a hospital means someone just died (although they may still be revived).

As I mentioned in Chapter 1, people who live in tropical regions tend to prefer bright saturated colors, while people who live in temperate zones tend to prefer more subdued colors. Children tend to prefer bright, saturated primary colors whether they live in tropical or temperate zones.

Then there's context. In Western culture, red is not only associated with stopping (stop signs and danger signals) and with sexy sports cars and dresses. It's also associated with fire (except possibly in towns where fire engines are painted yellow) and with danger, anger, blood, and war. And the association you come up with for the color depends on the context you see it in.

File this under interesting oddities: People don't even agree on what counts as white. In most of the U.S. and Europe, the preferred white has a slight bluish tinge, which is why people add bluing to their laundry. In Hawaii and Asia, the preferred white has a slight yellowish tinge. And that means whiter whites are a different color in New York than in Hawaii. (This is something to keep in mind if you go into the detergent business.)

Know your audience

The point is that when you pick the main color for your color scheme, you need to keep your audience and the context for the color in mind. Even health care workers understand red as a Bad Thing on a financial chart. But blue probably isn't a good choice in a get well card for a nurse. It may be a good choice for a chief financial officer.

If you're putting a presentation together for a group that you're not really a part of and don't know well, find someone who is and talk a little about what colors mean to that group.

If you get serious about color . . .

All this is a meager introduction to a subject that's worth an entire book. My goal here isn't to teach you a lot about the psychology of color, but just wake you up to the idea that there is a psychology of color. As I said in Chapter 1, the first step is to become aware of your own reactions to color.

> **If you want to learn more, you should pick up an art book that discusses color schemes and color harmony. I'll even recommend one: Bride M. Whelan's** *Color Harmony 2, A Guide to Creative Color Combinations.* **(It's published by Rockport Publishers, Inc. in Rockport, Massachusetts, and distributed by North Light Books, in Cincinnati, Ohio.)**
>
> *Color Harmony 2* **not only offers a book full of color schemes, but groups them by their psychological impact. You'll also find nuggets of information like: Yellow suggests activity and motion, lavender adds a sense of nostalgia, and red is always at the center of powerful color schemes that ring with vitality and awareness.**

Now that we've flirted with the psychology of color, let's look at some things that you probably don't need to know.

SPOT COLOR AND COLOR MATCHING SYSTEMS

> Some painters transform the sun into a yellow spot, others transform a yellow spot into the sun.
>
> Pablo Picasso

I spent fair amount of Chapter 3 and much of Chapter 6 talking about color matching. But there's a whole other kind of color matching that you should be aware of, namely, matching colors to a color matching system.

You may never use a color matching system. Correction: Make that you will probably never use one unless you get serious about graphics or desktop publishing. But if you mess around with color printing for very long, you'll probably come across programs or printers that support them. CorelDRAW 5, for example, includes color palettes for four different color-matching systems. Adobe Photoshop 3.0

includes choices for five systems in its Custom Colors dialog box. And even if you never use any of these systems sometimes it's useful to know what you're ignoring, if only to feel comfortable about ignoring it.

So what's a color-matching system? Basically, it's a way to make sure that when you send a color print job out to a print shop, the color that comes off the printing press is exactly the color you expect. All you have to do is pick the color from a book of color swatches. The color-matching system guarantees a match.

Probably the best known and most widely used color-matching system is Pantone, or, more formally, the Pantone Matching System, PMS. The Pantone system dates back to 1963, when computers filled rooms and were too expensive to use for anything as trivial as graphics. It's clearly aimed at graphics professionals.

PMS (which doesn't mean what you may be thinking)

Before you can understand the Pantone system, you have to understand the idea of spot colors. If you think of them as putting a special spot of color somewhere on the page, you won't be far off.

Spot colors

Except for primary colors, all the colors you get with four-color printing—which is to say, all the printed colors we've talked about in this book so far—are process colors. The printer creates them as part of the printing process, using cyan, magenta, yellow, and usually black. Spot colors aren't process colors. They get mixed to order, and they get printed separately from the process colors.

You can't print spot colors on a computer printer, because there's no way to print the additional color, much less mix the ink for the color. When you send something out to a professional print shop, on the other hand, the print shop can print each spot color separately (after mixing the ink to order) just as it prints cyan, yellow, magenta, and black as four separate colors.

The biggest drawback to spot color is price. Since each spot color gets printed on a separate pass, printing gets expensive if you need too many spot colors at once. So most graphic artists use spot colors sparingly. They might, for example, limit spot colors to the colors in a logo, which have to be just right.

The Pantone system lets you specify spot colors. It defines 736 colors, each of which is a mixture of some specific combination of nine Pantone Basic Colors plus Pantone Black and Pantone Transparent White. Each Pantone color gets mixed according to formula, and then printed as a spot color.

The universe of Pantone colors may be small, at just over 700 colors, but it covers a wider range than you can get from just four colors in four-color printing. You can use Pantone colors as a target and try to reproduce them as process colors, but you won't get all of them. Aside from the usual color-matching issues, some colors are simply outside the color gamut for four-color printing. The closest you'll get for those colors is an approximation.

All of which brings us to Pantone on the PC. (Or Mac. I mean PC in the generic sense, as in personal computer.)

Pantone on the Desktop

> Nothing is so good as it seems beforehand.
>
> George Eliot
> *Silas Marner*

The Pantone features that you'll find in programs like CorelDRAW and Adobe Photoshop, as well as other graphics and desktop publishing programs, are licensed from Pantone. (You can usually see the Pantone copyright notice as part of the program's startup notice.) They depend on RGB color lookup tables provided by Pantone to try to simulate Pantone colors on the screen. You can also find Pantone certified printers, which use CMYK color lookup tables, also licensed from Pantone.

You would probably suppose that if you're using a program with Pantone licensed software along with a Pantone certified printer, you would get a close match to Pantone colors when you print. You would, of course, be wrong.

You may match some colors. But there's no way to match any color outside the printer's color gamut. What you're doing when you use Pantone on the desktop is *simulating* the Pantone Matching System. Like the ads used to say for Beatlemania: It's not the real thing, but an incredible re-creation. Or, as one program warns on its opening screen: *Pantone Computer Video Simulations may not match Pantone-identified solid color standards.*

Of course, none of this is an issue unless you're planning to send something out to a print shop and want to use Pantone colors. In that case, anything you print on your own printer is simply a draft. Just understand that the simulations are approximations, and keep an eye on the difference between the simulated color and the one in the color sample book. If you're not sending anything out to a print shop, you can ignore the Pantone features entirely.

> **If you venture into the world of color-matching systems, be sure to start with a reasonably new color swatch book. The rule of thumb is to replace the swatch book once a year, to make up for fading inks, fingerprints, and other damage. If you want to explore color-matching systems and you don't know where to start or which one to use, ask around at the print shop you use (or plan to use). Someone there should be able to guide you.**

One last note: Some of the other color-matching systems you may run into include Trumatch, Focoltone, Toyo 88 ColorFinder 1050 (based on inks used in Japan), and ANPA (for newspaper applications). Feel free to ignore these too.

8 Color Photos

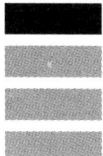

> A photograph is a secret about a secret. The more it tells you the less you know.
>
> Diane Arbus
> Quoted in Patricia Bosworth, *Diane Arbus: A Biography* (1985)

Up to now in this book, I've mostly practiced benign neglect when it comes to photos. I've mentioned them in passing, but I've focused on graphics. That's because working with photos adds a whole new set of issues to deal with—from getting the photo into your computer in the first place, to finding the disk space to store it.

Oh, yes. There's also the issue of printing it. That's when you get introduced to a new vocabulary, with terms like screen frequency and screen angles. (And if you don't know what those are, be assured you're in the majority.)

Even if you don't plan to print photos, you may still want to read this chapter, since much of the information applies to any bitmapped image, including drawings you scan in and drawings you create with a paint program on your computer. In truth, screen frequency, screen angles, and related issues come into play any time you print in dithered grays or dithered colors. It's just that you don't usually need to worry about them when you're printing graphics rather than photos.

That's why I'll be talking mostly about photos here, mentioning graphics only occasionally. If you understand these issues in context of photos, you can apply the same concepts to other images just as easily.

GETTING A PHOTO INTO YOUR COMPUTER

> A tourist is a fellow who drives thousands of miles so he can be photographed standing in front of his car.
>
> Emile Ganest

There are at least four ways to get a photo (or drawing, for that matter) into a computer: By scanner, by CD-ROM, by video capture board, and by digital camera. (Actually, I think that exhausts the logical possibilities, but let's stay with *at least* just in case someone comes up with another choice. You can't trust those pesky inventors. And, no, downloading a photo from the Internet doesn't count. The photo had to somehow get on the computer you're downloading from in the first place.)

Scanning It In

> Just because everything is different doesn't mean anything has changed.
>
> Irene Peter

Copiers, fax machines, and computers are all different. But if you take one-half of a copier or fax machine (the part that scans the page to copy or fax it) and find a way to plug it into a computer, you have a scanner.

Flatbed and page feed scanners

The vast majority of desktop scanners come in two varieties: Flatbed scanners and, for lack of a better name, page feed or sheetfed scanners. Flatbed scanners are similar to the scanners in most office copiers. You slap the photo (or whatever else you're scanning) face down on a flat sheet of glass, and the scanning mechanism moves under the glass to scan the image. Page feed scanners are similar to the scanners in most office fax machines. You feed the page into a sheet feeder, which grabs onto the page, moves it past the scanner mechanism inside, and occasionally mangles the page in the process.

Handheld scanners

A third choice is a handheld scanner. These can vary from the size and shape of an oversize mouse to about the size and shape of a three-hole punch. Whatever the size, you hold the scanning mechanism in your hand (no points for guessing that one), and sweep it across the page.

The mouse-size handheld scanners are suitable for scanning one band of a page at a time. Since most of these don't give you any easy way to patch the bands together into a single image, they limit the size image you can scan in. (And even the ones that come with software to let you stitch the bands together don't always do it well.) The larger versions are wide enough to cover the width of a page, so you can scan an entire page in one sweep. But because your hand controls the sweep, the quality of the image is usually less than you'll get with a desktop scanner.

Flatbed and handheld scanners have the advantage of letting you scan images from pages that won't feed through a sheet feed mechanism. Page feed scanners have the advantage of letting you stack several pages for scanning at once, which is really helpful if you're converting the pages to text using optical character recognition software, but irrelevant for scanning color photos. For our purposes, these three types of scanners are completely equivalent—as long as they scan in color. (But don't try to feed a book or a card-mounted photo through a page feed scanner.)

These three types of scanners are the ones you're most likely to use, but there are other kinds you should be aware of. Flatbed, page feed, and handheld scanners are designed to scan reflective images, meaning images that you look at by reflecting light off of them. You can also find slide scanners, which are designed to scan slides or transparencies and are aimed primarily at the graphic arts market. And you can find attachments for flatbed scanners that let them scan slides and transparencies as well.

In addition, you may occasionally run into mention of drum scanners. These are the el primo representatives of the breed. With drum scanners, you take the item to scan and tape it to a cylinder (that's the drum). The scanner then spins the drum while moving the scanning element over the page (or photo, or whatever). The bargain basement versions of drum scanners cost $35,000, which is why these are mostly found in shops that provide scanning services to others.

Figure 8.1 shows a photo that I scanned in at 120 dpi on a flatbed scanner. (A warning: There is room for confusion here, as I'll discuss a little later in this chapter, so don't take the 120 dpi too seriously.) This particular photo (which is not my backyard, by the way, but the view downhill from Windsor Castle) is 5 by 3.5 inches, which means, at 150 dpi, that the resolution for the entire photo is 750 by 525.

Figure 8.1 The view from Windsor Castle (at 150 dpi, or 750 by 525 for the entire photo).

Taking It Off a CD-ROM

> You furnish the pictures and I'll furnish the war.
>
> William Randolph Hearst

If Hearst were around today, he might be using stock photos to spruce up his newspaper. It's cheaper than paying photographers for new pictures, and a lot cheaper than firing a cruise missile. If you want to do the same with your desktop publishing output—from your client newsletter to birthday cards—the place to start is a CD-ROM. You can find any number of CD-ROMs filled with photos you can use without having to pay royalties.

Most of the photos in this book, for example, are from the photo sampler CD-ROM that comes with CorelDRAW 5. If you have CorelDRAW, and the sampler photos aren't enough for you, Corel (at 613-728-3733) will happily sell you additional CD-ROMs. There are lots of other sources too—Aris Entertainment in Marina del Rey, California, and Media Graphics International in Arvado, Colorado, to name two.

Photos on CD-ROMs usually take advantage of standard file formats like BMP, TIFF, JPEG, and Kodak's Photo-CD format. If these are all so much alphabet soup to you, don't worry about it. Most CD-ROMs with stock photos also include a browser program that lets you look through the photos and copy them to another program. And most CD-ROM packages will work on both the PC and Mac. Even so, before you pay any money, it's always best to make sure that the particular CD-ROM you're about to buy will work with the program you want to use it with. Ask before buying.

Figure 8.2 is a photo from the Corel Professional Photo series. I imported it, in Photo-CD format, into CorelDRAW, and exported it to TIFF format at 150 dpi. For this particular photo, that works out to 768 by 511 pixels for the entire photo.

Snapshots from a Video Capture Board

> The true picture of the past flits by. The past can be seized only as an image which flashes up at the instant when it can be recognized and is never seen again.
>
> Walter Benjamin
> *Illuminations*, "Theses on the Philosophy of History," no. 5 (1955; ed. by Hannah Arendt, 1968)

Video capture boards are just what they sound like. They're boards that fit in a computer slot and capture video signals.

Well, okay, they're not always boards. They can just as easily be boxes that sit outside the computer and plug into the serial or parallel port. That would make them video capture *devices*. But *devices* sounds so . . . formal. Let's just lump them all together as video capture boards.

Figure 8.2 A stock photo on CD-ROM, from the Corel Professional Photo series, at 150 dpi, or 768 by 511 pixels for the entire photo.

Of course, *capture* is ambiguous, since you can say that a television captures a picture simply by receiving a TV station. What I mean by capturing a video signal is taking a snapshot from the video signal, converting it to a digital picture, and saving the image to disk. Some video capture boards can capture full motion video as well as still pictures. That's useful if you're putting a multimedia presentation together. But since this book is about printers, let's ignore full motion video.

While we're at it, let's be clear what I mean by video signal. That's not the TV signal that travels from the TV station to your TV set (with or without cable) or from your VCR to the connector on your TV. Those are radio frequency signals that happen to be carrying video information. By video signal, I mean the signal that goes from, say, a video camera's video out jack to the video in jack on a monitor or VCR. When you plug a cable into your video camera on one side and your VCR on the other, the information that travels over the cable is the video signal.

Time for a little vocabulary lesson. The standard for video signals in the U.S. (and Japan) is NTSC format. The standard in Europe is PAL format. If you're in the U.S., you presumably want NTSC, since that's almost certainly what you'll find in any video cameras, VCRs, and camcorders you have. But video capture boards often support both.

Connections between different pieces of equipment—camera, VCR, monitor, and video board—can be by way of composite video, using RCA phono jack

style connectors (the kind you probably use on the cable that connects your stereo and speakers) or SuperVideo, a.k.a. S-Video, normally using a DIN connector (similar to the keyboard connector on most computers). If you have a choice of connectors on both your video capture board and the equipment you're plugging into it, choose the S-Video connector, which gives a somewhat better picture.

So, like I said before: A video capture board is just what it sounds like—a board (or sometimes not a board) that captures (or grabs a snapshot from) video signals (specifically NTSC or PAL video signals).

Frame grabbers

Another name for these gadgets, by the way, is frame grabbers. The logic behind the name is simple if you speak the right jargon. A video signal rewrites the entire screen some number of times per second—30 times per second for broadcast quality. Each full rewrite is a frame, much like a frame in a motion picture. And since capturing a still picture from a video signal means capturing a single full video frame, these guys are grabbing individual frames. That makes them frame grabbers.

Figure 8.3 is a captured video frame of a dog I found on the street. I put together a Dog Found poster by videotaping the dog with a camcorder, capturing this frame with a video capture board, and inserting the picture in a Word file. (This, by the way, was one of the smartest and most friendly dogs I've ever run across, and I was sorry when the owner showed up—which is a good argument for not having a lot of useful technology on hand to put together Dog Found posters.)

Figure 8.3 Have you seen this dog? This is a lost dog I found, videotaped, and captured (the image, not the dog) with a video capture board.

In any case, this particular photo is 160 by 120 pixels, which explains its postage stamp size. If you try to print it at too large a size, as in Figure 8.4, you run into a problem called pixelation.

Pixelation

With pixelation, the individual pixels show as visible squares. This problem tends to show up when you simply enlarge the image without making any other adjustments. There's a way to minimize this problem, which we'll get to later. It involves changing the overall resolution for the image so the individual pixels are smaller.

Figure 8.4 If you print a file at too large a size, you'll see the individual pixels as squares in the image.

Snapshots from a Digital Camera

> Using a camera appeases the anxiety which the work-driven feel about not working when they are on vacation and supposed to be having fun. They have something to do that is like a friendly imitation of work: they can take pictures.
>
> Susan Sontag
> *On Photography*, "Plato's Cave" (1977)

Depending on your point of view, you can think of a digital camera as a combination video camera and video capture board, or as a camera that uses digital memory instead of film. Either way, it's a gadget that looks and works more or less like a camera but stores its images in digital memory.

The typical digital camera lets you take some number of pictures—sometimes as few as five—and store them in the camera before you offload them to a computer. Depending on the camera, you may be storing the information on disk, in memory, or on a PCMCIA card. (That's one of those removable cards about the size of a credit card, that have been renamed to PC cards. After struggling to memorize the alphabet soup name, I refuse to use the newer, easier-to-remember name.) You then move the files to your computer, either by moving the disk or PCMCIA card to the computer and copying the files to your hard disk, or by transferring the files by cable through the parallel or serial port.

Resolution for a digital camera is usually pretty limited. If you look at your daily newspaper carefully, it's pretty easy to spot the photos taken with a digital camera. Just keep an eye out for pixelation.

Figure 8.5 is a photo I took with a Chinon digital camera, at 640 by 480 pixels in landscape orientation, or 480 by 640 in portrait mode, as shown.

Figure 8.5 This photo, taken with a digital camera, is 640 by 480 pixels (or 480 by 640, in this portrait orientation).

A LOOK AT RESOLUTION

> He has no resolution.
>
> Thomas Carlyle commenting on Samuel Taylor Coleridge
> Letter, 24 June 1824, to Carlyle's brother, published in *Collected Letters*, vol. 3

Some people may have a problem with a lack of resolution. But when you're talking about scanning and printing photos, the problem is too much resolution, or, rather, too many kinds of resolution, with completely different concepts masquerading under the same names.

Figure 8.5, taken with a digital camera, has a resolution of 640 by 480, which tells you the total number of picture elements, or dots, in the picture. (Although some people would argue that the term *picture element* should be reserved for talking about display resolution.)

Show that photo on screen, with a screen resolution of 640 by 480, and you have an interesting problem. (Ignore the inconvenient fact that the photo in Figure 8.5 is in portrait format. Assume you're looking at it on its side.) If the screen resolution is 640 by 480 and the picture is 640 by 480, you would expect the picture to fill the screen, yes? So what happens when you zoom out so there's some white space around the picture? What's the resolution now?

Answer: The screen resolution is still 640 by 480, and the picture resolution as stored in computer memory and on disk is still 640 by 480, but the picture you're seeing on screen is no longer 640 by 480. The resolution you're looking at depends on the number of screen pixels in the image on screen.

It gets worse.

In addition to describing the overall resolution in a picture or on a screen, most of us talk about resolutions in terms of dots per inch, or dpi. You may scan a particular image at a resolution of, say, 120 dpi. Your printer prints at, say, 600 dpi. If it uses dithering to get its colors, as most printers do, you use dithering cells, or halftone cells, that give you the equivalent of, say, 75 dpi.

What resolution? Or is it, which resolution?

So what's the resolution of the printed output?

Don't bother answering.

The point is that each kind of resolution means something different, even though they're all called resolution, and they're all usually given in dots per inch. If you want to understand what's going on, you need to keep the differences straight.

One good place to start is with clearly different terms. When you convert an analog image to a digital image—by scanner, video capture, or digital camera—you're actually taking samples of the original image or the scene you're photographing. When you scan something at so-called 120-dpi resolution, for example, you're taking 120 samples per inch. So the information in the scanned image is in *samples per inch*. Or, since it's a bitmapped image, you might think of it as the number of *bits per inch*.

The effective resolution for halftone cells is usually given in *lines per inch* and is usually called the halftone frequency, halftone screen frequency, or screen frequency, for reasons we'll come back to in a moment.

And since the printer resolution is the actual number of dots the printer can lay down in each inch, you should reserve dots per inch for talking about printers.

It also helps to stop talking about resolution, and talk instead about the specific kind of resolution—screen resolution (640 by 480 for VGA); total image resolution (the total number of elements in the picture—480 by 640 for that portrait photo in Figure 8.5); scanning, capture, or camera resolution (in samples per inch); printer resolution (in dots per inch); and effective resolution after halftoning (in lines per inch).

I'll call that last one halftone resolution, for lack of a better term. But keep in mind that halftone resolution is just another name for halftone frequency, which is the same as screen frequency, which is the same as halftone screen frequency.

If you manage to keep these different kinds of resolution firmly separate, you'll find that issues of resolution are much easier to deal with. If necessary, keep telling yourself that they're different things, even though they share the same name and are related to each other. Eventually, you'll believe it.

One other thing: Keep in mind that the resolution for a scanned image in samples per inch doesn't necessarily stay the same after you've scanned it into your computer. When you change the size of an image by scaling it up or down, for example, you're also changing the image resolution, in samples per inch.

Say you start out with a postage stamp size photo, at 2 by 2 inches, and scan it in at 120 samples per inch. But suppose you want to print it at 4 by 4 inches, so you stretch it—or scale it up—to the larger size with your favorite image editing program. The image will print at 4 by 4 inches, but the image resolution will now be only 60 samples per inch. And the result will be the same as if you started with a 4 by 4 inch photo and scanned it at 60 samples per inch.

This subtle distinction matters, because, as we'll discuss shortly, there is a best image resolution to use with any given halftone resolution. And the scanning resolution you choose should be based on the image resolution you'll wind up with after you finish messing with the scanned image. In other words, if you want to wind up with 120 samples per inch, and you plan to stretch the image to twice the original size, you should start by scanning at 240 samples per inch—assuming you have that option.

Halftones

> A bucket full of water does not splash about, only a bucket half-full splashes.
>
> Malayan proverb

I talked about dithering and halftones a bit in Chapter 5, by way of explaining the differences between multilevel and bilevel printers. When you're dealing with photos, it helps to know a little more about them.

For those who missed Chapter 5, I'll quickly point out that a multilevel printer can print individual dots in a range of shades. So if it's a monochrome printer, it can print dots in some number of grays as well as black or white. (More precisely, it gives you white by not printing any black. But I'll talk about printing white anyway.) If it can print enough shades of gray (or colors), it's a continuous tone printer—meaning that the change from one shade to the next is so subtle that the human eye sees it as a continuous range, rather than seeing discrete steps.

That's fine for multilevel printers, but most printers are bilevel. Each individual dot has to be black or white (a.k.a. not black). There ain't no gray. So bilevel printers have to fake gray by printing an assortment of black and white dots and letting your eye and brain do the mixing.

The technique is called dithering or halftoning, and the images are called halftones. Color printers work the same way to give you shades of colors, as I've already explained in Chapter 5. Since the concepts are the same for black and white and color and talking about all the different colors gets unnecessarily complicated, I'll stick with explaining how halftones work in black and white, except for issues where color makes a difference.

Halftone screens

Before computers, the standard way to get halftones was to take advantage of an etched screen, which was opaque except for a grid of thin etched lines. You would put the screen between a photographic transparency and film (or photosensitive paper) and then shine a light so the light would go through the transparency, through the screen, and fall on the film.

In this traditional approach to halftoning, the thin lines in the screen defract the light. The diffraction turns the continuous tone image on the photographic transparency into a collection of dots on the film. (But let's call them spots from here on. That will help avoid confusion when we get back to printers, which may need to use more than one printer dot in any given halftone spot.)

If you're not clear on how diffraction works, don't let that bother you. Just take my word for it that the physics works. Where lots of light gets through the transparency, you wind up with big black spots on the film. Where only a little light gets through, you wind up with tiny black spots. The result is a negative of the original transparency, with continuous tones from the original converted to a bunch of spots—a halftone. That halftone image is what you would use for printing, to let your bilevel printer fake gray.

As you've probably noticed, when you use a computer printer to print photographic images (or anything else with shades of gray), at no point do you shine a light through a transparency and an etched screen to create a halftone. What you may not have noticed is that you do the same thing electronically.

Screen frequency a.k.a. halftone frequency

When you print a photo or other gray scale bitmap, the image stored in memory or on disk is the closest thing your computer has to the continuous tone transparency in traditional halftoning. Although you don't have a physical screen, you define an electronic one, as so many lines per inch. (The screen may be in your graphics software, in your printer driver, or in the printer itself, but don't worry about that just yet. We'll come back to that issue later.) The name for the setting is typically screen frequency or halftone frequency.

The screen frequency defines the size of the halftone, or dithering, cell. If you have a 600-dpi printer, for example, and you define a screen frequency of 75 lines per inch (which is fairly typical), the size for each halftone cell will be 600 divided by 75, or 8 dots across and 8 down. With a 300-dpi printer, a 75-line-per-inch screen will give you a 4 by 4 halftone cell.

Since you can't depend on diffraction to automatically give you the right spot size with an electronic screen, your computer or printer has to calculate it instead. The calculation basically consists of determining a gray level for each halftone cell, and then printing as many dots as needed to hit that level of gray.

> We covered gray levels in Chapter 5 also. Rule 1 is that you can fake as many gray levels as you have dots in the halftone cell, plus one more for no dots. With 75 lines per inch for a 4 by 4 cell, for example, you can have 17 levels of gray, with anywhere from 0 to 16 dots filled in.
>
> Rule 2 is that the more dots in the cell, the more levels of gray you get, but the lower the effective resolution. A screen frequency of 75 lines per inch gives you a halftone resolution of 75 halftone cells, or spots, per inch. Drop the screen frequency to 60 lines per inch on a 300-dpi printer, and the halftone cell grows to 5 dots by 5 (300 dots per inch divided by 60 lines per inch). That gives you 26 shades of gray (5 times 5 plus 1), but it drops the halftone resolution to 60 spots per inch.

How the Different Resolutions Relate to Each Other

> . . . separate, distinct personalities, not separate at all, but inextricably bound, soul and body and mind, to each other . . .
>
> Judith Guest
> *Ordinary People,* Ch. 19 (1976)

There's more to say about halftoning, and we'll get back to it shortly, but we've gotten far enough to talk about how the different kinds of resolution are related to each other. That's something worth clearing up while you still have the different kinds of resolution fresh in mind.

To begin with, when you're scanning an image, there are four kinds of resolution you should care about: Printer resolution, halftone resolution, image resolution, and scanning resolution.

> You've probably noticed that I've listed the resolutions in reverse order from how you'll come across them. In real life, scanning is the first step and printing is the last. But you can't pick the right scanning resolution without knowing the printer resolution. More precisely, your choice of scanning resolution depends on the image resolution you want to wind up with after you've scaled or otherwise modified the image; your target image resolution depends on the halftone resolution, and your choice of halftone resolution depends on the printer resolution. So before you scan in a picture, think about what you're doing, working your way backward from printer to scanner.

Start with the printer resolution.

Choosing a printer resolution is usually a no brainer. If your printer has a top resolution of 300 dpi or 360 dpi (which you'll find in some ink jet printers), you'll want to use the best resolution, since anything lower than 300 dpi is pointless for photographs.

If your printer offers a higher resolution—600 by 300 dpi, or 600 by 600 dpi, or above—and you want the best output quality, you'll want to use the highest resolution you can get. In some cases, you may be more interested in speed than output quality, however, in which case you'll want to drop down to 300 dpi, assuming your printer gives you that option.

Next choose the halftone resolution.

Once you know the printer resolution you'll be using, you can decide on the halftone resolution. In some cases you don't have a choice. A lot of printers, particularly inexpensive ink jet printers, don't give you any options for setting the halftone resolution by any name—screen frequency, halftone frequency, or lines per inch.

If you can't find a screen frequency setting in the printer driver, front panel menu, or utilities that come with the printer, call the manufacturer and find out what screen frequency or frequencies it uses, and under what conditions. The printer may, for example, automatically use different screen frequencies at different resolutions, or it may use one screen frequency if you set the driver for photos and another if you set it for graphics. You need this information for choosing the image resolution.

That's important enough to bear repetition: You need this information for choosing the image resolution. If you get a tech support person whose talents are limited to making sure the printer is plugged in, and who doesn't know what a screen frequency is, be persistent. Patiently explain that it's the number of lines per inch in the halftone screen, and then insist that you need this information for choosing your image resolution.

Even if the printer uses one of the more sophisticated dithering schemes that we'll touch on a little later, you still need the screen frequency, or, in some cases, the effective screen frequency. The question you need to answer is, What screen frequency, or effective screen frequency, should you use for determining your image resolution?

And did I mention that you need this information for choosing your image resolution?

Well, there's one exception. If your printer uses a kind of screening called frequency-modulated screening, it won't have a screen frequency. But if that's what it uses, then that's what you need to know.

Other names for frequency-modulated screening include FM screening, FM dithering, FM halftones, and, of course, frequency-modulated dithering or halftones. Still another name, for a change of pace, is error diffusion. Sometimes FM screening shows up under the names diffusion dither and stochastic screening, which are simply two specific kinds of FM screens.

I've also seen printers that have a setting for halftone frequency in the driver, but ignore the setting or interpret it to mean something different than a simple screen frequency setting. You can find out for yourself whether the printer follows orders by printing two test prints with wildly different screen settings, like 10 lines per inch and 100 lines per inch. If you don't see a difference, call the manufacturer and find out what screen setting the printer uses.

If your printer lets you set the screen frequency, you may find some predefined settings in the driver. If so, you're generally best advised to stay with the predefined settings, even if the driver lets you enter any number you like.

In any case, if you can change the screen frequency, you may want to experiment a bit to see what the different settings do for different kinds of images. Keep in mind that the basic tradeoff in the printed image is between halftone resolution and the number of colors or shades of gray.

When you're printing a photograph, getting more colors is usually more important than getting a little extra resolution. But if you're printing a graphic, getting the extra resolution is probably more important, unless the graphic includes a gradient fill like the one in Figure 8.6.

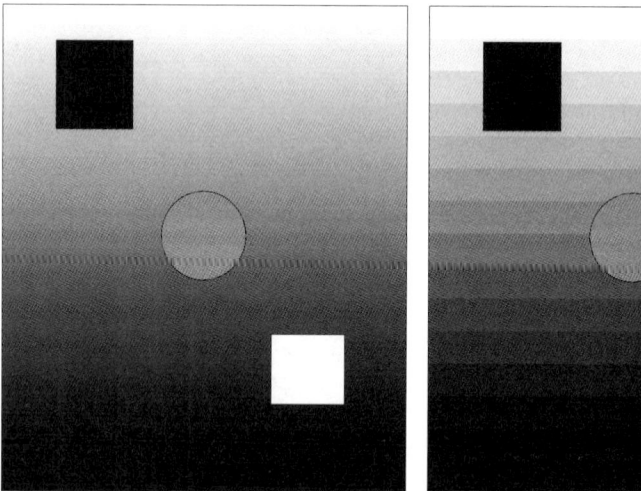

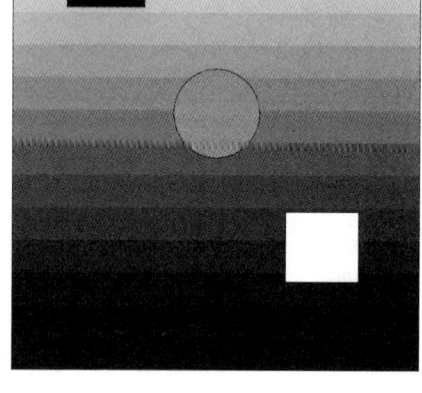

Figure 8.6 For graphics, resolution is usually more important than extra colors, unless you have a gradient fill like the background in these figures. Then too few colors translates to visible steps in the gradient fill, as on the right side.

The figure shows the same graphic twice. The version on the left uses 256 shades of gray in the gradient fill, which is why the fill changes gradually and continuously. The version on the right is set for 15 shades of gray, which is why it shows visible steps.

For those of you scratching your heads, wondering how you get 15 shades of gray—when a four-by-four cell translates to 17 shades and a three-by-three cell translates to 10 shades—the answer is that you're not locked into an full number of dots per halftone cell. A halftone screen of 80 lines per inch works out to 300 divided by 80, or 3.75 dots per cell. Multiply 3.75 by 3.75, and you get 14 dots per cell. That gives you 15 levels of gray, after you add 1 for no dots filled in.

I'll talk a little more about how to choose a screen frequency setting shortly—assuming, of course, that you have a printer that lets you set the screen frequency in the first place. For the moment, let's just assume you have a setting in mind and let's not worry about where it came from.

Choosing the image resolution

Once you know the halftone screen setting, or halftone resolution, figuring out the right image resolution is a snap. The rule of thumb is that the image resolution should be at least 1.5 to 2 times the halftone resolution. So if the halftone resolution is 75 lpi, the image resolution should be at least 113 to 150 samples per inch. Some people insist that 2.5 times the halftone resolution is a better rule of thumb, but the choice is partly a matter of how picky you are.

In printing a halftone image, each halftone cell can draw information from more than one sample in the image—if the information is there. So the more samples per inch in the image—up to matching the printer resolution—the better the output will look.

This is a case where you quickly run into diminishing returns, however. You'll get the most dramatic improvement by using 1.5 times the halftone resolution compared to matching the image and halftone resolutions. Boost the image resolution to 2 times the halftone resolution, and you'll see a noticeable difference, but not as dramatic. At 2.5 times the halftone resolution, the improvement will be even more subtle. And so on.

The price you pay for the extra quality is disk space and time for printing. A 4 by 4 inch picture at 24-bit color depth and 75 samples per inch takes 270 kilobytes (75 by 75 samples per square inch times 24 bits per sample divided by 8 bits per byte times 16 square inches).

Double the image resolution to 150 samples per inch, and the file size goes to 1.08 megabytes (150 by 150 times 24 divided by 3 times 16). Jump up to 300 samples per inch for image resolution, and the file size goes to 4.32 megabytes. (You can figure this one out for yourself.) If you get to 600 samples per inch, for a 600-dpi printer, the file size goes to a disk-eating 17.28 megabytes. And don't forget that the bigger the file, the longer it takes to send it to the printer, and the longer the printer takes to process it before printing.

The moral: Consider 1.5 times the halftone resolution as the absolute minimum for acceptable output. If you want higher than that, season to taste. Also consider buying a bigger hard disk, or better yet, a drive with removable cartridges.

There's one exception to this rule. (Isn't there always.) I mentioned already that if your printer uses something called FM screening, it doesn't have a screen frequency. And without a screen frequency, you can't pick an image resolution in terms of the screen frequency. (This does not require a course in logic.) So if your printer uses FM screening, there's a different rule of thumb; namely, pick an image resolution that's two-thirds to three fourths the printer resolution.

That means you want 200 to 225 samples per inch for a 300-dpi printer or 400 to 450 samples per inch for a 600-dpi printer. (Split the difference if your printer has different resolutions in horizontal and vertical directions, as with a 600 by 300 dpi printer.) Here again, this is partly an issue of what level of print quality you're comfortable with, so you ought to experiment with lower and higher settings.

Oh, there's another exception too. If you're using a true continuous tone printer, which doesn't use halftone screens, you'll want the samples per inch to match the printer resolution.

And finally, the scanning resolution

All of which brings us, finally, to what you need to know to get started: the scanning resolution. Once you know the image resolution you want, figuring out the scanning resolution is straightforward, if not quite as easy as figuring out the image resolution.

The hard part is deciding what size to print the image. Do whatever it takes to figure that out. Then compare the size of the final printout to the size of the original that you want to scan. Whip out a handy calculator and figure out the percentage difference.

If you're starting with a 2 inch by 2 inch original, for example, and you want the printed version at 4 inches by 4 inches, the final version is 200 percent of the original. So if you want an image resolution of, say, 150 samples per inch, you need to set the scanning resolution at 200 percent of the image resolution, or 300 samples per inch.

That was an easy one, but the logic works just as well with other numbers. If you're starting with a 3 inch by 5 inch original, for example, and you want the printed version at 4 inches by 6.7 inches, the final version is 133 percent of the original. So if you want an image resolution of 150 samples per inch, you need to set the scanning resolution at 133 percent of that, or 200 samples per inch.

If You're Not Using a Scanner

> The more things change, the more they remain the same.
>
> French adage

Did somebody ask, What about the other kinds of images—from video capture boards, digital cameras, and CD-ROMs? (Well, if you didn't ask, you should have.

It's a good question.) There are, in fact, a few differences in getting the right image resolution, but the differences are in the details. The same principles apply.

More precisely, everything, details and all, about printer resolution, halftone resolution, and image resolution is the same, no matter how you get the photo into the computer. The differences are in the choices of resolutions to bring in the image in the first place, and in how you get the image resolution to the level you want.

If you're using a CD-ROM that uses Photo-CD format, you'll have a choice of resolutions when you import the photo into a program file. Figure 8.7, for example, shows CorelDRAW's dialog box for setting both the resolution and color depth of a Photo CD format photo. You'll see this dialog box after you specify which photo to import, but before you actually import it. You should see a similar dialog box with other programs that support Photo-CD format.

Photo-CD format

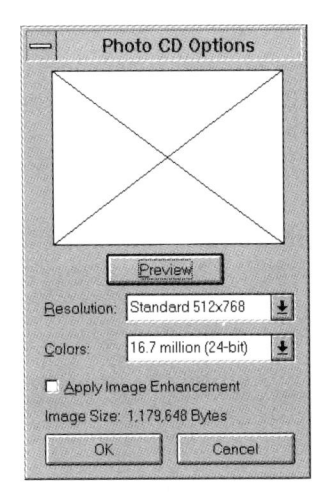

Figure 8.7 When you import a Photo-CD format photo, you can set the resolution and color depth.

As you can see in the figure, the resolution setting for Standard size is 512 (vertical) by 768 (horizontal). The other choices are Wallet, at 128 by 192; Snapshot, at 256 by 384; Large, at 1024 by 1536; and Poster, at 2048 by 3072.

If you know the final size for the printout, a little arithmetic will tell you what these total resolutions translate to as image resolutions. If you plan to print at, say, 3 inches across, a horizontal 256 pixels translates into 256 divided by 3, or 85 samples per inch. A horizontal 512 pixels, translates into 512 divided by 3, or 170 samples per inch.

Simply pick the Photo-CD resolution that matches the image resolution you want—or, unlike the winner on "The Price is Right," pick the one that comes closest without going under the magic number.

Other CD ROMs

With other CD-ROM formats, you won't have a choice of import resolutions, but you may find the same image stored in different resolutions on the same disk. One CD-ROM I have offers a BMPSMALL directory, with a set of photos at 320 by 240 resolution in BMP format, plus a BMPLARGE directory, with the same photos at 640 by 480 in BMP format, plus a TIFF directory, with the same photos yet again at 640 by 480 in TIFF format. Here again, if you have a choice of resolutions, do the math and then pick the resolution that comes closest to what you want without going under.

Video capture boards and digital cameras

If you're taking an image from a video capture board or a digital camera, you generally don't have much control over the resolution. With a video capture board, in fact, you may be stuck with a mere 160 by 120 for the entire picture, as in the photo in Figure 8.3.

If you want to print the picture at, say, 4 inches across, you'll wind up with a paltry 40 samples per inch. At this image resolution, you'll get obvious pixilation, with each pixel showing as a small square in the image, as demonstrated earlier, in Figure 8.4.

The good news is that there's a simple way to change the image resolution.

If you have a program that's designed for editing photos, like Adobe Photoshop or Corel PHOTO-PAINT version 5, which comes with CorelDRAW 5, you should find an option somewhere in the program for resampling. In PHOTO-PAINT, for example, choose Image Resample to open the dialog box shown in Figure 8.8. In Photoshop 3.0, choose Image Image Size to open the dialog box shown in Figure 8.9.

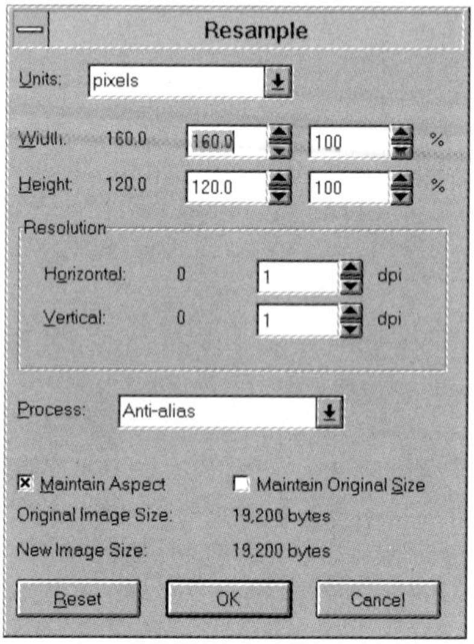

Figure 8.8 PHOTO-PAINT's Resample dialog box.

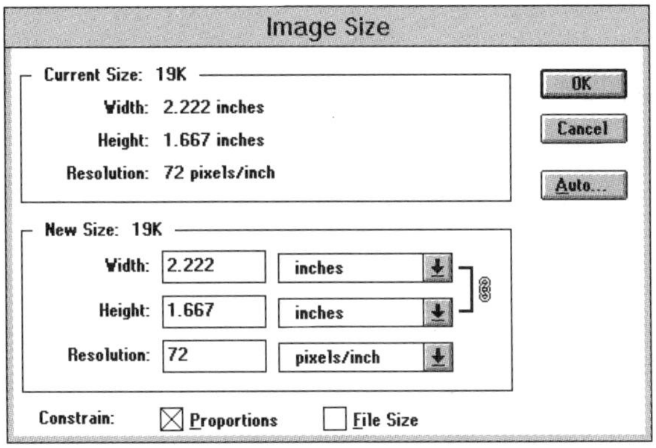

Figure 8.9 Photoshop's Image Size dialog box, for resampling images.

I won't get into the mechanics of how to use a resampling feature, since the specifics vary, depending on the program you're using. But as you can see in the figures, both programs let you set width and height for an image by a choice of units—with pixels as the default in PHOTO-PAINT and inches as the default in Photoshop. (Both programs offer pull-down lists to let you change the units.) When you set the width, height, and resolution, the programs change the image to match your settings.

What resampling does, basically, is change the image resolution by . . . well . . . uh . . . resampling it. If you have an image resolution of 40 samples per inch and you want 75 samples per inch, resampling will look at the data you have and convert it to a 75-sample-per-inch image.

Resampling manages this trick by the magic of interpolation. First it decides where to put the additional samples. Then it looks at nearby samples, and makes a best guess about an intermediate value for the new sample.

There happen to be several approaches to making that best guess, and some work better than others. If you have more than one choice in your graphics program, a good rule of thumb is that the approach that takes longest is probably doing the best job.

In general, resampling to move to a greater resolution works well for getting the right color in the middle of an object, but it tends to blur edges, giving photos a soft focus effect and graphics somewhat less than crisp edges. That's still better than pixilation, however.

Take a look at Figures 8.10 and 8.11. Figure 8.10 is a repeat of Figure 8.4, showing a 160 by 120 photo stretched to the point where the pixelation shows.

I started with the same file for Figure 8.11 as for Figure 8.10. But in this case, I used Corel PHOTO-PAINT to resample the image at five times the image resolution. At the same time, I upped the size in pixels by five—to 800 by 600—to keep

272 *Chapter 8*

Figure 8.10 Here's a repeat of Figure 8.4, complete with pixilation, so you don't have to turn back to the original to compare it to Figure 8.11.

Figure 8.11 Here's the same picture as in Figure 8.10, after resampling.

the picture from shrinking on the page. Assuming you're printing at 4 inches across, this resampling makes the difference between 40 samples per inch, at 160 by 120, and 200 samples per inch. I also used the anti-aliasing feature in PHOTO-PAINT, which helps to minimize jaggies on edges.

As you can see, the photo in Figure 8.11 shows the soft focus effect that I mentioned. And as you can see also, it's a real improvement over the sharp-edged individual pixels in Figure 8.10. But you don't have to settle for soft focus. Most graphics programs that are designed for photos also offer tools that can sharpen images by increasing the contrast between adjacent areas, which is another way of saying that they can sharpen edges. Figure 8.12 is the same picture again, after sharpening. The improvement shows most clearly around the dog's face and legs.

Figure 8.12 Here's that same dog again, after sharpening.

The particular sharpening tools you'll have available will vary depending on the program you're using. In some cases, you'll have only one choice, named Sharpen, or something equally appropriate. In other cases, like PHOTO-PAINT and Photoshop, you'll have a whole raft of sharpening tools.

If your graphics program offers a choice of tools, look for something called an unsharp mask, which, despite the name, sharpens the image with special attention to edges. Be aware that you can sharpen a picture too much, so if the program has settings that let you adjust the amount of sharpening, experiment with different settings. If the program doesn't have an unsharp mask feature, try whatever sharpening tools it offers.

Not so incidentally, you can use resampling to throw away some pixels as well as add some. If you've imported a photo from a CD-ROM, say, with far more samples per inch than you need, you can use resampling to lower the image resolution and cut down the file size.

Even more important than cutting down the file size when the image resolution is more than you need is throwing out the extra samples before they get to the printer. There are several ways to resample an image to get a lower image resolution, and some are better than others. The approach that most printers use is not one of the better ones. So you are always better off resampling with a program that's designed to resample intelligently, rather than letting the printer do it.

How Many Colors Are Enough?

> The purest and most thoughtful minds are those which love colour the most.
>
> John Ruskin

It's time to pick up one of the threads I left lying around a little earlier. When I was talking about choosing a halftone resolution, I skipped over the details of how halftones work. Part of the reason was that you may not have to worry about those details at all. If your printer doesn't give you the choice of setting the halftone screen, all you need to know is what screen setting your printer is using. In that case, you may want to skip over this section.

On the other hand, if you happen to have a printer that gives you the option of setting the halftone screen, it helps to know a few more of the details.

Most important, the tradeoff between resolution and the number of shades you get is easy to calculate. I covered the arithmetic already, in Chapter 5. But to save you the work of looking it up, I'll give a quick reprise here. Let's take bilevel printers first, since most printers are limited to full on or full off for each dot.

For bilevel monochrome printers, the number of shades of gray equals the number of printer dots in each halftone cell (or halftone spot), plus one for no dots filled in. As a formula, it looks like this:

```
Shades = Printer Dots per Halftone Spot + 1
```

or simply:

```
Shades = Printer Dots per Spot + 1
```

So a 4 by 4 cell, with 16 printer dots, allows 17 shades of gray; a 5 by 5 cell allows 26 shades, and so on.

For bilevel color printers, the math is the same for each color, but the total number of colors is much larger. More precisely, the total number of colors equals the number of shades for cyan times the number of shades for magenta (which gives you the number of cyan-magenta mixes) times the number of shades for yellow (which gives you the number of cyan-magenta-yellow mixes). (Since CMY printers can't give you a true black, you get a few extra colors with the added black in a CMYK printer, but not all that many. I'll ignore those here.)

In other words, the total number of colors equals the cube of the number of printer dots per halftone spot plus 1. Or, as a formula:

```
Colors = (Printer dots per spot + 1)³
```

So far, so good. Now let's take a closer look at how to figure out how many printer dots in a halftone spot.

For any given printer resolution, the number of printer dots along one edge of a halftone cell equals the printer resolution in dots per inch divided by the halftone resolution in spots per inch. Here's the formula for this one:

$$\text{Printer dots per halftone line} = \frac{\text{Printer dpi}}{\text{Halftone lpi}}$$

We've been here before. If you have a 600-dpi printer, a 75-lpi halftone screen will give you 600 divided by 75, or 8 dots across for each halftone spot. If you have a 300-dpi printer, the same 75-lpi halftone screen will give you 300 divided by 75, or only 4 dots across for each spot.

If your printer resolution is the same in both vertical and horizontal directions, you can square this to get the total number of dots in the halftone cell. Otherwise, you need to do this once for each dimension. So if your printer is 600 by 300 dpi and you use a 75-lpi screen, you have 8 dots in one direction and 4 in the other, giving you a total of 32 dots per halftone spot. The formula looks like this:

$$\text{Printer dots per spot} = \frac{\text{Horizontal dpi}}{\text{Halftone lpi}} \times \frac{\text{Vertical dpi}}{\text{Halftone lpi}}$$

And if we plug this formula for printer dots per halftone spot into the formula for colors that we came up with before, we get:

$$\text{Colors} = \left[\left(\frac{\text{Horizontal dpi}}{\text{Halftone lpi}} \times \frac{\text{Vertical dpi}}{\text{Halftone lpi}}\right) + 1\right]^3$$

If you're mathphobic, this is probably starting to look too much like something from an algebra book, but it's still basic arithmetic. If your color printer resolution is 600 by 600 dpi and you use a 75-lpi screen, the numbers work out like this:

$$\begin{aligned}
\text{Colors} &= \left[\left(\frac{600}{75} \times \frac{600}{75}\right) + 1\right]^3 \\
&= \left[(8 \times 8) + 1\right]^3 \\
&= 65^3 \\
&= 274{,}625
\end{aligned}$$

If you go up to a 100-lpi screen, the numbers work out to:

$$\text{Colors} = \left[\left(\frac{600}{100} \times \frac{600}{100}\right) + 1\right]^3$$
$$= \left[(36) + 1\right]^3$$
$$= 37^3$$
$$= 50,653$$

The same halftone screens with a 300 by 300 dpi printer give you 4913 colors at 75 dpi, or a paltry 1000 colors at 100 dpi. That's why 60 lpi is a typical setting for 300 dpi printing—with 25 dots in each halftone cell, and 17,576 colors.

For multilevel printers that don't offer enough levels to qualify for continuous tone output, the formula is slightly different. In this case, the number of colors also depends on the number of levels available for each color. So the formula becomes:

```
Colors = {Printer Dots per spot x [(Number of levels-1) + 1]}³
```

Having dragged you through this swamp of arithmetic, I now have to rush in and point out that what I've described is classic halftoning, with classic halftone cells. Many printers today take a more sophisticated approach. These more sophisticated halftone schemes generally go hand in hand with not letting you set the halftone screen in the printer driver. I'll touch on these a little later. For now, just be aware that even with these more sophisticated schemes, it's still appropriate to find out how many lines per inch, or effective lines per inch, the screen uses (except for FM screens, as I already pointed out). And it's still important to use the halftone resolution to determine the best image resolution. Now let's get to the payoff for all this math.

So, did someone ask how many colors are enough? (Besides me, I mean.) Well, ideally, you want the full 16.7 million colors that define true color. For those who are weak on calculating cube roots, that means 256 shades of cyan, magenta, and yellow. (That may sound familiar. I've pointed it out before in a different context.)

But here's a little secret: You don't really need 16.7 million colors for a picture to offer a continuous tone look. The human eye can detect between 7 and 8 million colors—at best. As I've mentioned elsewhere, as you get older, you lose color perception, just like you lose hearing, and the number of colors you can detect drops to just 2 to 3 million. The reason 16.7 million is the magic number for true color is mostly because the human eye can discriminate some colors better than others.

If you stop at 23-bit color (roughly 8.4 million colors), with the shades of color separated in even steps by some arbitrary scale, you'll find that for some colors— by which I mean for some hues and for some levels of saturation and brightness—you can move through several steps without seeing a difference. But with other colors, a single step makes an obvious difference. More important, it makes too much of a difference to shade gradually from one color to the next.

With 16.7 million colors, there are lots of cases where you have to move several steps before you see any difference in color. However, you also have enough colors so it's not too hard to arrange the steps to fill in the gaps for changes in colors that the eye is most sensitive to. (It's also not too hard to blow it and set the steps so you can see sudden visible changes where they should be continuous. But you have to work harder to mess up with 16.7 million colors than with 8.4 million.)

On the other hand, for lots of photos, you can't tell the difference between 16 bits (64,000 colors) and 24 bits (16.7 million colors). Even the 17,500 colors you get from a 60-lpi screen on a 300-dpi printer don't look too bad in most cases. (For the number of colors at least. The dithering patterns usually look pretty horrible.) And printers that use more sophisticated dithering techniques can offer more color depth for any given screen setting.

So while you're better off with more colors than fewer colors, the simple truth is that the best choice for screen setting depends on the particular image you're printing. If your printer driver gives you control over the setting, you may want to experiment a bit with different images to get a feel for which settings work best with which kinds of image.

With photographs, as I mentioned earlier, more colors is usually more important than better resolution, while with graphics, better resolution is usually more important. So you may want to try a lower number for the line screen setting when you print photographs than when you print graphics. (Assuming, of course, that you can set the screen frequency in the first place.)

Assorted Practical Issues

> The theoretical understanding of the world, which is the aim of philosophy, is not a matter of great practical importance to animals, or to savages, or even to most civilised men.
>
> Bertrand Russell
> A Free Man's Worship and Other Essays, ch. 1 (1976).

Aside from figuring out the right scanning resolution to use, there are several other practical issues you should be aware of when you're scanning a photo into your computer.

First on the list is the danger of moiré patterns. (This is a French word, by the way, which is why it often gets an accent over the *e*, even when it's written in English. It's pronounced moi-ray.)

Moiré patterns

A moiré pattern is basically an optical illusion you run into when you put one set of thinly spaced lines—or rows of dots—over another set. The human eye and brain like to play connect the dots, so you wind up seeing patterns that aren't really there. The patterns that you think you see in Figure 8.13, for example, are moiré patterns.

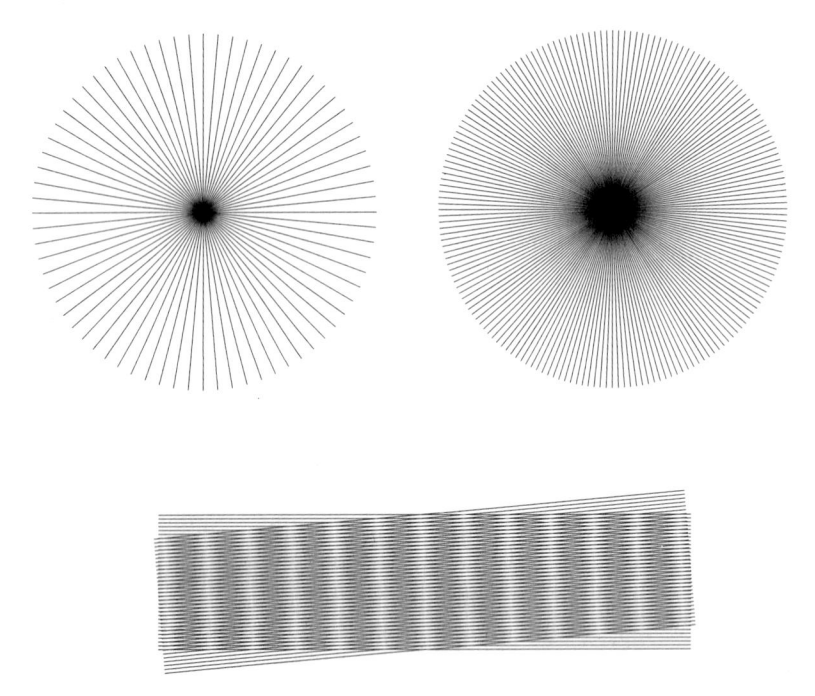

Figure 8.13 Moiré patterns are optical illusions of apparent patterns that aren't really there

Moiré patterns in scanned images

Moiré patterns can be an issue for scanning. Quite simply, if you scan an image that's printed as a halftone—from a magazine, say, or a newspaper—you're also scanning the halftone screen it was printed with. That halftone screen can interfere with the sampling grid in the scanner itself to give you a moiré pattern. Once neatly stored in the scanned file, it can interfere with the halftone screen you use when you print.

You can even run into moiré patterns with images that don't start out as halftones. Take a picture with venetian blinds in it, for example, or a picture of a man wearing a striped shirt, and the blinds or stripes can also interfere with the sampling grid. Once again, you'll wind up with moiré patterns.

That's the bad news. The good news is that if you work at it, you can usually get rid of the moiré pattern after you've scanned, or at least tone it down a lot. The basic trick is to use some sort of blurring filter in your graphics program to make the pattern go away, and then use a sharpening filter to sharpen up the image again. It won't be as sharp as when you started, but the scanned halftone screen should be gone. Be prepared to experiment a bit before you find the best way to make the moiré go away. A few programs—notably Light Source's Ofoto scanning program—offer Moire Removal as a choice right up there on the menu. (That's the Options menu in Ofoto). If you have a program that includes the feature, you're home free.

Who's Doing the Halftoning?

> No job is too small to botch.
>
> John Peer

Up to now, whenever I've mentioned halftoning, I've assumed that the printer or printer driver is doing the work. In truth, though, you can add the halftone screen at any point in the process—at the printer, the printer driver, the software application, or even at the scanner. What you can't do, or shouldn't do, is add halftoning at two different levels. That's a prescription for a moiré pattern.

I've been assuming the printer or printer driver is adding the halftone screen for good reason. You will usually get the best looking output that way.

Most color printers today—even some low price ink jets—offer sophisticated halftoning that's fine-tuned for the individual printer, with the halftoning handled by the printer itself for PostScript printers or by the printer driver for non-PostScript printers. Although you can override these halftone schemes and do your halftoning elsewhere, you'll almost always get worse results.

If you have an older color printer (or even a new one) that doesn't do anything very sophisticated for halftoning, you might be able to improve on the output by adding the halftone screen with your application. But I wouldn't bet on it.

Don't expect to find any halftoning features for embedded photos in your favorite word processor. But if you have a sophisticated graphics program, you'll often find some features that will let you override the default screening for the printer. Some programs also let you create special effects with halftone screens (which effects I'm not going to talk about). The more important issue, usually, is to make sure the feature isn't overriding your printer or printer driver when you don't want it to. If you use a graphics program, find out if it has a halftone feature, and, if so, how to make sure it's off.

Most, if not all, scanning programs offer an option for scanning in a black and white dithering mode a.k.a. halftone mode. (I haven't seen any with a color dithering mode, and I doubt I would want to use it if there were one.) Unless you are extremely short on disk space, I recommend that when you're scanning black and white photos (which are, of course, gray scale, not black and white) or scanning color photos as black and white (actually gray scale again), you stay with a gray scale mode. Again, the most important issue is to make sure you know where the dithering mode option is hidden, and make sure it's turned off.

Saving Disk Real Estate

> Small rooms or dwellings discipline the mind.
>
> Leonardo da Vinci

Speaking of disk space. If you store many 24-bit color images on your hard disk, you'll quickly discover one strong argument for removable disk cartridges. A 4 inch by 4 inch image scanned in at 200 samples per inch and 24-bit color depth is not quite 2 megabytes (200 times 200, or 40,000 samples per square inch times 16 square inches times 24 bits divided by 8 bits per byte). If you accumulate just ten images a week, that's 80 megabytes gone every month.

If you don't want to delete the images, the ideal solution is a removable cartridge disk, like SyQuest or Iomega removable cartridges. When you fill up one disk, you just move on to the next. But even then, the price of the cartridges makes saving disk space a Real Good Idea.

I've already mentioned your first line of defense: Don't go wild with image resolution. If 1.5 times the halftone resolution gives you acceptable looking output, don't go any higher. If you must go higher, don't go any higher than you have to. You certainly don't want an image resolution higher than your printer resolution.

Compressing files

Your second line of defense is to compress the files.

The first thing you need to know about compression is that it comes in two basic flavors: Lossy and lossless.

Lossless compression

Lossless compression doesn't lose any information in the process of compressing and decompressing. (Well, that makes sense.) It just wrings out all the extra space it can find in the file and packs it more tightly. (Don't take that description too seriously, but the concept is right.) It's something like squeezing everything into your suitcase at the end of a trip and making it fit, somehow.

Lossy compression

Lossy compression, in contrast, loses information. It's like throwing out some of your clothes to get the suitcase closed.

If you use, say, PKZIP, to compress files when you send them by modem, or you're using Drivespace, Stacker, or DoubleSpace disk compression schemes on your hard disk, you're already using lossless compression. And lossless compression is certainly what you want to use if you're compressing, say, a word processing document, where you can't afford to lose any of the information. But with picture files, losing a little information isn't necessarily a Bad Thing.

Lossless compression schemes can cut picture files in half or better. Lossy schemes can cut size by well over 90 percent. The only problem is that you have to be willing to lose a little picture quality to save the disk space. When a lossy compression scheme throws out information, it's gone forever.

The most widely used lossy compression scheme is JPEG, short for Joint Photographic Experts Group. You'll find it available as a choice in a range of programs, usually with an option to set the level of compression on a file-by-file basis.

If you experiment with JPEG compression, you'll find that you can use a higher compression with some pictures than with others before the picture quality changes noticeably. More important, you'll have to decide what level of quality you consider acceptable. If JPEG compression is available in your programs, invest some time in getting familiar with its possibilities and limitations.

If you're using a disk compression utility, like Stacker, DoubleSpace, or Drivespace, keep in mind that you're already compressing everything that goes on the disk. You're not likely to get any more benefit from using a lossless compression scheme when you save files to a compressed hard disk. Lossy compression schemes should still save you extra drive space, but not as much as on an uncompressed disk.

More on Halftoning

> Not many appreciate the ultimate power and potential usefulness of basic knowledge accumulated by obscure, unseen investigators who, in a lifetime of intensive study, may never see any practical use for their findings but who go on seeking answers to the unknown without thought of financial or practical gain.
>
> Eugenie Clark (b. 1922)
> *The Lady and the Sharks* (1969)

You can file this entire section under things you probably don't need to know. But since I keep talking about more sophisticated halftoning schemes, it's only fair that I give you a peek at what I'm talking about.

The simplest approach to filling a halftone spot starts at the center of the halftone cell and grows the spot outward, as shown in Figure 8.14. This approach imitates halftone spots on film, which use a single spot of various sizes. But with a 300-dpi printer, and even a 600-dpi printer, it has the disadvantage of showing up as an easy-to-see pattern—particularly in areas where the same color repeats over a large part of the page.

Growing the spot

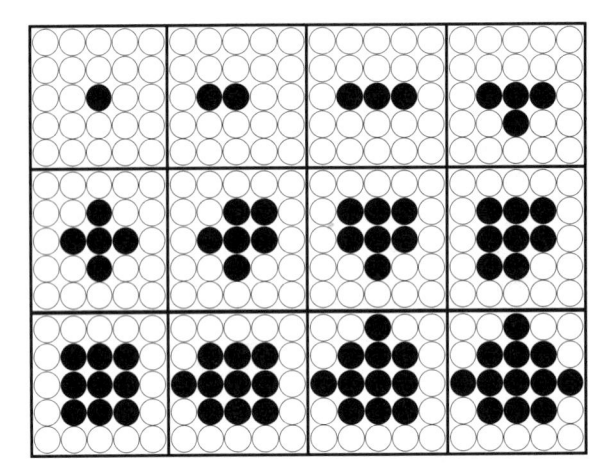

Figure 8.14 The simplest approach to filling a halftone spot starts in the middle, and grows the spot.

A sophisticated variation on growing the spot from the center is to divide each halftone cell into four quarters and grow a separate spot in each quarter.

Regular pattern halftones

One step up from this classic approach to halftones is a regular pattern halftone: *Pattern*, because instead of growing the dot from the center, it uses a pattern of dots spread throughout the halftone cell. *Regular*, because it uses the same pattern of dots in each cell with any given level of gray. Figure 8.15 shows an example of several shades of dithered gray with a regular pattern halftone. The figure uses a four-by-four cell, because it's easier to design a four-by-four pattern than a five-by-five pattern.

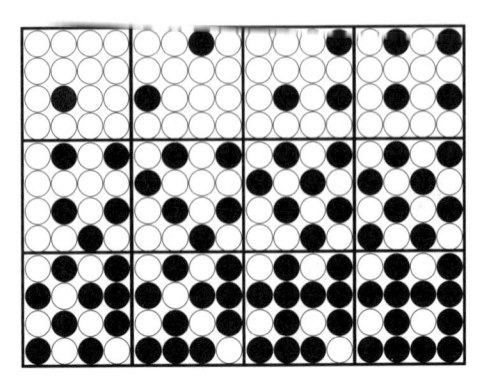

Figure 8.15 Regular pattern halftones offer a more sophisticated approach to dithering.

Supercells

The next step up from regular pattern halftones is supercell halftoning. Supercell halftones are a little too complicated to explain quickly here. But the basic concept is to combine some number of halftone cells into a larger supercell. This lets you fake intermediate gray levels by splitting the dots among the cells.

Say what?

Here's the basic idea in a drastically oversimplified example. Suppose you have one cell with four dots. That lets you have five gray levels—0, 25, 50, 75, and 100 percent. Now suppose you treat the one cell as if it were joined with another cell that also has four dots. And suppose you want to get a 37.5 percent gray level. Well, you can't do it with either cell by itself. But you can do it by putting one dot in one of the cells and effectively sharing it between them, making one cell 25 percent and the other 50 percent, but treating the two cells as one supercell.

There's a lot more to supercells than this. And I repeat that this explanation is drastically oversimplified. But it gives you some sense of what supercell screening is about. If your printer uses supercells, odds are that it won't let you mess with the halftone screen settings. And you shouldn't.

FM screening (not on your radio dial)

I mentioned frequency-modulation screening (a.k.a. FM screening, FM dithering, FM halftones, frequency-modulated dithering, frequency-modulated halftones, or error diffusion) earlier in this chapter without explaining what it was. Basically FM screening differs from standard halftones by not changing the size of the halftone spots. Instead, FM screening uses the same size spots throughout the image, but uses more of them in dark areas and fewer in light areas. In other words, it modulates, or changes, the number of spots instead of the size of the spots.

Figure 8.16 shows what diffusion dithering looks like at a somewhat grainy 100 pixels per inch. Figure 8.17 shows the same photo with diffusion dithering at

Figure 8.16 Diffusion dithering, at 100 pixels per inch.

284 *Chapter 8*

Figure 8.17 Diffusion dithering, at 75 pixels per inch.

Screen angles

an even grainier 75 pixels per inch. Although you might not believe it from these two samples, because of the low resolution, FM screening is generally one of the better choices for printing photos.

Have I mentioned screen angles lately?

Don't answer. That's a rhetorical question. I mentioned them earlier in this chapter without explaining what they were. Briefly, the screen angle is the angle of the halftone screen. If the screen is parallel to the bottom of the page, the angle is 0 degrees. If it's at an angle to the page, the angle is higher. (Brilliant deduction.) The standard angle for monochrome printing is 45 degrees, because the screen is least obvious at that angle.

When you print in color, you get a separate screen for each color. So the issue with color printing is what angle to use for each color. And the answer is to use the angles that keep you from getting moiré patterns.

Some programs and printer drivers give you the option of setting the screen angles and setting the angle for each color separately. If you get seriously and deeply into color printing, you may find situations where, indeed, you might want to mess with the screen angle, but that's mostly for people who are preparing something for sending out to a print shop. If you're printing on a desktop printer, the best advice (if your driver lets you change screen angle) is to keep your hands off the setting. The default screen angles are designed to minimize moiré patterns. Unless you're getting moiré patterns, leave the angles alone.

GAMMA: THE THIRD LETTER IN THE GREEK ALPHABET

> The world no doubt is the best or most serviceable schoolmaster; but the world's curriculum does not include Latin and Greek.
>
> E. V. Lucas

You can add any number of special effects, filters, and other enhancements to a photo with a high-end graphics program. The one that earns special mention here is gamma correction, because it's a key feature whose function is less than obvious.

I mentioned way back in Chapter 3 that gamma correction lets you change brightness and contrast in a way that brings out details better in both light and dark areas. I also promised to show you an example when I came back to the subject in this chapter.

The easiest way to see what gamma correction does is to compare it to adjusting brightness and contrast. Figure 8.18 shows a scanned photo with a dark foreground and light sky, complete with clouds. The obvious problem is that the entire foreground is so dark that it's essentially a silhouette.

Figure 8.18 This shot of Vermont wearing its peak autumn colors shows no detail at all.

One way to try for more detail is to crank up the brightness, as in Figure 8.19, but then the sky gets completely washed out, with no sign of any clouds.

Figure 8.19 Crank up the brightness, and you get some detail in the dark areas, but the clouds disappear.

Changing the contrast doesn't help much at all for this particular picture. In Figure 8.20, I've the turned the contrast down a bit, so the dark colors aren't all shifted to nearly black, the way they are in the original. The trees show just a bit

Figure 8.20 Turn down the contrast, and you'll also get more detail in the dark areas, but the light areas lose contrast, making the clouds blend in to the sky.

more detail, but the sky is noticeably darker, and the image generally grayer, as if seen through a neutral gray filter. (Neutral gray filters don't shift color—that's why they are called neutral—they only affect the amount of light, or brightness.) Basically, I've regained some of the darker tones in the trees by lopping off the lightest tones in the sky.

The problem with both the contrast and brightness controls is that you have to apply them evenly for the whole picture—for both the dark and light areas. Raise the brightness to brighten the dark area, and you have to brighten the light areas just as much. Lower the contrast to improve the dark area, and you have to lower it for the rest of the picture just as much.

What you really need to improve this picture is some way to crank up both the brightness and contrast in the dark area without changing them much in the light area. And that's what gamma correction can do for you.

In Figure 8.21, I've adjusted the gamma upwards. As you can see, the dark area is both brighter and more contrasty than in any of the other pictures. Even better, the light area has changed only a little from the original, and you can still see the clouds in the sky.

Figure 8.21 Gamma correction does the trick.

Quite simply, as I've said before, gamma correction lets you adjust both brightness and contrast, and adjust them differently in dark areas than in light areas. This is called nonlinear adjustment. And what it means is that you get a different adjustment in dark areas and light areas.

As with most graphics tools, the best way to get a feel for how gamma correction works is to try it. I'd also suggest comparing the gamma correction to results you can get by changing brightness and contrast. Once you learn how to use gamma correction (assuming it's available in your graphics program), you'll find that it's one of the most valuable tools you've got for working with photos.

COLOR MATCHING WITH SCANNERS

> Everything that lives strives for color.
>
> Johann Wolfgang Von Goethe

Color matching is just as much an issue between scanner and printer as between screen and printer. In fact, it's more important in some ways. Any time you scan a photo into your system, you'll want to know that the colors in the printed version that comes out bear some relation to the colors you scanned in.

The good news is that most tools for matching scanner and printer colors are a lot easier to use than the tools for matching screen and printer. Typically, software that offers color matching between scanner and printer comes with either a hardcopy sample or a standard image on disk.

If the software comes with a hardcopy sample—which you'll find in the CorelDRAW package for example—you scan the sample, then print it out, and scan the printed sample. The software compares the scanned version of the printout with the colors it expects to see and generates a color correction table. You can then set this table as the default to use when scanning photos in the future.

If the software generates its own sample image, you follow pretty much the same procedure. You print the sample and then scan it. Here again, the software compares the scanned version with the colors it expects to see and generates a color correction table.

Details vary from one program to the next, of course, but the procedure is usually straightforward. And foolproof. So there isn't anything for me to add here. Just be aware that calibrating your scanner for color matching is a Good Idea. And if you have software that will do it, do it.

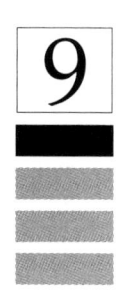

9 Get to Know Your Printer Driver

> Do not be too timid and squeamish about your actions. All life is an experiment.
>
> Ralph Waldo Emerson

If you're like most people, you probably stay with the default settings for your printer on the assumption that the defaults were carefully chosen to give the best looking output for the largest range of images. Or that they're at least a reasonable compromise for getting pretty good output for a wide range of images.

Wrong.

I can't begin to count the number of times I've tested a printer and wound up with rotten-looking output, only to be told, *You shouldn't use the default settings.* Oh.

Sometimes the settings you need to change are the color correction settings or the halftone settings. Sometimes the settings are as simple as picking the right paper from a list of choices, or setting the driver for graphics, photographs, or both. But no matter which settings you need to change, you can't change them without going to your printer driver and learning how to take advantage of it.

In this chapter, we'll take a look at the choices in some representative drivers. Let's start with a couple of ground rules:

First, I'll be talking about Windows and Windows 95 drivers, because I happen to work primarily on a Windows system and that's what I have handy. If you're a Mac user, don't let that throw you. The look and feel of the screens may change slightly between PC and Mac, but the choices are pretty much the same.

Second, I'll assume through most of this chapter that you know how to get to the driver setup screens. For those who don't, here's the road map:

You can get there from most programs by choosing File Print Setup, or by choosing File Print, then Setup. (Assuming, of course, you pick the right printer along the way.) With some Windows drivers, however, you won't get to see all the options if you go to the driver from a program. (I don't know of any good reason for this, but it's a fact you have to live with.)

You can also reach the drivers in Windows and Windows for Workgroups 3.1x by opening the Control Panel, choosing the Printers Icon, highlighting the printer name, and choosing Setup.

In Windows 95, you can choose the My Computer icon on the desktop, then choose the Printers folder, highlight the printer name, and choose File Properties. If you're using a Windows 3.1 driver in Windows 95, you need one more step: Go to the Details tabbed card, and choose setup. On the Mac you can change the printer driver from within the chooser, but you can set the printer driver settings from within each program.

> **If the driver for your printer happens to be included here, that's fine, but don't feel left out if it isn't. The point is not to teach you how to use some specific drivers, but to arm you with a strategy for using *any* printer driver. If you follow through all the examples in this chapter, you should be able to look at virtually any color printer driver, understand the vast majority of the choices, and spot the oddball choices immediately, so you'll know the right questions to ask. You'll be much better off coming out of this chapter with general concepts that you can apply anywhere, rather than worrying about details in specific drivers.**

FULL MANUAL CONTROL

> As of now I am in control here.
>
> Alexander Haig
> Comment in the wake of the attempted assassination of President Reagan, as reported in *Time* magazine, April 18, 1981

The NEC SuperScript 3000 printer driver is a good place to start, both because it offers so many choices and because it gives you complete manual control over most of them. Figure 9.1 shows the main setup screen for the driver.

Mundane choices

Most of the choices in Figure 9.1 are standard fare for just about any printer—whether color or monochrome. Starting at the upper left corner, with the Multiple Copies box, the Copies text box lets you specify the number of copies to print for each page you send to the printer.

> **If you ever print multiple copies, you probably already know that you can set most programs for multiple copies. The general rule is that if you let the program handle the multiple copies, it will also automatically collate the pages. However, it will take more time to print, since the program has to do its thing with each page (okay, process the page) each time it hands a page off to the printer driver. If you let the printer handle the multiple copies, you have to collate the pages yourself. But you cut down the printing time, since the program processes each page only once.**

For photos or complex graphics, this means it usually makes more sense to let the printer, rather than the program, handle the multiple copies. With simple graphics, however—and particularly with ribbon-based color printers—the processing time is relatively small compared to the printing time. You may find that saving the time doesn't make up for the extra work collating the pages.

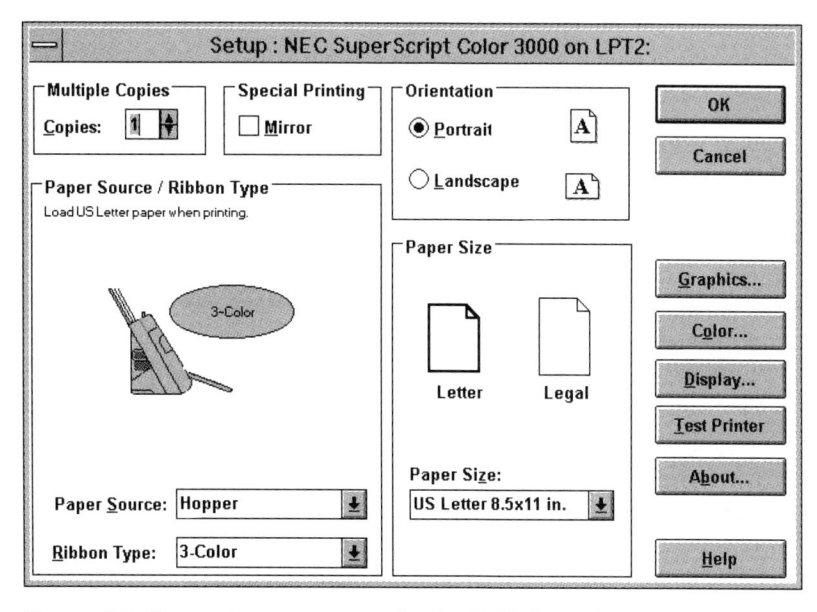

Figure 9.1 The main setup screen for the NEC SuperScript 3000 color printer driver offers mostly basic choices.

Next over is the Special Printing box with a check box for Mirror printing. Add an X to this box and you'll get a mirror image of what you see on screen. Why, you may ask, would you want a mirror image? The only reason is for printing a mirror image on the back side of transparencies.

To the right of the Special Printing box is the Orientation box, with a choice of Portrait and Landscape modes. There's nothing special here either. Portrait prints with the short dimension of the paper along the top and bottom. Landscape prints with the long dimension along the top and bottom. Pick the one that matches the way you want to print.

Just below the Orientation box is the setting for paper size, which for this particular printer is limited to letter and legal size. Here again, we're not dealing with rocket science. Just pick the one that matches the paper you're printing on.

Finishing the circle clockwise is the Paper Source/Ribbon Type box. The choices for Paper Source, in this case, are Hopper—which is NEC's term for the input tray—and Manual. You should be able to handle this one, as long as you know where the paper is. (Well, *duh*.)

Ribbon type   More interesting is the Ribbon Type text box. As you might guess from the name of the option, the SuperScript Color 3000 is a ribbon-based printer. The Ribbon Type text box lets you tell the driver which ribbon is loaded. The choice of ribbons will obviously depend on the particular printer, but you'll need to nail down the jargon the printer uses for its ribbons.

The SuperScript 3000, for example, has three-color ribbons for both thermal wax and thermal dye modes, but the 3-Color choice in the driver is strictly for thermal wax printing. If you're using a three-color thermal dye ribbon, the choice is called Photo. (This is one of those misguided attempts to make things easier by not telling you what's really going on.) Just to confuse matters a little more, the box for the thermal dye ribbon is labeled 3-Color Dye Sublimation Ribbon. *Sigh.*

> **One interesting oddity in the SuperScript Color 3000 driver is that the printer tells the driver which ribbon is loaded. That means you shouldn't have to, but you do. If the ribbon type is set wrong, the printer driver will stop at print time, tell you it's the wrong ribbon, and ask whether to continue.**
>
> **If you have a printer that does this sort of thing, be sure to find out what happens if you tell it to go ahead and print. If it follows the setting in the driver, you'll certainly want to bail out. If it ignores the driver setting, you'll probably want to print. But be sure you check that the right paper is loaded first.**

That covers everything in the dialog box except the buttons that go down the right side. You should be able to figure out the OK and Cancel buttons without my help. We'll skip over the Graphics and Color buttons for the moment. Next down is the Display button. This brings up a dialog box that lets you tell the driver what status information to show you during printing. That's a useful feature, but not worth going into here. The Test Printer button prints a test page to confirm that everything's working; the About button gives information about the driver version; and the Help button calls up the driver's Help screens.

Graphic options   That's all you need to know about those buttons. Let's back up to the Graphics button. Choose it, and the driver will open the dialog box shown in Figure 9.2.

Now we're getting to the interesting stuff. The one setting in the Print Quality box at the top of the dialog box is for Ink Density. Since this is a ribbon-based thermal printer, the ink density is controlled by the amount of heat at the printhead. More heat transfers more ink to the paper, and the best setting depends on the paper you're using.

This happens to be an unusual option for a ribbon-based printer. However, you'll find equivalent features on most ink jet printers, which transfer more ink to the paper by . . . uh . . . spraying more ink on the paper.

Fine-tuning the amount of ink   Regardless of the type of printer, you can take advantage of this sort of setting to fine-tune the printer for the paper you're using. A few test runs should tell you pretty quickly what the best setting is for any given paper. I found that with laser paper, the Darkest setting gave me acceptable output with reasonably solid coverage in solid areas, though still not as solid as with NEC's own thermal transfer paper.

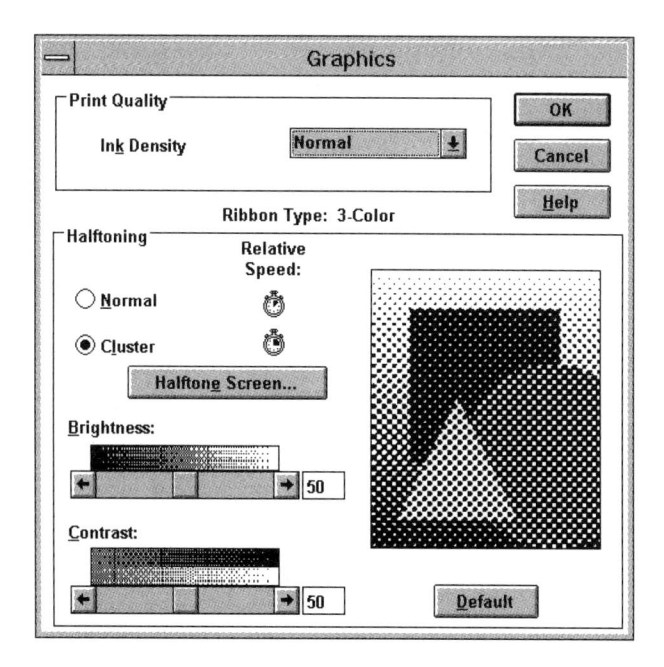

Figure 9.2 The Graphics dialog box in the SuperScript 3000 driver lets you tweak the output.

The more typical equivalent of this option, which you'll find on most ink jet printers, lets you choose a type of paper. The paper setting determines, among other things, how much ink the printer puts on the page.

Next down comes the Halftoning box. The brightness and contrast controls in this box do just what you would expect from using brightness and contrast controls on a television set all your life. If the printed image needs some tweaking, and the program you're printing from doesn't offer its own controls, you can use these settings to adjust the brightness and contrast. (The Default button in the lower right corner of the dialog box resets everything back to the defaults.)

The more interesting option in the Halftoning box is the choice between Normal and Cluster. A quick look at the driver's help file will tell you that these are the halftone settings.

Pick Normal, and you get a predefined halftone screen that you don't have any control over. Pick Cluster, and you get a different kind of dithering pattern, which is a bit slower than the Normal choice, but which also gives you control over halftone screen frequency and screen angle. If you pick Cluster, you can then choose the Halftone Screen button to open the Halftone Screen dialog box shown in Figure 9.3.

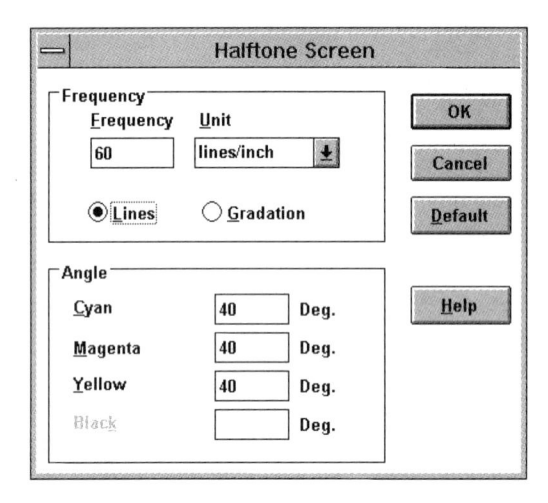

Figure 9.3 The Halftone Screen dialog box lets you set screen frequency and screen angle.

As you can see in the figure, the dialog box lets you enter screen frequency and screen angles. One neat feature in this dialog box is that you can switch between seeing the lines-per-inch setting for screen frequency and seeing the number of gray levels it gives you. Just choose the Lines button, as shown in the Frequency box, for lines per inch, or Gradation for shades of gray. As I've suggested elsewhere, you'll generally want to leave the screen angle alone.

Finally, if you back out to the main Setup dialog box and choose the Color button, you'll see the Color dialog box shown in Figure 9.4. You've seen this before, in Chapter 3, as part of an exercise in color (mis)matching.

Color matching and mismatching

Since we've been over most of this dialog box before in detail, I'll just take a whirlwind tour here. The Color Coordinate choice is best thought of as a color correction feature. By any name, it lets you modify the colors. The choices for this particular printer are Screen Match, Enhanced Color, Grayscale, and None.

The Quick Match box is one of the unusual extras in this driver. Adding an X to the box modifies the way the driver handles the Screen Match and Enhanced Color choices. So, it effectively gives you two more color correction options.

Except for color corrections that are designed to simulate what a file will look like if you print it on a commercial press, color correction choices are strictly pot luck. You can pretty well bet that a choice like Grayscale will let you print color images in black and white (by which I mean shades of gray, of course). But you'll have to test the other choices to see what they do.

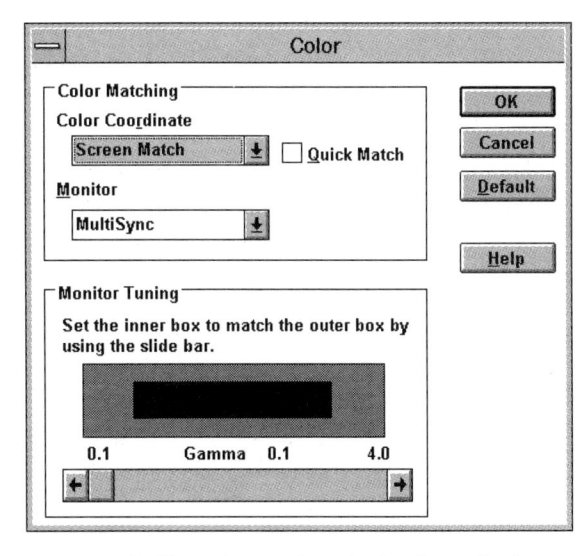

Figure 9.4 Changing settings in the SuperScript 3000 Color dialog box can change the colors the printer prints.

The Monitor box lets you pick a monitor from a list. This gives the driver a better idea of what it's supposed to match when you choose Screen Match. The Monitor Tuning box lets you set the driver for your specific monitor, as I discussed at length in Chapter 3.

And that's all there is to understanding a printer driver. Don't believe me? Then let's look at another one.

AUTOMATIC PILOT

> It is critical vision alone which can mitigate the unimpeded operation of the automatic.
>
> Marshall McLuhan

Since we started with a fully manual driver, it's only fair to jump to the other extreme and look at a fully automatic driver.

Well, maybe that's an exaggeration. I suppose a *fully* automatic driver wouldn't let you set anything at all, and there aren't any drivers that have quite reached that point. There are, however, some that leave you with very little to think about. Consider, for example, the HP DeskJet 660C driver, shown in Figure 9.5

The basics The Orientation, Copies, and Paper Size options are pretty much the same as for the NEC driver that we just looked at. One extra item worth mention is the

296 *Chapter 9*

Ordered Printing check box. If you're printing multiple copies of a document, putting an X in this box collates the copies. That's equivalent to letting your program handle the multiple copies. It even gives you the same slowdown in print speed.

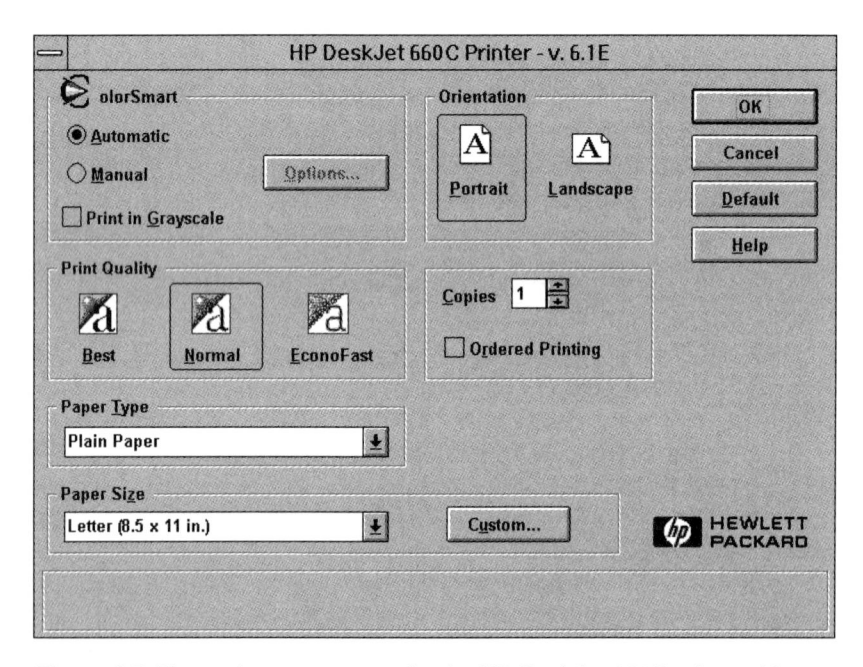

Figure 9.5 The main setup screen for the HP DeskJet 660C printer driver may be all you'll ever need.

If you're printing a single copy of a document, adding the X tells the driver to print the pages in reverse order—with the last page printing first and the first page last. The reason you might want to print in reverse order is that this particular printer rolls its pages out face up. So if you print in normal order, the second page comes out face up on top of the first, the third on top of the second, and so on. When you're done, you have to shuffle the pages yourself to reverse the order.

I'll also mention in passing that there are lots more predefined paper sizes for the DeskJet 660C than for the NEC. I counted 15 choices, including Index Card and Envelope, as well as Letter and Legal. Also notice the Custom button to the right of the Paper Size box. This opens another dialog box that lets you set a custom paper size.

Paper type   The more interesting setting for our purposes is Paper Type. The driver lists six choices, including Plain Paper, Ink Jet Paper, Glossy Paper, and Transparencies, with extra choices for glossy paper and transparencies to pause after each page.

As you may remember from the ink jet section of Chapter 5, picking the right setting isn't always as simple as matching the choice to the actual type of paper you have. Briefly, for those who skipped Chapter 5, when you change paper type, you change a number of settings at the same time. And if you're using anything but a specific brand and type of paper recommended by the printer manufacturer, you have to experiment to find the best setting. (That's the *Reader's Digest* version. If you want to know more, take a look at Chapter 5.) But that's not the interesting part.

The interesting part is that when you're driving on automatic, with the Automatic option in the ColorSmart box, the only choices you have that affect color, halftoning, and print quality are Paper Type, Print Quality, and the option to Print in Grayscale, which is just below the Automatic and Manual buttons.

Automatic settings

When you choose a paper type in automatic mode, the driver not only sets things like color correction and dithering automatically, it won't even show you what settings it's using. In some cases, it even limits your choices in print quality. If you choose HP Premium InkJet Paper or HP Glossy, the driver will set Print Quality to Best. It will let you change to Normal, if you like, but not to EconoFast. (This makes good sense. If you're using paper that has a premium price, there's no sense wasting it on draft quality output.)

Most printer drivers with this sort of automatic mode do an impressive job of picking the right settings for you. You may want to experiment with the manual choices to get a better feel for your printer. But unless you are unhappy with the output for a particular image, you're usually best advised to simply leave the driver in automatic. Even so, when you print, make sure you take advantage of the driver's features by setting the paper type and print quality. And don't forget to check that the grayscale setting is on or off, as appropriate.

When you're ready to delve into manual control on this sort of driver, you can usually find a manual setting, cleverly named Manual in the dialog box in Figure 9.5. In this particular driver, once you choose Manual, you can take advantage of the Options button in the ColorSmart box. Choose the button, and you'll open the dialog box shown in Figure 9.6.

The first thing to notice about this dialog box is that you don't get as many options as in the NEC SuperScript 3000 driver. In particular, you won't find any way to set line screen or frequency, which is typical for drivers that lean towards automatic control.

The second—and more important—thing to notice is that the options you get are all pretty much the same as for the NEC printer, even though the names are slightly different.

The Intensity setting is the equivalent of the SuperScript's Ink Density; the Color Control setting is the equivalent of the SuperScript's Color Coordinate; and the Pattern and Scatter Halftoning settings are the equivalent of the SuperScript's Normal and Cluster Halftoning settings. More precisely, the two drivers offer different dithering schemes, but both offer a choice in dithering scheme. (And, in case you're wondering, the Scatter choice in HP DeskJet driver is for frequency-modulated dithering, which I discussed in Chapter 8.)

Do you begin to see a pattern yet?

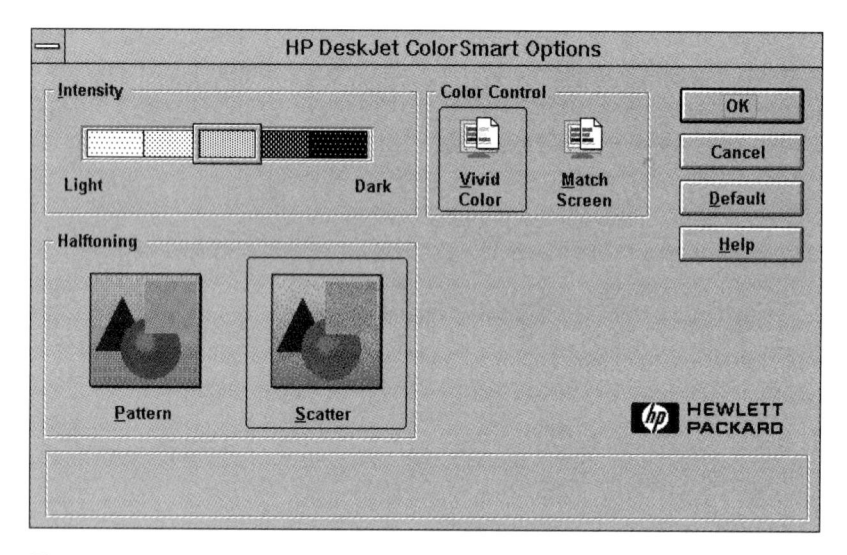

Figure 9.6 Even the manual control options for the DeskJet 660C driver are a bit limited.

POSTSCRIPT

> There are only three kinds of people in the world: those who can count, and, those who can't.
>
> Unknown

As it happens, the NEC SuperScript 3000 printer that we started with is a GDI printer, and the HP DeskJet 660C is a PCL printer. (This should not be a surprise, considering that it's from Hewlett-Packard.) What we haven't looked at yet is a driver for a PostScript printer, for the third major category of printer language.

Let's fix that now. Figure 9.7 rounds out the threesome, with the first level setup screen for the Tektronix Phaser 340.

PostScript drivers come in several strikingly different formats, but they all have essentially the same set of choices. This one, which is based on the Microsoft Windows driver, is the least visually attractive, but it's a place to start. We'll look at another one later.

Get to Know Your Printer Driver **299**

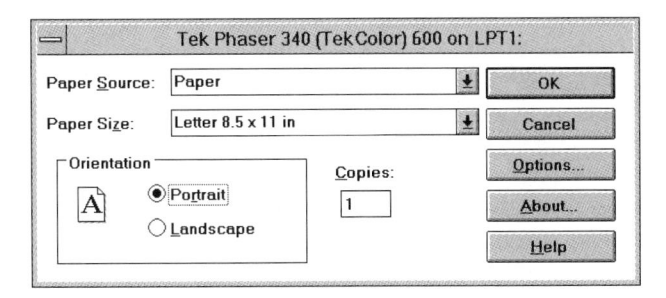

Figure 9.7 The first setup screen for a typical PostScript driver deals with just the basics.

As you can see in the figure, this first dialog box covers the basics. It lets you set the paper source, paper size, orientation, and number of copies to print. To get to some more choices, you can choose the Options button to open the dialog box shown in Figure 9.8.

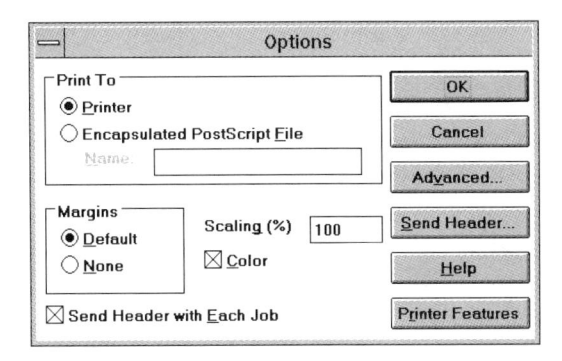

Figure 9.8 You should rarely need to change these standard PostScript options.

The Options dialog box includes settings that you'll rarely need to change, starting with the choices in the Print To box, which let you choose between printing directly to a printer or to a file.

> **Printing to a file can be a useful trick.** How so, you ask? Suppose you've created a file on one computer that doesn't have a printer attached, and you want to print it from another computer that doesn't have the program you created the file in. You could spend a lot of time moving printers and cables around, or installing the program on the second computer. Or you can print the file to disk, move the print file (for lack of a better term) to the second

computer, and use a copy command to copy the file to the printer. The DOS command, for example, would be:

`COPY MYFILE LPT1:`

or

`COPY MYFILE PRN`

Neat trick, huh?

The Margins box under the Print To box lets you tell the driver what margins to report to your software. Most of the time, you'll want this set to Default so your software knows how much of the page is off limits. If you're set at Default and try setting too small a margin in Microsoft Word, for example, Word will warn you that you're trying to print in the nonprintable area. If you're set at None, Word will let you set the margins to zero. Then anything you want to print in the nonprintable area will get lopped off.

Set the feature and take your chances.
The Scaling option does just what it says. Sometimes. When it works, it scales the image size up or down by some percentage. However, it doesn't work with all programs. If you're using a program that depends entirely on the driver for printing, the feature works. If you're using a program that largely ignores the driver, except for basic communications with the printer, the scaling won't work. Or worse. With CorelDRAW, for example, changing the scaling doesn't change the size of the image at all. Instead, it moves the image to a different part of the page.

Unfortunately, the programs that are most likely to ignore the driver are graphics and desktop publishing programs, precisely the software you're most likely to be interested in for serious color output.

Speaking of color output, the Color check box is another feature that works or doesn't work depending on the software you're using. When it works, an X in the check box tells the driver to print in color. If you remove the X, the driver prints in shades of gray. When it doesn't work, the setting has no noticeable effect on anything.

Next down is the option to Send Header with Each Job. This one needs a little explanation. Briefly, PostScript printers need some information sent to them at least once when they wake up. The information is in something called a header.

If you prefer, you can wipe the X out of this check box. If you choose the Send Header button on the right side of the dialog box, you can send the header once manually or create a file that you can send to the printer whenever you like. That will save a little time at the beginning of each print job, but then you have to remember to send the header each time you wake up the printer.

The safest way to make sure the printer has the header information when it needs it is to send it at the beginning of each print job. And that's why you'll usually want an X in this check box.

All of which brings us to the stack of buttons on the right side of the dialog box. These include the Send Header button (which I won't bother with), the usual OK, Cancel, and Help, plus two buttons of interest: Advanced and Printer Features. Let's start with Advanced. Choose it, and the driver will open the dialog box shown in Figure 9.9.

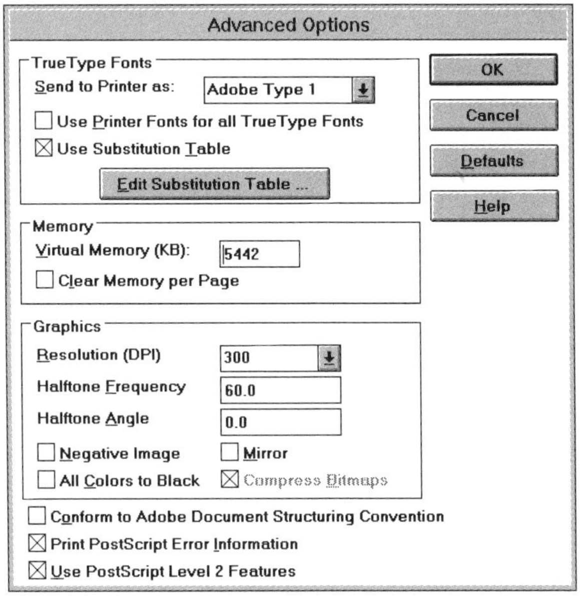

Figure 9.9 You'll find these Advanced options in virtually any PostScript driver.

I'm going to ignore the TrueType Fonts box at the top of the dialog box and the Clear Memory per Page option in the Memory box. To explain them, I'd have to go into all sorts of details about fonts, which belong in a book on desktop publishing, not a book on color printing.

The virtual memory size in the Memory box is one of the few things you can usually count on the printer manufacturer to set correctly. (You won't see this option on the Mac, because the driver gets its information directly from the printer.) If you want to check it out, however, you may be able to. If you have Windows or Windows 95, you'll find a file in your /WINDOWS/SYSTEM directory called TESTPS.TXT. If you copy it to your printer, it will usually print a few lines, including one that reads:

```
Max Printer VM (KB):
```

with a number after it, and one that reads:

```
Max Suggested VM (KB):
```

with a number after it. You can then plug the maximum suggested VM (KB)—or virtual memory in kilobytes—into the Virtual Memory (KB) text box in the dialog box.

Don't be surprised if the TESTPS.TXT file doesn't print on your printer. I tried it on two PostScript printers and found it printed just fine on one, but didn't print anything on the other. And these were both Adobe PostScript printers. If the file doesn't print, stay with the virtual memory setting the printer manufacturer supplied in the driver or call the manufacturer and ask what setting to use.

Next down is the Graphics box, with the options we're most interested in.

The Resolution, Halftone Frequency, and Halftone Angle choices should be old friends by now. But here's a warning: You'll find these choices available even for printers that ignore them. You'll even find them in the PostScript drivers for thermal dye printers, and thermal dye printers don't dither. (At least, not normally.) Which means they don't have halftones. Which means they don't have halftone frequencies or halftone angles. So don't take these settings too seriously. As I've said elsewhere in this book, you'll have to check with the printer manufacturer to find out what the printer is actually doing.

The four check boxes at the bottom of the Graphics box are less straightforward than you might suppose. The Negative Image and Mirror check boxes—like the Scaling and Color features in the Options dialog box—may or may not work, depending on your software.

Here again, with programs that take full advantage of the driver, these features work as promised, giving you a negative or mirror image or both as appropriate when there's an X in the check boxes. But with programs that largely ignore the driver, the features don't work.

With CorelDRAW, for example, the program simply ignores the Mirror check box and rides roughshod over the driver setting. But if you put the X in the Negative Image check box, you'll wind up with a printer error. With Word, everything works as advertised. The printer will even give you the negatives of colors, so that yellow turns to blue in the negative, red turns to cyan, and violet turns to green.

The All Colors to Black option is supposed to turn a color image into black and white at the printer. I've yet to see it work with any program or any printer.

The Compress Bitmaps option lets you speed printing by sending bitmapped images to the printer in compressed format. If you have an X in the Use PostScript Level 2 Features check box at the bottom of the dialog box, you won't be able to turn the Compress Bitmaps feature off. If you don't have the PostScript Level 2 features turned on, you'll be able to turn the Compress Bitmaps feature on or off. In general, if you're printing on a PostScript Level 2 printer, you'll want to turn on the Level 2 features. Otherwise, you'll want both features off.

Just under the Graphics box is the Conform to Adobe Document Structuring Convention check box. Unless someone—at a print shop, for example—asks you to give him or her a file in this format, you'll want to leave this blank. If you need to use this feature, be very clear that this is a different kind of file than the one you can create by choosing Print To Encapsulated PostScript File in the Options dialog box. To create a file with the Document Structuring Convention, a.k.a. DSC, format, you need to set this option, then print to a file from your application program, which usually means using a Print to File command in the program.

Finally in this dialog box is the Print PostScript Error Information check box. If you have an X in this box, your printer should print an error message when there's a PostScript problem. If you find these error messages useful, make sure there's an X in the box; otherwise, get rid of it. (More rocket science.)

If you close the Advanced Options dialog box and back up to the Options dialog box, you'll find one other button of interest, labeled Printer Features. Choose this button, and you'll get the one dialog box in the PostScript driver that's custom designed for the specific printer the driver came with. Figure 9.10 shows the version for the Tektronix Phaser 340.

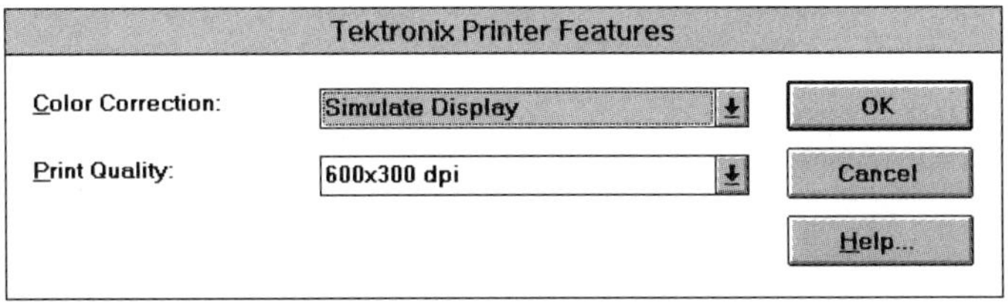

Figure 9.10 The features dialog box doesn't always have a lot of features in it.

As you can see, there are only two categories of features for this particular printer: Color Correction and Print Quality. You already know all about color correction. I'll just mention that this is where you're most likely to find a grayscale option that's guaranteed to work. The Print Quality option in this case lets you choose between 300 by 300 dpi and 600 by 300 dpi—something that you can't do with the Resolution choice elsewhere in the driver.

And that's all there is to a typical PostScript driver. I hope you've noticed that for all the issues that relate to graphics and color—from halftone screens to color correction—the options in all three drivers we've looked at are essentially the same.

More PostScript

> Why do I do this every Sunday? Even book reviews seem to be the same as last week's. Different books—same reviews.
>
> John Osborne
> Jimmy, *Look Back in Anger*, act 1

I mentioned earlier that there are several versions of PostScript driver that look different from each other, but still offer essentially the same features. Figure 9.11 should prove the point.

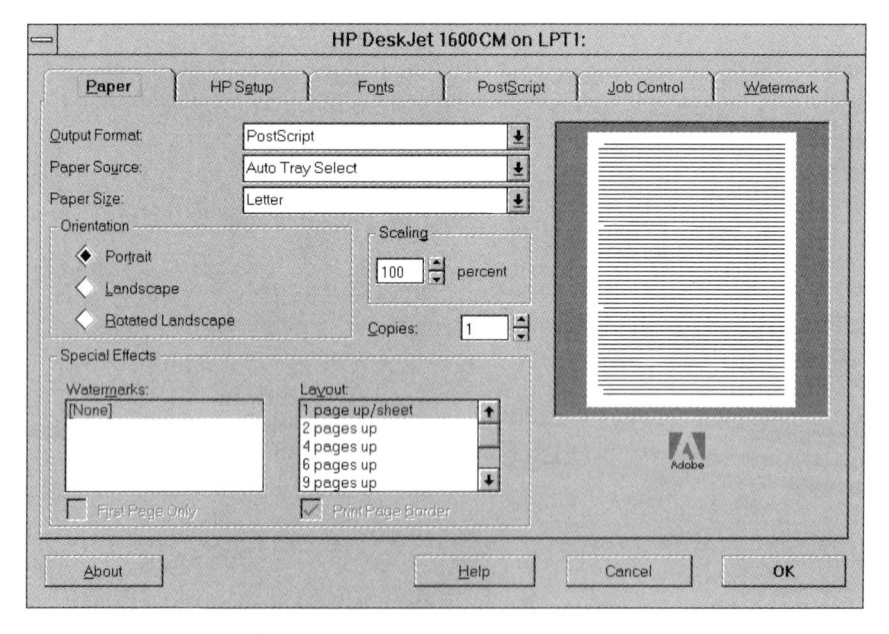

Figure 9.11 Some PostScript drivers look like this.

The tabbed-card format for this driver, which happens to be for the HP DeskJet 1600CM, is a lot prettier to look at than the version we've just been through, but if you compare the choices on the Paper tabbed card showing in the figure, you'll find that they pretty well match the choices on the first level setup dialog box and the Options dialog box we've just looked at.

There are also a few additional features in this driver, including a watermark feature that lets you print a page with, say, DRAFT or CONFIDENTIAL across it.

But you won't find any new features relating to graphics or color, which are the ones we're interested in.

The HP Setup card, shown in Figure 9.12 is equivalent to the Printer Features dialog box in the driver we just looked at. As you can see, there's nothing new here either. These are the same options you already saw in the PCL driver for the DeskJet 660C.

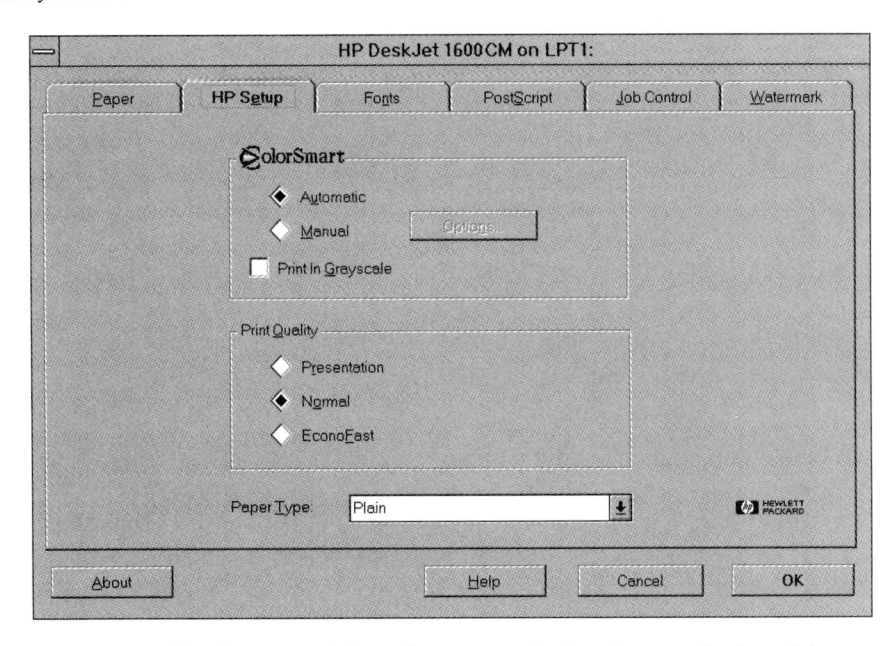

Figure 9.12 The Setup card gives the custom choices for a particular printer.

As I said way back at the beginning, once you follow through the examples in this chapter, you should be able to look at virtually any color printer driver and understand the vast majority of the choices. If you don't believe me, go find a driver at random and see if I'm right.

WINDOWS 95

> He that will not apply new remedies must expect new evils.
> Francis Bacon

Still here? That's good, because there's one other thing you might like to know about: Windows 95.

The key to understanding Windows 95 drivers is that they're no different in any important respect from the Windows drivers we just looked at. They look different, but the range of choices is essentially the same.

Well, there is one difference. Some Windows 95 drivers include color-matching features. In those cases, you'll find a Color Control box on the Graphics tabbed card, with choices for No Image Color Matching and Use Image Color Matching. If you choose to use it, you can open another dialog box and tell the driver which color-matching method to use. (And you already know all about color matching from Chapter 3.)

All of which is good and well, but even if the driver offers color matching, you need a program that supports it. According to Adobe, applications that generate their own PostScript code, which include most high-end graphics programs, can override the driver settings for color control, and many do. So before you take the driver settings too seriously, find out whether the program you're using takes them seriously also.

AND FINALLY...

> People must not do things for fun. We are not here for fun. There is no reference to fun in any act of Parliament.
>
> A. P. Herbert.
> Lord Light, in *Uncommon Law*, "Is it a Free Country?" (1935)

All of which brings us to the end of this look at color printers. By now, you should have a good grounding in what you need to know when you print in color. But there are lots of subtleties you can learn only by doing, and the subtleties change from one printer to the next, which means you've got to teach yourself.

So my final advice is: Don't take your printing too seriously. When things don't print the way you expect them to, step back, take a deep breath, and try again. Experiment. Do something different. Enjoy the colors along the way. And, most of all, have fun. Really.

Glossary

Absorption spectrum—A measure of how much light of each wavelength a given object absorbs. The absorption spectrum of any given object helps determine its color. A white piece of paper, for example, absorbs very little light of any wavelength, which means it reflects all wavelengths, which is why we see the paper as white. Put some red ink on the page, and the ink will absorb green and blue light, reflecting red wavelengths only, which is why we see the ink as red.

Achromatic color scheme—A color scheme that consists solely of gray or just black and white. This color scheme is often called monochrome since it's what you would expect from a monochrome printer. However, a monochromatic color scheme, which you'll find defined later in this glossary, is actually something quite different.

Additive primary colors—Red, green, and blue—the three colors of light that you can mix together in varying intensities to come up with any other color. These are called additive primaries because you literally add the colors together when you mix them. With the subtractive primary colors that printers use, you mix the pigments together so they can absorb—or subtract—colors from reflected light.

Addressability—The number of addressable points on a monitor screen or printed page. For a monitor screen, the addressability is completely determined by the resolution. At VGA's 640 by 480 resolution, the number of addressable dots is 640 times 480, or 307,200 dots. For a printer, the number of addressable points depends on both the resolution and the maximum printing area. A 300 dot per inch resolution in a printer with an 8.25 inch by 11.25 inch printing area works out to about 8 million addressable dots (300 times 8.25 times 300 times 11.25).

Aliasing—Also called the jaggies. A staircase effect that shows up on edges of lines and objects. If a line or edge is supposed to be smooth but isn't, it's suffering from aliasing.

A-size printer—Any printer whose maximum paper is A size or a little larger. A-size paper is 8½ by 11, the U.S. standard for letter size. Most A-size printers can also print on 8½ by 14 inch legal-size paper. A few, which are also known as super A-size printers, can print on paper that's larger than letter size in both dimensions.

Banding—Any unwanted effect of bands that shouldn't be there. Ink jet printers often leave bands on printed output, because the printhead prints in bands, spraying ink across the page one band at a time. The lines between bands often indicate the path of a clogged ink nozzle.

Another common kind of banding shows up when colors or shades of gray that should gradually shade into each other break up instead into distinct bands, with abrupt changes in color or shade. This is one case where a picture is certainly better than words. The background in the figure labeled Banding is a gradient fill that's supposed to change gradually. The bands are pretty obvious.

Banding The background in this graphic is a gradient fill that should change gradually, instead of changing in distinct bands.

Bidirectional printing   Printing both left to right and right to left with a printhead that moves horizontally across the page. Printers with printheads that move across the page can either print a band each time the printhead goes across the page in either direction, or they can print only when the printhead is moving in one direction, left to right. Printing in both directions, or bidirectional printing, is faster, but is more likely to leave visible traces of the printhead's path, in the form of bands.

Bilevel printer—Any printer that doesn't vary the intensity of its dots. Most printers are bilevel, with no intermediate steps between full color and no color. Any particular spot on the page either gets a full intensity dot, or none at all. The only way bilevel printers can print any colors beyond the basic eight (three primary plus three secondary colors plus black and white) is by dithering. To print continuous tones, you need a multilevel printer, which is covered elsewhere in this glossary.

Bitmap (or Bit map) image—Also called raster graphics; an image that's literally defined bit by bit, mapping each bit to a position on a grid, like a mosaic built from small tiles. (In this context, a bit is the same thing as a pixel, which is covered elsewhere in this glossary.) A scanned photograph, for example, is a bitmapped image. So are the graphics you can draw in paint programs like Paintbrush, which will let you zoom in on an image so you can see and work with individual bits. When you edit bitmapped images, you're literally replacing individual bits with other bits, either retail, one bit at a time, or wholesale, by painting over an entire area with a painting tool. All this is very different from working with object-based graphics, which define images with mathematical descriptions of lines, curves, and fills. You'll find object-based graphics discussed elsewhere in this glossary.

Bleeding—The tendency of ink from an ink jet printer to spread a bit, as it's absorbed by the paper fibers before it dries. Some people draw a distinction between bleeding, blooming, and wicking. Others use the three terms interchangeably. For those who draw a distinction, bleeding applies only to two colors spreading into each other. Blooming describes the tendency of individual dots to spread to a larger size. Wicking describes the tendency of the ink to follow individual fibers in the paper as it spreads.

Whether you draw a distinction between these terms or not, when ink spreads into the paper, edges on text and lines lose sharpness. There's some advantage to this too. The tendency to spread hides dithering patterns in graphics, including the dithering patterns in dithered colors. For purposes of this book, bleeding refers to any spreading of the ink into the paper.

Blooming—Depending on who you talk to, either another name for bleeding—the tendency of ink from an ink jet printer to spread a bit before it dries—or the specific tendency of individual dots to spread out into larger dots as the paper absorbs them. People who use the second definition generally consider blooming to be distinct from bleeding, and reserve bleeding to describe two different color inks spreading into each other.

Brightness—A measure of how light or dark a color is in the HSB, or hue-saturation-brightness, color model. Zero brightness, for any hue or saturation, is black.

B-size printer—Any printer whose maximum paper is B size or a little larger. B-size paper is 11 by 17 inches, the U.S. standard for tabloid size. Some B-size printers, which are also known as super B-size printers, can print on paper that's larger than standard tabloid size in both dimensions.

Chroma—A measure of how much hue there is in a given color, or how colorful it is. Chroma, which is the measurement of colorfulness in the Munsell color system, is similar to saturation in the HSB (hue-saturation-brightness) color model. The difference is that chroma tells you how colorful a color is in relation to white. Saturation tells you how colorful a color is relative to its brightness. If you shine a light on the side of solid color ball, the saturation will be pretty much the same across the face of the ball, because you make allowances for changes in brightness. However, the chroma will be lower on the dark side of the ball, because there's less color if you compare it to white.

Chromaticity—A somewhat arcane concept that combines hue and saturation. Since you can define any color by hue, saturation, and brightness, you can define any color by chromaticity and brightness.

CIE standards—A collection of standard approaches to describing colors, as defined by the Commission Internationale de L'Éclairage, an international standards body. The name translates to International Commission on Lighting, or International Commission on Illumination, but it's usually abbreviated to CIE. Unlike the RGB or CMYK systems for describing color, the CIE standards aren't pegged to a particular monitor or printer. That makes them a good starting point for trying to match colors from, say, one printer to another. PostScript Level 2 incorporates the CIE standards.

CMY—Short for cyan-magenta-yellow, the three primary colors that printers use to create all the colors they can print. Printers and other equipment that use cyan, magenta, and yellow are CMY devices. CMY devices naturally follow a CMY color model, which defines colors by the amount of cyan, magenta, and yellow in each color.

CMYK—Short for cyan-magenta-yellow-black. In theory, cyan, magenta, and yellow should let you create all the colors the human eye can see, including a dark black. Real cyan, magenta, and yellow pigments, however, fall short of the ideal, and the black you get from mixing the three colors is more often a dark brown or blue. Most printers and other CMY devices make up for this shortcoming by adding black as a separate color, which turns them into CMYK devices.

Coated paper—A paper for ink jet and thermal wax transfer printers that's coated on one side. Most so-called coated paper is similar in look and feel to plain copy paper, but coated paper for thermal wax transfer printers holds wax better than plain paper can, and coated paper for ink jet printers doesn't absorb ink as much as plain paper, so the colors are more vibrant. Not all papers with coatings on them are called coated paper. Glossy paper, for example, has a glossy coating on one side of the paper, but it's called glossy paper, not coated paper.

Color depth—Also called color resolution. The number of colors a printer or video display offers. The term is analogous to talking about the depth on the bench for a sports team. The more good players you have sitting on the bench, the more depth you've got. And more colors for a printer or display means more color depth. The most common color depths are 8 bit (256 colors), 16 bit (65,536 colors), and 24 bit (roughly 16.8 million colors).

Color gamut—The complete range of colors for a given device; for a printer, all the colors the printer can print; for a monitor, all the colors the monitor can show. Each printer and each monitor has its own color gamut.

Color-matching system—Any of several systems for specifying colors from a book of color swatches. Any color-matching system essentially guarantees that the color you pick is the color you'll see in the output from a printing press. Some computer printers can simulate a color-matching system, but only some colors will match the color swatches. The rest will be approximations.

Color model—Any method for describing or specifying colors. The red-green-blue, or RGB, color model, for example, lets you specify colors as a specific amount or percentage of red, green, and blue. Similarly, the cyan-magenta-yellow, or CMY, color model lets you specify colors as a specific amount or percentage of cyan, magenta, and yellow. The hue-saturation-brightness, or HSB, color model lets you specify colors by hue, saturation, and brightness. Other color models include the CIE color model, developed by the Commission Internationale de L'Éclairage, and several variations on the CIE model. The CIE color model has the advantage of being an international standard.

Color resolution—Also called color depth; the number of colors a printer or video display offers. All other things (like resolution, for instance) being equal, most people will see a continuous tone image (read: photograph) as having a higher resolution if it has more colors to draw on in creating it. This tendency to see more colors as adding resolution naturally leads to talking about the number of colors available in a printer, say, as the color resolution for that printer.

Color space—A mathematical representation of a color model. In the RGB color model, for example, a specific amount of red, green, and blue specifies both a particular color and a point in the RGB color space.

Color wheel—A wheel-shaped arrangement of colors that's meant to help choose colors that work well together. There are twelve basic colors in the color wheel (plus lighter and darker versions of the same hues). These include three primary colors, three secondary colors, and six tertiary colors. Artists have a set of rules about how to combine colors from each group to create pleasing color schemes.

Colorant—In a printer, the material that carries the color. Colorants include the dye in a thermal dye printer, the wax in a thermal wax printer, the ink in an ink jet printer, and so on. An informal equivalent is to refer to all colorants as ink.

Complementary colors—Colors that lie directly opposite each other on an artist's color wheel. If you stare at a color for at least 30 seconds, and then turn your gaze to a neutral background, the color you'll see as the afterimage is the complement to the original color. With light, complementary colors add up to white, the same way that red, green, and blue add up to white.

Composite black—As distinct from true black, a black in a CMY or CMYK printer that's made by mixing cyan, magenta, and yellow. With most printers, composite black is distinctly off-black, usually with a brown or blue tinge.

Continuous tone image—Depending on context, either an image where colors (or shades of gray) actually vary continuously, as in a photograph, or should vary continuously. You can take a photograph that's been scanned as a continuous tone image, for example, and print it with a printer that can't print continuous tones. The printed result won't have continuous tones, but it will be an example of how the printer handles continuous tone images.

Continuous tone printing—A printing technique that varies color continuously, at least to the limit of what the human eye can see. To get continuous tones, a printer has to be able to mix colors together at the same spot and vary the intensity of color in small steps by varying the amount of color in each dot. Thermal dye printers, for example, overlay transparent dyes on top of each other and vary the intensity of each color. (More precisely, they vary the amount of heat to control the amount of dye in each dot of color.) True continuous tone printers offer all the colors the human eye can see without any dithering. Some printers claim continuous tone when what the manufacturer really means is that the printer can vary the intensity of color somewhat to reduce the amount of dithering, but not enough to eliminate the need for dithering altogether.

Cool colors—Blue, blue-green, and violet. Cool colors, as opposed to warm colors, are colors that tend not to catch the eye, and, therefore, make good background colors in graphics. Green and magenta can also be cool colors, but that depends on the colors around them. If you surround them with blue, blue-green, or violet, the eye will interpret them as warm colors. If you use them with yellow, orange, red, or brown, the eye will interpret them as cool colors.

CRT—Either a cathode ray tube or a monitor. Technically, a CRT is the actual display in virtually all desktop monitors and television sets—the picture tube. However, lots of people, and marketing departments, use CRT as a synonym for CRT-based monitor, although I've yet to hear anyone say cathode ray tube when they mean a monitor.

Cylindrical section display—A display shaped like a section cut out of a large cylinder. Most cylindrical section displays use the Sony Trinitron cathode ray tube. These displays curve in the horizontal direction but not in the vertical direction. That means they don't distort the image as much as the spherical section displays that have been the standard display shape until recently, but they distort the image more than a flat display or flat square display. You'll find flat, flat square, and spherical section displays all covered elsewhere in this glossary.

Deep Color—Also called high color. Technically, at least 16-bit color (65,536 colors) but less than 24-bit color (roughly 16.8 million colors). More meaningfully, enough colors so at least some photos will show with true photographic quality, but not enough to guarantee that every photo or graphic with continuous tones will show without noticeable banding (literally bands of different colors where there should be a gradual change in color) or posterization (a similar effect that shows sudden shifts in colors that should change gradually). posterization and banding are both covered elsewhere in this glossary, complete with samples of each effect.

Diffusion dither—One of two kinds of frequency-modulated screening techniques. The other is stochastic screening. FM screens differ from traditional halftone screens by keeping the same size halftone spot and simply using more of them in dark areas than light areas. Traditional halftone screens keep the number of halftone cells constant and vary the size of the spots.

Dithering—A printing technique that varies color (or shades of gray) by defining a matrix of dots and controlling the number of dots of each color within the matrix, or cell. Dithering effectively reduces resolution for a printer, with each cell acting as a single pixel. With a six by six matrix, for example, a 300-dpi printer is reduced to an effective 50 dpi, which explains why you can see individual dots in a photo printed on most 300-dpi printers.

Dithering pattern—A pattern of dots that often shows in dithered colors or shades of gray. Dithering patterns show up because most dithering techniques repeat the same pattern of dots over and over, like a repetitive pattern on a tiled floor. The figure labeled Dithering shows dithering patterns.

Dithering The dithering patterns are different for each shade of gray.

Dot Pitch—The distance, on a CRT monitor screen, between the center of one phosphor dot and the center of another dot of the same color, two rows below. Dot pitch is not the same as dot size, but the two are related, so that a smaller dot pitch goes hand in hand with a smaller dot size.

Drawing program—A graphics program that's object oriented. A graphic can be a bitmap or an object. If it's a bitmap (which is covered elsewhere in this glossary), the graphics program stores it as a pattern of bits, or picture elements. If it's an object (which is also covered here), the program stores it as a mathematical formula that it converts to bits only when it draws the image on the screen or at the printer.

Object-oriented graphics tools are usually called drawing tools, like the drawing features in Word, for example. Object-oriented programs, or drawing programs, often have the word *draw* in their names, as in CorelDRAW. Graphics programs that let you draw . . . uh . . . make that *create and edit* bitmaps, are called paint programs, and often have the word *paint* in their names, as in Paintbrush.

Dual-component toner—Toner that requires a separate developer, the other choice being mono-component toner, which doesn't need a developer. For more information on both, take a look at the entry for mono-component toner elsewhere in this glossary.

Dual mode or dual technology printer—A printer with both thermal dye transfer and thermal wax transfer modes. Dual mode printers generally compromise quality slightly in one mode, but they let you save money in thermal wax transfer mode when printing draft output or graphics.

Dye sublimation printer—A common mispronunciation for thermal dye transfer printer. So called dye-sublimation printers use dye, but they don't sublime, so they ain't dye sublimation printers. But lots of people call them that, or call them dye subs for short, so don't let that bother you.

Electrophotographic printer—A laser or laser-like printer. Laser, LED, and LCD printers all use a technique called electrophotography to put images on paper. In each case, the printer uses light to draw the image of a page on a drum as an electrostatic charge. The drum then picks up toner and transfers it to the paper. These printers differ mainly in the source of the light—a laser, LED, or LCD. Also in this category is the ion-deposition printer, which uses an ion beam instead of light to draw the image on the drum, also as an electrostatic charge.

Error diffusion—An approach to halftoning that doesn't use halftone cells for producing gray scale and color images. Error diffusion also goes by several other names, including frequency-modulated screen, which you'll find elsewhere in this glossary.

Flatbed scanner—A type of scanner that's similar to the scanner on a typical office copier. The scanner offers a flat glass surface for whatever you're scanning. The scanning mechanism moves under the glass, scanning as it goes. The other choices are page feed scanners and handheld scanners, both of which are covered elsewhere in this glossary.

Flat display—A display that's literally flat, rather than a section of a sphere or cylinder. Because most displays are curved, flat displays appear slightly concave to most people at first, but they're easy to get used to. Their key advantage over other kinds of displays is that because they are flat, they don't distort the image. You'll also find flat square, cylindrical section, and spherical section displays covered elsewhere in this glossary.

Flat square display—A display that's relatively flat, compared to a standard spherical section. In truth, a flat square display is neither flat nor square. Like most displays, it's wider than it is high. And like the older spherical display format, it's a section of a sphere. However the sphere that a flat square display is based on is much larger than the sphere that a spherical section display is based on. As a result, the display looks flat, and you don't get the distorting effect of looking at a picture drawn on a large beach ball. Other choices for display shapes are flat and cylindrical section. Both of these, as well as spherical section displays, are covered elsewhere in this glossary.

Four-color ribbon—A ribbon with cyan, magenta, yellow, and black panels. For most printers, you need black as a fourth color to ensure that blacks won't come out with a brown or blue tinge. However, four-color ribbons are more expensive per image than three-color ribbons, because the extra panel means that for any given length of ribbon, you get fewer images.

Four pass three-color ribbon—A ribbon with cyan, magenta, and yellow panels, along with a fourth panel for laying down a coating that lets it print on plain paper. These ribbons are also called plain paper ribbons. There was a time when four-pass ribbon meant the same as four-color ribbon, but now that you can get four-pass, three-color ribbons, the phrase *four-pass ribbon* is ambiguous.

Frame grabber—A video capture board that captures individual video frames only. Video signals rewrite the screen some number of times each second—30 times per second for full motion, broadcast quality video. Each full screen is a frame, much like the frames in motion pictures. Video capture boards can capture a video signal and convert it to digital pictures. Some video capture boards can capture single frames or full motion video with equal ease. Others can grab single frames only. The ones that grab single frames are frame grabbers.

Frequency-modulated screen (also FM screen, FM halftones, FM dithering)—Also called error diffusion. A kind of halftone screen that doesn't use halftone cells for producing gray scale and color images. In frequency-modulated screens, the halftone spots are all the same size, but the frequency of those spots changes, so there are more of them in dark areas than light areas. This is in sharp contrast to traditional halftone screens, which use a fixed number of halftone spots but vary the size of the spot. Diffusion dither and stochastic screening are two specific kinds of FM screen.

Full bleed image—Any image that's large enough to completely cover a specified size of paper so the image effectively bleeds off the edge of the page. A-size paper, for example, is 8½ by 11 inches, so a full bleed A-size image, is 8½ by 11 inches or a little larger. To print a full bleed A-size image, you need paper that's larger than A-size.

GCR—Acronym for gray component replacement, which is covered elsewhere in this glossary.

GDI printer—A printer that uses the Windows graphical device interface, GDI, as its printer language. The graphical device interface is the set of commands that Windows uses to put images on the screen. GDI printer drivers don't translate images from GDI to some printer language; they simply use the same commands for the printer that Windows is already using for the screen.

GDI printers can't print directly from DOS programs and can't even print from a DOS window without special drivers. Usually, however, GDI printers are also available in other versions for other operating systems, so you can, for example, get the printer for Windows or for the Mac.

Glossy paper—A type of paper, for ink jet printers only, with a glossy coating on one side. Ink jet printers generally produce their best looking output on glossy paper, printing on the glossy side. Not so incidentally, glossy paper is not considered coated paper, even though it has a glossy coating. Coated paper generally has much the same look and feel as plain paper.

Gray component replacement (GCR)—A technique for replacing a combination of cyan, magenta, and yellow in printed colors with an equivalent amount of gray. In the CMYK color model, equal values of cyan, magenta, and yellow create gray or black. So any color that consists of a combination of all three primary colors consists of a gray component, plus additional parts of one or two of the primaries. Gray component replacement replaces some or all of that composite gray component with black ink.

Halftone screen—In traditional halftoning, an opaque screen, using glass or film, with thin etched lines to let light through; in computer-based halftoning, the electronic equivalent. To create a halftone in traditional halftoning, you place a screen between a continuous tone transparency (similar to a slide) and film. You then shine a light so it goes through the transparency, then the screen, and falls on the film. Because of diffraction, the light going through the thin lines on the screen forms black spots at the film, transforming the original continuous tone image into a halftone.

In computer-based halftoning, you set the screen frequency in lines per inch, which determines how many dots at the printer go into each halftone cell. Instead of letting diffraction determine how large the black spot is in each halftone cell, the computer or printer calculates the gray level for the cell and uses the gray level to determine how many black dots to print in that cell.

Halftone screen frequency (or halftone frequency)—The number of halftone cells in one dimension of a halftone screen. Halftone screen frequency is often called halftone frequency or screen frequency. This is usually given in lines per inch, but you can also think of it as the number of halftone spots per inch. You can also think of it as halftone resolution, since it's actually the effective resolution you get after halftoning.

Halftoning—A way of fooling the eye and brain into seeing shades of gray from a mixture of black and white dots (or shades of any given color from a mixture of dots in that color and white). For computer printers, halftoning depends on dividing a picture into halftone cells and defining a level of gray for each cell by the mix of black and white dots in that cell. If a cell is, say, four by four dots, it can have anywhere from 0 to 16 black dots, for 17 levels of gray. For color printing, the same technique works for each primary color—so that a four-by-four cell gives 17 levels of cyan, 17 levels of magenta, and 17 levels of yellow, all of which can combine to give 17 times 17 times 17, or 4913 different colors.

Handheld scanner—Any scanner that's meant to be held while scanning. Handheld scanners can range from about the size of a mouse to the size of a three-hole punch. The one thing they all have in common is the mechanism they use to scan across the page. That mechanism is your hand. The other choices are flatbed and page feed scanners, both of which are covered elsewhere in this glossary.

High color—Alternate pronunciation for deep color, which is at least 16-bit color (65,536 colors) but less than 24-bit color (roughly 16.8 million colors). For more details, take a look at the entry for deep color elsewhere in this glossary.

HSB—Short for hue, saturation, brightness. The HSB color model is one of the more common choices in various programs for modifying colors. Hue comes closest to describing the raw color in a given color—red, green, blue, orange, and so on. Saturation measures how much of the color is there. Pink is a red hue with low saturation. Zero saturation with any hue is white, black, or gray. Brightness measures how light or dark the color is. Zero brightness with any hue or saturation is black.

HVC—Short for hue, value, chroma. The Munsell color system uses these three components for describing color. Hue means the same as in the HSB system, coming closest to describing the color that's in the color. Value means the same as brightness in the HSB system, measuring how light or dark the color is. Chroma is similar to saturation in the HSB system, measuring how much of the color there is.

Hue—Describes the color in a given color. Pink and red both have the same hue. Similarly, blue and light blue both have the same hue. The concept of hue is part of several color models, including the HSB, or hue-saturation-brightness, color model.

Ink jet printer—A printer that creates images by spraying liquid ink on a page. Technically, an ink jet printer can use either standard ink, which dries by evaporating after it hits the page, or it can use melted wax, which dries by cooling after it hits the page. However, most people (including me) limit this category to printers that use ink rather than wax.

Interlaced resolution—A monitor resolution that the monitor reaches by drawing each image in two passes—drawing every other line on the first pass and filling in the blank lines on the second pass. Interlacing lets monitors reach higher resolutions than they can manage without interlacing, but at the cost of a distinct flickering of thin horizontal lines, as the screen first draws one set of lines on the screen and then the next.

Ion-deposition printer—A printer that works similarly to a laser printer but uses an ion beam instead of a laser to draw the image of a page on a drum. Ion-deposition printers don't have the same crisp, clean edges for lines and text that you would expect from a laser printer, but they offer speeds up to about 90 pages per minute.

Jaggies—The informal (and far more descriptive) name for aliasing. By either name, the jaggies are ragged edges on lines and objects that are supposed to be smooth.

Laser printer—A printer that uses a laser to draw the image of a page as an electrostatic charge on a drum. The drum uses the electrostatic charge to pick up toner, and then transfers the toner to paper. The printer then fuses the toner to the paper with heat. Laser printers are known for their relatively high resolution and crisp, clean edges. Color laser printers are somewhat cumbersome to maintain, because they need four toner cartridges.

LCD printer—A printer that uses an LCD to draw the image of a page on a drum as the first step in printing. Except for the light source, LCD printers are essentially identical to laser printers.

LED printer—A printer that uses LEDs to draw the image of a page on a drum as the first step in printing. Except for the light source, LED printers are essentially identical to laser printers.

Letter-size printer—Alternate pronunciation for A-size printer, which is covered elsewhere in this glossary.

Metamerism—The phenomenon that two colors can look identical to each other under some lighting conditions but not under others. Any two colors that meet this criterion are called metamers or a metameric pair. The standard example of metamerism is the jacket and pants that match under the fluorescent lighting in a store but don't match in daylight.

Moiré pattern—An optical illusion in the form of an interference pattern. Moiré patterns can show up when you overlay one set of thinly spaced lines or rows of dots over another. This can be a problem for printing halftone images, which consist, after all, of rows of dots. If you scan a halftone image from, say, a magazine, the halftone grid in the scanner can interfere with the halftones to give you a moiré pattern. Similarly, if you let your software add a halftone screen, and then print with the printer driver adding a halftone screen, there's a good chance that the two screens will give you a moiré pattern.

Monochromatic color—Alternate pronunciation for pure color, which is covered in more detail elsewhere in this glossary. By either name, a pure color consists of a single wavelength of light, or a small range of wavelengths.

Monochromatic color scheme—A color scheme that uses a single hue, but varies saturation and brightness; A monochromatic color scheme has nothing to do with monochromatic color. A combination of dark red, red, light red, and pink would be a good example of a monochromatic color scheme. So would dark blue, blue, and light blue. Don't confuse a monochromatic color scheme with using black and white or shades of gray. If you're using grays only, the saturation is zero, the hue is irrelevant, and the color scheme is achromatic.

Mono-component toner—Also called single-component toner. Toner that doesn't require a separate developer. The other choice is dual-component toner, which separates out the colored toner particles from the developer particles that help deliver the toner to the page. Laser printers that use mono-component toners are a little easier to set up and maintain than those that don't, since they don't need a developer as a separate consumable. More important is that most printers with mono-component toners generally have better formed text characters and graphics, with crisper, cleaner edges than you'll find in printers with dual-component toners. They also print solid areas more evenly.

Multilevel printer—Any printer that can vary the intensity of its dots. Multilevel printers have some number of steps, or levels, between full on and full off for each dot. True continuous tone printers, which offer 16.7 million colors without dithering, are multilevel printers with 256 levels for each primary color. Any given dot can be some combination of cyan, magenta, and yellow, with each color at any of 256 levels. Some printers offer multilevel printing that's way short of 256 levels for each color. But any increase in the number of levels lets a printer print more colors with a given size halftone cell or use a smaller halftone cell for a given number of colors. Printers that aren't multilevel are called bilevel.

Munsell color system—A color model created by Albert Munsell. The Munsell color system describes colors in terms of hue, value, and chroma. Hue means the same as hue in the HSB (hue, saturation, brightness) model and is the closest to describing the pure color. Value means the same as brightness in the HSB model and describes the lightness or darkness of the color. Chroma is similar in concept to saturation in the HSB model, as a measure of how much hue is in the color.

Noninterlaced resolution—A monitor resolution that the monitor can reach without resorting to interlacing. Interlacing, which is covered elsewhere in this glossary, leaves a telltale flicker on the screen, which is at least distracting and can leave you with a headache. The only resolutions you should consider using are noninterlaced.

Nonprintable areas—The top, bottom, left, and right margins on a page where a given printer can't print. Most printers have some sort of dead space where they can't print. Thermal wax transfer and thermal dye transfer printers have particularly large nonprintable areas. These printers need wide margins so they can grip the paper and keep it carefully aligned on each pass through the printer, with one pass for each color.

Object-based graphics (also object-oriented graphics)—Also called vector objects, or vector graphics. Any graphic image that defines lines, curves, and fills as mathematical formulas. The other choice, called bitmapped graphics (which is covered elsewhere in this glossary), defines the image as an assortment of individual bits mapped to particular positions on a grid. Programs that define shapes as formulas can easily scale the shapes up or down and keep edges smooth. Changing the size of bitmapped graphics can be a problem, since the program has to guess where to add or subtract bits.

Page feed scanners—A type of scanner that feeds pages through a page feed mechanism. Page feed scanners are similar to the scanners on most office fax machines. A sheet feeder drags pages though the scanner, while the scanner mechanism itself stays still. Page feed scanners typically let you set up a stack of several pages to feed though the scanner automatically. However, they have severe limits on the maximum weight paper they can handle. And you certainly can't feed a book page through a sheet feeder—not as long as it's attached to the book. Flatbed and handheld scanners, which are both covered elsewhere in this glossary, don't have that problem.

Paint program—A graphics program that lets you create and edit bitmapped images, or bitmaps, as opposed to graphic objects. Bitmaps (which are covered elsewhere in this glossary) define an image as a collection of individual bits in specific locations—or, if you prefer, they map the bits to a grid. Paint programs often have the word *paint* in their names, as in Paintbrush. The other choice for graphics is to define lines, curves, and fills by mathematical formulas. This lets the program treat a line, for example, as an object instead of a collection of bits. Object-oriented programs are called drawing programs.

Pantone Matching System (PMS)—Arguably the best known color-matching system. Color-matching systems, which are mostly of interest to professional graphic artists, let you pick a color from a book of color swatches for printing on a printing press. The color-matching system guarantees that the color you get back from the printer will match the color swatch.

PCL—One of the most widespread printer languages. Hewlett-Packard created PCL and keeps updating it as new printers come out, but you'll find PCL in lots of other printers as well. The language comes in lots of variations too. Most Hewlett-Packard ink jet printers use PCL 3. The LaserJet II used PCL 4. The LaserJet III used PCL 5, but not the same version of PCL 5 as the LaserJet 4.

Phase change printer—Alternate name for wax jet printer. The name is based in physics. The wax in wax jet printers goes from solid when you put it in the printer to liquid when it melts to solid when it cools on the page. Since a change from liquid to solid or solid to liquid is a phase change, that makes these phase change printers, but this particular name has never been popular, and that's not likely to change.

Pixel or picture element—The smallest unit of a picture. In a color image, a pixel is the smallest unit that you can define a color for.

Pixelation—A tendency for the individual pixels, or picture elements, in an image to show up as visible squares. In general, you'll get pixelation if the resolution for the image is too low for the size of the image. For any given size, in inches, the fewer the pixels across and down, the more likely you'll see pixelation.

Plain paper ribbon—A special ribbon that lets thermal wax transfer printers, which normally need coated paper, use standard copier paper instead. In addition to the color panels, plain paper ribbons have an extra panel for adding a coating to the paper. The colors then print over the coating.

Posterization—An effect that limits the number of colors, or shades of gray, available so that photos look a bit like drawings. Some programs offer posterization as an artistic effect that you can add to images. You can also get posterization when you don't want it if a printer or video card doesn't offer enough colors to give you the gradual changes that the photo needs. The picture labeled Posterization shows what a slightly posterized photo looks like.

Posterization The posterization in this photo shows up both in the scuba diver's skin, with abrupt changes in the shade of gray, and in the water surface in the background.

PostScript—One of the more common printer languages for higher end printers. PostScript was originally from Adobe, which licenses Adobe PostScript to various printer manufacturers. Other printers use PostScript clones. Both Adobe PostScript and the clones come in two versions, Level 1 and Level 2. Level 2 includes a built-in color model that serves as a standard to help match colors from one printer to the next.

Primary colors—For printers and monitors, the three colors that a given device mixes to create all other colors. For monitors, the primary colors are red, green, and blue. For printers, they're cyan, magenta, and yellow. For artists, the primary colors serve a somewhat different purpose, since few, if any, artists limit themselves to just three colors of paints for creating all the other colors they use. The primary colors in the artist's color wheel are blue, red, and yellow. Rather than serving as the starting point for creating other colors, they are part of a scheme for choosing colors that will work well together.

Printer language—A set of commands for controlling a printer. The two most widely used printer languages for color printers are PCL and PostScript, although both of these come in more than one version. Most other common languages are named after the printers or printer companies that created the language in the first place, such as Epson or IBM. Some printer languages aren't really printer languages as such. Windows, for example, uses a set of commands for putting images on the screen called the graphical device interface, or GDI. A Windows GDI printer uses the same GDI commands.

Process color—Color produced by printing with cyan, magenta, yellow, and black—or cyan, magenta, and yellow. Any color printer attached to a desktop computer is limited to process colors. Printing presses can also print spot colors, which are specific colors mixed to order and printed separately from cyan, magenta, yellow, and black.

Pure color—Also called monochromatic color; color that consists of a single wavelength of light or a small range of wavelengths. Pure color looks identical to colors created by mixing other colors—to the human eye at least. However, there are practical differences between pure color and mixed color. For example, two samples of pure colors that match under one kind of light will match under any other. Two samples of mixed colors that match under, say, fluorescent light won't match under other lighting conditions, such as daylight, unless they have exactly the same mix of colors.

Raster (or raster graphics)—Another name for bitmapped graphics. By either name, raster graphics define images bit by bit, and they stand in contrast to object-oriented graphics, which define images as a mathematical description of lines, curves, and fills. Object-oriented graphics and Bitmapped graphics are also defined, in more detail, elsewhere in this glossary.

Rasterization—The process of converting an image into a collection of bits. Since all printers use dots to print graphic images, they need to convert the image to a collection of dots, a.k.a. a bitmap, before they can print. If the image starts out as an object-based graphic, rasterizing the image converts it from an object, or a collection of objects, to a bitmap. If it starts out as a bitmap, rasterization maps the bits in the image to the dots available at the printer. Map a line 300 dots across one to one with a 300-dpi printer, for example, and the line will come out to one inch. Map the dots one to-one with a 600-dpi printer, and the line will be one-half inch. But if you map each dot to two dots across on a 600-dpi printer, the line will be one inch on a 600-dpi printer also.

Registration—The alignment of different parts of an image. When you put an image together from different pieces—by printing each color separately for the entire page, for example, and then printing the next color, and the next—each piece has to be carefully aligned with the other pieces. The alignment, or registration, controls how well the pieces fit together.

RGB—Short for red-green-blue, the three primary colors that monitors use to create all the colors they can show. Monitors and other equipment that uses red, green, and blue are RGB devices. RGB devices naturally use an RGB color model, which (surprise) defines colors by the amount of red, green, and blue in each color.

RIP (Raster Image Processor)—The electronics in a printer that rasterize an image for the printer to print. Not all printers include RIPs. Some use drivers that let the computer do the work, so the computer feeds the predigested, already-rasterized image to the printer.

Saturation—The amount of hue in a given color. Pink and red, for example, are both the same hue. Red is more fully saturated. If you pass a white light through a prism to break it into the spectrum, the colors of the spectrum are fully saturated.

Screen—Short for halftone screen, which is covered elsewhere in this glossary.

Screen angle—The angle of a halftone screen. If the screen is parallel to the edge of a page, it's at 0 degrees. If it's rotated by 45 degrees, the screen angle is 45 degrees. In color printers, the screen angle is different for each color ink. In general, the default screen angles—in either monochrome or color printing—are designed to minimize the visibility of the screen. With color printers, the angles are designed to minimize moiré patterns.

Screen frequency—Alternate pronunciation for halftone screen frequency. Screen frequency is the number of halftone cells in a halftone screen and is usually given in lines per inch. Think of it as the effective resolution you get after halftoning.

Secondary colors—For printers and monitors, the three colors you get when you mix each possible pair of primary colors. For monitors, the secondary colors are cyan (a mixture of green and blue), yellow (red and green), and magenta (red and blue). For printers, they're red (yellow and magenta), green (cyan and yellow), and blue (cyan and magenta). For artists, the secondary colors on the artist's color wheel—green, violet, and orange—are the three colors that are midway between each pair of primary colors. The color wheel is not concerned with mixing colors, but rather with helping design color schemes.

Shade (of color)—A fully saturated color in the artist's color wheel, with black added. Shades differ from tints, which start with the same fully saturated hue and add white. This distinction between shades and tints is part of the art vocabulary of color, not the printing vocabulary. In printing, every variation in lightness for a given hue is a different shade.

Sheetfed scanner—Alternate pronunciation for page feed scanner. By either name, this works like the scanner in a typical fax machine, pulling the page though a sheet feed mechanism.

Simultaneous contrast—The tendency of a central area to change appearance depending on a surrounding area. A face that's perfectly visible in room light, for example, can turn into a silhouette if the background changes from a closed window shade to bright sunlight. Another example is that the same patch of green can look bluish against a yellow background or yellowish against a blue background.

Single-component toner—Another name for mono-component toner, which is covered elsewhere in this glossary.

Solid ink or solid wax printer—Alternate pronunciations for wax jet printer.
   Let's take these in reverse alphabetical order:
   The name *solid wax* makes some sense, since the wax starts as a solid before the printer melts it and ends up as a solid after it's on the paper. But when the printer is actually doing its stuff, the wax is liquid, so you could just as easily call these liquid wax printers (even though nobody does).
   The *ink* sneaks in here because you can think of wax as an ink, in a generic sense at least. More important, you could build printers that work the same way as solid wax printers, but melt polymers or other materials instead of wax. By defining the category as solid ink rather than solid wax, you can stick all such printers in a single category, rather than having a separate name for every printer that uses a different kind of ink. (Well, different kind of colorant, if you want to get picky about it, but don't expect anyone to know what a solid colorant printer is.)

Spectrum—Often shorthand for the visible spectrum, which includes all the wavelengths of light the human eye can see; more generally, all the wavelengths of light in a beam of light or in light reflected from an opaque sample. The spectrums (or spectra) from two different color samples can be quite different, even though the two colors look identical in some lighting conditions.

Spectrophotometer—A device for measuring spectra (or spectrums, but people who use spectrowhatsits are much more likely to say spectra).

Spherical section display—A display shaped literally as a section of a sphere, like a piece cut out of a large beach ball. These displays curve in both the horizontal and vertical directions, which distorts the image noticeably. Until recently, most displays were spherical sections. Most 14-inch monitors today are spherical sections as well. However the standard size for monitors is gradually moving to 15 inches, and most 15-inch monitors use flat square displays, which look flat so that they don't distort the image. Other choices in display shape are cylindrical section and flat displays, which are both covered elsewhere in this glossary.

Spot color—Any color mixed to order and printed separately from cyan, magenta, yellow, and black. Computer printers can't print spot colors, because there is no way to add a custom color ink. With a printing press, however, you can create a separate printing plate for each spot color and print each custom color in its own pass.

Stochastic screening—One of two kinds of frequency-modulated screening techniques. The other is diffusion dither. FM screens differ from traditional halftone screens by keeping the same size halftone spot and simply using more of them in dark areas than light areas. Traditional halftone screens keep the number of halftone cells constant and vary the size of the spots.

Subtractive primary colors—Cyan, magenta, and yellow—the three colors of ink you can mix together to come up with all the other colors a printer is capable of printing. These are called subtractive primaries because the pigments in the ink absorb, or subtract, specific colors from reflected light. Cyan ink, for example, absorbs red, which leaves blue and green in the reflected light.

Super A-size paper—Any paper format that's somewhat bigger than A size in both dimensions. Unlike A-size paper, which is defined as 8½ by 11 inches, there is no specific size definition for super A size. The significance of super A-size paper is that it's big enough to hold a full bleed A-size image, which means an image that's 8½ by 11 inches, or a little larger.

Super A-size printer—Any printer that can print on super A-size paper. Most, but not all, super A-size printers can take advantage of super-A size paper to print full bleed A-size images (8½ by 11 inches or a touch larger).

Super B-size paper—Similar to super A-size paper in concept; only the size is different, with B size defined as 11 by 17 inches, and super B size as somewhat bigger in both dimensions. Here again, the significance of the super size is that it's big enough hold a full bleed image, B size in this case, which means an image that's 11 by 17, or a little larger.

328 *Glossary*

Super B-size printer—Any printer that can print on super B-size paper. Most, but not all, super B-size printers can take advantage of the paper to print full bleed B-size images.

Tabloid-size printer—Another name for B-size printer, which is covered elsewhere in this glossary, and includes Super B-size printers in the same category.

TAC—Acronym for total area coverage, which is totally covered in a nearby area of this glossary.

Tertiary color—The six colors on the artist's color wheel that are neither primary nor secondary. There are a total of twelve basic colors on the color wheel: three primary colors (red, yellow, blue), three secondary colors (orange, green, violet) with one secondary color between each pair of primary colors, and six tertiary colors (red-orange, yellow-orange, yellow-green, blue-green, blue-violet, red-violet) with each tertiary color between a primary color on one side and a secondary color on the other.

Thermal dye transfer printer—A ribbon-based printer that heats the ribbon to release a dye that's absorbed by a special, polyester-coated paper. Thermal dye transfer printers, or thermal dye printers for short, are known for printing high quality continuous tone images such as photographs. They're also known for their high cost per page.

Thermal wax transfer printer—A ribbon-based printer that heats the ribbon to melt wax onto paper. Thermal wax transfer printers, or thermal wax printers for short, are known for printing high-quality graphics with fully saturated colors. They do a particularly good job of printing saturated colors on transparencies.

Three-color ribbon—A ribbon with cyan, magenta, and yellow panels. For most printers, you need black as a fourth color if you want to avoid blacks with a brown or blue tinge. However, a few printers can give you a dark black with just three colors. More important is that three-color ribbons cost less per image than four-color ribbons because one less panel for each image means that for any given length of ribbon, you get more images.

Three-pass ribbon (also three-pass three-color ribbon)—Alternate pronunciation for three-color ribbon, but with a twist. For a long time, three-color ribbon and three-pass ribbon meant the same thing, because thermal wax and thermal dye printers run each page through the printer once for each color. But then some printer manufacturers started selling plain paper ribbons for thermal wax printers.

The plain paper ribbons add a fourth panel that lays down a coating on the paper first. The colors print over the coating. That means a three-color plain paper ribbon is a four-pass ribbon, and a three-color ribbon can have either three or four passes. This matters because more passes take longer to print.

So when you're talking about thermal wax printers, a three-color ribbon can be three or four passes, but a three-pass ribbon can only be three colors. Thermal dye printers need special, polyester-coated paper, so for thermal dye printers, a three-color ribbon is always a three-pass ribbon.

Tint (of color)—A fully saturated color in the artist's color wheel, with white added. Tints differ from shades, which start with a fully saturated color and add black. The distinction between shades and tints is part of the art vocabulary of color, not the printing vocabulary. In printing, every variation in lightness for a given hue is a different shade.

Total area coverage (TAC)—The maximum coverage of a page. In theory, four-color printers can have a maximum coverage of 400 percent by covering 100 percent of the page with each of four inks. In practice, that's overkill, and few printers produce satisfactory output with over 300 percent. Most printers do best with a maximum of 260 to 280 percent. Some programs let you define the percentage of total area coverage to use for your printer, and they modify the output to match.

True color—Technically, at least 24-bit color (roughly 16.8 million colors). More meaningfully, true color offers a large enough selection of colors so the human eye will see any photograph as truly photographic quality, with colors shading naturally into each other, without any abrupt changes where there shouldn't be any.

UCR (undercolor removal)—A technique for controlling a printer so that some or all of a mixture of cyan, magenta, and yellow inks gets replaced with an equivalent amount of black. The point of undercolor removal is that using equal values of cyan, magenta, and yellow theoretically adds up to a neutral gray or black in any case. Substituting black ink gives a more truly hueless color (if you accept gray and black as colors).

Unidirectional printing—Printing in one direction, left to right, with a printhead that moves horizontally across the page. Printers with printheads that move back and forth across the page, such as ink jets, can either print in both directions, printing one band left to right and the next right to left, or they can print in one direction only, printing a band left to right, returning to the left side without printing, printing another band left to right, and so on. Printing in one direction only, or unidirectional printing, takes longer to print each page, but often does a better job of aligning the bands, so they don't show in the printed image.

Value—A measure of how light or dark a color is in the Munsell color system. A value of zero is black.

Vector objects, or vector graphics—Alternate names for object-oriented graphics, which are defined elsewhere in this glossary.

Video capture board—A board that goes in a computer expansion slot and can capture video signals and digitize them. Some video capture boards are actually boxes that sit outside the computer and plug into the parallel or serial port. These are actually video capture devices, but for purposes of this book, they count as video capture boards. Some video capture boards can capture full motion video; others capture only single frames.

Video signal—The signal that travels between two pieces of video equipment, such as a camera and VCR, and carries the video information. The standard for video equipment in the U.S. and Japan is NTSC. The standard in Europe is PAL.

Warm colors—Red, orange, and yellow. Warm colors tend to catch the eye, which makes them a good choice for foreground colors in graphics or for specific text or objects you want to draw attention to. Green and magenta can also be warm colors, depending on the colors around them. Put them in a sea of blue, blue-green, or violet, and they'll seem warm. Use them with yellow, orange, red, or brown, and they'll seem cool.

Wax jet printer—A printer that melts solid wax to a liquid, which dries on the page by cooling; also called phase change, solid ink, and solid wax printer. Wax jet printers come in two varieties. One kind sprays ink directly on a page, just like an ink jet printer. The other sprays the ink on a drum, which transfers it to paper much like a laser printer transfers toner to paper.

The claim to fame for both kinds of wax jets is vibrant, fully saturated colors. The version that sprays directly on paper is a poor choice for transparencies, because the wax drops dry to tiny lenses. The version that uses a drum is a good choice for transparencies, because rolling the drum against the paper to transfer the wax also flattens the drops of wax.

Wicking—Depending on who you talk to, either another name for bleeding—the tendency of ink from an ink jet printer to spread a bit before it dries—or the specific tendency for ink to spread along a fiber or fibers in the paper. Those who use the second definition generally consider wicking as distinct from bleeding and reserve bleeding to describe two different color inks spreading into each other.

Index

Absorption spectrum, 100
Achromatic color scheme, 246
Additive primaries in mixing colors, 101–105
Aliasing, 147
Analogous color scheme, 243

Backgrounds
   color choices, 77
   rules for using text and color, 80–81
   transparencies, 77–78
Banding, 182–183
   checking output, 190, 193
   clogged nozzles, 188
   example, 182
   printer settings and paper types, 187
Bidirectional printing, 184, 185
Bilevel laser printers, 199
   halftones, 262–263
   number of colors used, 274–277
Bitmapped images (raster graphics), 135–136
   file size issues, 149–150
   loaded into object-oriented programs, 143–144
   mapping bits to a grid, 136–139
   monitor display mechanism, 150–151
   paint programs, 141
   scaling, 149
   scanned images, 138–139, 261
Bits
   number of colors displayed, 161–162
BJC-600e printer, 26, 122, 125, 187–188, 194
Black
   additive and subtractive primaries in mixing colors, 102–105
   four-color printing, 8
   lack of, in CMY model, 8
   need for, in four-color printing, 8

Black and white printers. *See* Monochrome printers
Black and white printing. *See* Monochrome printing
Bleeding, 11, 24
Blooming, 11
Blue, 3
   additive and subtractive primaries in mixing colors, 101–105
   differences between monitors and printers, 96, 98–99, 119–120
   eye cones and color perception, 101
   mixing with other colors, for monitor display, 4–5
   primary, secondary, and tertiary colors, 240–241
   using text and color, 81
Brightness, 37–39. *See also* Lightness
   black and white copies of color graphics, 88
   HSB (hue-saturation-brightness) model, 37–39, 224
   making edges stand out, 78–79
   monitor control, 45
   using text and color, 80
B size paper, 214
Buying a printer, 215–217
   applications to be used, 216–217
   percentage of coverage per page, 216
   price per page, 215–216

Calibrating
   monitors, 225–231
   printers, 231–236
Camera, digital
   resolution, 260, 270–273
Camera resolution, 261

331

332 *Index*

Canon, 185
   BJC-600e printer, 26, 122, 125, 187–188, 194
Capture resolution, 261
Cartridges, ink jet
   refilling, 191–192
   three-color, 191
CD-ROM photographs, 256, 269
Charts
   black and white copies of color graphics, 81–91
   consistency in design, 69–70
   less is more approach, 68–69
Chromaticity
   calibrating, 226
   description, 221–223
CIE standards, 220
   description, 221–223
CMY devices, 6, 106, 109
CMY (cyan-magenta-yellow) model
   additive and subtractive primaries in mixing colors, 101–105
   description, 6
   lack of black, 8
CMYK devices, 106
CMYK (cyan-magenta-yellow-black) model, 220
   additive and subtractive primaries in mixing colors, 101–105
   advantages, 114
   choosing, 114–116
   defining, in CorelDRAW, 7, 8, 111–113
   description, 7
Coatings, paper, 17, 175–176, 185
Color
   basics, 219–236
   psychology of, 47–49, 248–250
   for a third dimension, 72–74
   use of terms, 239–242
Color depth, 160, 162–168
   dithering, 164–165
   number of colors needed, 163–164
   posterization, 166–168
   video cards, 169
Color LaserJet printer, 210
Color matching, 35–36, 105–133
   matching the printer to the screen, 121–123
   matching the screen to the printer, 123–128
   scanners, 288
Color matching systems, 250–252

Color models
   choosing, 114–116
   CIE standards, 220, 221–223
   color space, 6–7
   CMY (cyan-magenta-yellow) model, 6
   CMYK (cyan-magenta-yellow-black) model, 7, 220
   HSB (hue-saturation-brightness) model, 37–39, 224
   HSL (hue-saturation-lightness) model, 224
   HSV (hue-saturation-value) model, 224
   HVC (hue-value-chroma) model, 223–224
   limitations, 220
   Munsell system, 223–224
   RGB (red-green-blue) model, 6–7, 220
Color monitors, 95–133
   adjusting, 45–46
   basics, 152–172
   calibrating, 225–231
   choosing a size, 153–158
   color depth, 162–168
   color gamuts, 106–113
   comparison with colors on the printed page, 44–47
   differences between vertical and horizontal resolution, 148
   differences with colors for printing, 96, 98–99, 111–113, 117–120
   effect of colored bezels, 169–172
   lighting conditions, 46, 118
   matching printing colors to (*see* Color matching)
   number of colors displayed, 160–162
   number of colors needed, 163–164
   perception of white, 117–118
   shapes, 157–158
   size of image displayed, 153
   testing for resolution settings, 148–149
   video cards, 168–170
Color perception
   changing conditions, 43–44
   differences between monitors and printers, 96, 98–99, 111–113, 117–120
   effect of colored bezels, 169–172
   eye rods and cones, 100–101
   incandescent versus fluorescent lighting, 36–37, 221
   lighting conditions, 46

Index **333**

matching colors, 35–36, 105–117
monitor background, 45
on the printed page versus on the monitor, 44–47
psychology of color, 47–49, 248–250
simultaneous contrast, 40–41
size of color area, 41–42
surrounding colors, 39–41
Color printers, 9–32, 174–180
   color gamuts, 106–117
   dedicated color, 31–32
   ink sensors, 190–191
Color printing
   comparison with colors on a monitor, 44–47
   four-color (*see* Four-color printing)
   HSB (hue-saturation-brightness) model, 46, 224
   margin widths, 52–53, 205
   photographs, 253
   preventing streaks, 60–61, 62–66
   rasterizing images, 151–152
   three-color (*see* Three-color printing)
   transparencies, 27, 178
Color quality
   dot matrix printers, 10
   faxes, 91
   ink jet printers, 11
   judging output appearance, 192–195
   laser printers, 21
   photographs, 193–194
   printer language, 25
   thermal dye printers, 17
   thermal wax printers, 14
   transparencies, 194–195
   wax jet printers, 13
Color resolution, 160–162
Color ribbons, 8–9, 55–62
   changing, 61–62
   cleaning the printhead, 62
   dual mode printers, 60–61, 207
   dust protection, 60–61
   plain paper ribbons, 56–58
   changing, 61–62
   thermal dye printers, 18, 55–56, 204
   thermal wax printers, 13–14, 18, 28, 29, 55–56, 204
   three- and four-color, 8–9, 56, 59–60
   types, 55

Colors
   knowledge about, for color printing, 34–35
   matching colors, 35–36, 105–117
   mixing, for monitor displays, 4–5, 95, 98–99
   mixing, to produce other colors, 2–3
   warm and cool categories, 48–49
   See also specific colors
Color schemes, 70, 237, 242–248
   achromatic, 246
   analogous, 243
   backgrounds, 77–78
   complementary, 144
   consistency, 69–70
   less is more approach, 67–69
   making edges stand out, 78–79
   monochromatic, 71–72, 245–246
   opposing, 243
   picking the main color, 250
   primary and secondary, 243
   rainbow colors, 75, 247–248
   reasons for using, 70
   sample output in graphics programs, 75–76
   sources for ideas, 76
   split complementary, 144
   temperature scale, 247
   tertiary triad, 144
   for text, 80–81
   warm and cool colors, 71, 245
Color space, 6–7
Color spectrum, 2–3, 221
Color theory, 238–242
   color wheel variations, 238–239
   use of terms, 239–242
Color wheel
   complementary colors, 241–242
   illustration, 238
   primary colors, 240
   secondary colors, 240–241
   tertiary colors, 241
   use of terms, 239–242
   variations, 238–239
Complementary colors, 241–242
Complementary color scheme, 244
Compression, types, 280–281
Cones, color perception, 100–101
Consistency in design, 69–70
Contrast
   backgrounds, 77

334 *Index*

Contrast (*cont.*)
  monitor control, 45
  simultaneous contrast, 40–41
Cool colors
  backgrounds, 77
  color schemes, 71, 245
  psychology of color, 48–49, 248–250
Copy paper, 174. *See also* Plain paper
  choosing, 54
  printer settings, 187–188
  results in printing, 26–29, 54
Costs
  buying a printer, 215–217
  color printer prices, 22–23
  paper usage, 27, 29, 179, 205
  percentage of coverage per page, 216
  price per page, 215–216
  printing draft copies in black and white, 66–67
  ribbons, 206, 207, 215
  thermal dye printers, 17, 206
  thermal wax printers, 197, 205
  three-color ribbons, 9
  wax jet printers, 195, 197
Cyan
  additive and subtractive primaries in mixing colors, 102–105
  color wheel, 240
  differences between monitors and printers, 96, 98–99, 119–120
  mixing with other colors, for printer output, 1, 97–98

Daisywheel printers, 10
Design
  backgrounds, 77–78
  color for a third dimension, 72–74
  color matching systems, 250–252
  consistency, 69–70
  differences in grays, 91–94
  layout and readability, 67
  less is more approach, 67–69
  making edges stand out, 78–79
  monochromatic color schemes, 71–72
  printing draft copies in black and white, 66–67
  progression of rainbow colors, 75

  sample output in graphics programs, 75–76
  text and color, 80–81
  using a color scheme, 70
  warm and cool colors, 71
DeskJet 560C printer, 111, 185, 186, 187
DeskJet 660C printer, 295–298
DeskJet 1200C printer, 111, 125, 187, 210–211, 233
DeskJet 1200C/PS printer, 25, 30
DeskJet 1600CM printer, 304
Developer, in laser printers, 203
Device independence, in PostScript, 210–211
Digital camera, resolution, 260, 270–273
Dithering
  color depth, 164–165
  description, 5–6
  granularity of spots and size of the cell, 201
  halftones, 263
  laser printers, 21, 198
  monochrome printing, 199–200
  number of color combinations, 200
  photographs, 200–201
  resolution versus colors, 202
  scanning, 198, 280
  thermal dye printers, 16
  wax jet printers, 13
Dithering cell, 263
DOS, 25
Dot matrix printers
  color quality, 10
  command sets, 26
  printing process, 10
Draft copies, printing in black and white, 66–67
DRAM, 170
Drawing programs, 141–143
Drivers
  fax, 90
  printer (*see* Printer drivers)
  video, 155
Dual mode printers
  best way to use, 207
  cartridges, 191
  costs, 207
  description, 18–19
  ribbons, 60, 61–62, 207
Dumb printers, 212–213
  advantages, 212
  disadvantages, 212
  PCL and PostScript usage, 212

Dust protection for ribbons, 60–61
Dye sublimation printers, 15–16

Electrophotographic printers, 19, 20. *See also* Laser printers
Enhanced PCL 5, 209
Epson command sets, 26
Epson Stylus Color printer, 177
Expenses. *See* Costs
Eye rods and cones, 100–101

FARGO Primera Pro printer, 113, 148
Faxes
  black and white copies of color graphics, 82, 88–91
  choice of modes, 89
  from a computer, 89–90
  from a fax machine, 88–89
  testing pages, 90–91
Fax machines, 254
  faxing graphics, 88–89
Fax modem, 90
Fax programs, 90
Flatbed scanners, 254–255
Fluorescent lighting, color perception, 36–37, 221
Fonts
  scaleable, in PCL, 209
  transparencies, 77
  TrueType, 211, 301
Four-color printing, 8–9
  changing, 59–60
  need for black in mixing colors, 8
  ribbons with color printers, 8–9
Four-color (CMYK) ribbons, 8, 55
  advantages, 9
  three-color ribbons versus, 56
  when to swap with a three-color ribbon, 60
Frame grabbers, 258
Frequency-modulated (FM) screening, 265, 268, 283–284

Gamma correction, 129–131, 285–288
  calibrating a monitor, 227–228, 229
  description, 130–131
  setting, 131

Glossy paper, 177–178
Graphical device interface (GDI), 26, 212
Graphics
  black and white copies of color graphics, 81–91
  color for a third dimension, 72–74
  consistency in design, 69–70
  differences in grays, 91–94
  dot matrix printers, 10
  faxing, in black and white, 82, 88–91
  judging output appearance, 192–193
  laser printers, 21
  less is more approach, 68–69
  readability and good design, 67
  thermal dye printers, 17
  thermal wax printers, 205
  warm and cool color schemes, 71
Graphics programs
  file size issues, 149–150
  sample output options, 75–76
  scaling a bitmapped image, 149
Gray component replacement (GCR), 234–235
Gray scale
  design of graphics, 74
  faxing pages, 89
  halftones, 262–264
  posterization, 166–168
Green, 3
  additive and subtractive primaries in mixing colors, 102–105
  color wheel, 240
  differences between monitors and printers, 96, 98–99, 119–120
  eye cones and color perception, 101
  mixing with other colors, for monitor display, 4–5
  psychology of color, 249

Halftone cell, 263, 276
Halftone resolution, 261, 264, 265–267
  Halftones, 262–264
  dithering, 263
  frequency-modulated (FM) screening, 265, 268, 283–284
  growing the spot, 281–282
  printer settings, 293–294
  regular patterns, 282

Halftone resolution (*cont.*)
  screen angles, 284
  screen frequency, 263–264, 268
  screens, 263
  supercells, 283
Handheld scanners, 254–255
Hewlett-Packard (HP)
  Color LaserJet printer, 210
  DeskJet 560C printer, 111, 185, 186, 187
  DeskJet 660C printer, 295–298
  DeskJet 1200C printer, 111, 125, 187, 210–211, 233
  DeskJet 1200C/PS printer, 25, 30
  DeskJet 1600CM printer, 304
  HP-GL/2, 209
  LaserJet 4 printer, 210–211
  PCL, 25, 208, 209
High-end color printers, 22–23
HSB (hue-saturation-brightness) model
  advantages, 115
  description, 37–39
Hue
  backgrounds, 77
  black and white copies of color graphics, 88
  description, 37–39
  HSB (hue-saturation-brightness) model, 37–39, 224
  HSL (hue-saturation-lightness) model, 224
  HSV (hue-saturation-value) model, 224
  HVC (hue-value-chroma) model, 223–224
  monochromatic color schemes, 71–72
  using text and color, 80
HSL (hue-saturation-lightness) model, 224
HSV (hue-saturation-value) model, 224
HVC (hue-value-chroma) model, 223–224

IBM command sets, 26
Image resolution, 264, 267–268
Images
  bitmapped (*see* Bitmapped images)
  consistency in design, 70
  dithering, 5–6
  object-based (*see* Object-based images)
  resampling, 270–273
Incandescent lighting
  color perception, 36–37, 221

Ink
  paper usage, 28–29
  percentage of coverage per page, 216, 234
  printer settings, 292–293
  sensors, 190–191
  spraying from nozzles, 186–191
  spreading (bleeding), 11, 24
Ink jet printers, 181–195
  advantages, 180
  banding, 182–183, 187, 188, 193
  as both a color and monochrome printer, 32
  cartridges, 191–192
  categories, 180–181
  clogged nozzles, 188–191
  color quality, 11
  differences with wax jet printers, 195
  disadvantages, 180
  four-color, 181
  ink sensors, 190–191
  judging output appearance, 192–195
  paper usage, 26, 28–29, 30, 54, 175–178
  preventing streaks, 65–66
  price per page, 215
  printing draft copies in black and white, 66–67
  printing process, 11, 182–186
  printing transparencies, 30, 194–195
  resolution, 11, 23
  self-test, 188–189
  settings, 184–186
  spreading of ink, 11
  three-color, 181
Ink sensors, 190–191
Ion-deposition printers, 19, 21

JPEG compression, 281

Language. *See* Printer language
LaserJet 4 printer, 210–211
Laser paper
  choosing, 54
  printer settings, 188
  results in printing, 29, 30, 46, 54
  simultaneous contrast, 41
  testing a plain paper ribbon, 56–58

Laser printers, 197–204
　advantages, 198
　bilevel and multilevel, 198–203
　as both a color and monochrome printer, 32
　buying, 215
　color quality, 21
　continuous tone, 21, 198, 262
　developer replacement, 203
　disadvantages, 198
　dithering, 21, 198
　paper usage, 26, 29, 54
　PCL 5C, 210
　price per page, 215–216
　pricing, 22
　printing draft copies in black and white, 66–67
　printing process, 19–20
　printing transparencies, 30
　resolution, 21, 23, 24
　toner replacement, 203–204
　use of term, 20
Layout
　printer language, 25
　readability and good design, 67
LCD (liquid display) monitors, 152, 158–160
　display mechanism, 159
　number of colors displayed, 160–162
　size measurement, 159–160
LCD printers, 19, 20. *See also* Laser printers
LED printers, 19, 20. *See also* Laser printers
Lighting
　incandescent versus fluorescent, 36–37, 221
　matching colors, 35–36
　monitor colors, 46
　perception of white, 118
Lightness
　HSL (hue-saturation-lightness) model, 224
　shades on a color wheel, 240
　using text and color, 80
Lossless compression, 280–281
Lossy compression, 280
Low-end color printers, 23

Macintosh computers, 24, 152, 153
Magenta
　additive and subtractive primaries in mixing colors, 102–105
　color wheel, 240
　differences between monitors and printers, 96, 98–99, 119–120
　mixing with other colors, for printer output, 4, 97–98
　primary, secondary, and tertiary colors, 240–241
Margins
　larger image size, 52–53
　ribbon printers, 205
Matching colors. *See* Color matching
Media Graphics International, 256
Memory
　compressing files, 280–281
Metamerism, 221
Mid-range color printers, 23
Misregistration, 182–184
Models
　choosing, 114–116
　color space, 6–7
　CMY (cyan-magenta-yellow) model, 6
　CMYK (cyan-magenta-yellow-black) model, 7
　HSB (hue-saturation-brightness) model, 37–39
　RGB (red-green-blue) model, 6–7
Modems, fax capability, 90
Moiré patterns, 277–279
　example, 279
　scanning, 278–279
Monitors. *See* Color monitors
Monochromatic color scheme, 245–246
Monochrome printers
　combined with color output, 31–32
　laser versus copy paper usage, 41
　PCL, 208, 210
Monochrome printing
　black and white copies of color graphics, 81–91
　dithering, 199–200
　dot matrix printers, 10
　monochrome masters, 84–88
　monochrome ribbons, 58
　on any printer, 180
　printing draft copies, 66–67
　printing on color printers in monochrome mode, 85–86
　testing color ribbons, 56, 58
　wax jet printers, 196

338 Index

Monochrome ribbons, 55
   uses, 58
Multilevel laser printers
   dithering, 199–202
   printing photographs, 202
MultiSync monitor, 132
Munsell system, 223–224

N
NEC
   4FG monitor, 125
   SuperScript Color 3000 printer, 92, 129–132, 290–295, 298
Networks, color printers, 22
NTSC format, 257, 258

O
Object
   drawing, in CorelDRAW, 141–143
   resizing, 140–141
   use of term, 139–140
Object-based images (vector graphics), 136
   bitmapped images in object-oriented programs, 143–144
   drawing an object, 141–143
   monitor display mechanism, 151
   resizing an object, 140–141
Object Linking and Embedding (OLE), 143–144
Operating System Specific, printer language, 26
Opposing color scheme, 243
Options dialog box, printing in monochrome mode, 86
OS/2, printer drivers, 24

P
Page feed scanners, 254–255
Paintbrush, 113, 148
   images loaded into object-oriented programs, 143
   mapping bits to a grid, 136–138
   scaling a bitmapped image, 149
Paint programs, 141
PAL format, 257, 258
Pantone Matching System (PMS), 251, 252
Paper, 26–30, 53–54
   categories, 174
   choosing, 54
   coatings, 17, 175–176, 185
   color variations, 54
   costs, 27, 29, 179, 215–216
   determining which side to print on, 176
   ink jet printers, 26, 28–29, 30, 54, 175–178
   larger image size, 52–53
   laser printers, 26, 29, 54
   margins in printing, 52–53, 205
   paper sizes, 52–53
   percentage of coverage per page, 216, 234
   perception of white, 117–118
   price per page, 215–216
   printer settings, 186–188, 296–298
   results with copy paper, 27–28, 54
   results with laser paper, 29, 30, 54
   sources, 54
   spreading (bleeding) of ink, 11, 24
   thermal dye printers, 17, 27, 53, 178, 214–215
   thermal wax printers, 26, 27–28, 29, 30, 54, 57, 58, 175–177
   wax jet printers, 26, 29–30, 53
   weight variations, 54, 175
Paper Direct, 54
PC cards, 259
PCL (Printer Control Language), 25, 208–210, 298
   color printers, 210
   levels, 209–211
   monochrome printers, 208, 210
   versions, 25, 208–209
PCMCIA card, 259
Perception of color
   additive and subtractive primaries in mixing colors, 101–105
   changing conditions, 43–44
   differences between monitors and printers, 96, 98–99, 111–113, 117–120
   effect of colored bezels, 169–172
   eye rods and cones, 100–101
   hue, saturation, and brightness, 38–39
   incandescent versus fluorescent lighting, 36–37
   lighting conditions, 46
   matching colors, 35–36, 105–117
   monitor background, 45
   on the printed page versus on the monitor, 44–47
   psychology of color, 47–49, 248–250
   simultaneous contrast, 40–41
   size of color area, 41–42

surrounding colors, 39–41
wavelength, 99, 100
Phase change printers, 12. *See also* Wax jet printers
Phaser 340 printer, 30, 65, 83, 92, 113, 116–117, 121–122
Phaser 540 printer, 203
Photo-CD format, 269
Photographs
   bitmapped images, 138–139
   digital camera, 259–260, 270–273
   dithering, 200–201
   dot matrix printers, 10
   frame grabbers, 258
   gamma correction, 285–288
   images loaded into object-oriented programs, 143
   judging output appearance, 193–194
   loading off a CD-ROM, 256, 269
   paper for printing, 26
   printing, 253
   resolution, 260–268
   scanning, 254–255
   thermal dye printers, 17
   video capture board, 256–258, 270–273
Pixels
   LCD monitor display, 159
   mixing colors for monitor display, 4–5
   monitor size and resolution, 156–157
Plain paper, 174–175. *See also* Copy paper
   advantages, 179–180
   bidirectional printing, 185
   costs, 179, 205
   premium, 175
   thermal wax printers, 205
   variations, 174
   weight, 175
Plain paper ribbon, 56–58
Polyester-coated paper, 17, 175–176
Posterization, 166–168
PostScript, 25, 148, 208, 210–212
   device independence, 210–211
   dumb printer usage, 213
   halftoning, 279
   Level 1, 212
   levels, 212
   Level 2, 25, 212, 220
   printer drivers, 298–305
   printing in monochrome mode, 86
   versions, 25

Premium plain paper, 175
Pricing, measuring, per page, 215–216
Primary colors, 3
   additive and subtractive primaries in mixing colors, 101–105
   color wheel, 240
   eye cones and color perception, 101
   forming secondary colors, 96–97
   mixing, for monitor display, 4–5, 95
   psychology of color, 49
Primary color scheme, 243
Primera Pro printer, 113, 148
Printer Control Language. *See* PCL
Printer drivers, 289–306
   halftoning, 279
   matching the screen and printer, 128–133
   PostScript, 298–305
   printer language, 24–25
   Windows 95, 305–306
   See also PCL; PostScript
Printer language, 24–26, 208–213
   categories, 24, 208
Printer resolution, 264, 265
Printers. *See* Black and white printing; Color printers
Printhead
   banding, 182
   cleaning, 62
   ink spraying from nozzles, 186–188
   misregistration, 182–184
Printing. *See* Color printing
Printing process
   banding, 182–183
   bidirectional, 184, 185
   dithering, 5–6
   dot matrix printers, 10
   ink jet printers, 11, 182–186
   laser printers, 19–20
   misregistration, 182–184
   printer settings, 186–188
   resolution, 23–24
   saturation, 38
   specific to operating system, 26
   spreading (bleeding) of ink, 11, 24
   thermal dye printers, 15–16, 18
   thermal wax printers, 13–14, 18
   unidirectional, 184, 185
   wax jet printers, 12
Projectors, 31

Proofing transparencies, 78
Psychology of color, 47–49, 248–250

Quality of color
    dot matrix printers, 10
    ink jet printers, 11
    laser printers, 21
    thermal dye printers, 17
    thermal wax printers, 14
    wax jet printers, 13

Rainbow colors, 75, 247–248
Raster graphics. *See* Bitmapped images
Raster image processors (RIPs), 151
Red, 3
    additive and subtractive primaries in mixing colors, 101–105
    differences between monitors and printers, 96, 98–99, 119–120
    eye cones and color perception, 101
    mixing with other colors, for monitor display, 4–5
    primary, secondary, and tertiary colors, 240–241
    psychology of color, 249
    using text and color, 81
Refill kits, cartridges, 191–192
Resampling, 270–273
Resizing an object, 140–141
Resolution, 23, 24, 260–284
    black and white copies of color graphics, 87
    colors in dithering, 202
    digital camera, 270–273
    faxes, 89
    ink jet printers, 11, 23
    kinds, 261–262
    laser printers, 21, 23, 24
    moiré patterns, 277–279
    number of colors, 274–277
    Photo-CD format, 269
    printed output, 261
    printer, 265
    samples per inch, 261, 262
    scanning, 260–268
    screen frequency, 265–266, 268
    size of image displayed, 153
    testing a printer for settings, 148–149

    use of term, 24
    video capture board, 270–273
    video cards and memory, 168–169
    wax jet printers, 13, 23
    See also 600 dots per inch (dpi) printing
RGB devices, 6, 106, 152
RGB (red-green-blue) model, 114, 220
    additive and subtractive primaries in mixing colors, 101–105
    calibrating a printer, 235–236
    defining, in CorelDRAW, 6
    description, 6–7
    Pantone Matching System (PMS), 252
Ribbons. *See* Color ribbons; Monochrome ribbons
Rods
    color perception, 100

Samples per inch, 261, 262
Saturation, 37–39
    backgrounds, 77
    black and white copies of color graphics, 88
    HSB (hue-saturation-brightness) model, 37–39, 224
    HSL (hue-saturation-lightness) model, 224
    HSV (hue-saturation-value) model, 224
    making edges stand out, 78–79
    printing process, 38
    psychology of color, 49
    size of color area, 41–42
    using text and color, 80, 81
Scaling a bitmapped image, 149
Scanning
    bitmaps, 138–139
    color matching, 288
    dithering on laser printers, 198, 280
    moiré patterns, 277–279
    photographs, 254–255
    resolution, 260–268
Scanning resolution, 261, 264, 268
Screen frequency, 263–264, 265–266, 268
Screen resolution, 261
Screens. *See* Halftones
Secondary colors, 240–241
Secondary color scheme, 243
Self-test
    checking clogged nozzles, 188–189
    preventing streaks, 66

Shades, use of term, 239–240
Shading, posterization, 166–168
Sharpening tools, 273
Simultaneous contrast
   color perception, 40–41
   description and example, 39–40
   on laser paper, 41
600 dots per inch (dpi) printing, use of term, 24
16-bit color, 167
Size of monitor
   choosing a monitor, 153–155
   LCD display measurement, 159–160
   resolution, 155–157
Slide scanners, 255
Solid ink printers, 12. *See also* Wax jet printers
Solid wax printers, 12. *See also* Wax jet printers
Sony Trinitron tube, 157
Split complementary color scheme, 244
Spot color, 250–252
Star SJ-144 printer, 14, 26, 55
Streaks, 62–66
   checking output, 190
   dust protection for ribbons, 60–61
   examples, 61, 64, 65
   ink jet and wax jet printers, 65–66
   self-testing, 66
   thermal wax and thermal dye printers, 62–65
Stylus Color printer, 177
Subtractive primaries in mixing colors, 102–105
Supercells, 283
SuperScript Color 3000 printer, 92, 129–132, 290–295, 298
SuperVideo (S-Video), 258

Tektronix, 12, 13, 16
   Phaser 340 printer, 30, 65, 83, 92, 113, 116–117, 121–122
   Phaser 540 printer, 203
   540 Plus printer, 21
Temperature scale, 247
Tertiary colors, 241
Tertiary color scheme, 244
Text, rules for using text and color, 80–81
Thermal dye printers, 204–205
   color quality, 17
   costs of using, 17, 206
   differences with thermal wax printers, 16–17

dual mode printers, 18–19, 53
need for precise registration, 205
paper sizes, 214–215
paper usage, 17, 27, 53, 178
preventing streaks, 62–65
printing graphics, 17
printing process, 15–16, 18
printing transparencies, 30, 31
resolution, 23
ribbons, 18, 55–58, 204
use of term, 16
similarities with thermal wax printers, 18
Thermal dye transfer printers, 15. *See also* Thermal dye printers
Thermal wax printers, 204–205
   color quality, 14
   costs, 197, 205
   differences with thermal dye printers, 16–17
   dual mode printers, 18–19, 53
   need for precise registration, 205
   paper usage, 26, 27–28, 29, 30, 54, 57, 58, 175–177
   preventing streaks, 62–65
   printing graphics, 205
   printing process, 13–14, 18
   printing transparencies, 30
   resolution, 23
   ribbons, 13–14, 18, 28, 55–58, 204
   similarities with thermal dye printers, 18
Thermal wax transfer printers, 13. *See also* Thermal wax printers
Three-color printing
   advantages, 181
   cartridges, 191
Three-color (CMY) ribbons, 8, 55
   four-color ribbons versus, 56
   when to swap with a four-color ribbon, 60
3-D graphics, 73–74
Tints
   use of term, 239–240
Toner
   ink jet printers, 191–192
   laser printers, 203–204
Total image resolution, 261
Transparencies
   backgrounds, 77–78
   judging output appearance, 194–195
   printing, 27, 178

Transparencies (*cont.*)
  proofing, 78
  results with different printers, 30–31
  testing, 31
Trinitron tube, 157
TrueType fonts, 211, 301
24-bit color, 167–168
Two-bit color, 161
Typewriters, 10, 174

Undercolor removal (UCR), 233–234
Unidirectional printing, 184, 185

Vector graphics. *See* Object-based images
VESA local bus (VLB), 170
VGA display, 145, 154
Video capture board
  example of scanned photograph, 257
  formats, 257–258
  resolution, 270–273
  scanning, 256–258, 261
Video cards
  amounts of memory at common resolutions, 168–169
  calibrating a monitor, 231
  color depth, 169
Video driver, 155
Video RAM (VRAM), 170
Virtual Memory, 302

Warm colors
  color schemes, 71, 245
  psychology of color, 48–49, 248–250
Wavelength
  color perception, 99, 100, 221
Wax jet printers, 195–197
  as both a color and monochrome printer, 32
  buying, 215
  color quality, 13
  costs, 195, 197, 215
  differences with ink jet printers, 195
  paper usage, 26, 29–30, 53
  PCL 5C, 210
  preventing streaks, 65–66
  price per page, 215–216
  printing draft copies in black and white, 66–67
  printing process, 12
  printing transparencies, 30
  resolution, 13, 23
  types, 196–197
  use of term, 12–13
Weight of paper, 54, 175
White
  additive and subtractive primaries in mixing colors, 101–105
  differences between monitors and printers, 117–118
  psychology of color, 249
White point, 229, 230–231
Wicking, 11
Windows
  fax programs, 90
  graphical device interface (GDI), 26, 212
  printer drivers, 24
  printing in monochrome mode, 86
  TrueType fonts, 211, 301
Windows 95, 301
  printer drivers, 24, 305–306
WRAM, 170

Yellow
  additive and subtractive primaries in mixing colors, 102–105
  differences between monitors and printers, 96, 98–99, 119–120
  mixing with other colors, for printer output, 4, 97–98
  primary, secondary, and tertiary colors, 240–241

Zenith Flat Tension Mask tube, 157